Inequality and Development Challenges

BRICS ■ NATIONAL SYSTEMS OF INNOVATION

Series Editors: **José E. Cassiolato,** Federal University of Rio de Janeiro, Brazil.
Maria Clara Couto Soares, Federal University of Rio de Janeiro, Brazil.

This series of books brings together results of an intensive research programme on aspects of the national systems of innovation in the five BRICS countries — Brazil, Russia, India, China and South Africa. It provides a comprehensive and comparative examination of the challenges and opportunities faced by these dynamic and emerging economies. In discussing the impact of innovation with respect to economic, geopolitical, socio-cultural, institutional and technological systems, it reveals the possibilities of new development paradigms for equitable and sustainable growth.

Books in this Series

The Role of the State
Editors: Mario Scerri and Helena M. M. Lastres
ISBN 978-0-415-84254-9

Inequality and Development Challenges
Editors: Maria Clara Couto Soares, Mario Scerri and Rasigan Maharajh
ISBN 978-0-415-71032-9

The Promise of Small and Medium Enterprises
Editors: Ana Arroio and Mario Scerri
ISBN 978-0-415-71036-7

Transnational Corporations and Local Innovation
Editors: José E. Cassiolato, Graziela Zucoloto, Dinesh Abrol and Liu Xielin
ISBN 978-0-415-71038-1

Financing Innovation
Editors: Michael Kahn, Luiz Martins de Melo and Marcelo G. Pessoa de Matos
ISBN 978-0-415-71039-8

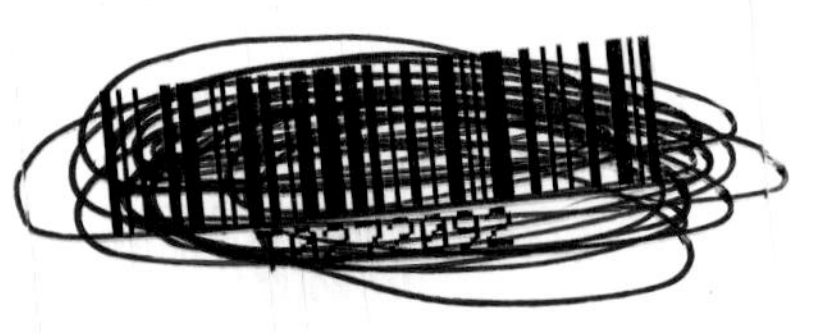

BRICS ■ National Systems of Innovation

Inequality and Development Challenges

Editors

Maria Clara Couto Soares
Mario Scerri
Rasigan Maharajh

LONDON AND NEW YORK

First published 2014 by Routledge

2 Park Square, Milton Park, Abingdon, Oxfordshire OX14 4RN
711 Third Avenue, New York, NY 10017

Routledge is an imprint of the Taylor & Francis Group, an informa business

First issued in paperback 2017

Typeset by

Glyph Graphics Private Limited
23, Khosla Complex
Near Samrat Apartments
Vasundhara Enclave
Delhi 110 096

British Library Cataloguing-in-Publication Data
A catalogue record of this book is available from the British Library

ISBN 978-0-415-71032-9 (hbk)
ISBN 978-1-138-56102-1 (pbk)

Contents

List of Abbreviations

AI	Africa Institute
AIDS	Acquired Immunodeficiency Syndrome
ARC	Agricultural Research Council
ATM	Automatic Teller Machine
BBBEE	Broad-based Black Economic Empowerment
BC	Backward Classes
BEE	Black Economic Empowerment
BNDES	National Bank for Economic and Social Development
BRICS	Brazil, Russia, India, China and South Africa
BRT	Bus Rapid Transit System
CDOT	Centre for Development of Telematics
CHIPS	Chinese Household Income Project Survey
CNI	National Confederation of Industry-Brazil
CNPq	National Council for Scientific and Technological Development
CSIR	Council for Scientific and Industrial Research
CSLS	Centre for the Study of Living Standards
CULS	China Urban Labour Survey
CUT	Central University of Technology
CV	Coefficient of Variation
DoL	Department of Labour
DPE	Department of Public Enterprise
DSIR	Department of Scientific and Industrial Research
DST	Department of Science and Technology
DTI	Department of Trade and Industry
ECLAC	Economic Commission for Latin America and the Caribbean
FASIE	Foundation for Assistance to Small Innovational Enterprises
FDI	Foreign Direct Investment
FERA	Foreign Exchange Regulation Act
FET	Further Education and Training
FFC	Financial and Fiscal Commission
FINEP	Studies and Projects Finance Organisation

FIRE	Finance, Insurance, Real Estate, and Business Services
GC	Gini Coefficient
GDP	Gross Domestic Product
GER	Gross Enrolment Ratio
GERD	Gross Domestic Expenditure on Research and Development
GGP	Gross Geographic Product
GNI	Gross National Income
GRP	Gross Regional Product
HDI	Human Development Index
HEI	Higher Education Institutions
HEMIS	Higher Education Management Information System
HET	Higher Education Training
HIV	Human Immunodeficiency Virus
HRS	Household Responsibility System
HS	Harmonised System
HSRC	Human Sciences Research Council
IBGE	The Brazilian Institute of Geography and Statistics
ICT	Information and Communication Technologies
INEP	National Institute of Studies and Research on Education
IPEA	Institute of Applied Economic Research
IPEADATA	Economic Applied Research Institute Database
IPO	Initial Public Offering
IPR	Industrial Policy Resolution
IPS	Industrial Policy Statement
IT	Information Technology
LABS	Laboratory for Accelerator Based Services
LLL	Lifelong Learning
MBA	Master of Business Administration
MCT	Ministry of Science and Technology
MDIC	Ministry of Development, Industry and Foreign Trade
MOHRSS	Ministry of Human Resources and Social Security of the People's Republic of China
MPCE	Monthly Per Capita Expenditure
MRTP	Monopolies and Restricted Trade Policies
MSER	Middle School Enrolment Ratio
MSEs	Micro and Small Enterprises

NACI	National Advisory Council on Science and Technology
NCEUS	National Commission for Enterprises in the Unorganised Sector
NGO	Non-Governmental Organisation
NIS	National Innovation System
NRD	National Experimental Research and Development Survey
NSDP	Net State Domestic Product
NSI	National System of Innovation
OBC	Other Backward Castes
OECD	Organisation for Economic Co-operation and Development
PASTER	Programme aimed at Technological Self-Reliance
PC	Personal Computer
PEA	Economically Active Population
PINTEC	Survey on Technological Innovation
PL	Poverty Line
PNAD	National Household Sample Survey
POF	Consumer Expenditure Survey
PPP	Purchasing Power Parity
PSER	Primary School Enrolment Ratio
R&D	Research and Development
RFBR	Russian Foundation for Basic Research
RSA	Republic of South Africa
RSFSR	Russian Soviet Federative Socialist Republic
S&T	Science and Technology
SALT	South African Large Telescope
SC	Scheduled Castes
SCE	Secondary Certificate Examination
SEBRAE	The Brazilian Service of Support for Micro and Small Enterprises
SECEX	Department of Foreign Trade
SET	Science, Engineering, and Technology
SET4W	Science, Engineering and Technology: Permanent Sub-Committee of NACI
SETA	Sector Education and Training Authority
SEZ	Special Economic Zone
SIM	Subscriber Identity Module
SIP	Statement on Industrial Policy

SIRO	Scientific and Industrial Research Organisations
SME	Small and Medium Enterprise
SMS	Short Message Service
SPR	Science Policy Resolution
ST	Scheduled Tribes
StatsSA	Statistics South Africa
STI	Science, Technology and Innovation
TDDP	Technology Development and Demonstration Programme
TNCs	Transnational Corporations
TPS	Technology Policy Statement
TVEs	Township and Village Enterprises
ULC	Unit Labour Costs
UNDP	United Nations Development Programme
USD	United States Dollar
USSR	Union of Soviet Socialist Republics
VC	Venture Capital
ZAR	South African Rand

List of Figures

List of Tables

Foreword

Inequality is one of the most deeply rooted characteristics of underdevelopment. It is also present in highly industrialised countries, but its magnitude and consequences in developing countries are overwhelming. Moreover, a marked difference in the level of inequality has been suggested as a main cause of divergences in the process of development (Lindegarde and Tylecote 1998).

There are two characteristics concerning inequality worth recalling. One is that fighting inequality is like fighting a mobile target. Once something important, for instance, an innovation capable of saving children, is available only for some children, inequality rises. To keep inequality at bay is a permanent task. The second characteristic is that inequality is perceived as particularly damaging for social cohesion. As Albert Hirschman put it, tolerance to inequality is '... like a credit that falls due at a certain date. It is extended in the expectation that eventually the disparities will narrow again. If this does not occur, there is bound to be trouble and, perhaps, disaster' (1981: 40). Fighting inequality is one of the means to consolidate democracy.

Inequality has, obviously, many faces. The following quote gives an accurate perspective on the issue:

> To speak of a social inequality is to describe some valued attribute which can be distributed across the relevant units of a society in different quantities, where 'inequality' therefore implies that different units possess different amounts of this attribute. The units can be individuals, social groups, communities, nations; the attributes include such things as income, wealth, status, knowledge, and power (Wright 1994: 21).

Throughout this book, the reader will find that several such units are analysed, including those characterised by gender, ethnicity, geography, and class. The attributes are also diverse, and are combined in such a way that the issue of quality of life and life opportunities is highlighted for the different nations that constitute the BRICS group.

Innovation has to do with inequality, and as this book rightly points out, inequality also influences innovation. From a developmental point of view, a main issue is to orient innovation efforts in a direction that diminishes inequality, and to make inequality a point of departure for innovation efforts. The way inequality is conceptualised is important in this regard. If the concept is restricted to income inequality, the role of innovation appears to be mainly related to economic growth. Innovation is associated in this way to the positive trickle-down effect that economic growth is expected to have on inequality. The problem in this regard is twofold. On the one hand, even with pro-active social redistributive policies, historical experience shows that people left behind form a hard core of important dimension. On the second hand, if inequality is expressed in highly differential qualities of social services, like education or health, inequalities in the quality of life are impossible to diminish only with money, even if differences in income are narrowed. This is due to the fact that the investments needed to narrow the gap of well-being in its multiple aspects, if intended by simply 'individual catching-up', are prohibitive. Here innovation is called into action.

The ways in which innovation can help to fight inequality depend on the type of inequality, but some general comments can nevertheless be made. As Everett Rogers remarks, innovation will probably enhance inequality there where inequality is already high. But this will not happen if innovation is designed directly to enhance equality. This is not a usual goal for innovation, but it is a possible goal for it. Innovation for equality can be unusual, but still is innovation, meaning that it must provide a solution for a problem involving something new, be it the solution itself or the way the solution is conceived or built. For innovation purposes problems need to be transformed by some agent in demands for solutions, with all the specifications that such solutions should fulfill. Specific communities, different kinds of associations (like Doctors without Borders) and business firms are examples of such agents in the case of equality-related innovations; public policy is probably the strongest one everywhere, but particularly so in developing countries.

The National Systems of Innovation approach is particularly suited for the idea of innovation directed to fight inequality. Inclusive innovation systems is a concept that suggests the kind of dynamic that links problems stemming from inequality, agents able to put forward a demand for solutions, innovation capabilities that help to solve the problems, and policies fostering the production and use of the solutions found. But inclusive innovation systems can only be built within existing innovation systems, and will shape differently for different attributes and different units, to use Wright's terminology. The reader will find in this book all the information and the analyses needed to understand how inequality looks like in the BRICS countries, and how the actual systems of innovation of these countries behave. The reader will be able, then, to make his/her own synthesis and, in dialogue with the authors, figure out how innovation can help to fight inequality. The opportunity to do this, so rare, so timely, so welcome, is a contribution of the book to the wedding of innovation and solidarity.

Montevideo
June 2010

Judith Sutz

References

Hirschman, A., 1981. *Essays in Trespassing. Economics to Policy and Beyond.* New York: Cambridge University Press.

Lindegarde, S. and A. Tylecote, 1988. 'Resource Rich Countries' Success and Failure in Technological Ascent, 1870–1970: The Nordic Countries versus Argentina, Uruguay and Brazil'. Paper presented at the 12th International Economic History Congress, 24–28 August, Seville.

Rogers, E. M., 1995. *Diffusion of Innovations*, Fourth edition. New York: Free Press.

Wright, E. O., 1994. *Interrogating Inequalities.* New York: Verso.

Preface

This series is the result of a collaborative effort of several people and institutions. The contributions presented here consolidate the findings of the project 'Comparative Study of the National Innovation Systems of BRICS' sponsored by the International Development Research Centre (IDRC). The project is rooted in a larger research effort on BRICS national innovation systems being developed in the sphere of the Global Research Network for Learning, Innovation and Competence Building Systems — Globelics. The Globelics initiative on BRICS economies brings together universities and other research institutions from Brazil, Russia, India, China, and South Africa. The aim is to strengthen an original and less dependent thought, more appropriate to understanding development processes in less developed countries.

First and foremost, we would like to thank Professor Bengt-Åke Lundvall, the coordinator of Globelics, who supported and promoted the BRICS project from the outset in 2003 and organised the First International Workshop of the BRICS Project in Aalborg, Denmark, in 2006. Without his leadership and enthusiasm the project could not have taken off.

We owe special thanks to project researchers and coordinators for their engagement in project activities and accessibility which helped overcome difficulties that naturally emerge from the geographical and cultural diversity of BRICS. We are also very grateful to those who provided the necessary administrative and secretarial support that resulted in the good performance of this project, especially Luiza Martins, Fabiane da Costa Morais, Tatiane da Costa Morais, and Eliane Alves who helped in editing activities and whose support was crucial for formatting the manuscript and organising the tables and figures. Max dos Santos provided the technical IT support for the research network.

The core ideas analysed in this series were discussed at international seminars organised in Brazil (2007), South Africa (2008), India (2009), and again in Brazil (2009) under the auspices of the BRICS Project, gathering scholars, academics, policy makers, businessmen, and civil society representatives. Our understanding of this complex theme has evolved considerably thanks to the seminar participants' constructive criticism. We are grateful to them as well as to all the other people not named here who also helped in the implementation of the project.

None of this work would have been possible without financial support. The support given by the IDRC was essential for the completion of this project and we are very obliged to them and their staff for their support. We would especially like to thank Richards Isnor, Federico Buroni, Gustavo Crespi, Veena Ravichandran, Isabel Bortagaray, and Clara Saavedra. We are also grateful to Bill Carman and Michelle Hibber, then IDRC Publishers, for the technical assistance provided in the preparatory work that led to this publication.

Supplementary grants were received from various agencies of the Brazilian Ministry of Science and Technology, especially the Studies and Projects Finance Organization (FINEP), the National Council for Scientific and Technological Development (CNPq). In particular, we would like to thank the general secretary of the Ministry of Science and Technology, Dr Luiz Antonio Elias, and the president of FINEP, Luis Fernandes, who have given enthusiastic support to the BRICS project since its inception.

Introduction

BRICS National Systems of Innovation

José E. Cassiolato and Maria Clara Couto Soares

Preamble

The world is experiencing significant transformations in its geopolitical and economic constitution. The processes of transformation have accelerated over the last decades. A significant part of the growth potential of the world economy nowadays and for the coming decades resides in some fast-developing countries. Brazil, Russia, India, China, and South Africa (BRICS) have displayed such potential for dynamic change. In a historic rupture with past patterns of development, the BRICS countries are now playing a major role in alleviating the current global crisis whilst revealing new and alternative progressive paradigms.

Much beyond the emphasis given by international agencies to the identification of investment possibilities in the BRICS production structures or to the prospects presented by their consumer markets, our perspective in analysing the BRICS countries is inspired by their significant development opportunities, as well as their several common characteristics and challenges, and the learning potential they offer for other developing countries. Identifying and analysing these opportunities and challenges will help to uncover alternative pathways towards fulfilling their socio-political-economic development potential within the constraints of sustainability.

The central focus of this book series is the National System of Innovation (NSI) of the five BRICS countries. Each book deals with a key component of the innovation system, providing the reader with access to analyses on the role played by the state, the financing, direct investment and the small and medium enterprises, besides approaching a particularly relevant — though still not extensively studied — aspect of the BRICS economies: the challenge of inequality and its interrelations with the NSIs of these countries.

The research endeavour that generated the publication of this book series has gathered universities and research centres from all the BRICS countries, as well as policy makers invited to discuss the outcomes. The research development and the comparative analysis of its results are intended to bring to light the challenges and opportunities of the BRICS countries' national innovation systems from the points of view of these same countries. Part of the effort undertaken was addressed to the construction of a shared methodology aimed at advancing the comprehension of the specificities of innovation systems in each country. This was done in view of the need for improvements in the analytical framework used for the analysis of the national innovation systems located in countries outside the restricted sphere of developed countries. Special attention was paid to the political implications. However, instead of searching for generalisable policy recommendations, it was sought to identify and analyse bottlenecks that are common to the BRICS economies, their complementarities and competition areas, as well as other aspects of major importance for supporting decision makers and that are able to incite reflection about the subject of innovation and development in other less developed countries.

It is worth mentioning that the research consolidated in this publication is rooted in a larger research effort on BRICS national innovation systems being developed in the spheres of Globelics[1] and RedeSist (the Research Network on Local Productive and Innovative Systems) at the Economic Institute of the Federal University of Rio de Janeiro.[2] Globelics is an international academic network which uses the concept of innovation systems (IS) as an analytical tool aimed at the comprehension of the driving forces that push economic development. It aims to advance the use of the IS perspective on a world basis. Established in 2002 and inspired by renowned scholars from the field of economics of innovation such as Christopher Freeman (1987) and Bengt-Åke Lundvall (1992), the Globelics network has, among others, the purpose of encouraging knowledge exchange between less developed countries, thus fostering mutual learning across innovation research groups in Latin America, Africa and Asia. With this, it is sought to strengthen an original and more autonomous approach to understanding the development processes in developing countries. On the other hand, the focus put by the Globelics network on the study of innovation systems of BRICS results from the recognition that understanding the particular dynamics which connects the knowledge base with innovation and economic performance in each of the five BRICS countries is, today, a precondition for better appreciating the direction that the world economy will be following (Lundvall 2009). It is within such analytical field that the contribution offered by this book series is inserted.

In the following sections we (*a*) present the broad conceptual approach of NSI used as the guiding analytical framework for the research gathered under this book series; (*b*) characterise the increasing importance of the BRICS countries in the global scenario; and (*c*) introduce the five-book collection on NSIs in the BRICS countries.

NSI and Development — A Broad Perspective

One of the most fruitful ways of thinking developed in advanced countries in the last 30 years came from a resurrection and updating of earlier thinking that emphasised the role of innovation as an engine of economic growth and the long-run cyclical character of technical change. A seminal paper by Christopher Freeman (1982) pointed out the importance that Smith, Marx and Schumpeter attached to innovation (ibid.: 1) and accentuated its systemic and national character (ibid.: 18). Freeman also stressed the crucial role of government policies to cope with the uncertainties associated with the upsurge of a new techno-economic paradigm and the very limited circumstances under which free trade could promote economic development. Since it was formulated in the 1980s, the system of innovation (SI) approach has been increasingly used in different parts of the world to analyse processes of acquisition, use and diffusion of innovations, and to guide policy recommendations.[3]

Particularly relevant in the SI perspective is that since the beginning of the 1970s, the innovation concept has been widened to be understood as a systemic, non-linear process rather than an isolated fact. Emphasis was given to its interactive character and to the importance of (and complementarities between) incremental and radical, technical and organisational innovations and their different and simultaneous sources. A corollary of this argument is the context-specific and localised character of innovation and knowledge. This understanding of innovation as a socially determined process is in opposition to the idea of a supposed techno-globalism and implies, for instance, that acquisition of technology abroad is not a substitute for local efforts. On the contrary, one needs a lot of knowledge to be able to interpret information, select, buy (or copy), transform, and internalise technology.

Systems of innovation, defined as a set of different institutions that contribute to the development of the innovation and learning capacity of a country, region, economic sector, or locality, comprise a series of elements and relations that relate production, assimilation, use, and diffusion of knowledge. In other words, innovative performance depends not only on firms and R&D organisations' performance but also on how they interact, among themselves and with other agents, as well as all the other forms by which they acquire, use and diffuse knowledge. Innovation capacity derives, therefore, from the confluence of social, political, institutional, and culture-specific factors and from the environment in which economic agents operate. Different development trajectories contribute to shape systems of innovation with quite diverse characteristics requiring specific policy support.

It is this understanding of the systemic nature of innovation that allows for two crucial dimensions of the SI approach to be explicitly discussed: the emphasis on historical and national trajectories and the importance of taking into account the productive, financial, social, institutional, and political contexts, as well as micro, meso and macro spheres (Freeman 2003; Lastres et al. 2003). Although all of these contexts are relevant for a discussion about development, two in particular should be singled out that are pertinent to this study. One is the financial context, recognised by Schumpeter (1982 [1912]) in his *The Theory of Economic Development*. For him, entrepreneurs, to become the driving force in a process of innovation, must be able to convince banks to provide the credit to finance innovation. In this sense, any discussion about innovation systems has to include the financial dimension.[4] The other is the idea that space matters, that the analysis of systems of innovation should be done at the national (Freeman 1982; Lundvall 1988) and local levels (Cassiolato et al. 2003).

The national character of SI was introduced by Christopher Freeman (1982, 1987) and Bengt-Åke Lundvall (1988) and has been widely used as an analytical tool and as a framework for policy analysis in both developed and underdeveloped countries. As a result, research and policy activities explicitly focusing on SI can be found in most countries and a rapidly growing number of studies of specific NSIs have been produced. Although some authors tend to focus on the NSI in a narrow sense, with an emphasis on research and development efforts and science and technology organisations, a broader understanding of NSI (Freeman 1987; Lundvall 1988) is more appropriate. This approach takes into account not only the role of firms, education and research organisations and science and technology institution (STI) policies, but includes government policies as a whole, financing organisations, and other actors and elements that influence the acquisition, use and diffusion of innovations. In this case emphasis is also put on the role of historical processes — which account for differences in socio-economic capabilities and for different development trajectories and institutional evolution — creating SI with very specific local features and dynamics. As a result, a national character of SI is justified.

Figure 1 is an attempt to show both the narrow and the broad perspectives on NSI. The broad perspective includes different, connecting sub-systems that are influenced by various contexts: geopolitical, institutional, macroeconomic, social, cultural, and so on. First, there is a production and innovation sub-system which contemplates the structure of economic activities, their sectoral distribution, degree of informality and spatial and size distribution, the level and quality of employment, the type and quality of innovative effort. Second, there is a sub-system of science and technology which includes education (basic, technical, undergraduate, and postgraduate), research, training, and other elements of the scientific and technological infrastructure such as information, metrology, consulting, and intellectual property. Third, there is a policy, promotion, financing, representation, and regulation sub-system that encompasses the different forms of public and private policies both explicitly geared towards innovation or implicitly, that is, those that although not necessarily geared towards it, affect strategies for innovation. Finally, there is the role of demand, which most of the time is surprisingly absent from most analyses of SI. This dimension includes patterns of income distribution, structure of consumption, social organisation and social demand (basic infrastructure, health, education).

Figure 1: *The Narrow and Broad Perspectives on NSI*

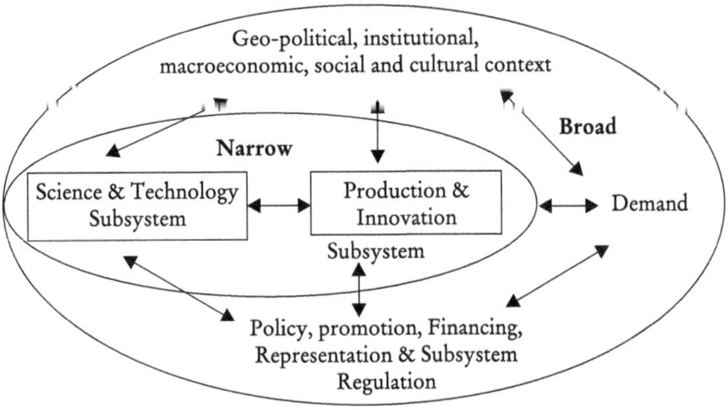

Source: Adapted from Cassiolato and Lastres (2008).

This portrayal of the national innovation system framework is a corollary of an understanding that

- innovation capacity derives from the confluence of economic, social, political, institutional, and culture-specific factors and from the environment in which they operate, implying the need for an analytical framework broader than that offered by traditional economics (Freeman 1982, 1987; Lundvall 1988);
- the number of firms or organisations such as teaching, training and research institutes is far less important than the habits and practices of such actors with respect to learning, linkage formation and investment. These shape the nature and extensiveness of their interactions and their propensity to innovate (Mytelka 2000; Johnson and Lundvall 2003);
- main elements of knowledge are embodied in minds and bodies of agents or embedded in routines of firms and in relationships between firms and organisations. Therefore, they are localised and not easily transferred from one place/context to another,

for knowledge is something more than information and includes tacit elements (Lundvall 1988);
- the focus on interactive learning and on the localised nature of the generation, assimilation and diffusion of innovation implies that the acquisition of foreign technology abroad is not a substitute for local efforts (Cassiolato and Lastres 1999);
- national framework matters, as development trajectories contribute to shape specific systems of innovation. The diversity of NSIs is a product of different combinations of their main features that characterise their micro, meso and macroeconomic levels, as well as the articulations among these levels (Freeman 1987; Lastres 1994).

From the specific point of view of less developed countries (LDCs) the usefulness of the SI approach resides precisely in the facts that (*a*) its central building blocks allow for their socio-economic and political specificities to be taken into account and (*b*) it does not ignore the power relations in discussing innovation and knowledge accumulation. As this book argues, these features are particularly relevant in the analysis of the BRICS countries' innovation systems. As the analysis of economic phenomena also takes into consideration their social, political and historical complexity, policy prescriptions are based on the assumption that the process of development is influenced by and reflects the particular environment of each country, rather than on recommendations derived from the reality of advanced countries. A number of development studies followed these ideas, arguing that technical change plays a central role in explaining the evolution of capitalism and in determining the historical process through which hierarchies of regions and countries are formed. Furtado (1961), for instance, established an express relation between economic development and technological change pointing out that the growth of an economy was based on the accumulation of knowledge, and understood development within a systemic, historically determined, view. Although original, these contributions have a close correspondence with Myrdal's (1968) proposition that: (*a*) contexts and institutions matter; (*b*) positive and negative feedbacks have cumulative causation; (*c*) cycles may be virtuous or vicious, and with Hirschman's (1958) point that interdependencies among different activities are important.

The need to address paradigmatic changes and the problems and options deriving from the upsurge of information technologies led to the outbreak in Latin America in the 1980s of a series of interconnected work from the innovation perspective. Building on Furtado's work on changes associated with the industrial revolution, authors like Herrera (1975) and Perez (1983) analysed the opportunities and challenges associated with the introduction of these radical changes in the region. It was only then that the innovation and development literature started to integrate the empirically validated knowledge about learning inside firms with the contributions stemming from the work of Freeman, Perez, Herrera, and others on new technologies, changes of techno-economic paradigms and systems of innovation. What gave special impetus to this direction was the empirical work focusing on technological capability building as part of a broader national innovation system. The role of government policies in orienting the speed and direction of technological changes was also highlighted (Freeman and Perez 1988).

Development processes are characterised by deep changes in the economic and social structure taking place from (technological and/or productive) discontinuities that cause and are caused by the productive, social, political, and institutional structure of each nation. Development is also seen as a systemic process, given the unequal capitalism development in the world. The recognition of national specificities of these processes is also fundamental. We found the same stress on the national character of development processes in List's work (1841), and on the NSI idea of Freeman (1982) and Lundvall (1988) in Furtado's (1961) discussion about the transformation of national economies where their structural complexity is manifested in a diversity of social and economic forms. For Furtado, it is in this transformation that the essence of development resides: structural changes 'in the internal relations of the economic and social system' (ibid.: 103) that are triggered by capital accumulation and technological innovations. The emphasis on diversity, and the recognition that: (*a*) both theory and policy recommendations are highly context dependent, (*b*) the economy is firmly embedded in society, and (*c*) knowledge and technology are context-specific, conform some general identities.

Furtado (ibid.) established a direct relation between economic development and technological innovation pointing out that the growth of an advanced economy was based on the accumulation of new scientific knowledge and on the application of such knowledge to solve practical problems. The Industrial Revolution set into motion a process of radical changes based on technical progress that has lasted till now and that is at the root of how the world economy is conformed. In essence, those changes: (*a*) rendered endogenous the causal factors related to growth into the economic system; (*b*) made possible a closer articulation between capital formation and experimental science. Such articulation has become one of the most fundamental characteristics of modern civilisation. As pointed out by Furtado (ibid.), the beginning of such a process took place in the countries that were able to industrialise and create technical progress first, and the quick accumulation made possible in the development of this process became the basic engine of the capitalist system. For this reason, there is a close interdependency between the evolution of the technology in the industrialised countries and the historical conditions on the basis of which such development was made possible. As the behaviour of the economic variables relies on parameters that are defined and evolve into a specific historical context, it is quite difficult to isolate the study of economic phenomena from its historical frame of reference (Furtado 2002). This assertion is more significant when analysing economic, social and technological systems that are different from each other, as in the underdeveloped economies. In this context, underdevelopment may not, and should not, be considered as an anomaly or simply a backward state. Underdevelopment may be identified as a functioning pattern and specific evolution of some economies. Social and economical peripheral structure determines a specific manner under which structural change occurs (industrialisation during the 1950s and 1960s) and technical progress is introduced. Hence different outcomes from those in developed countries are to be expected (Furtado 1961; Rodriguez 2001).

The neo-Schumpeterian perspective also argues that economic development is considered a systemic phenomenon, generated and sustained not only by inter-firm relations, but most significantly by a complex inter-institutional network of relations. Innovation is eminently a social process. Therefore, development — resulting from the introduction and diffusion of new technologies — may be considered as the outcome of cumulative trajectories historically built up according to institutional specificities and specialisation patterns inherent to a determined country, region or sector. Each country follows its own development trajectory according to its specificities and possibilities, depending fundamentally on their hierarchical and power position in the world capitalist system. The more distant underdeveloped countries are from the technological frontier, the larger will be the barriers to an innovative insertion in the new technological paradigm. More serious than technological asymmetries are knowledge and learning asymmetries, with the implication that access, understanding, absorption, domination, use and diffusion of knowledge become impossible. However, even when the access to new technologies becomes possible, most of the time they are not adequate for the reality of underdeveloped countries and/or these countries do not have a pool of sufficient knowledge to make an adequate use of them. This occurs because the learning process depends on the existence of innovative and productive capabilities that are not always available. On this aspect, Arocena and Sutz (2003) argue that there are clearly learning divides between North and South that are perhaps the main problem of underdevelopment nowadays.

The Increasing Relevance of the BRICS Countries

The BRICS denomination was originally used to connect the dynamic emerging economies of Brazil, Russia, India, China, and South Africa as continental countries bearing a strategic position in the continents of the Americas, Europe, Asia, and Africa. The BRICS are also joined by their large geographical and demographic dimensions. Collectively, they were home to 42.2 per cent of the world population as of 2010 representing nothing less than 2.9 billion people. In addition, the five countries account for approximately 30 per cent of the earth's surface, holding significant reserves of natural resources such as energy and mineral resources, water and fertile lands. As well, BRICS countries have 24.3 per cent of world biodiversity; Brazil alone embracing 9.3 per cent of the total (GEF 2008).

Moreover, it is the recent performance of these economies and their macroeconomic indicators that make them more and more the focus of surveillance and analysis. In fact, the BRICS countries display a growing economic importance. In 2000, the five countries accounted for 17.1 per cent of the world GDP in public–private partnership (PPP). Their share increased to 25.7 per cent in 2010, with China and

India accounting for 13.6 per cent and 5.5 per cent respectively, followed by Russia (3 per cent), Brazil (2.9 per cent) and South Africa (0.7 per cent) (IMF 2011).

The participation of the BRICS countries in world GDP is expected to rise sharply in the years to come. The impact of the financial crisis and global recession on developed world economy over the last three years has only lent support to this expectation, beyond attracting attention to the BRICS economies' capacity to remain immune or quickly recover from the crisis. Large domestic markets, pro-active investment policies, monetary and tax policies with anti-cyclic capacity, presence of major public banks, and high level of reserves are elements increasingly recognised as having helped at least some BRICS economies to be less affected by the crisis.

While growth slowed in all major regions, China and India continued to grow rapidly in 2009 and 2010 (Table 1). In other BRICS countries the crisis rebounded fast. In Brazil, the GDP fell 0.2 per cent in 2009, but the economy surpassed pre-crisis growth rates in 2010 (7.5 per cent). South Africa showed a GDP decrease by 1.8 per cent in 2009 and had a 2.8 per cent increase in 2010. In Russia, heavily dependent on commodities like oil and gas, the economy has been hit more severely by the global crisis. It experienced shrinking of almost 8 per cent in 2009 but the GDP growth recovered to 3.7 per cent in 2010, beating the developed economies' growth rates. Prospects for 2015 show the five economies representing 29.5 per cent of the world economy.

The economic performance of the BRICS countries has, however, varied widely during the last decades as shown in Table 1. China has maintained its position as the fastest growing economy worldwide. India has also grown significantly and regularly. Brazil has had an irregular performance, well below its potential, but showed an enhancement in the second half of the 2000s. Russia, after the severe 1990s crisis that resulted in a decline of 40 per cent in its real GDP, has recovered and South Africa has had a small improvement in its economic performance that remains below its potential.

These different performances were accompanied by significant changes in the productive structure of the five countries, which reflect dissimilar development strategies.

The competitiveness of China's industrial sector is the main source of the country's impressive economic growth. The share of industry

Table 1: *BRICS: Average Rates of Growth of Real GDP (1980–2015) (percentage)*

	1980–1990	*1990–2000*	*2001–2005*	*2006*	*2007*	*200[illegible]*	*2009*	*2010*	*2015**
Brazil	2.8	2.9	2.8	3.7	5.7	5.1	–0.2	7.5	4.1
Russia	–	–4.7	6.2	7.4	8.1	5.6	–7.9	3.7	5.0
India	5.8	6.0	6.9	9.8	9.3	7.[illegible]	6.5	9.7	8.1
China	10.3	10.4	9.6	11.6	13.0	9.0	8.7	10.3	9.5
South Africa	1.6	2.1	4.0	5.4	5.1	3.[illegible]	–1.8	2.8	2.8
Developed Countries	3.1	2.8	1.9	2.8	2.5	0.[illegible]	–3.2	3.0	2.3

Source: UNCTAD (2010) for the period 1980–2008 and IMF (2011) for 2009–2015 data. See http://unctadstat.unctad.org/ReportFolders/reportFolders.aspx (accessed 15 March 2011).

Note: *Estimate.

in the composition of China's GDP is unusual and growing: it was around 40 per cent in 1990 and reached 48 per cent in 2009. In contrast, in 2008, 56.1 per cent of the Chinese labour force still remained in rural areas. The relative share of the agricultural sector, which accounted for 30.2 per cent in 1980, is constantly falling, to 11 per cent of GDP in 2009. The share of services grew from 21.6 per cent in 1980 to 41 per cent in 2009.

Really impressive is the mounting share of China's manufacturing sector in world manufacturing GDP (Figure 2). In 1990, it represented 3.1 per cent of global manufacturing GDP, achieving 21.2 per cent in 2009.

Figure 2: *Manufacturing Sector: BRICS' Share in World GDP (1970–2009)*

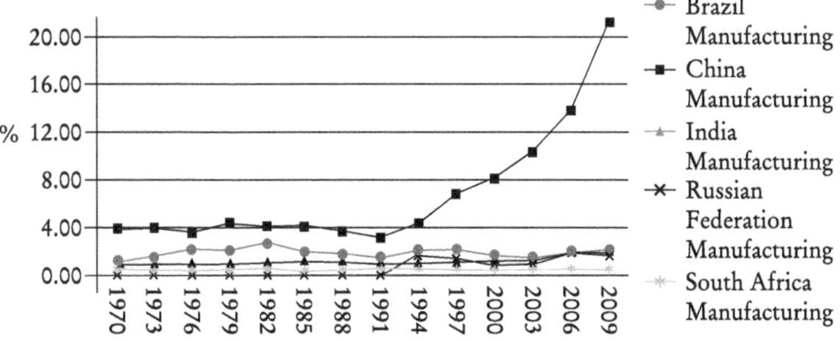

Source: UNCTAD (2009). See http://unctadstat.unctad.org/ReportFolders/reportFolders.aspx (accessed 15 March 2011).

China has diversified its industrial system to a significant degree during the last 25 years and the share of technologically intensive sectors in industrial output in 2009 reached 42 per cent of the total value added by the manufacturing sector. In the other four countries this share is around 15 per cent.[5] In addition, some major differences in the characteristics of the BRICS countries' manufacturing sectors should be noticed.

Brazil has gone through a structural transformation since the late 1980s, with a significant reduction of the share of industry in total GDP (declining from 41.7 per cent in 1980 to 25.4 per cent in 2009) and a high growth of services (from 50 per cent to 68.5 per cent in the same period). It is worth emphasising that agricultural goods that have had an important role in the country's trade surplus were responsible for only 6.1 per cent of GDP in 2009, showing a fall from 9.0 per cent in 1980. In Brazil, as in Russia and South Africa, the products based on natural resources and commodities have a relatively greater share of national GDP than in China and India.

Russia's economic development is heavily dependent on energy and raw material resources. As in Brazil, the contribution of manufacturing sector to GDP in Russia has declined since the 1980s, decreasing from 44.6 per cent in 1983 to 32.9 per cent in 2009. The share of defence-related industrial complex in manufacturing is significant, together with the strong production base in non-electric machines and equipment. The oil and gas industry alone accounts for more than 10 per cent of the gross value added. The share of services in total GDP has grown in the last two decades achieving 62.4 per cent in 2009 while agriculture has decreased its participation accounting for only 4.7 per cent in 2009.

The Indian economy is essentially service-led. Skills in the manufacturing sector are relatively modest and concentrated in non-durable consumer goods and in the chemical-pharmaceutical complex. However, some manufacturing segments in the automobile complex and in certain basic industries have been developing rapidly in recent years. Since the mid-1980s, the contribution of industry to India's GDP has been almost constant and around 26 per cent, but from 2004 to 2009 it increased to 28.3 per cent. India's capacity in the area of services is significant, particularly those linked to information and communication technology (ICT). The share of services in GDP has grown from 39 per cent in 1980 to 54.6 per cent in 2009. Although the agricultural sector is declining in India's GDP, it still represented 17.1 per cent in 2009 (compared to 36.8 per cent in 1980) and constitutes an important determinant of the overall economic growth.

The services sector has also been playing a more important role in the South African economy. The share of this sector in GDP was 45.4 per cent in 1980 and increased to 65.8 per cent in 2009. The development of the financial sector and the growth of tourism have contributed to this growth. Finance, real estate and business services are expanding their share with regard to government services. South Africa's industrial sector is heavily based on natural resources, mainly steel and non-ferrous metals, with some increases in capacity occurring in non-durable consumer goods and the automobile sector. The share of industry-added value in total GDP value decreased from 48.4 per cent in 1980 to 31.4 per cent in 2009. The metal and engineering sectors dominate the manufacturing sector. Although agriculture is responsible for a small share of South Africa's GDP (3 per cent in 2009), it still represents an important source of employment. The minerals and mining sector remains important also with respect to both employment and foreign trade.

The changes observed in the participation of BRICS countries in international trade were even more significant (Table 2). Their share in merchandise trade value more than doubled in the short period of 2000–10, exports rising from 7.5 to 16.4 per cent and imports from 6.2 to 14.9 per cent. However, the contribution of the five countries varied significantly. The most notable fact is the well-known growth of China in the merchandise trade value: its exports mounted from 3.9 per cent to 10.4 per cent of world exports reaching US$ 1.58 trillion in 2010, and imports increased from 3.4 per cent to 9.1 per cent in the same period.

Table 2: *BRICS: Merchandise Trade Value (in billion of current US$) and Share in World Total (2000–10) (percentage)*

	2000		*2005*		*2010*	
Exports	*Value*	*%*	*Value*	*%*	*Value*	*%*
World	6,448.57	100.00	10,495.70	100.00	15,174.44	100.00
Brazil	55.12	0.85	118.53	1.13	201.915	1.33
China	249.20	3.86	761.95	7.26	1,578.270	10.40
India	42.38	0.66	99.62	0.95	221.406	1.46
Russia	105.57	1.64	243.80	2.32	400.424	2.64
South Africa	31.95	0.50	56.26	0.54	85.700	0.56
	2000		*2005*		*2010*	
Imports	*Value*	*%*	*Value*	*%*	*Value*	*%*
World	6,662.89	100.00	10,800.15	100.00	15,353.26	100.00
Brazil	58.64	0.88	77.63	0.72	191.46	1.25
China	225.02	3.38	660.21	6.11	1,396.20	9.09
India	51.52	0.77	142.84	1.32	328.36	2.14
Russia	49.13	0.74	137.98	1.28	273.61	1.78
South Africa	30.22	0.45	64.19	0.59	96.25	0.63

Source: UNCTAD (2010).

India also experienced a sharp increase of exports, reaching 1.46 per cent of the world total in 2010. Fostered by Chinese growth and commodities boom, the share of Brazil and Russia in world exports grew rapidly from 2000 to 2010, increasing almost four times. South Africa is the only BRICS country that still shows less than

1 per cent of world exports. On the import side, India and Russia increased their share in world imports more than fivefold. Except India and South Africa, the other BRICS countries managed to keep a surplus in their merchandise trade in 2010. In India inflows on account of invisibles have been helpful in financing the growing deficit in merchandise trade.

The BRICS economies have significantly increased their openness to international trade in the last decades. They have raised their exports and imports both in volume terms as a share of GDP, but the level of trade openness has varied quite a lot (Table 3). The greater changes occurred in China and India, particularly since the 1990s when they speeded up their international trade flows. Currently, China, South Africa and Russia are the BRICS economies with the higher levels of openness. The Brazilian economy, despite the liberalisation process in the 1990s, remains the most closed amongst the BRICS countries.

Table 3: *BRICS: Foreign Trade (in million of current US$) and Share of GDP (percentage)*

	Exports + Imports				
Countries	*1970*	*1980*	*1990*	*2000*	*2010*
Brazil	8.719	25.412	61.212	113.762	393.379
China	4.833	38.919	11.471	474.227	2,972.960
India	4.792	28.839	51.144	93.941	540.489
Russia	–	–	349.249	136.973	627.323
South Africa	8.352	50.411	48.6	56.782	161.953
	Exports + Imports (GDP)				
Countries	*1970*	*1980*	*1990*	*2000*	*2010*
Brazil	13.0	10.3	14.0	17.6	18.8
China	5.3	12.9	29.9	39.6	50.6
India	7.9	15.7	15.8	20.4	31.3
Russia	–	–	36.1	52.7	42.4
South Africa	45.7	61.2	43.4	42.7	44.5

Source: United Nations (2010b); World Bank (2011).

The bilateral trade flows between BRICS countries have been relatively restricted. However, since the first half of the 2000s there was a widespread increase of exports and imports flows between the five economies, but particularly a stronger presence of China as an important trade pole for the other four countries (Baumann 2009). In 2009, China surpassed the US as the main trade partner of Brazil and also emerged as the second main trade partner of India and Russia. The converse does not however hold, as these four economies don't match their respective rankings insofar as they are neither the top import suppliers nor export destinations for China. China exports to Brazil, India, Russia, and South Africa at a more intense pace than it imports from them. In addition, the latter are concentrated on a few primary goods intensive in natural resources while China's exports are much more diversified and led by manufactured goods. Therefore, despite the fact that intra-BRICS trade has increased in recent years, the flows are still restricted in size and unbalanced in terms of the different rhythms and compositions of the BRICS bilateral commercial transactions.

In the last decades, the BRICS countries have been the recipients of significant amounts of foreign direct investment (FDI). Brazil received the greatest share of FDI of all BRICS economies until the first half of the 1980s. Although China has surpassed Brazil since 1985, Brazil continued to be a major destination for FDI during the 1990s, most notably during the process of privatisation that took place during that decade. Since the 2000s Russia and India have been strengthening their relevance as FDI inflow destinations. In 2010, the BRICS countries received 17.6 per cent of global FDI inflows. Especially since 2005, there was a sharp increase of BRICS' FDI outflows. With the exception of South Africa, BRICS countries more than tripled their FDI outflows from 2005 to 2010, raising their participation in the world total from 3.6 per cent to 11.1 per cent in the period (Table 4).

BRICS countries also followed different development strategies regarding FDI. Particularly remarkable has been the Chinese policy to attract multinational companies since the beginning of the 1990s. Inserted in a broader strategy aiming to expand its technological knowledge and later to strengthen the domestic industries and enterprises, China imposed conditions — such as the establishment of joint ventures and that R&D be carried out locally — that had to be met before the subsidiaries were to operate in China or sell in its markets. Brazil, Russia and South Africa — countries that liberalised their economies with few restrictions — got more portfolio investment, but most of the investment received by the manufacturing sector was used to buy up local companies. In China and India, where the capital account was not liberalised, FDI seems to have been concentrated in new investments in production and innovation.

Table 4: *BRICS: Foreign Direct Investment, Inflows and Outflows Share in the World Totals*

	Selected Years								
FDI Inflows (%)	*1970*	*1975*	*1980*	*1985*	*1990*	*1995*	*2000*	*2005*	*2010*
Brazil	2.94	4.53	3.53	2.54	0.48	1.29	2.34	1.53	3.90
China	NA	NA	0.11	3.50	1.68	10.96	2.90	7.37	8.50
India	0.34	0.32	0.15	0.19	0.11	0.63	0.26	0.78	1.98
Russian Federation	NA	NA	NA	NA	NA	0.60	0.19	1.31	3.31
South Africa	2.50	0.71	−0.02	−0.80	−0.04	0.36	0.06	0.68	0.13
FDI Outflows (%)									
Brazil	0.01	0.38	0.71	0.13	0.26	0.30	0.19	0.29	0.87
China	NA	NA	NA	1.01	0.34	0.55	0.07	1.39	5.14
India	0.00	0.00	0.01	0.01	0.00	0.03	0.04	0.34	1.11
Russian Federation	NA	NA	NA	NA	NA	0.17	0.26	1.45	3.91
South Africa	0.12	0.44	1.46	0.08	0.01	0.69	0.02	0.11	0.03

Source: UNCTAD (2010).

Other relevant macroeconomic indicators could be added — such as the impressive share of BRICS in international monetary reserves (about 40 per cent of the total) — but the interest in these five emerging economies goes beyond this area. Together with their expanding economic relevance, these countries are claiming a rising geopolitical influence. They have been important players in their geographic areas of influence. However, they are pushing to have an increasing voice in the international high-level decision-making institutions, particularly through reforms in the UN system and in the Bretton Woods organisations. New dialogue spaces bringing together BRICS countries, such as the IBSA (India, Brazil and South Africa), BRICS (Brazil, Russia, India, China, and South Africa), and BASIC (Brazil, South Africa, India, and China) signal concrete steps to move forward the cooperation and coordination within and amongst these countries, which intends to go further than the mere economic sphere.[6]

Their growing leverage in international relations together with other emerging countries is associated with a repositioning of the balance of power on the world stage, which was intensified by the recent world crisis. BRICS countries want to see these changes reflected in the institutions of global governance. Since their economies will probably continue to account for a sizeable portion of the increase in global GDP in the near future, it is expected over time that BRICS will exert increasing financial and political influence, even if limited by their considerable differences and constraints to form a coherent political bloc anytime soon.[7]

The increased influence of these countries took place during a period marked by intense transformations in the global society. One of these remarkable changes is the integration in the economy of a significant portion of previously marginalised segments of the BRICS population. The highly populated China and India led this process in terms of world shares, but Brazil also had an important participation (Chapter 2, this volume). The present and potential dimension of BRICS domestic markets as well as the policies adopted by some BRICS countries aiming to reduce their dependence on developed countries' consumer markets has been drawing increasing attention in the last years. According to one estimate, two billion people from BRICS will join the global 'middle class' by 2030 (Wilson and Dragusanu 2008) representing a huge impact on the demand profile with expected reflexes on global investments as well as on innovation.

Simultaneously, several hurdles remain for the BRICS to overcome. One of them is the growing social gap caused by the unequal distribution of recent economic growth. While the percentage of the population below the poverty line has decreased over the past 30 years in most of the BRICS countries, inequality is still a major issue for these economies. In fact, the BRICS countries, except Brazil, show a trend of increasing income inequality that — particularly since the 1990s — has been following the rapid economic growth. Moreover, despite the improvements in recent years, Brazil is still among the countries with the worst distribution of income, together with South Africa that found itself in an even worse situation.[8] In addition, India and Russia are among those with the largest percentage of the population living below the poverty line.[9] Furthermore, beyond the income dimension, inequality has a multi-dimensional character in the BRICS countries. This challenge is exacerbated by race, gender, ethnic, and geographic dimensions and therefore demands more integrated solutions (Chapter 1, this volume).

One of the problems associated with the high poverty levels and the perverse distribution of income is the limited access to quality public services — education, health, housing and infrastructure, safety and security, etc. These problems are common to the five countries, where a significant portion of the population lacks access to essential goods and services, and demand urgent redress. This situation is reflected in poor human development indices in the BRICS countries. Other undeniable challenges faced by BRICS are unemployment, poor quality employment and increasing informality.

Another evident challenge in all five countries is the huge regional disparity in human and economic development. There is also a large gap between the rural and urban population. In general, the wealthier regions are those that are more industrialised. Practically 60 per cent of the total GDP of Brazil originates in the states of the southeast. The Chinese economic development model favours the coastal provinces, while other provinces in the interior are much less developed. In South Africa, economic activity is concentrated in Gauteng province and in the western part of Cape Town. The industrial development of Russia occurred principally around cities such as Moscow, St Petersburg, Nizhny Novgorod, and Ekaterinburg. India also shows significant inequalities between the rich regions to the south and the northern regions of the country as well as between the rural and urban populations. Therefore, regional redistribution of income and access to essential goods and services is another significant challenge that these five countries have in common (Chapter 1, this volume).

The negative environmental impact of recent growth is another huge challenge to be faced by BRICS countries. According to CDIAC-UN data for 2008, the BRICS countries are responsible for emitting 35.3 per cent of the world's total CO_2.[10] China is ranked as the world's largest emitter, accounting for 21.9 per cent followed by the United States (17.7 per cent), India (5.4 per cent) and Russia (5.3 per cent). South Africa and Brazil are responsible for 1.4 per cent and 1.2 per cent of global emissions respectively, and occupy the 13th and 17th positions internationally. If we take the example of China, we observe that fossil-fuel CO_2 emissions in the country have more than doubled in the 2000 decade alone. Energy efficiency is a big problem in China and energy consumption per product is about 40 per cent higher than in the developed world. Other environmental problems are also critical. For instance, 40 per cent of river and 75 per cent of lake water is polluted leaving 360 million rural people without clean water. As in China, the environmental impacts in other BRICS countries are also mounting.

Other than extending the existing problems in BRICS countries, one general and common issue should be emphasised. This relates to the sustainability of its current growth trajectory. This is true in terms of growing inequality, increasing environmental impacts, as well as regional and other imbalances. However, there are some recent changes that may open better future prospects.

All the BRICS countries have an important role to play in shaping the future of the world economy, but China will probably have a more prominent role in this respect. The Chinese system of innovation has been undergoing some changes in order to address two new proclaimed goals: the building of a 'harmonious growth' and the development of 'indigenous innovations' (AeA 2007). The harmonious growth aims at reducing the growing social and environmental imbalances. China's emerging 'high-growth with low-carbon' strategy has been emphasised by recent policy decisions, together with measures directed to reduce rural–urban social gaps. The indigenous innovation goal refers to the efforts to make China less reliant on foreign technology through the building of a new kind of relationship between national and foreign players in the process of developing and using new technologies.[11] China is pursuing these goals especially by linking innovation to domestic needs and by giving increased priority to domestic consumption.[12]

For Brazil, India, Russia, and South Africa, Chinese success may lead to strategies towards strengthening domestic technological capabilities and fostering clean technologies. Nevertheless, the differentiated role of the BRICS countries in the configuration of global power and the global economy will in some way constrain the evolution of BRICS national systems for innovation. In addition, their NSIs are highly dependent on their historical development and on how the different domestic actors interpret global developments as well as how they position themselves in the national and international economies. Yet, more flexibility for setting up new industrial and technological policies may be expected.

Introduction to Books 1–5

This book series attempts to cover five themes that are crucial to an understanding of the National System of Innovation of BRICS. The first book *The Role of the State*, edited by Mario Scerri (South Africa) and Helena M. M. Lastres (Brazil) aims at exploring the relationship between the state and the national systems of innovation in BRICS countries. An evolutionary approach has been adopted in order to capture the nature of the state in the respective countries and thus understand the historical and ideological basis for its role in the evolution of the NSI in the five countries. As a background, it is argued that debates on the role of the state in the development process, especially since the 1980s, have often focused on the apparent dichotomy between market-driven and state-driven development. This is a rather wasteful diversion, since it should be accepted as a starting premise that the state is essential to the structural transformation that is required for development.

The second book addresses an aspect of the NSI that is normally absent from the discussion: the relation between innovation and inequality. The objectives of the book *Inequality and Development Challenges*, edited by Maria Clara Couto Soares (Brazil), Mario Scerri and Rasigan Maharajh (South Africa) are to trace the trends in interpersonal and inter-regional inequality within BRICS in an evolutionary perspective and to analyse the co-evolution of inequality and the innovation system to highlight how the various elements of innovation and the production system and inequality mutually reinforce.

The book is driven to improving our understanding of this issue. The inequality concept is considered in its multi-dimensional character, embracing a phenomenon that goes beyond the mere income dimension and is manifested through forms increasingly complex, including, among others, assets, access to basic services, infrastructure, knowledge, as well as race, gender, ethnic, and geographic dimensions. The book adopts the broad approach of the national system of innovation to analyse the relations between BRICS innovation systems and inequality, departing from a co-evolutionary view.

As shown in the book chapters, innovation can affect inequalities in different ways and through distinct trails that are influenced by national conditions, and shaped by public policy interventions. Although innovation does not constitute the main factor of influence on inequality, it is suggested that distinct strategies for technological change may lead to different outcomes in distributive terms, thus either aggravating or mitigating inequality. Based on this understanding, the book corroborates the hypothesis that inequalities need to be explicitly taken into account in development strategies since the benefits of science, technology and innovation are not automatically distributed equally. Therefore, advancing the comprehension of inter-relations between innovation and inequality may be helpful to find ways to shape the national innovation systems so that they reduce rather than increase inequalities.

The third book aims at analysing the contribution of small- and medium-scale enterprises (SMEs) in the national system of innovation. The objective of the book *The Promise of Small and Medium Enterprises*, edited by Ana Arroio (Brazil) and Mario Scerri (South Africa) is to explore three main research goals. In the first place, to provide an overview of the main characteristics of micro, small and medium firms in the Brazilian, Russian, Indian, Chinese and South African national systems of innovation as a basis to examine the contribution of SMEs to the economy of each country. A second goal is to bring to the forefront crucial issues in the discussion of industrial and technological policies for small firms, including the recent evolution and future trends of policies and instruments, their applicability and coordination, as well as a discussion of the macro-economic, legal and regulatory environment. A final research objective is to draw out initiatives to promote innovation in SMEs that address common bottlenecks in BRICS countries and that can contribute to policy design and implementation by these and other countries.

The fourth book discusses the relationship between transnational corporations and the national system of innovation of BRICS countries. In the book *Transnational Corporations and Local Innovation*, edited by José E. Cassiolato (Brazil), Graziela Zucoloto (Brazil), Dinesh Abrol (India), and Liu Xielin (China) the thesis of technological globalisation is taken with some caution, refuting the idea that R&D activities would be inexorably internationalised. In fact, technological innovative activities in TNCs have been transformed, in relation with the financialisation of transnational corporations (TNCs), as evidenced by the rise of their intangible assets (which includes R&D, patents, and trademarks) and a reorientation of R&D expenditures towards non-scientific activities and very downstream development.

The book chapters present a detailed presentation of the relation of the position and evolution of TNC in the country. Subsequently, there is a discussion on the local factors affecting innovation by TNCs and local firms in the country. Government policy towards TNCs has been important but as the Chinese experience shows, access to local buoyant markets has also been vital. Other issues discussed refer to how the government protects local companies from the competition of TNCs. Spillovers of TNCs to local BRICS enterprises have also been analysed and the immediate conclusion is that there is hardly any convincing evidence regarding either the existence or non-existence of spillovers. An in-depth analysis of outward FDI has also been conducted.

Finally, the fifth book deals with finance and funding in the national system of innovation. The objective was to analyse institutional character and support instruments for the innovation financing process in BRICS, focusing on institutional structure and innovation policy. This book, *Financing Innovation*, edited by Michael Kahn (South Africa) and Luiz Martins de Melo and Marcelo G. Pessoa de Matos (Brazil) contributes to understanding the varied approaches to the financing of innovation. It draws on the experience of five diverse countries each of which has undergone dramatic structural adjustment in the last two to three decades. The experience of the BRICS countries presents a unique set of case studies of the transition from largely closed centrally planned and state-driven economic and science policy to a more open and market-led situation. The contributing authors examine the varying approaches to the provision of support to the full range of activities that contribute to innovation ranging from scholarship support to doctoral students, to R&D tax incentives and the provision of seed capital.

The significance of financing investments in innovation has been pointed out as an important structural bottleneck that is yet to be solved by the private financial institutions. If, on the one hand, the internationalisation, deregulation and globalisation of financial markets signals the possibility of resources at lower costs, on the other, the characteristics of investments in innovation such as the length of time needed for development, the uncertainty and the risk, point to the need of setting national institutional arrangements.

Notes

1. Available at http://www.globelics.org (accessed 3 December 2011).
2. Available at http://www.redesist.ie.ufrj.br (accessed 3 December 2011).
3. This is also true in Latin American countries, where it is being applied and understood in close connection with the basic conceptual ideas

of the structuralism approach developed in the region since the 1950s under the influence of the Economic Commission of Latin America and Caribbean. In fact, since the mid-1990s, the work of RedeSist — the Research Network on Local Productive and Innovative Systems — based at the Economics Institute of Rio de Janeiro, Brazil, has been using such a dual frame of reference.

4. See, for instance, Mytelka and Farinelli (2003); Freeman (2003); Chesnais and Sauviat (2003).
5. The following data on BRICS countries' value added by sector (per cent of GDP), 1980–2009 is based on the UNCTAD *Handbook of Statistics* (2010).
6. The IBSA Dialogue Forum was established in June 2003 in Brasilia, Brazil.
   BRIC was formally constituted in June 2009 at a summit of the four countries in Yekaterinburg, Russia. In 2011, South Africa joined the group, which changed its denomination to BRICS.
   BASIC of the G4 was formed during the international climate change negotiations in December 2009 in Copenhagen, Denmark.
7. There are several economic and geopolitical factors that restrict a greater convergence of interests among BRICS countries in multilateral negotiations. The analysis of these constraints goes beyond the limited scope of this concept note, but we could cite the aforementioned relatively low degree of trade complementarities between BRICS as an important one.
8. In 2008, Gini indexes were respectively 0.54 and 0.67 according to Brazilian and South African national institutes of statistics.
9. According to World Bank statistics, the population below poverty line was 28.6 per cent in India and 30.9 per cent in Russia in the mid-2000s.
10. It is important to mention that CDIAC-UN data considers only global carbon dioxide emissions from the burning of fossil fuel, but not emissions from deforestation or other greenhouse gases, including methane.
11. The US Information Technology Office in Beijing refers to indigenous innovation as a term combining three distinct elements: *yuanshi* (original, or genuinely new); *jicheng* (integrated, or combining existing technologies in new ways); and *yinjin* (assimilated, or making improvements to imported technologies). See http://www.usito.org/ (accessed 8 January 2013).
12. In November 2008, China launched a US$ 584 billion anti-cyclical package. According to the HSBC report on climate change (Robins 2009) almost 40 per cent of the total package resources were allocated to 'green' themes. Among others, it combined the search for a lower carbon pattern with the offering of better transport conditions for lower income people placed in rural areas, fostering a niche for the development

of innovations capable of attending to the specificities of this domestic market segment.

References

American Electronics Association (AeA), 2007, 'China's Fifteen Year Science and Technology Plan: What does it Mean to Spawn "Indigenous Innovation"?', *Competitiveness Series*, vol. 14, April, 2.

Arocena, R. and J. Sutz, 2003. 'Knowledge, Innovation and Learning: Systems and Policies in the North and in the South', in J. E. Cassiolato, H. M. M. Lastres and M. L. Maciel (eds), *Systems of Innovation and Development: Evidence from Brazil*. Cheltenham: Edward Elgar, 291–310.

Baumann, R., 2009. 'El Comercio entre los Países "BRICS"', LC/BRS/R.210, Comisión Económica para América Latina y el Caribe (CEPAL), Santiago de Chile, August.

Carbon Dioxide Information Analysis Center–United Nations (CDIAC–UN), 2008. 'Global, Regional, and National Fossil-Fuel CO_2 Emissions'. http://cdiac.ornl.gov/trends/emis/overview.html (accessed 1 March 2011).

Cassiolato, J. E. and H. M. M. Lastres, 1999. *Globalização e Inovação Localizada: experiências de sistemas locais no Mercosul*. Brasília: Instituto Brasileiro de Informação em Ciência e Tecnologia.

——, 2008. 'Discussing Innovation and Development: Converging Points between the Latin American School and the Innovation Systems Perspective', Working Paper no. 08-02, Globelics Working Paper Series, The Global Network for Economics of Learning, Innovation, and Competence Building System.

Cassiolato, J. E., H. M. M. Lastres and M. L. Maciel (eds), 2003. *Systems of Innovation and Development: Evidence from Brazil*. Cheltenham: Edward Elgar.

Chesnais, F. and C. Sauviat, 2003. 'The Financing of Innovation-related Investment in the Contemporary Global Finance-dominated Accumulation Regime', in J. E. Cassiolato, H. M. M. Lastres and M. L. Maciel (eds), *Systems of Innovation and Development: Evidence from Brazil*. Cheltenham: Edward Elgar, 61–118.

Economist, The, 2010. 'A Special Report on Innovation in Emerging Markets', 15 April.

Freeman, C., 1982. 'Technological Infrastructure and International Competitiveness', Draft Paper submitted to the OECD Ad Hoc Group on Science, Technology and Competitiveness, Organisation for Economic Co-operation and Development, Paris. http://redesist.ie.ufrj.br/globelics/pdfs/GLOBELICS_0079_Freeman.pdf (accessed 24 September 2012).

Freeman, C., 1987. *Technology Policy and Economic Performance: Lessons from Japan*. London: Frances Pinter.

——, 2003. 'A Hard Landing for the "New Economy"? Information Technology and the United States National System of Innovation', in J. E. Cassiolato, H. M. M. Lastres, and M. L. Maciel (eds), *Systems of Innovation and Development: Evidence from Brazil*. Cheltenham: Edward Elgar, 119–40.

Freeman, C. and C. Perez, 1988. 'Structural Crisis of Adjustment, Business Cycles and Investment Behaviour', in G. Dosi, C. Freeman, R. Nelson, G. Silverberg, and L. L. Soete (eds), *Technical Change and Economic Theory*, London: Pinter, 38–66.

Furtado, C., 1961. *Desenvolvimento e Subdesenvolvimento*. Rio de Janeiro: Fundo de Cultura.

——, 2002. *Capitalismo Global*. São Paulo: Paz e Terra.

Global Environmental Facility, 2008. 'Index Table — Biodiversity'. http://www.thegef.org/gef/node/1805 (accessed 16 February 2011).

Herrera, A., 1975. 'Los Determinantes Sociales de la Politica Cientifica en America Latina', in J. Sábato (ed.), *El Pensamento Latinoamericano en Ciencia-Tecnologia-Desarrollo-Dependencia*. Buenos Aires: Paidos, 98–112.

Hirschman, A., 1958. *The Strategy of Economic Development*. New Haven: Yale University Press.

Instituto de Pesquisa Econômica Aplicada (IPEA), 2008. 'PNAD-2007: Primeiras Análises: Pobreza e Mudança Social', *Comunicados da Presidência*, 1(9), Instituto de Pesquisa Econômica Aplicada, Brasília.

International Monetary Fund (IMF), 2011. 'World Economic Outlook Database', September 2011. http://www.imf.org/external/pubs/ft/weo/2011/02/weodata/index.aspx (accessed 4 October 2011).

Johnson, B. and B.-Å. Lundvall, 2003. 'Promoting Innovation Systems as a Response to the Globalising Learning Economy', in J. E. Cassiolato, H. M. M. Lastres and M. L. Maciel (eds), *Systems of Innovation and Development: Evidence from Brazil*. Cheltenham: Edward Elgar, 141–84.

Lastres, H. M. M., 1994. *The Advanced Materials Revolution and the Japanese System of Innovation*. London: Macmillan.

Lastres, H. M. M. and J. E. Cassiolato, 2005. 'Innovation Systems and Local Productive Arrangements: New Strategies to Promote the Generation, Acquisition and Diffusion of Knowledge', *Innovation: Management, Policy & Practice*, 7(2): 172–87.

Lastres, H. M. M., J. E. Cassiolato and M. L. Maciel, 2003. 'Systems of Innovation for Development in the Knowledge Era: An Introduction', in J. E. Cassiolato, H. M. M. Lastres and M. L. Maciel (eds), *Systems of Innovation and Development: Evidence from Brazil*. Cheltenham: Edward Elgar, 1–33.

List, F., 1841. *National System of Political Economy.* New York: Cosimo.

Lundvall, B.-Å. 1988. 'Innovation as an Interactive Process: From User-Producer Interaction to the National System of Innovation', in G. Dosi, C. Freeman, R. Nelson, G. Silverberg, and L. L. Soete (eds), *Technical Change and Economic Theory*. London: Pinter, 349–69.

——, 1992. *National System of Innovation: Towards a Theory of Innovation and Interactive Learning*. London: Pinter.

——, 2009. 'The BRICS Countries and Europe', in J. E Cassiolato and V. Vitorino (eds), *BRICS and Development Alternatives: Innovation Systems and Policies*. London: Anthem Press, xv–xxi.

Myrdal, G., 1968. *Asian Drama: An Inquiry into the Poverty of Nations.* London: Penguin Books

Mytelka, L. K., 2000. 'Local Systems of Innovation in a Globalized World Economy', *Industry and Innovation*, 7(1): 15–32.

Mytelka, L. K. and F. Farinelli, 2003. 'From Local Clusters to Innovation Systems', in J. E. Cassiolato, H. M. M. Lastres and M. L. Maciel (eds), *Systems of Innovation and Development: Evidence from Brazil.* Cheltenham: Edward Elgar, 249–72.

Perez, C., 1983. 'Structural Change and the Assimilation of New Technologies in the Economic and Social System', *Futures*, 15(5): 357–75.

———, 1988. 'New Technologies and Development', in C. Freeman and B.-Å. Lundvall (eds), *Small Countries Facing the Technological Revolution.* London: Pinter, 85–97.

Ravallion, M., 2009. *The Developing World's Bulging (but Vulnerable) 'Middle Class'.* Washington DC: World Bank.

Robins, N., 2009. 'A Climate for Recovery: The Colour of Stimulus Goes Green', HSBC Global Research. http://www.research.hsbc.com (accessed 2 December 2011).

Rodríguez, O., 2001. 'Prebisch: actualidad de sus ideas básicas', *Revista de la CEPAL*, 75: 41–52.

Schumpeter, J. A., 1982 [1912]. *The Theory of Economic Development: An Inquiry into Profits, Capital, Credit, Interest, and the Business Cycle (1912/1934).* New Jersey: Transaction Books.

United Nations Conference on Trade and Development (UNCTAD), 2009. *UNCTAD Handbook of Statistics 2009.* Geneva; New York: United Nations. http://unctadstat.unctad.org/ReportFolders/reportFolders.aspx (accessed 15 March 2011).

——, 2010. *UNCTAD Handbook of Statistics 2010.* Geneva; New York: United Nations. http://unctadstat.unctad.org/ReportFolders/reportFolders.aspx (accessed 15 March 2011).

United Nations, 2010a. 'United Nations Statistical Databases', United Nations Statistic Division. http://unstats.un.org/unsd/databases.htm (accessed 20 March 2011).

United Nations, 2010b. 'United Nations Commodity Trade Statistics Database', United Nations Statistic Division. http://comtrade.un.org/ (accessed 20 March 2011).

Wilson, Dominic and Raluca Dragusanu, 2008. 'The Expanding Middle: The Exploding World Middle Class and Falling Global Inequality', Global Economics Paper no. 170, Goldman Sachs, 7 July.

World Bank, 2010. 'World Economic Indicators Database 2010'. http://data.worldbank.org/data-catalog/world-development-indicators (accessed 25 March 2011).

——, 2011. 'World Development Indicators Database 2011'. http://siteresources.worldbank.org/DATASTATISTICS/Resources/GDP_PPP.pdf (accessed 1 July 2011).

1

The Co-evolution of Innovation and Inequality

Mario Scerri, Maria Clara Couto Soares and *Rasigan Maharajh*

Empirical evidence consistently confirms the relevance of science, technology and innovation in advancing economic development (OECD 1992, amongst others). The analysis of the distributive effects of innovation in the circuits of production, distribution, consumption, and waste management, however, remains largely underdetermined. The complex relationship between inequality, innovation systems and development therefore provides scholars with major opportunities to contribute new insights into an important intellectual domain. The analysis of economic systems through an innovation systems lens has opened up the theoretical space for the analysis of the co-evolution of economic systems and society and of the multiplex causalities of the various interlinked sub-systems. The understanding of the dynamic inter-relations between innovation systems and inequality constitutes a formidable challenge given its complexity, contestation and interdisciplinary character. However, despite the magnitude of the task, a better understanding of the relationship between innovation systems and inequality allows for the evaluation of different options for configuring technological and institutional change and for opening up the possibility for policies that may promote development alternatives which normatively aspire towards greater equality and social cohesion. This book is driven by the imperative shared by both the academic and policy communities to seek to improve our collective understanding of these issues. The book adopts the broad version of the national systems of innovation (NSI) approach to analyse the relations between the innovation systems of the BRICS (Brazil, Russia, India, China, and South Africa) countries and inequality, proceeding from a co-evolutionary perspective.

The early works on the systems of innovation approach to the analysis of economic dynamics date back to the 1980s (Freeman 1982a, 1982b; Freeman and Lundvall 1988). Since then the SI approach has been increasingly used to analyse processes of acquisition, use and diffusion of innovations besides orienting policy recommendations in both more developed and developing countries. The initial attempts to present a countervailing theory to the neoclassical orthodoxy were based on a narrow approach to the analysis of innovation systems, with a specific focus on research and development and on organisations directly connected to science and technology. While the narrow approach is still adopted in innovation system literature, the eventual broadening of the understanding of innovation systems and the convergence of the innovation systems approach with the Latin American structuralist approach to development economics (see Cassiolato and Lastres 2008) has brought in a greater analytical and normative capacity to the analysis of national systems of innovation. This broader approach incorporates governmental policies, social institutions, financing organisations, and all other agents and elements that affect the acquisition, use and dissemination of innovations. This approach also includes informal institutions, as established routines and practices which, through processes of socialisation and internalisation, govern social, economic and political interactions. It is this broad perspective which is particularly important to the subject addressed by the book, since it allows a better understanding of how the innovation process takes place and how it is linked with local specificities and distributional issues (see Cassiolato et al. 2008).

An important contribution of the broad approach to the analysis of innovation systems is the recognition of the importance of the socio-economic and political context in which the system is embedded, due to its influence on the configuration of the capabilities of organisations, regions and countries for developing, disseminating and using innovations. In this approach, innovation is considered as deeply dependent on the local specificities of social, political and economic relations, being therefore directly affected by both history and the particular institutional context of countries or regions where it occurs. Therefore innovation and learning reflect the combination of prevailing institutions and the socio-economic structures. The extension of the definition of institutions to include formal institutions not directly connected to science and technology and even further to informal institutions as established forms of routines, practices and interpersonal relations allows for an integrated approach to the analysis of the sources of enduring patterns of inequalities of various forms.

Before we proceed further, however, we need to expand on the rationale for the inclusion of the question of inequality in this series of studies of the various aspects of national systems of innovation in the BRICS countries. This is a legitimate query since in some respects the problem of inequality is substantively different from the other issues addressed in this series. The relationships between the national system of innovation and the state, finance, the small and medium enterprise sector, and transnational corporations and foreign direct investment are immediately apparent and self-evident as relationships between formal institutions. The phenomenon of inequality, in terms of its root causes and effects, is usually seen to belong more to the area of social, rather than economic, studies, even though the degrees of inequality are usually estimated using economic measures. Marxian analysis is, of course, the one main exception to this rather generalised statement, given its direct focus on the economic sources of class divisions and inequality and the innovation systems approach is in its way similar to a refined Marxian approach in its consideration of the totality of the phenomenon and its multidimensional relationship with the economy. This is enabled by the extension of the definition of the economy under this approach beyond the neoclassical reductionist version and by its erosion of the misleading distinction between the 'economic' and the 'social' spheres.

The detrimental effects of inequality are usually seen in terms of their impact on social stability and on the value system of the democratic ideal. We therefore need to see why the issue of inequality, measured in various ways, should be included as a legitimate component of this series of studies on the various aspects of the BRICS systems of innovation. One reason for inclusion is the empirical evidence that this group of countries experience high levels of inequality as an outcome of their currently pursued developmental trajectories. The concerns generated by this phenomenon are however global, and as such, the inclusion of inequality in the analysis of the specific systems of innovation affords a degree of congruence between innovation studies and those of the global political economy. The basic assumption is that the nature of the specific systems of innovation, and their evolutionary paths, has a non-trivial effect on the manifestation of significant levels of inequality in its various dimensions. From this perspective, the five chapters that follow seek to understand the history of inequality and the manner in which inequality is being affected by economic policies in general and by industrial, trade and innovation strategies in particular. At the same time these chapters reflect on the effects of inequality, in their specific manifestations on the evolutionary paths of the respective national systems of innovation of the five economies.

Before proceeding further, it is important to define inequality. Broadly speaking, inequality may be seen to have at least two major aspects: opportunity and outcomes. The two facets are of course strongly related but are not identical. Opportunity refers to what we may call the 'life chances' of individuals and groups, whose determinants include a myriad factors deriving from economic, political and social contexts. Opportunity is difficult to measure except through proxy variables, including income, wealth, the various features of human capital, and access to the means for self-development.[1] In this context, human capital can be seen as an enabler of personal life choice options. From this perspective we can avoid an economic reductionist assessment of inequality by contextualising measurements of human capital within a context of political and social constraints. Outcomes, on the other hand, are more easily measured, usually in terms of income, wealth and consumption patterns. While the two aspects of inequality are not identical, the endurance of a specific pattern of inequality of outcomes over time would tend to entrench corresponding patterns of inequality of opportunity. The concept of inequality is therefore considered in its multidimensional character, embracing a phenomenon that goes beyond the mere income dimension and is manifested through increasingly complex forms, including, among others, assets, access to basic services, infrastructure, and knowledge, as well as race, gender, ethnic and geographic dimensions. The different forms of inequality, whether class, gender, ethnicity, or geographic, have distinct implications on the effects of inequality and on the required counteracting policies. These forms often intersect, as with, for example, a correlation between race and class or the relationship between ethnicity and geographical setting, to create new configurations of the manifestation and the root causes of inequality. There are therefore two major features of the definition of inequality. The first is its expression in class, gender, ethnicity, and geographical forms, as discussed earlier. The second dimension to the definition concerns its manifestation in terms of income, wealth, education, health, etc., which determine both the quality of life and life opportunities. The focus on inequality in terms of opportunity and prospects highlights the structural nature of inequality which establishes it as an institution within the web which makes up the national system of innovation.

The types of inequality considered in this book, and the relative emphases placed on them, obviously differ across the five studies and are quite specific in terms of their underlying structures and histories. In the case of the two NSIs which emerged from centrally planned economies into new varieties of capitalism, the main focus of the respective studies is on class and geographical inequalities. This focus is most pronounced in the case of China, whereas in the Russian study, gender inequality is also included. The Russian study also identifies families with children as being particularly disadvantaged since the disintegration of the Soviet Union with the consequence of a recognised disincentive to have and raise children. In the case of India, inequality measures refer to religious groupings, as well as class and region. The Brazilian study also includes ethnicity, in terms of racial classification, alongside class and region. The history of South Africa obviously dictates that the conjuncture of race and class be considered in the assessment of the institution of inequality, along with geography and gender (Maharajh 2011). The choice of the types of inequality which have been considered in the respective country studies also carries implications for the complexity of the problematic posed by the proposed co-evolution of innovation and inequality. The wider the range of the types of inequality which are considered as relevant for a particular system, the greater is the potential for interrelations and causalities among the various types and sources of inequality. This tends to render both the phenomenon of inequality and the possibilities for its solution through policy more complex. The treatment of specific inequalities in these five studies is obviously not exhaustive, both in terms of inclusion and of emphasis. It represents, rather, a context-specific ranking of the types of inequality in terms of their relevance in the co-evolution between innovation and inequality.

The idea of co-evolution between innovation and inequality offered by Cozzens and Kaplinsky (2009) is a welcome contribution to the understanding of this complex relationship. They suggest that 'innovation and inequality co-evolve, with innovation sometimes reflecting and reinforcing inequalities and sometimes undermining them'. The causal relations between innovation and inequality can also run in the opposite direction with high degrees of endemic inequality shaping the evolution of national systems of innovation. Here we can find the source of mutual self-reinforcing mechanisms between innovation and inequality which over time entrench and deepen the structural inequality of incomes, wealth and, more crucially, the life chances of different sections of populations. This forms the basis for a path-dependent vicious circle of innovation deepening inequality which further determines an evolution of the system of innovation which adjusts for the economic constraints posed by acute inequality, primarily in terms of the type and spread of human capabilities and learning capacities. This path dependency, especially given long historical reinforcement, would almost inevitably require state intervention to break this vicious cycle.

Fundamentally, the basis for the co-evolution between innovation and inequality is the fact that the foundations of inequality form one of the informal institutions of national systems of innovation. The treatment of inequality, and its basis, as an institution is premised on the assumption that the inequalities which we consider exhibit a degree of persistence over time. It follows that inequality emerges from established practices and relationships which endure, are structural and are subject to analysis stemming from an established theoretical basis. In this sense both the sources of inequality and the specific type of inequality itself can be considered as informal institutions. From this perspective we can therefore proceed to explore the factors which tend to reproduce inequality and it is only on this basis that we can eventually derive corrective policy recommendations. The study of the sources and effects of inequality thus becomes an integral part of the analysis of systems of innovation. Several theoretical approaches can be brought into the investigation of inequality as one of the institutional components of a national system of innovation and, given the political economy basis of the study of systems of innovation, these approaches almost necessarily tend to be contentious. Thus class inequalities are obviously subject to Marxian analysis while racial and ethnic inequalities would merit approaches to identity politics and the analysis of ethnic conflict, with gender inequality requiring the application of gender economics. Regional inequalities would probably best be approached from a more traditional development economics basis. These various approaches must not be seen as compartmentalised since the various forms which inequality can take are often conflated in a singular, contextually specific, local manifestation. Thus, for example, a roughly theoretically integrated approach is required to analyse the effects of globalisation on the shape and changes in inequalities of various forms within the context of specific NSIs as well as the more commonly studied effects on the inequalities between NSIs. In this way a more complex assessment of the systemic effects of the modern manifestation of globalisation can be brought to bear on to an issue which has come to occupy a prominent place in the analysis of the development of the international political economy.

The potency of the institution of inequality in terms of its specific manifestation differs dramatically across systems and again this is one of the examples where specificity matters crucially. In the case of South Africa, for example, it is impossible to understand the NSI without an understanding of apartheid, a unique example of entrenched inequality arising from a system of legislated racial discrimination which affected almost all aspects of life (Scerri 2009; Maharajh 2011). The uniqueness of this case among the BRICS systems of innovation is that until relatively recently racial discrimination in South African was a formal institution. Inequality in India, on the other hand, rises from a political economic context which has, since independence, been democratic and has outlawed discrimination on the basis of caste, religion, ethnicity, or gender. The enduring inequality in India is a deeply rooted informal institution and it is perhaps this very informality which makes it so difficult to eradicate simply through legislation.

Inequality and poverty have historically defined Brazil's and South Africa's political economy and continue to constitute a worrying reality, notwithstanding recent improvements in the case of Brazil. The trend of increasing inequality in both China and India wherein the 'Gini has overtaken the growth rates' has attracted the attention of a number of scholars. Thus, as highlighted in this book, inequality is a peculiar trait of these countries comprising a key factor for understanding both the configuration and the dynamic of the national innovation systems of BRICS. Figure 1.1 shows the evolution of the Gini index from the early 1990s to the late 2000s in the BRICS countries.

We are of course fully aware that the referred trends are not confined to the BRICS economies. Inequality is shown to have increased in the global economy at an unprecedented rate over the last three decades, a period when knowledge intensity in the production process and international trade dramatically increased. This validation of

Figure 1.1: *Change in Inequality Levels, Early 1990s versus Late 2000s* (Gini Coefficient of Household Income**)*

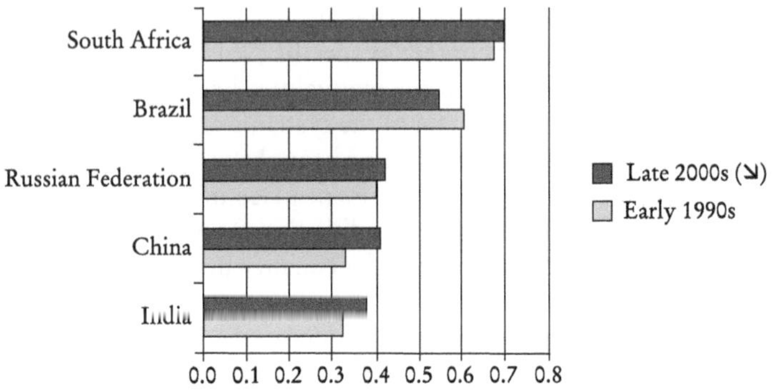

Source: OECD–EU (2011).
Note: *Figures for the early 1990s generally refer to 1993, whereas figures for the late 2000s generally refer to 2008.
**Gini coefficients are based on equivalised incomes for OECD countries and per capita incomes for all EEs except India for which per capita consumption was used.

the logic of the Prebisch-Singer theorem (see Singer 1950; Prebisch 1950) of the deteriorating terms of trade between developed and developing economies and the perverse effect of the neoclassical factor price equalisation theorem on the globalisation of class divisions should come as no surprise. On the one hand the increasing prominence of knowledge intensity as a determinant of international competitiveness tends to increase the inequality among NSIs. On the other, the accelerating rate with which knowledge and the access to knowledge has come to create competitive advantage at the interpersonal level has increasingly sharpened inequalities within NSIs. It seems, therefore, that NSIs can thrive even in the presence of large and enduring structural inequalities.

This then is the conundrum which faces both the analyst and the politician. The drive to reduce inequality and eradicate poverty can obviously stem from a principled ethical stance entrenched in a variety of political agendas and ideologies. This however, is not always sufficient to bring about the necessary structural changes, especially in the face of the ubiquitous allure of the neoliberal 'trickle down' theory of the much vaunted welfare effects of free markets. It has to be clearly demonstrated that significant enduring inequalities within any NSI ultimately severely restrict its development and compromise its long-term viability. The immediately obvious argument for this proposition is premised on the deleterious effects of sustained inequalities on the development of broad-based human capital and human capabilities and the severe constraints which they impose on internal systems of consumption. The former effect imposes supply side restrictions on innovation, while the latter imposes constraints on the demand side of the innovation system. Beyond these effects there is also the other, more generic implication of sustained significant inequalities for the long-term political legitimacy, social stability and economic dynamicism of the political economy of the NSI.

Innovations, whether as technology or institutional change, can spur economic growth and engender the structural transformation of an economy. However, the operation of systems of innovation and capability formations might either redress or exacerbate inequality. While a positive correlation is frequently observed between advances in science, technology and innovation and the deepening of socio-economic gaps, this is not a necessary outcome.[2] Indeed, this study is partially driven by the hope that a better understanding of the relationships which determine this apparently common correlation, or even causality, may eventually enable policy formulations which would directly address these particular deleterious effects of innovation. The relevant question here is whether an innovation system can be separated from the logic and accumulated trajectory of its political economy. This aspiration is particularly relevant to highly unequal developing economies where fostering innovation usually increases inequalities and 'the trend toward higher inequality is probably stronger in a global knowledge-based and innovation-driven economy [with] people with greater capabilities, power, and social capital [being] better situated to innovate, to take profit from innovations, and to learn by innovating' (Sutz and Arocena 2006: 7).

As shown in all the chapters in this book, innovation can affect inequalities in different ways and through distinct paths which are influenced by national conditions and shaped by public policy. Although innovation does not constitute the main factor of influence on inequality, it is suggested that distinct strategies for technological change may lead to different outcomes in distributive terms, thus either aggravating or mitigating inequality. Based on this understanding, this book corroborates the hypothesis that inequalities need to be taken explicitly into account in development strategies since the benefits of science, technology and innovation cannot be assumed to be automatically distributed equally. Therefore, advancing the comprehension of the interrelations between innovation and inequality may be helpful to find ways to shape the evolution of NSIs so that they reduce rather than increase inequalities. It is here that we need to make a distinction between innovation and systems of innovation. The relationship between innovations, especially technological innovations, and inequality, can perhaps be traced through the factor biases of innovations and their effects on existing distributions of income, wealth and economic and political power. A comprehensive deconstructive analysis of these relationships, however, can only be adequately assessed from within the theoretical context of the systems of innovation approach, defined broadly enough to incorporate most aspects of the political economy and extending considerably beyond the orthodox definition of the economic sphere. It is only within this context that the intimate relationship between innovation and issues of inequality and the attendant one of poverty can be thoroughly explored in their various multidirectional sets of causalities. The systems of innovation approach also allows for a proper dynamic analysis of the shifts of these various interlocked relationships over time, affected by, and affecting, the various interlocking political economies within which they are set.

Given the fact that the analysis of the relationship between systems of innovation and inequality has a relatively short history, this book is not rooted in a body of concepts already sufficiently developed and able to provide a solid basis for guidance to the research. The reflection on the subject in this book is built on the experience of the BRICS countries. The terms of reference of this study are not confined to contributing to a better understanding of the relations between inequality and the NSI in these countries; they are also driven by a recognised urgent need to support a programme of political action aimed at the promotion of development from a perspective focused on social inclusion. This is a case where praxis, based on sound theory and empirical investigation, is urgently called for. In this regard, we hope that the analyses presented in this book may stimulate discussion of the implications of the analysis for public policies in BRICS countries and may also have some influence on policy-making contexts in other countries.

The following five chapters present the BRICS case studies and each chapter shares a loosely common structure so as to facilitate cross system comparisons. The overall objectives of each chapter are twofold. The first is to trace the trends in interpersonal and inter-regional inequality within economies from an evolutionary perspective. The relevant period of analysis obviously differs, depending on the specific histories of individual countries, but in general it covers the past 70 years. The second is to analyse the co-evolution of inequality and innovation system in order to provide some understanding of the mutually reinforcing relationship between the various elements of the innovation and production system on the one hand, and inequality on the other.

Each chapter starts with the characterisation of poverty and inequality patterns in the country concerned, tracing the trends in interpersonal, inter-regional as well as in other forms of inequality (race, class, gender, ethnicity, geographic locality, and others as appropriate for the country) within the economy over the last few decades, from an evolutionary perspective on the political economy in question. In the analysis of the grounding of the patterns of inequality, the individual chapters attempt to place the observed trends against the historical, political and cultural background of inequality. The analysis of the co-evolution of inequality and innovation system follows this section. The attempt here is to analyse how (and whether) the various elements of the NSI and inequality mutually reinforce each other. To this effect, each chapter examines how the policies and institutions of the national systems of innovation and production co-evolve with inequality at personal and regional levels. This enquiry also empirically highlights how these policies and institutions have reinforced greater structural heterogeneity, the informalisation of employment along with widening of productivity in a context of unequal access to education, health, knowledge infrastructure (e.g. access to mobile networks, the internet, etc.), financial infrastructure, R&D infrastructure and other relevant elements of the national systems of innovation. Within the context of the evolution of the policy framework, the shift away from public sector orientation to private sector domination, with unequal access to global production network, market-driven trade and investment, etc., within the context of rapidly accelerating globalisation will be examined. Thus the co-evolution of NSIs and inequality will be examined within the changing context of the national systems of innovation and production. As already indicated, the main indicators of inequality which are used in this book cover both inequalities of opportunity and those of the more immediate conditions of life. The former set of measures includes access to health and education, access to knowledge infrastructure and access to financial infrastructure. In this regard the chapters also pay specific attention to regional disparities in competence-building institutions and production. These measures provide some indication of the entrenchment of the institutions of inequality. The more immediate measures of inequality which are used include wages, the assessment of inter-sectoral wages/productivity differentials and their bearing on inequality, and the patterns of employment, specifically with respect to the formal/casual divide. The final section of each of the country chapters identifies some salient features of the relationships between the shape of the specific national systems of innovation and specific prevalent forms of inequality which require the attention of policy makers and also draws out a brief list of recommendations for future policy.

It is evident that the BRICS systems of innovation exhibit high degrees of inequality of different forms. The origins of the current patterns and rates of inequality are quite diverse. Thus, for example, South Africa emerges from a state of legalised racial discrimination which, in terms of biopolitics, represents an extreme example of the governance of every aspect of racial divisiveness, from job and residential allocation, the right to engage in business, the right to education, and the freedom to associate, including the area of sexual relations. The Brazilian original social matrix, determined by the concentration of land and of political power, as well as by external dependency, imposed its imprint on the entire process of historical constitution and evolution of Brazilian nation. Throughout different political regimes, the strength of political coalitions, particularly those of landowners and capitalists in relation to urban waged workers and the rural mass, underpinned the inertial and iniquitous distributive patterns observed in Brazil.

Both Russia and China were formed by variations of the egalitarian ideal of communism but both are now witnessing an alarming increase in the rates of inequality over the last two decades. In the case of Russia, the collapse of the Soviet Union and the sudden plunge into an extreme *laissez faire* variety of capitalism during the 1990s had a devastating effect on income and wealth distribution. In the case of China, the accelerated evolution of the political economy into a distinctly Chinese variety of capitalism has also generated a hitherto unprecedented level of inequality in its wake. India, a constitutional parliamentary democracy since its independence, has addressed endemic inequality consistently through policy over the past six decades; the fact that inequality in its various forms still remains such a serious concern is indicative of the ubiquitous and pernicious nature of the informal institutions which underlie endemic inequality.

The nature of the co-evolution of the national system of innovation and inequality is obviously different for the five economies given their historical specificities. Despite the very real specificities of the NSIs studied here the common conclusion that emerges is that in the absence of appropriate policy measures, the evolution of NSIs within the post-1980s context of market liberalisation tends to reproduce, reinforce and even intensify structural inequalities. This is as should be expected since the alteration of the structural context within which private corporations operate does not fall within the role of those corporations. It is rather the role of the state to alter the structure within which the private sector functions. Thus in the case of Russia and China, the two economies which, following their very specific paths, have emerged from a totally planned economy into some variety of capitalism we see an almost inevitable increase in inequality. In the case of Russia the dismantling of the Soviet welfare system and its inadequate substitution in the transition to a capitalist system of innovation has been the main cause of the relationship between inequality and the particular evolution of the NSI. In the case of China, this co-evolution related to the shift to a highly specific variety of capitalism has also increased inequality, not so much in terms of class stratification as geographically, between rural and urban populations. In China, while absolute poverty levels are being reduced, inequality is still increasing. In the case of India, the initial stage in the evolution of the NSI, from independence until the early 1980s, was state led on the basis of import substitution and inward industrialisation and, with a strong redistributive component, was accompanied by falling levels of inequality. In the second phase of the evolution of the innovation system within a more market-driven policy environment the nature of the co-evolution between the system of innovation and inequality has altered, with increasing inequality as, for example, employment grows at a significantly slower rate than output. In the case of South Africa the stimulation and promotion of innovation by the state has largely proceeded without an effective programme for the incorporation of the majority of the population into the formal, skills intensive sectors of the economy. As a consequence, we see a positive relationship between the direction of the evolution of the NSI and inequality. The co-evolutionary aspect of these relationships is highlighted in the chapter on Brazil, which indicates that while the structure of the innovation system, and its development, does little to alleviate inequality, the structure of inequality has also restricted the absorption of technology and the development of an indigenous technological base. In all five cases, therefore, the indication seems to be quite clear that the set of strong and multidirectional causalities in the co-evolution between innovation systems and inequality can only be addressed adequately by state policy. In the absence of public policy which is explicitly designed to alter the nature of this co-evolution, the logic of the development of a capitalist system of innovation almost inevitably has negative distributional effects across the system. This is why it is useful to view inequality, in its various related forms, as an institution within the broader institutional web which makes up the NSI. This perspective should enhance the design of appropriate policy measures aimed at aligning the progression on the system of innovation with the reduction of inequality. This need has become even more pronounced since the global alteration in policy environments since the 1980s.

Finally, we need to accept that the studies presented in this book constitute an initial step in a longer-term research programme which this topic merits. The level of complexity of this area of research and its strong and increasing relevance not only to individual NSIs but to the global system certainly requires a more thorough and exhaustive analysis of the co-evolution of inequalities and systems of innovation for each of the BRICS economies as separate works.

The comparative analyses presented in this book raise a number of questions which still need to be explored. In the first place the bulk of the studies focus on the effects of particular evolution paths of systems of innovation on inequality, defined in a number of ways. However, as already discussed briefly, causality also works in the opposite direction with endemic inequality determining the evolutionary path of systems of innovation, through, for example, the human capital implications for choice of technology and industrial structure. This is due to the fact that in the BRICS systems of innovations, entrenched inequality is a strong non-trivial component of the informal institutional underpinning of these national systems of innovation. The effects of this institution in its various specific manifestations on the nature of the NSI still have to be assessed in detail in future research.

The importance of considering this specific institution of the BRICS systems of innovation emerges from the studies in this book which clearly indicate that it is still a defining institution in the system of innovation. From this position we may tentatively propose that one of the watersheds in the evolution of the innovation systems of the BRICS economies will occur when the specific institutions of inequality cease to be a significant identifier of these systems.

Another area which, while addressed in the various chapters, also merits further exploration is the effect of rapid globalisation on inequality, not merely in terms of current measures but also with regards to the altering of the parameters of inequality. It is now common knowledge that the modern process of globalisation tends to influence the national specificity of systems of innovation and the simultaneous effect which is relevant to considerations of inequality is the degree to which the introduction of access to globalised means of production deepens the intra-national gaps in the conditions of life and in life chances.

Finally, a fundamental question about the nature of inequality still needs to be addressed and this has to do with the relationships among the various types of inequality. At this stage we are still largely in the process of measuring different forms of inequality and locating them within a specific NSI. Congruence in measurements often indicates some strong correlations among various forms of inequality but we still need to grapple with the issue of causality, especially from a historical perspective, in order to understand the root causes of the multifaceted complexity of inequality and the nature of its embedment within NSIs to the point of becoming an integral part of the institutional framework of these systems. It is particularly in this area that the future development of this research project could fruitfully co-opt other disciplines than economics in order to provide the kind of inter-disciplinary methodology required for the thorough investigation of this problematic. There is in these five studies, to various degrees, already a hint of an inter-disciplinary approach. Certainly history has been firmly brought in, in each case. Ideological shifts have also been alluded to in some of the studies, although again the space constraint prohibits the development of the rich analysis which this aspect opens up.

It is hoped that this book has started a new debate with the convergence of two areas of interest — the co-evolution of systems of innovation and inequality with the consideration of the BRICS economies as a specific and distinct field of application. The project has also proceeded in the conviction that the study of inequality through the perspective of the systems of innovation approach not only enriches our understanding of this particular aspect of economic dynamics but also provides the theoretical foundation for policy formulations which are more appropriate for addressing the problems of structural inequalities. All of these studies identify some sort of trade-off between equity and growth with some countries experiencing a stronger correlation between growing inequality and the development of their national system of innovation. The one system where this 'perverse' correlation is least pronounced is India, due to the fact that the first stage of the evolution of its system of innovation, from independence to the early 1980s, was guided by a policy framework explicitly designed to reduce poverty and inequality. This starting base has served to mitigate the effects of the market liberalisation drive which followed. What is evident is that the link between growth and inequality has to be broken through revisiting the foundations of the systems of innovations which we have studied. This need is captured by the statement at the end of the chapter on China that 'we need a new philosophy of development and innovation' if we hope to break this link. From this stance the one case which may potentially offer a policy 'demonstration effect' is that of Brazil. Unlike the case of India, the Brazilian economy has shifted from an entrenched relationship between inequality and the structure of its NSI onto a development path which has over the last decade seen inequality systematically reduced through economic policies which specifically place social development at the top of the economic agenda. This offers sound empirical evidence to support the theoretical proposition that the co-evolution between innovation and inequality can indeed be turned into a virtuous one, given the correct policy environment.

Notes

1. Sen (1999: 296), among others, cautions against the possible pitfalls in the adoption of the concept of human capital when he points out that 'human beings are not merely the means of production, but also the end of the exercise'. Sen also states that '[w]e must go *beyond* the notion of human capital, after acknowledging its relevance and reach. The broadening that is

needed is additional and inclusive, rather than, in any sense, an *alternative* to the "human capital" perspective.' However, a broad enough definition of human capital and an emphasis on the fundamental distinction of human from other forms of capital should enable the appropriate deployment of this potentially powerful analytical construct within a systems of innovation approach, while subverting its appropriation by neoclassical and neoliberal economics. One of the benefits of this deployment would be the erosion of the distinction between the economic and the social spheres and the dangerously misleading separation of the means and the ends of development policy.

2. As pointed out by some authors: 'when the issue of inequality [is] investigated, we often find that diffusion of innovations widens the socio-economic gap between the higher and the lower status segments of a system' (Rogers 1995: 125).

References

Cassiolato, J. E. and H. M. M. Lastres, 2008. 'Discussing Innovation and Development: Converging Points between the Latin American School and the Innovation Systems Perspective', *Globelics Working Paper Series* (08-02).

Cassiolato, J. E., M. C. C. Soares and H. M. M. Lastres, 2008. 'Innovation in Unequal Societies: How Can it Contribute to Improve Equality?' *Seminario Internacional Ciencia, Tecnología, Innovación e Inclusión Social*, United Nations Educational, Scientific and Cultural Organisation, Montevideo, May.

Cozzens, S. E. and R. Kaplinsky, 2009. 'Innovation, Poverty and Inequality: Cause, Coincidence, or Co-evolution', in B.-Å. Lundvall, K. J. Joseph, C. Chaminade, and J. Vang (eds), *Handbook on Innovation Systems in Developing Countries*. Cheltenham: Edward Elgar.

Freeman, C. 1982a. 'Technological Infrastructure and International Competitiveness', Draft Paper submitted to the Organisation for Economic Co-operation and Development Ad Hoc Group on Science, Technology and Competitiveness, Organisation for Economic Co-operation and Development, Paris.

——, 1982b. *The Economics of Industrial Innovation*, Second edition. Boston: MIT Press.

Freeman, C. and B.-Å. Lundvall (eds), 1988. *Small Countries Facing the Technological Revolution*, London: Pinter.

Maharajh, R. 2011. *Innovating beyond Racial Capitalism: A Contribution towards the Analysis of the Political Economy of Post-apartheid South Africa*, Lund Studies in Research Policy 3. Lund: Lund University.

Organisation for Economic Co-operation and Development (OECD), 1992. *Technology and the Economy: The Key Relationships*. Paris: Organisation for Economic Co-operation and Development.

——, 2011. *Divided We Stand: Why Inequality Keeps Rising*, Paris: Organisation for Economic Co-operation and Development.

Organisation for Economic Co-operation and Development–European Union (OECD-EU), 2011. Database on Emerging Economies and World Bank Development Indicators. http://www.oecd.org/dataoecd/40/13/49170475.pdf Stat link http://dx.doi.org/10.1787/888932535432 (accessed 10 January 2012).

Prebisch, R., 1950. *The Economic Development of Latin America and its Principal Problems*, Washington DC: Economic Commission of Latin America and United Nations Department of Economic Affairs.

Rogers, E. M., 1995. *Diffusion of Innovations*, Fourth edition. New York: Free Press.

Scerri, M., 2009. *The Evolution of the South African System of Innovation since 1916*. Newcastle: Cambridge Scholars Publishing.

Sen, A., 1999. *Development as Freedom*. Oxford: Oxford University Press.

Singer, H., 1950. 'The Distribution of Gains between Investing and Borrowing Countries', *American Economic Review*, 40(4): 473–85.

Sutz, J. and R. Arocena, 2006. 'Integrating Innovation Policies with Social Policies: A Strategy to Embed Science and Technology into Development Process', *International Development Research Centre Strategic Commissioned Paper*, April.

2

Inequality, Innovation System and Development: The Brazilian Experience

Maria Clara Couto Soares and
Maria Gabriela Podcameni

The relevance of science, technology and innovation to the promotion of economic growth and competitiveness is widely recognised (Furtado 1961; Freeman 1987). However, the distributive effects of innovation and the dynamic relationships between innovation and inequality still remain largely unexplored.

This chapter seeks to contribute to the improvement of our understanding of these issues with a focus on Brazil. The chapter adopts a broad approach to the national system of innovation (NSI) (Freeman 1987; Lundvall 1992; Cassiolato and Lastres 2008) and utilises the Latin American structuralist perspective (Prebisch 1951; Furtado 1968) to examine the relations between the Brazilian innovation system and inequality.

Despite the improvements in recent years, Brazil is still one of the most unequal countries in the world. If on the one hand it is necessary to further understand how poverty and inequality exert a particular influence on the process of generating, disseminating and using innovations, on the other hand, it is necessary to advance in the study of the distributive impacts of the innovation system in the country.

The present work corroborates the hypothesis that advancing the comprehension of interrelations between innovation and inequality may be helpful in identifying alternatives for technological development capable of contributing simultaneously to economic growth and social inclusion. Although innovation is not the main contributor to inequality, it is believed that distinct strategies for technological change may lead to different outcomes in distributive terms, thus either aggravating or mitigating inequality (Cozzens and Kaplinsky 2009).

In addition to this brief introduction, the chapter is organised as follows: the next section characterises poverty and inequality patterns and trends in Brazil, showing how the structural, multifaceted and broad character of inequality in the country affects the innovation process in different ways. The following section highlights how the policies and institutions that constitute the NSI co-evolve with inequality at personal and regional levels. Showing how the asymmetries of the NSI can be observed in their different dimensions and sub-systems, this section also empirically illustrates how the dynamic of Brazilian innovation system has not contributed to breaking the vicious cycle of inequality. Finally, in the last section some concluding remarks are presented. It is argued that integrating excluded and precariously included population in adequate consumption conditions, together with the improvement in the generation of public social services could represent both an opportunity and a huge challenge for innovation policies. In that sense, interlinking social, production and innovation policies might get the Brazilian innovation system to contribute as much to the improvement of dynamic competitive advantages, as to the construction of a more just and equitable society and, therefore, a more sustainable development.

Poverty and Inequality in Brazil — Patterns and Trends

Historical roots: the structural character of inequality in Brazil

Brazil ranks as the ninth global economy, with Gross Domestic Product Purchasing Power Parity (GDP PPP) of 2,169,180 million US$ and Gross National Income (GNI) per capita PPP of 10,920 US$ in 2010 (World Bank 2011). In spite of these economic indicators being far from characterising a poor country, in 2009 there were 39.6 million poor people and 13.5 million people living under conditions of extreme poverty in the country, comprising altogether 28.7 per cent of Brazilian population (IPEA 2009c).[1] This sharp contrast reveals a country where the origin of poverty is neither in absolute nor in relative scarcity of resources. It results from a society that is deeply unfair, where unequal distribution of income and of national wealth has historically characterised and continues to characterise the socio-economic structure of the country.

The high indexes of poverty and the deep inequality are not recent in Brazilian society. Indeed, inequality has consolidated in the country as a historical legacy inherited from colonisation. The original social matrix, founded on concentration of both land and political power and on foreign dependence, imposed its mark on the whole process of historical constitution and evolution of the Brazilian nation. The coalitions formed in Brazil by the distinct economic and political power of the social classes, particularly those of land owners and of capitalists in relation to urban wage-earners and to rural workers, comprise the central mark of Brazilian capitalism. The strength of these coalitions lies in the inertia of the unfair distributive pattern that prevails in Brazil.[2]

Thus, a remarkable characteristic of inequality in Brazil is the persistence of unequal income and wealth concentration throughout the various periods, political regimes and development patterns experienced by the country. As emphasised by Pochmann (2007a), in spite of the significant economic advances reached, particularly between 1933 and 1980 (period that comprised the process of national industrialisation), the country failed in accomplishing the basic reforms of capitalism (agrarian, tax and social), which made it impossible for Brazil to adequately face the problems related to wealth concentration and social exclusion. Not even the public assets were universalised, so as to offer equal opportunities in education, health, housing and transport to the population.

As will be shown later, there is a strong concentration of poverty in the northern and northeastern regions and in rural areas and small municipalities. Among others, the main deficiencies found are: lower schooling levels; worse quality of dwellings; lower access to infrastructure services and to consumption durable goods. Despite its apparent homogeneity, poverty in Brazil hides quite distinct social contexts. It results as much from reproduction of outdated forms of insertion in production and from anachronistic institutions, particularly observable in the rural setting, as from unemployment and low earnings for unspecialised labour predominantly in urban areas (Medeiros 2003).

In other words, without being restricted to social minority groups, poverty and inequality in Brazil are present in multidimensional and heterogeneous ways, with strong concentration that is both regional and sectoral (rural/small cities). Therefore, in order to confront inequality, we will require broad public policies aimed at fostering growth, reducing the concentration of wealth and building up participation and social cohesion, which also accounts for the territorial heterogeneity where distinct social and power relations take place.

In recent years, and particularly as of 2001, a continuous process — unprecedented in the country's recent history — of reduction in income inequality has been observed. Between 2001 and 2009 inequality measured by Gini dropped 9.7 per cent, one of the fastest in the world along the period. This improvement in the distributive pattern offers potentially interesting opportunities for the country, which will be examined further along in this chapter.

In the following section, we seek to underline the distinct processes that characterised the unequal distributive profile in Brazil. The analysis starts from the post–World War II period and is structured according to three periods: (*a*) imports substitution industrialisation, characterised by accelerated growth with concentration of income; (*b*) crisis and neoliberal trade liberalisation, characterised by aggravation of poverty and inequality; (*c*) recent period of moderate growth with income distribution.

Imports substitution industrialisation (1950 to the end of 1970s)

In Brazil, the process of imports substitution industrialisation has, more incisively than in other Latin-American countries, marked a long period of high economic growth. From the 1950s until the end of the 1970s, this process has been accompanied by deep structural changes, which turned the country from a primary-exporting economy to a complex industrial economy rated among the greatest in the world.

The performance of the country during this period was indeed amazing. Between 1965 and 1980 Brazil experienced an average rate of growth of the value added for the manufacturing sector of 9.5 per cent per year, only surpassed by three Asian countries (South Korea, Singapore and Indonesia). The industrial structure — which has developed by means of a strategy that included protection, promotion and regulation — presented, in the beginning of the 1980s, a high degree of inter-sectoral integration and production diversification, very similar to that of most Organisation for Economic Co-operation and Development (OECD) countries (Cassiolato 2008).

In spite of these advances, the model of imports substitution industrialisation was not able to provide accumulation of the capabilities required for positive techno-innovative dynamics. As Furtado (1961, 1968) noted, the establishment of a production system aimed at satisfying the consumption needs of the Brazilian upper class had adverse effects. It justified settling an industrial park based on foreign investment and predominantly imported technology, whose links with pre-existing capabilities were weak, thus leading to poor multiplier effects in the economy.

The inadequacy of the adopted technological pattern became evident, on the supply side, when new technology was imported without the concomitant process for incorporation and generation of the required capabilities for the endogenisation of the technological progress. It restricted the process of knowledge accumulation and learning within the country. On the demand side, import of technologies aimed at reducing workforce, in a country with high unemployment rates, reinforced a concentrative consumption pattern, which was unable to instil dynamism in the domestic market. It created restrictions to economies of scale and reinforced production heterogeneity, ending up by feeding back the subordinated pattern of technical progress.[3]

Furthermore, in the absence of basic reforms, particularly the agrarian reform, the industrialisation process was unable to modernise at the same pace as other sectors, the archaic agricultural sector. The result was the sharpening of the differences of both productivity and income between urban and rural areas. The great availability of workforce, created by the urban explosion, by low productivity of agriculture and by concentration of land tenure, in face of a technological pattern aimed at reducing the use of work-force in the industrial sector exerted a depressing impact on the basis of urban wages and led to the loss of almost half the value of the minimum wage in the period 1960–80.[4] That is, the productivity gains resulting from industrialisation ended up being appropriated by a small part of the population. Worth remembering is the fact that this sharp compression of wages has been facilitated by the strong political repression that prevailed in the country during the period of military dictatorship, which spanned from 1964 to 1985.

Consequently, although there was a reduction of absolute poverty in that period, income distribution became still more concentrated, sharpening inequality.

Crisis and trade liberalisation (1981–2000)

As of the beginning of the 1980s, the cycle of growth with structural changes has been interrupted. Marked by the crisis of foreign indebtedness, this period was characterised by great turbulences — high and increasing inflation rates, unemployment, disarrangement of the labour market, growth of informality in the production system, dropping of the minimum wage and of wages in general, and growth of employment in the services sector to the detriment of industrial employment, among others. Moreover, the state has sunk into financial and fiscal crisis that made it unable to lead the industrialisation process at the same time that domestic private agents, still defended by protectionist barriers, significantly reduced their investments. As a result, the 1980 decade has aggravated the already high income concentration, with the Gini coefficient reaching a peak of 0.636 in 1989.

The inflationary acceleration of the 1980s and beginning of 1990s was the main mechanism of income concentration and, together with the unstable economic growth, led the labour market to a precarious situation, with stagnation and decrease of real earnings. Year 1985 ends the period of military dictatorship in the country; in 1988 a new constitution was approved and in 1989 the first direct election for president of the republic was held, which elected a centre-right government. With the end of hyperinflation in 1994 and the implementation of some social rights assured by the new Constitution, there was a significant reduction of poverty and growth of earnings in the first deciles of the distribution.[5] However, the low economic growth, the significant reduction of industrial employment and the stagnation of formal employment did not allow the positive effects of price stabilisation on the lowest incomes to last (Medeiros 2003, 2006).

The neoliberal economic reforms adopted throughout the 1990s, including deregulation, privatisation, trade and financial liberalisation, as well as the resulting changes in economic and social structures, have consolidated a new distributive coalition in Brazil. Constituted by the new financial groups, by the foreign capital mobilised by privatisations and by industrial and agribusiness exporters, this coalition consolidated a model of macroeconomic policy based on orthodox fiscal policies, high interest rates, growing debt and insertion in international trade subordinated to the financial flows of the balance of payments. This policy ended up introducing a serious distributive conflict between the payment of accrued liabilities of the debt (thus benefiting a new group of moneylenders) and the social expenditures aimed at income transfer, affecting not only the minimum wage but also investments in public services such as education, health, housing and sanitation.[6]

In this context, during the 1990s, social exclusion has expanded from those traditional social segments of disadvantaged people towards social strata that once used to be socially included.[7] These new socially excluded people, most of them belonging to urban areas of rich regions of the Brazilian centre-south, started to encompass a significant part of the working class, which was subject to labour insertion characterised by precariousness and instability. These are social segments that were deprived of better labour conditions and became threatened by underemployment, long lasting unemployment and greater age vulnerability. Such segments comprise even groups with high schooling levels, whose individual and collective capabilities could not be either developed or used for lack of opportunities.

Growth with income distribution (2001–10)

Between 2001 and 2010, Brazil underwent a period of moderate growth (3.6 per cent GDP average increase in the period) with low inflation rates. As of 2003, with the election of a new centre-left government, such growth has been combined with policies that aimed to guarantee real increases of minimum wages, to expand cash transfer programmes, as well as to offer credit alternatives to lower income levels.

The marked reduction of poverty rates in this decade, which decreased from 50.3 per cent to 28.7 per cent of Brazilian population between 2001 and 2009, particularly reflects the significant improvement in the pattern of income distribution in the country, combined with more substantial growth rates between 2004 and 2010 (IPEA 2010a).

The governmental programmes of income transfer had strong impacts on the reduction of extreme poverty and contributed to changing income inequality in the poorest segments of Brazilian population. According to IPEA, in 2009, 34.1 per cent of the population, especially that with lowest earnings, was protected by some of the mechanisms of income guarantee. Also on the grounds of cash transfer programmes, the poorest municipalities of the country presented growth rates higher than those of the richest ones, thus contributing to the reduction of inequality between poor and rich regions of the country. Among cash transfer programmes, social security transfers related to real increases of minimum wage and conditional programmes such as Brazil's Family Allowance Programme (Bolsa Família), played a fundamental role in re-distribution of income.

Introduced in 2003, Bolsa Família was intended to unite several income transfer programmes run at the municipal, state and federal levels since 1995. Designed as an expression of the development of direct monetary transfers to families or individuals, its key assumption is that linking income transfers to poor families with structural policies and programmes (mainly in the fields of education, healthcare and jobs) could break through the vicious cycle of poverty in the present and halt its future replication. In 2009 Bolsa Família reached 5,561 municipalities and 12.4 million families benefiting 49.2 million people (about 26 per cent of the population).

As of 2004, the gradual increase of formal employment in the lower strata of the occupational pyramid, together with improvement of the minimum wage real value and raise of labour revenues, were the most important factors for explaining the income improvement for population as a whole. According to Neri (2009), in the period 2001 to 2008, increased wages explain 67 per cent of the reduction of inequality, followed by social programmes (17 per cent), especially the Bolsa Família, and social security benefits (16 per cent).

Even with the emergence of the world crisis in 2008, data published by IPEA shows that poverty and inequality kept decreasing in Brazil having diminished 1.5 per cent in 2009. That is, in contrast to other periods of economic slowdown in the country, the current period is unusual in that the poverty rates not only did not rise but even decreased one year after the manifestation of the crisis. According to IPEA (2008b), the explanation for this distinct trajectory was the adoption of public policies aimed at guaranteeing real increases in the minimum salary as well as at building a network of income guarantee for the poorest people as of 2003. These policies have decisively contributed to avoiding the decline in the socio-economic situation, as observed during the previous periods of strong economic slowdown in Brazil, configuring an effective network for protecting the income of the poorest segments.

It is interesting to note that one of the reasons for the relatively fast recovery of Brazilian economy from the international crisis was the dynamism of its domestic market, which was strengthened by the inclusion of more than 28 million people that emerged from poverty and indigence in the period 2003–09 (Neri 2009; IPEA 2010a).

Therefore, in contrast to the period of imports substitution industrialisation, when rapid economic growth was accompanied by significant income concentration, the recent period of growth (although more modest) has been accompanied by decrease of inequality, thus reflecting not only advances in the process of democracy building in the country, but also the outcomes from specific policies aimed at income redistribution. This process has contributed to the reduction in social polarisation, reflected in the expansion of intermediate classes which, until then, presented a relatively small participation in the population distribution.

In the next section, we analyse some impacts of the improvements of income distribution during the 2000 decade, with special emphasis on an issue that has gained increasing attention in the international sphere: the expansion of the so-called 'middle class'.

Interpersonal inequality in Brazil

Income and Wealth

As already mentioned, during the period characterised by strong growth of Brazilian economy, the decades of 1960 and 1970, there was a reduction in absolute poverty, although accompanied by high income concentration. The Gini index in this period rose from 0.536 in 1960, to 0.593 in 1979 (Centre for Social Policies at the Getúlio Vargas Foundation [CPS/FGV]). In the decade of 1980, the impacts of the debt crisis and of inflationary acceleration inverted the process of reduction of poverty and indigence in the country, and aggravated the already significant income concentration. Between 1981 and 1989, the percentage of poor and extremely poor people rose, respectively, from 38.9 per cent to 39.5 per cent and from 16.1 per cent to 18.1 per cent of total population. The Gini index reached its apex in 1989, rising from 0.584 to 0.636 during the period.

During the first years of the 1990s, with the hyperinflation and the accelerated liberalisation of the economy, poverty and indigence deepened both in terms of proportion and in absolute terms. In 1993, the percentage of poor people reached 41.1 per cent and that of indigents 19 per cent, altogether comprising more than 60 per cent of Brazilian population, equivalent to 85.3 million people. The plan for economic stabilisation, adopted in 1994 and the regulation of BPC, The Continuous Cash Benefit Programme, in 1996, have contributed to the reduction of poverty and indigence to 33.3 per cent and 14.1 per cent respectively that year.[8] This level remained relatively stable until 2001. In absolute terms, however, the number of poor people and indigents increased from 69.9 to 78.2 million during the period.

As of 2001, an accelerated and continuous fall in the rates of inequality is observed in Brazil. It decreased from 0.596 to 0.538 in the period between 2001 and 2009, according to the Gini index (Figure 2.1). It was one of the fastest rates of change in the whole world during this period.

It is worth noting that, since 2003, the decrease in poverty and indigence is observable not only in terms of a percentage, but also in absolute terms. Between 2003 and 2009, more than 30 million people left the condition of poverty and indigence. This period coincides with the change in government and the implementation of policies aimed at income distribution associated with the recovery of real value of the minimum wage.

In spite of its expressive drop, the per capita income inequality in Brazil remains extremely high, placing the country among the 10 per cent most unequal in the world. As may be seen in Table 2.1, in 2009, the richest 10 per cent of the population still possessed more than 40 per cent of total income, whereas the poorest 40 per cent retained around 10 per cent of total income. What is worse, however, is the fact that the very small group of the richest 1 per cent of population has a share of the income (12.1 per cent) higher than that of the 40 per cent of the whole Brazilian population (10.2 per cent) (IPEA 2008a) resulting in a distributive profile that is deeply unfair.

If, in addition to the pattern of income distribution, wealth distribution is also taken into account, the inequality scenario gets worse.[9] That is, when the analysis of income distribution in Brazil is expanded beyond its personal dimension (labour revenues), so that it includes the distinct forms of capital revenues (interests, profits, rents, leases), what can be noticed is a relatively small participation of the labour

Figure 2.1: *Evolution of Inequality per capita Family Income in Brazil: Gini Coefficient (1977–2009)*

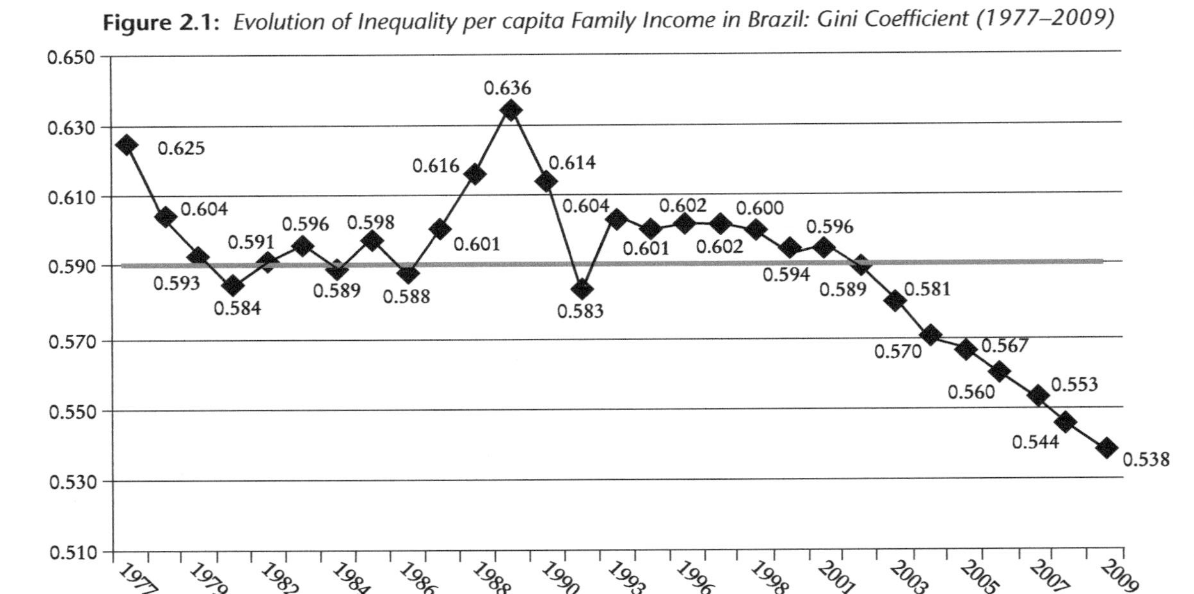

Source: Authors' elaboration based on 1977–2009 data from the Ipeadata database (IPEA 2010b).

Table 2.1: *Indicators of Inequality in per capita Income in Brazil (2009)*

Indicators	*Amount*
Percentage of income appropriated by the poorest decile (%)	
First	0.95
Second	3.08
Third	6.16
Fourth	10.24
Fifth	15.47
Sixth	22.13
Seventh	30.39
Eighth	41.28
Ninth	57.19
Percentage of income appropriated by the highest 1%	12.1
Gini coefficient	0.542
Theil-T index	0.597
Ratio between the rent appropriated by the 10% richest and the poorest 40%	16.67
Ratio between the rent appropriated by the 20% richest and the poorest 20%	18.98

Source: Barros et al. (2010).

incomes in the national revenue, which has direct consequences for the income distribution in the country.

According to Pochmann (2008), between 1980 and 2005, the participation of labour income in the national revenue lost 11 percentage points, decreasing from 50 per cent to 39 per cent. The author points out that the advancing process of Brazilian wealth financialisation, which started in 1981, was the main factor causing this strong reversion of the functional distribution of income in favour of incomes of property.[10] Only from 2006 on has the functional income distribution improved, the labour income rising to 43.6 per cent in 2008.

Consumption

Latin American structuralist literature had long ago signalled the problem of under-consumption in less developed countries with high income concentration, and pointed out that, among other ways, this problem should be addressed by means of redistributive policies. Better conditions of income should favour consumption and production, and thus would foster new investments and could also promote technological development and reduce the extreme heterogeneity of the production structure (Furtado 1968).

The pattern of inequality examined earlier has had a strong impact on both the consumption patterns and the structure of demand in the Brazilian economy. The huge disparity between rich and poor social segments when it comes to consumption may be estimated by looking at the average monthly expenditures of the Brazilian families by income bands. In the period from 2008 to 2009, expenditures by the 10 per cent richest families were 9.6 times higher than those of the 40 per cent poorest families. In rural areas, the gap was 10.3 times (IBGE 2008-9a). The existing disparity also can be observed when one analyses the consumption patterns by kinds of expenditure according to income bands (Figure 2.2).

The results confirm the inequalities in the consumption profile of Brazilian families. The value of food expenditures in the highest income families is almost triple the national average and nearly six times that of low-income families. The particularly sharp disparities in transport and housing also stand out as shown in Figure 2.2. In relation to spending on transport the great emphasis on spending with individual transport by families with higher incomes is noted. But the variable that has the greatest inequality among income classes is the 'acquisition of property' to the extent that most spending on real estate acquisition is made by the 20 per cent of the richest families in Brazil (IPEA 2010a).

Household access to personal computers and the Internet — both of which play a significant role in access to employment opportunities — is also asymmetrical among different classes of the Brazilian population. The average percentage of Brazilian households with access to personal computers and broadband is relatively low — 20.3 per cent in 2009. However, we observe that the shortage of access is strongly concentrated in lower income population. In spite of some regional asymmetries, the main factor in inequality is, in fact, the income. The segments with incomes above 20 minimum wages have a rate of computer and broadband access of 83.5 per cent compared to 2.6 per cent of households with income until 1 minimum wage, or 4.6 per cent of the households with income from 1 to 2 minimum wages (IBGE 2008a).

In 2008, 75 per cent of Brazilian households had income up to 2 minimum wages. Therefore, in the knowledge-based economy, the existence of strong asymmetries in both the access and in the capacity of using the information technologies available in Brazil is an important obstacle which contributes to the reproduction of inequalities and hinders capability building.

Figure 2.2: *Evolution of the Average Monthly Household Expenditure for Some Types of Spending according to the Classes of Monthly Income of Families*

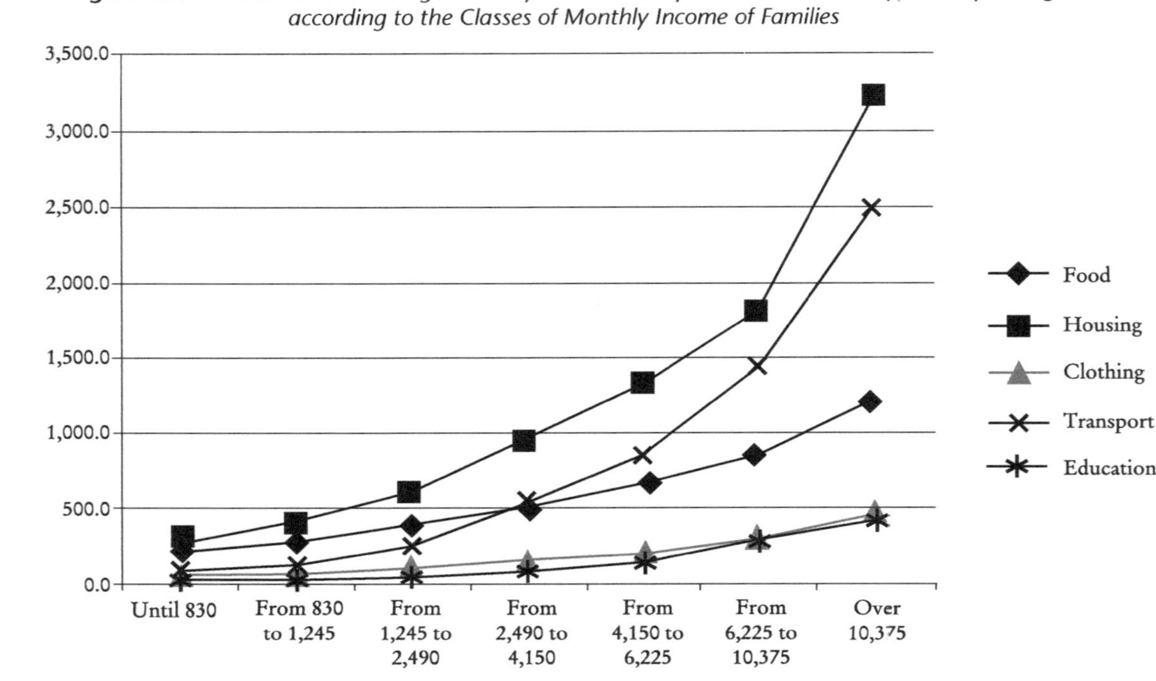

Source: IBGE (2008–09b).

The differences observed in the consumption pattern by income bands are expressed as much in quantitative as in qualitative terms. That is, besides consuming fewer goods, the poorer families tend to purchase goods and services of lower quality (and price), compatible with their purchasing power. Table 2.2 illustrates this phenomenon, by comparing the acquisition of substitute food products according to the per capita income band.

The major disparity in the pattern of consumption of substitute products in the higher and lower income bands is just one example of the deep heterogeneity of Brazilian structure of demand. This latter ends up inducing an extreme heterogeneity in the Brazilian production structure, which is aimed at market segments that are quite differentiated in terms of income. In other words, the sharp inequality in consumption patterns tends to determine a production structure that is much more heterogeneous than that of countries with better income distribution.

A facet of such heterogeneity in Brazilian production structure may be observed, for instance, in the coexistence of distinct production systems of quite distinct technological base within a same sector (and frequently within a same industrial plant) directed to different markets in terms of income.[11] The existence of high income disparity in the country allows for the survival of production activities characterised by very low productivity based on spurious competitive advantages, which is focused on the low income consumer market.[12] Concomitantly other products are aimed at the country's rich socioeconomic elite market that adopts consumption patterns similar to those of developed countries. The production structure aimed at the segment of those with high purchasing power is characterised by greater dynamism, by producing goods containing greater value added and by the use of capital-intensive techniques, generally based upon imported technologies. Therefore, inequality contributes to the high heterogeneity in the production structure, also with direct impacts on the dynamics of the innovative systems as will be seen later.

The nature of the final product has significant implications on the relative welfare of distinct groups of consumers. Product innovation is a locus where income inequality clearly shapes innovation, once the products are aimed at particular income ranges. In Brazil, the industrialisation process was primarily directed at satisfying the consumption patterns of high income ranges. There was no concern with building industrial, technological and services structures aimed

Table 2.2: *Annual Household per capita Food Purchase (kg) by Income Bands (2009)*

		Annual Household Per Capita Food Purchase (kg)					
		Family Monetary and Non-Monetary Monthly Income Bands (R$)					
*Products**	*Total*	Up to 830	Over 830 to 1,245	Over 1,245 to 2,490	Over 2,490 to 4,150	Over 4,150 to 6,225	Over 6,225
Premium beef	6,073	2,848	4,312	5,696	7,968	9,592	11,332
Sale beef	6,888	6,030	6,999	7,324	7,358	6,945	6,279
Fresh cow milk	9,792	9,925	12,766	11,384	7,743	6,226	5,403
Pasteurised cow milk	25,641	11,636	18,145	25,417	35,563	41,515	40,206
Crystalline sugar	5,548	8,152	6,998	5,285	3,010	4,109	3,680
Refined sugar	3,160	2,464	3,162	3,417	3,321	3,864	2,972
Olive oil	0,178	0,046	0,102	0,127	0,171	0,356	0,634
Soy oil	6,342	5,748	6,618	6,772	6,554	6,449	5,277
Sugarcane rum	0,188	0,224	0,262	0,162	0,201	0,090	0,115
Beer	5,632	1,623	3,049	4,606	7,827	9,431	15,444
Cola soft drinks	12,663	4,674	6,780	12,044	18,541	19,838	26,659
Other soft drinks	2,740	1,515	1,993	2,586	3,461	4,246	4,778

Source: Authors' elaboration based on IBGE (2009a).
Notes: *substitute products.

at serving the consumption and basic needs of the vast majority of the population. As mentioned before, the production sectors aimed at lower income people in Brazil are characterised by lesser technological innovation intensity and low innovation content. Therefore, due to the lack of policies aimed at changing this trend, inequality has been also reproduced on the side of consumption.

Corroborating with the Latin American structuralist literature, the redistributive policies adopted in the 2000s in Brazil are favouring both the consumption and production structures, as well as fostering new investments in the country. As will be pointed out, these changes open room for improving the dynamism of the Brazilian innovation system.

Reduction in consumption disparities

Between 2001 and 2008, the growth of income of the poorest 10 per cent of the Brazilian population was 8.1 per cent per year, almost thrice greater than the national average of 2.8 per cent and more than five times that of the richest 10 per cent, which was only 1.4 per cent in the period. Concurrently, the share of the national revenue appropriated by the poorest grew almost 30 per cent in the period (IPEA 2009b). Figure 2.3 shows the average growth rate of per capita family income by deciles of the distribution, between 2001 and 2008.

These advances had direct repercussions on the expansion of intermediate income ranges in Brazil.

A study was carried out based on PNAD data analyses of the behaviour of the Brazilian middle class in the period from 1992 to 2008 (Neri and Carvalhaes 2008; Neri 2009).[13] According to this study, the growth of the so-called middle class was initiated in the middle of the 1990s by the process of economic stabilisation (although its quick expansion has occurred particularly from 2001 on), followed by the period of significant reduction of income inequality. In 1993, the middle class represented 30.9 per cent of Brazilian population, rising to 49.2 per cent in 2008 and reaching 50.5 per cent in 2009.

Table 2.3 shows the evolution of the social classes in Brazil revealing a significant expansion of classes A, B and C and contraction of classes D and E in the period 2003–08. The growth in the Brazilian intermediate class — which emerged from classes D and E — represented the incorporation of 21 million people in the market of consumer goods in the period.

Figure 2.3: *Average Growth Rate of per capita Family Income by Distribution Deciles: Distribution of the Last Year (2001–08)*

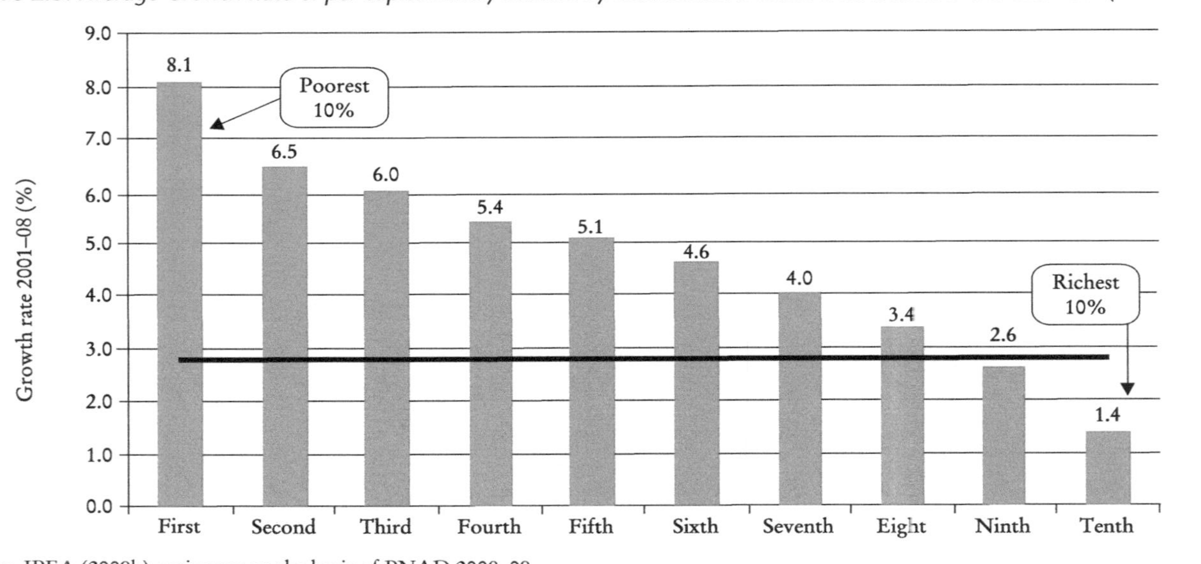

Source: IPEA (2009b), estimates on the basis of PNAD 2008–09.

Table 2.3: *Evolution of Social Classes in Brazil (2003–08)*

Classes	Class Definition (US$)*	Cumulative Variation in the Period		Situation at the End of the Period (2008)	
		People (millions)	Percentage (%)	People (millions)	Participation in Total Population (%)
E	0–562	(19.5)	(43.0)	29.9	16.0
D	562–780	(1.5)	(8.9)	45.3	24.4
C	780–3,362	25.9	31.0	91.0	49.2
AB	3,362	6.1	37.1	19.4	10.4

Source: Neri (2009).
Notes: *Calculated on the basis of 2007 PPP assessment.

Besides directly impacting demand, the increase of consumption shaped by the rise in purchasing power of the lower income ranges together with the expansion of access to credit also exerts influence on the profile of production investments. Additionally, it opens a broad range of opportunities for innovation. The way and the dynamics for taking these opportunities, however, depend on how the various elements that comprise the national innovative system interact. Public policies, in this context, may play a key role.

Several industrial and services segments, involving many enterprises in Brazil (not limited to the larger ones), started to introduce changes in their production processes in order to reduce costs, simplifying

Box 2.1

Nestlé Brazil has been betting on the expansion of lower class market since 2005. Surveys conducted by the company revealed a major growing potential in classes C and D, which represent more than 80 per cent of food consumption in the country. Based on the specificities of this potential consumer base, the firm started to produce cheaper products and built a distribution structure able to overcome the hindrances related to poorer consumers' lack of access to the big supermarket chains. The company invested in a new plant located close to the consumer market of the northeast, the poorest region of the country, where the products are miniaturised and packaged at a lower cost. The distribution chain set up by the firm comprises 6,000 women, most of them denizens of the neighbourhood in market areas served by the firm, working as representatives for direct selling of the company's most popular products. Nestlé finances products stocks and the sales representatives are managed by the administrative structure of the company. According to Nestlé Brazil, the company currently counts on 120,000 outsourced workers. Such strategy has allowed the company to open significant markets among low income populations and it expects that within five years products aimed at these populations will represent 7 per cent of its turnover.[14]

or miniaturising products, designing new products, introducing decentralised distribution channels, among other strategies, seeking the incorporation of lower income consumers who up to now were excluded from their markets. However, the innovation 'intensity' of these changes is still apparently low. Of course, this is a new process that deserves further examination.

Finally, it is worth noting that the impacts of intermediate class expansion on the national system of innovation (NSI) go beyond the consumption aspect, and include the effects of improving capabilities and learning, among many other aspects. For example, the middle-class segments tend to invest more in education than those of lower income ranges. Not only because they generally can do without the income of children's labour, thus assuring the priority of education for longer than the poorest segments, but also because they can provide better quality education to the children. The same situation occurs in healthcare. Both of these are considered significant factors in building increased human capabilities required by the knowledge-based economy.

In the next sections, we analyse other aspects of inequality in Brazil, beyond income, wealth and consumption. Factors such as the extreme regional heterogeneity, colour differences, gender issues and asymmetries of occupational character are also relevant mechanisms for reproducing and perpetuating inequality, increasing the distance between rich and poor Brazilians.

Inter-regional inequalities

Brazil is constituted by five big regions and 27 federated units; throughout its vast territory it presents six distinct biomes. Despite the advances of the 2000s decade, the country is characterised, since its colonial period, by deep regional asymmetries. More than 50 per cent of Brazilian GDP is concentrated in the southeastern region, and São Paulo state alone represents 34 per cent. By comparing Brazilian regions, we observe significant disparities, corroborated by a number of indicators.

The situation of regions in the north and northeast deeply contrasts with the situation of the regions in the south and southeast in terms of product, consumption, poverty and schooling as shown by the data in Table 2.4, among many other aspects. These imbalances are aggravated by the fact that the northeast is the second most populated region in

Table 2.4: *Selected Regional Indicators*

Regions	*Area %*	*Population %*	*Gross Regional Product %*	*Average Household Spending R$*	*Poor People %*	*Extreme Poverty %*	*Schooling Rate %*
Southeast	10.86	42.0	56.0	3.135	11.8	3.2	60.5
South	6.77	14.5	16.6	3.030	11.6	3.3	57.4
Central-west	18.87	7.3	9.2	2.591	11.6	3.4	54.7
Northeast	18.25	28.1	13.1	1.700	39.6	15.5	39.2
North	45.25	8.1	5.1	2.006	32.5	9.9	39.1

Source: IBGE (2009a); IBGE (2008–09c); IPEA (2009c).

the country, which is inhabited by 55.1 per cent of the country's total poor and extremely poor population. The 39.7 per cent out of the total population living in the northeast and 29.1 per cent out of all those who live in the north earn until one minimum wage; these percentages decrease to 18 per cent and 18.1 per cent in the south and southeast, respectively. Illiteracy rate reached 17.7 per cent in the northeast whereas in the south it was 5 per cent (IBGE 2008–09c).

The same pattern can be observed with regard to inequality in the access to potable water, basic sanitation, garbage collection, and to health and electricity services. Whereas in the southern and southeastern regions at least 95 per cent of the population has access to potable water, in the north this percentage falls to 63 per cent. In terms of basic sanitation, data behaviour is similar, with more than 90 per cent coverage in the southeastern region and only 64 per cent in the north (IPEA 2006). Although inadequate housing is a widespread problem in the country, regional inequalities are quite evident. The worst housing conditions are found in northern Brazil, where only 32.1 per cent of the urban population is considered to have adequate housing conditions (IPEA 2008a).

In terms of knowledge and learning, access to information and infrastructure is fundamental for the development of both individual and collective capabilities. Sharp regional asymmetries in the access to personal computers, internet and other ICT infrastructure are a further challenge to the reduction of the extreme inequality and the heterogeneity that prevail in Brazil.

In brief, Brazil presents inequality between regions as much from the viewpoint of the production structure concentration, as from the point of view of the infrastructure of S&T, or in relation to the access to basic services, among other aspects. These regional inequalities impact the dynamics of the NSI both directly and indirectly.

Inequality across ethnicity, colour and gender

Brazil is one the most ethnically racially diverse countries in the world. Brazilian population is composed primarily by descendents of the indigenous people, Portuguese settlers, African slaves and other groups of immigrants (European, Japanese, Syrian-Lebanese, etc.) who settled in Brazil, principally between 1820 and 1970.

In 2010, the population of 190.7 million people was composed of 91 million whites (47.7 per cent), 82 million coloured (43.1 per cent),

15 million blacks (7.6 per cent), 2 million Asian (1.1 per cent), and 818,000 indigenous people (0.4 per cent) (IBGE 2010a). For historical reasons, ethnic groups are not uniformly distributed throughout the country: the south is predominantly white (55.2 per cent) and the northeast is mostly Afro-Brazilian (69 per cent back and coloured).

According to IBGE/PNAD, in 2007, 77.6 per cent out of all people over 25 years who count 15 or more years of study were white; only 17.2 per cent were coloured and 3.5 per cent black. According to the School Census of 2007, among the white youngsters aged 16 years, 70 per cent had completed the mandatory basic school. Among the black population in this age range, only 30 per cent reached this schooling level. Among white children between eight and nine years old attending school, the illiteracy rate is about 8 per cent. For black children in this same age range, the rate is doubled. Inequalities persist in secondary school and higher education, as shown in Table 2.5. Also significant is the huge inequality evidenced by the distribution of household income per capita among the 10 per cent poorest and the richest 1 per cent by colour. Once 74 per cent of the 10 per cent poorest are black or coloured, 86.2 per cent of the 1 per cent richest are white.

Table 2.5: *Selected Indicators by Race (2007), Brazil*

Indicator	*White %*	*Black & Coloured %*
People with 15 or more years of study (people over 25 years)	77.6	20.7
Completion of elementary school (young people up to 16 years)	70.0	30.0
Completion of high school (young people up to 19 years)	55.0	33.0
Completion of higher education	13.4	4.0
Distribution of monthly income per capita: 10% poorest	26.1	73.2
Distribution of monthly income per capita: 1% richest	85.7	12.4

Source: IBGE (2007); IPEA (2007); Ministry of Planning (2007).

With regard to gender inequality, although Brazil does not present the educational disparities characteristic of many underdeveloped countries, some asymmetries must be mentioned. In terms of labour income, gender disparity is clear, even if it has progressively reduced.

Considering people over 10 years old, the average monthly income of men in 2006 was 80.8 per cent higher than that of women in the same year — a difference quite significant, but nonetheless lower than the 140.4 per cent observed 10 years before (IBGE 2006a). This inequality in terms of income is observed in every income range and also in all regions of the country. The study on gender and poverty made by Melo (2005) further reveals that, in terms of distribution of the occupied population, women tend to work in less organised economic activities, through informal contracts; they are also more vulnerable to unemployment, and represent a significant portion of unpaid labour, which reinforces the precarious nature of women's occupations.

Summing up the preceding analysis, we may say that inequality in Brazil has a structural, multidimensional and heterogeneous character. It is precisely due to the complexity of the relations between wealth and poverty in the country that the use of the concept of social exclusion is becoming widespread. Such concept seeks to embrace the phenomenon that goes beyond mere income inequality and is manifested through forms that are increasingly more complex, including, among others, the territorial, gender, colour/ethnic dimensions emphasised in this work. Social exclusion is understood here as a division between those who enjoy living and work conditions comparable to the existing development pattern and those who do not; added to this deficit is the notion of inhibition to the development of potential capabilities due to the lack of opportunities.

Of course social exclusion is a constitutive part of capabilities deprivation (Sen 2000). Exclusion from facilities and benefits to which others have access means lack of opportunities — not just in terms of access to medical and educational services or decent housing, but also to those stemming from knowledge advancement and its application in diverse innovations. The limited access to the chances that technical changes open in various spheres of daily life constitutes a factor that feeds exclusion and inequality at the same time as it restricts accumulation of capabilities in the country.

One of the *sine qua non* conditions for reaching innovation societies is advancing towards fair societies (Dalum and Lundvall 1992). Furthermore, studies have indicated that development is limited in the presence of extreme inequalities and in the absence of persistent efforts aimed at strengthening the accumulation of capabilities in both those producing and those using knowledge and innovation (Sutz 2008).

The broad structural character of inequality in Brazil has various impacts on the process of innovation in the country and on the formation and evolution of the NSI. Inequality affects the process of innovation as much on the side of the supply as on that of demand. It restricts capabilities and learning; jeopardises the generation, dissemination and use of innovation; sharpens the heterogeneity of the production and innovation system; and restricts the process of internalisation of technological progress, among other aspects. Indeed, the understanding of inequality as the constitutive part of the context and the institutionality that surrounded the formation and development of the recent NSI becomes crucial, both from the analytical and from the normative points of view.

Co-evolution of innovation system and inequality

As shown in the previous section, the NSI in Brazil is permeated by structural characteristics of a highly unequal and heterogeneous country. In this section we highlight how the policies and institutions that constitute the NSI and production co-evolve with inequality at personal and regional levels. Therefore, if, on the one hand, inequality affects the NSI restricting the endogenisation of technological progress and limiting the capacity of acquisition, use and diffusion of innovations in the country, on the other hand, the dynamic of the Brazilian innovation system has not contributed to breaking the vicious cycle of inequality.

The following analysis shows how the asymmetries of the NSI can be observed across different dimensions and sub-systems, both reflecting and contributing to the reproduction, exclusion and inequality in the country. This section will also empirically highlight how these policies and institutions have reinforced greater structural heterogeneity and regional asymmetries along with widening of productivity in a context of unequal access to education, knowledge and R&D infrastructure, financial infrastructure, and other relevant elements of the innovation system.

Disparities in production and innovation institutions

The analysis by Survey on Technological Innovation (PINTEC), the governmental database of innovation in Brazil, shows a relatively low average in innovation rate, cooperation rate and expenditure with innovation activities over sales (Table 2.6). Brazilian averages in all these indicators are quite inferior to that observed in the OECD countries.

Table 2.6: *Innovation Indicators: Extractive and Manufacturing Industries (2000–08) (percentage)*

Activities	*2000*	*2003*	*2005*	*2008*
Innovation rate				
Industry	31.52	33.27	34.41	38.60
Extractive industry	17.19	21.97	23.08	23.70
Manufacturing industry	31.87	33.53	33.57	38.40
Cooperation rate				
Industry	11.04	3.75	8.46	10.38
Extractive industry	24.63	2.71	12.85	14.13
Manufacturing industry	10.86	3.77	7.14	10.04
Expenditure with innovation activities over sales				
Industry	3.84	2.46	3.04	2.85
Extractive industry	1.47	1.61	1.80	0.88
Manufacturing industry	3.89	2.48	2.80	2.60

Source: IBGE (2008c).

Besides the low innovation dynamism, PINTEC's database also shows that most firms' efforts are concentrated on the dissemination of innovations. Expenditures related to innovation are primarily directed at the acquisition of machinery and equipment, and not at R&D. If we single out innovations that represent only new products for the market, the situation worsens, with the innovation rate dropping to only 3–4 per cent (IBGE 2008c). The strategies for human resources training and for capabilities building are also incipient, as are cooperation activities among companies.

However, two relevant aspects must be considering when we use PINTEC. First, the indicators used refer to average values. Therefore, they do not consider the weights of different industry sectors in the production structure of the country, and do not capture the broad variance of the innovation process resulting from the extreme heterogeneity of the Brazilian production structure. A second problem is the fact that, until 2003, PINTEC comprised only firms from manufacturing and extractive industries, and did not include either the services sector or agro industry.[15] These latter sectors, however, are responsible for about 80 per cent of domestic production and are a major contribution to the innovation process in Brazil. Thus, the focus by PINTEC on sectors that hold high rates of innovation and the use of average innovation rates create a huge distortion of Brazilian reality. However, a detailed analysis of innovation activity in the Brazilian production system is out of the scope of this work.[16]

Evaluation of the co-evolution of inequality, and the innovation and production sub-systems in Brazil, must highlight how the specificities of the size of the establishments and the geographical concentration of production and innovation activities reinforce inequalities in the country. With this in mind, our use of PINTEC data will take into account these limitations of its indicators in analysing innovation (Cassiolato 2008).

Regional specificities

The spatial dynamics of Brazilian production and innovation structures reveals strong territorial inequality in social and economic terms. Almost 80 per cent of Brazilian firms are concentrated in the southeastern and southern regions. The state of São Paulo alone concentrates more than 31 per cent of Brazilian industrial capacity (PIA 2009). The high concentration of firms, formal employments, infrastructure and financial institutions in the southeast reinforce its capacity for leveraging big projects of investments and creates a cycle that reinforces inequality over the country.

Naturally, the high regional concentration is not limited to industrial aspects, and is followed by a strong socio-economic inequality. Table 2.7 shows that the north and northeast regions have the worst indicators.

The uneven distribution of both industrial chains and educational institutions reproduces and strengthens regional disparities, through the concentrations of innovative process. From the point of view of innovation, regional disparities are even more pronounced. According to PINTEC 2008, more than 50 per cent of innovative enterprises are located in the southeastern region; together with the southern region, this percentage rises to 81 per cent. Indeed, a significant part of innovations introduced in both product and in processes in Brazil is concentrated in only six of the federated units.

These characteristics influenced the dynamic of the national system of innovation, making the major part of the production and innovation capacities restricted to the richest areas of Brazil.

Table 2.7: *Selected Regional Indicators (2008)*

Regions	*Participation on GNP**	*PIB per capita (US$)**	*Industrial Enterprises (%)**	*Industrial Employment (%)****	*Average Salary (minimum wages)**	*Higher Education Institutions (%)***	*Functional Analphabetism*****
Southeast	56.0	11.049	52.6	52.5	3.5	49	15.2
South	16.6	9.955	27.4	25.3	2.7	19	15.5
Central-west	9.2	11.108	5.7	5.3	2.7	7	22.0
Northeast	13.1	4.083	11.2	13.5	2.2	15	30.8
North	5.1	5.571	3.1	3.4	2.5	9	18.5

Sources: Authors' elaboration.
Notes: *IBGE (2008a); **CNPq (2009); ***Ministry of Labour and Employment (2009); ****IBGE (2010b).

Asymmetries by Size of the Establishments

The Brazilian production system comprises a high number of micro and small enterprises (MSEs). Official data point that, in 2006, there were 5.37 million MSEs registered in the country, which were responsible for 20 per cent of the GDP. In that year, MSEs represented altogether 94 per cent of the total number of firms in Brazil, contributing with 38 per cent of formal employment but accounting for only 22 per cent of total wages and remunerations in Brazilian economy (Arroio 2009). In other words, a significant part of the Brazilian population relies on the performance of MSEs but their participation in income generation is still relatively low.

The activities of a large majority of MSEs in the country are characterised by low technological complexity, with extensive use of unqualified labour, operating in traditional industries such as food and beverages, clothing and footwear, in which barriers for entry are low. Many MSEs limit their activities to local or regional markets where requirements regarding service and product quality, and the levels of competition, are considered to be smaller (Arroio forthcoming). Additionally, these enterprises generally face limitations in terms of human resources qualifications, of resource availability for innovation activities, and of technological cooperation.[17]

On the other hand, the production segments comprising firms of relatively greater size tend to play a more significant role in the governance of the Brazilian innovation and production system. The conditions for firms to engage in the process of capability building are still rather unequal in the country, with the better opportunities and conditions offered to the larger enterprises.

Therefore, for different reasons, MSEs in Brazil face difficulties in access to policy instruments and programmes oriented at fostering better production and innovation performance. Their presence in the production systems characterised by greater technological content in Brazil is reduced.[18] In addition, given the feeble competitive conditions MSEs usually have, wealth and quality employment tend to remain concentrated in larger enterprises, ending up by reinforcing inequality. Policies capable of reinforcing their competitive status could diminish the heterogeneity of the NSI as well as contribute to the reduction of inequalities.

The next section analyses the characteristics of the Brazilian labour market, given the direct correlation between the characteristics of the labour market and the innovation performance of the system as a whole.

Labour market and wages

Brazil has established itself as an essentially urban country (84 per cent of the population lives in cities) and most jobs can be found in the third sector (60 per cent) — agribusiness relied mainly on mechanisation (IBGE 2010a).

A striking feature of the Brazilian labour market is the persistently high degree of informality. Informality is even more intense in the northern states of the country. This may be explained by the low participation of industrial activities in the economy of this region, where the prevailing jobs can be found either in services or agriculture.

Urban informality increased by 10 points between 1991 and 2001, due to the continuous liberalisation of the economy in the 1990s, reaching 56 per cent in 2001. Two sectors responded most to this change: processing industry and services. The former, which usually hires personnel under formal contracts, was deeply affected by liberalisation policies, causing both a reduction of the total number of jobs and the creation of precarious jobs; while the later, characterised by informal hiring, absorbed a great number of the employees who previously held industrial jobs (IPEA 2009d).

However, since 2001, it is possible to observe a sharp drop in the rate of informality in Brazil. During 2001–09, the average number of people formally occupied grew from 44 per cent to 51 per cent, informally decreasing from 56 per cent to 49 per cent (Figure 2.4). The rise in formal work occurred in practically all occupations (IPEA 2009d).

This trend can be considered a significant change in the Brazilian labour market, since the access to some services and rights is restricted to formal workers. In addition, the decrease in informality generates positive impacts on tax collection for funding welfare.

From 2001 to 2009 there was also a reduction in unemployment: the average annual unemployment rate for 2009 was estimated at 10 per cent against 18 per cent in 2001 (Ministério do Trabalho e Emprego [Ministry of Labour and Employment, MTE]/Departamento Intersindical de Estatística e Estudos Socioeconômicos [Inter-union

Figure 2.4: *Percentage of Formal Jobs and Informal Occupations*

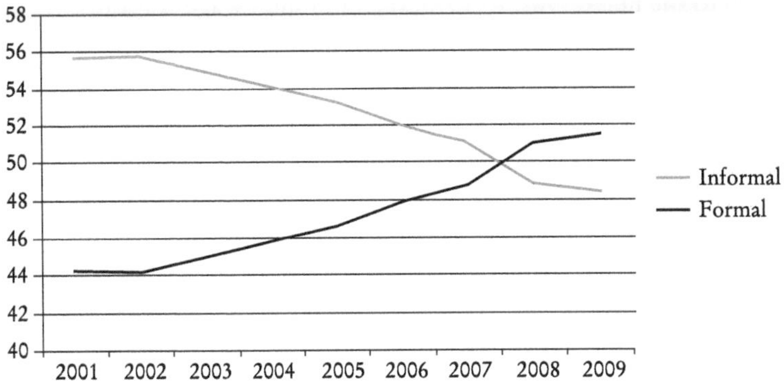

Source: IPEA (2009d).

Department of Statistics and Socioeconomic Studies, DIEESE]/ Pesquisa de Emprego e Desemprego [Survey of Employment and Unemployment, PED]). In Brazil, industry is the sector with the higher proportion of formal employment. The increase in employment in industry after years of contraction would have influenced formal economy as a whole. The intense recovery of output growth, especially since 2004, combined with employment-elasticity of 0.7, allowed for the first time in many years the expansion of occupation and an increased productivity.

It is possible to say that output growth recovery of the Brazilian economy associated with the increase in the formal employment contracts represents significant changes in the still very precarious labour market. The differences in the income by sector and, especially, by type of occupation are still very significant.

Regarding the distribution of national income, a downward trend of the per capita share of labor income in the national income since 1960s can be noticed. In the 1999–2000 biennium, for example, the weight of labour income represented only 40 per cent of national income, compared to 56.6 per cent in 1959–60. In the first decade of this century, however, Brazil showed a distinct trend from that observed during the last 50 years, combining a reduction of inequality in personal income distribution with a rising share of labour income in national income. In the biennium 2008–09, the weight of labour in national income increased 9.5 per cent compared with 1999–2000.

The minimum wage, created in 1940, fell sharply in its value from 1960 to the mid-1990s. In 1993, the minimum wage was only 40 per cent of its value in 1960. The process of recovery stared in 1994 and two recovery phases can be recognised: from 1994 to 2003 there was a relatively weak increase of about 1 per cent per year; and from 2004 to 2010 when the increase reached more than 10 per cent per year (IPEA 2011a).

Figure 2.5 illustrates the process comparing the evolution of minimum wage with Gini index for two types of income — labour and household income per capita. Authors such as Pochmann (2005) and Saboia (2007) have shown that the real increases in the minimum wage had important impacts on both the reduction of salary range and on the overall inequality of employed people income.

Nevertheless, earning minimum wage still cannot meet the basic needs and does not ensure elimination of poverty in Brazil. Therefore, a continuous improvement of minimum wage is an important public policy that would combat both the overexploitation of workers and the income inequality in the country.

Competence building institutions: Access to knowledge and S&T infrastructure

The learning process is directly related to accumulated knowledge and it demarcates the possible range of generation and assimilation of new knowledge or technical advances.[19] Due to the cumulative character of the learning process, basic education received in childhood constitutes a major pillar for the process of capability building. Moreover, in view of the requisites of the new techno-production paradigm, continued education figures as a chief factor in competitiveness, allowing for a continuing upgrading of qualifications. The strengthening of the NSI is, therefore, closely related to the development of a quality and continuous educational system, which helps individuals assimilate and generate new knowledge, thus enhancing the capabilities of the innovation system as a whole. Thus, assuming the relevance of the educational system for NSI development, this section presents the main data regarding the Brazilian educational and infrastructure systems, seeking to understand their main characteristics and implications for NSI.

Figure 2.5: *Evolution of the Minimum Wage and Gini Index for the Labour Income and Household Income per capita (1959–2009)*

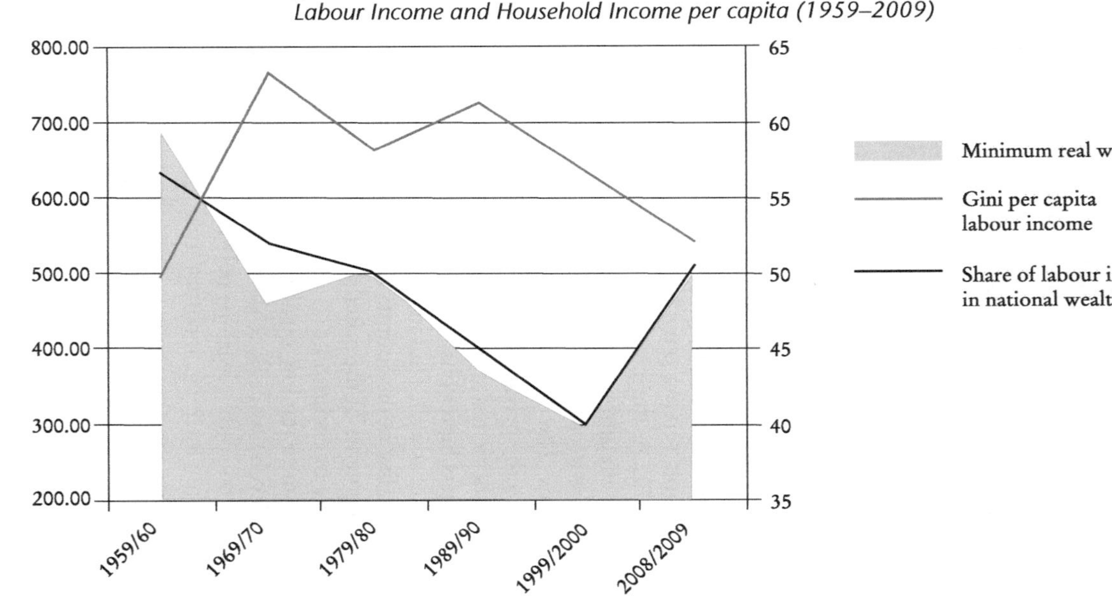

Source: IPEA (2011a).

Basic Education (Primary and Secondary Education)

In Brazil, 14.1 million people are illiterate (IBGE 2009a). Adding the so-called functional illiterates (people over 15 years old with less than four years of schooling), this percentage reaches 20.3 per cent of the population in 2009. Thus, in spite of decreasing trends, illiteracy rates in Brazil are among the greatest in Latin America.

The northeastern region presents a rate that is almost double of the Brazilian average, standing at 18.7 per cent, and quite higher than the south and southeast rates, which do not exceed 6 per cent. Both in the northeast and in Brazil as a whole, nearly 90 per cent of illiterate people are in the age range of 25 and over; the greatest concentration is represented by old people. For the geographical disparities, we observe that almost a quarter of the rural population is illiterate. As for the urban/metropolitan population, this rate is 16.7 per cent. The distribution of illiterates by colour shows the high disparity: 40.8 per cent are black, 41.1 per cent are mixed race and 18.1 are white (ibid.).

Elementary education in Brazil is predominantly public, with private schools serving only 14.6 per cent of students (Ministry of Planning 2010). As the major part of Brazilian students is concentrated in the public education system, the drop of education quality observed in the last two decades has a strong impact on the capabilities level of the Brazilians. The decrease in quality of the basic public education in relation to the private system produces a duality in the quality of education. The richest strata of the population, having access to private education, gets better chances of accessing higher education and the labour market as well. Thus in effect, the educational system promotes social inequality in the country, as it offers distinct opportunities to different segments of the population, reflecting and reproducing the vicious circle of exclusion.

In addition to the low quality of education (at both primary and secondary levels) available to the majority of the population, the non-existent lifelong public learning in Brazil negatively impacts domestic capabilities for learning, incorporating, disseminating, and generating innovation. Furthermore, it limits the development of important sources of diversity in social agents and institutions, thus jeopardising the national innovation system.

Higher Education

The number of students that have completed an undergraduate course in Brazil has increased significantly through the last 10 years. In 2001, only 400,000 students concluded an undergraduation course. In 2010, this number was 900,000, showing an increase of 125 per cent. In spite of the significant increase, higher education in Brazil is still very inaccessible (INEP 2011).

In 2010, 14.4 per cent of the population aged 18 to 24 years (age range expected for entry into higher education), were enrolled in higher education. Access is different in each region. While in the south, 19.2 per cent of young people in the age group analysed attended higher education in 2010, in the northeast the index was below 10 per cent. Among youths aged 18 to 24 years in rural areas, only 4.3 per cent had access to higher education, compared with 18.2 per cent of the population living in the city. There is also inequality in access between blacks (8.3 per cent) and whites (21.3 per cent) (IPEA 2011b).

The regional distribution of higher superior institutions is also highly unequal: in 2008, 49 per cent of universities and other higher education institutions were located in the southeastern region, while 19 per cent were in the northeast, 17 per cent in the south, 9 per cent in centre-west, and only 6.5 per cent in the northern region (Ministry of Planning 2010).

It is possible to say that the precariousness and the heterogeneity of the basic educational system spread to the higher education, which is also marked by the presence of strong asymmetries. Table 2.8 shows the unequal access to higher education of the population between 18 to 24 years. The table shows, for example, that 64 per cent of the population in university age and that earns less than one minimum salary has not completed primary school.

Table 2.8: *Schooling Level of Population between 18 and 24 Years Old according to Household Per capita Income, Brazil (percentage)*

	Per capita Income in Fractions of the Minimum Wage					
Levels of Schooling	*0 to 1/2*	*More than ½ to 1*	*More than 1 to 2*	*More than 2 to 5*	*More than 5*	*Total*
Not completed primary school	27	37	28	7	1	100
Completed primary but not high school	15	30	37	16	3	100
Completed high school but not higher education	11	27	39	18	5	100
Access to higher education	2	11	26	27	35	100

Source: IBGE (2007).

In Brazil, the higher education system represents an extension of the exclusion that occurs throughout the basic and secondary educational system, where mostly the upper class can access quality education and, thus, get access to university.

Postgraduate System and Research Institutions

A positive characteristic of NIS in Brazil is both the quantity and the quality of its science and technology (S&T) infrastructure. Data from CNPq shows that in 2008 there were 22,797 research groups, with approximately 105,000 researchers working at 422 research institutions. On the other hand, one of the most negative characteristics of Brazilian NIS is the high concentration of resources, as much in terms of infrastructure as in terms of human capabilities, in the most developed regions of the country.

It is worth mentioning that, as of the mid-1980s, a gradual decentralisation of policies and investments in S&T has occurred.[20] This process has deepened in the 1990s with the weakening of federal government policies in the area, and led state governments to improve their institutional basis and to develop initiatives, programmes and policies aimed at innovation in the ambit of the states. Almost all states created their own foundations and funds in support of research, besides developing specific programmes to support R&D activities performed by the production sector. However, in spite of the mentioned decentralisation, there remain deep regional disparities in both the allocation of resources and in the S&T infrastructure of the country, as will be shown in the following text.

In the mid-1960s, Brazil decided to invest in the preparation of researchers, with public universities as its main institutional basis. According to Velho (2007), throughout the 1970s, nearly 800 new masters and doctorate courses were created and, in the beginning of the 1990s, the number of courses already reached little more than 1,000, comprising every knowledge area.

By the end of 2009, there were 2,314 institutions of higher education: 245 public and 2,069 private. From 2008 to 2009, the number of public and private institutions increased 3.3 per cent and 2.6 per cent respectively. The undergraduate courses grew by 13 per cent over 2008. Another relevant issue is the technology courses, which grew by 26.1 per cent from 2008 to 2009. The number of Brazilian higher education enrollment increased from 3.5 million to 5.9 million in seven years (2002–09) (Census of Higher Education, 2009 [Ministry of Planning, Budgeting and Management 2009]).

Nevertheless, it is worth emphasising that the postgraduate system, in spite of its internationally acknowledged quality, has a low level of interaction with the Brazilian production structure (Velho 2007).

There is also a high spatial concentration of the centres of excellence and of technological services in the country. According to data from CNPq's Directory of Research Groups in Brazil, in 2000, the country had 224 research institutions, a number that jumped to 422 in 2008. In 2008, almost half the research institutions were concentrated in the southeast region. The strong concentration in this region is still observed in terms other indicators (number of research groups, researchers, technical professionals, etc.) (Figure 2.6).

Figure 2.6: *Profiles of the Regions in the Directory of Research Groups in Brazil and CNPq Support, Brazil (2008) (percentage)*

	Groups	Institutions	Research Lines	Students	Researchers	Technicians	PhD Researchers
South	23	19	22	23	22	19	20
Southeast	49	49	48	48	47	56	53
North	5	9	5	4	6	6	4
Northeast	17	15	18	19	18	14	16
Centre-west	6	7	6	6	8	5	7

Source: CNPq (2010a).

Vocational Learning and Training

One of the main reasons for the shortage of qualified work-force in Brazil is the mismatch between the current supply of vocational courses and the demand in the sectors that present more intensive growth, such as services and some industrial segments. Even though the supply of vocational learning has been increasing, it is still insufficient.

The number of enrolments in the last years in the technical education system in Brazil has increased significantly: between 2002 and 2010 there was an increase of 75 per cent in the number of enrolments in the vocational education. However, the number of students in vocational education is still considered as insufficient (Ministry of Planning 2010).

Another problem that aggravates the scarcity of technical courses in Brazil is the poor efforts of firms in terms of training and building capabilities of their human resources. Based on PINTEC 2008, we may observe that Brazilian innovative enterprises invested an average 82,000 US$ during 2008 in human resources activities, like training and capabilities building. Considering solely the innovative enterprises of the industrial segment, this amount corresponded to only 0.80 per cent of the net income from sales.

An expansion in the supply of vocational technical courses on the part of the public sector, and more initiatives by firms regarding the supply of human resources training is crucial for amplifying the possibilities of workforce inclusion of youth coming from the secondary education, and for enhancing the capabilities and promoting the development of the country.

Access to financial infrastructure

The financial dimension has a key relevance in the innovation process. Indeed, as the outcomes of the innovation process are not always predictable, to foster and finance it comprises a challenge, and the financing of investments in innovation is still pointed out as a strong bottleneck to innovation in many countries (de Melo 1994).

In Brazil, some analysts argue that the financial system has not been helpful to the economic development (Studart 1995). Although already in the 1960s the country counted on a reasonably articulated system of public financial institutions capable of implementing a long-term credit policy, the same was not observed at the private banks' side.

Even in the period of intense economic growth allowed by imports substitution industrialisation, private banks in Brazil kept the strict character of their actions, essentially aimed at credit for consumption. For many reasons, the capital market in the country has also not consolidated as a source of financing for enterprises, although some advances have been observed in recent years (de Melo and Rapini forthcoming).

Accordingly, in the absence of a long-term financing private banks' market operating in the country, and in view of the limitations of the domestic capital market, the financing of the enterprises has been carried out predominantly with resources originated from the firms' retained profits and from public and foreign credits. The main source of public credit for investment in the country is made available through the National Bank for Economic and Social Development (BNDES).[21] The foreign credit, extremely important until the end of the 1970s, has had its significance relatively reduced since the emergence of the foreign debt crisis in the 1980s decade.

The Brazilian financial system currently comprises a complex system. Nevertheless, as in the past, it remains unwilling to provide long-term financing to the enterprises operating in the country. Data on financing to enterprises indicates the predominant use of own resources in firms' expansion strategies, followed by long-term debt (particular through BNDES or foreign credit) and, to a lesser extent, by financing through issuing capital stock shares (Moreira and Puga 2000).

It is worth mentioning that a characteristic mark of the financial system in Brazil is its regional concentration, which follows the concentration of the production system and S&T infrastructure. As shown in Table 2.9, in the 2003–08 period the southeast region absorbed 56 per cent of credit operations (including public and private sources).

Table 2.9: *Regional Performance: Participation in Credit Operations in Brazil (2003–08)*

Region	*Participation in Credit (%)*	*Participation in GNP (%)*
Southeast	56	56
South	19	17
Northeast	8	13
North	6	5
Centre-west	11	9

Source: BNDES 2010 and IBGE/Regional Accounts 2008.

According to de Melo and Rapini (forthcoming), the existence of large international groups, leaders in the more dynamic markets, makes them independent and disconnected from the Brazilian financial institutions, whose capital is predominantly national. At the same time, the large national groups stay, in general, closed, avoiding opening their capital because of concerns about losing control of their enterprises. The disconnection between the banking system and the large industrial capital blocks is responsible for the inexistence of large private national groups of international magnitude, with financial capacity and capability for production conglomeration, capable of facing competition on the international market alongside large groups from developed countries and even from other emerging countries.

Another asymmetry highlighted by these authors is related to the technological and innovation capabilities. The lack of leadership by Brazilian enterprises in the dynamic sectors prevents the complete internalisation of innovation, causing a rupture between the capacity for generating knowledge, forming human resources for R&D and the effective introduction in the production and innovation system. This issue cannot be solved only with the increase of resources for innovation. These are important and necessary, but do not solve the central question of the separation of R&D produced outside the country by multinational companies, leaders in the dynamic sectors, and introduced in the country without the need of an internal effort of innovation. Thus, what should be the NSI's central and strongest attribute is in fact its congenital defect: the weak economic and technological competence of Brazilian enterprises (ibid.).

The analysis of financing innovation in Brazil shall, then, take into account the characteristics and asymmetries of the national financial system described here.

Financing and Funding Innovation

According to PINTEC data, in 2001–08, 58.2 per cent of the enterprises that made expenditures in internal R&D activities were located in the southeastern region and 27.9 per cent in the south. This strong geographical concentration of firms that invest in internal R&D activities perpetuates regional imbalances in the fields of greater knowledge content and learning. The same can be said regarding the small and micro enterprises. The high participation of self-financing in investments for innovation (nearly 90 per cent of investment in R&D activities in Brazil is financed with firms' own resources), in spite of being compatible with the worldwide pattern, points to a disadvantaged position of micro and small enterprises insofar as these firms can count only on the relatively minor availability of retained profits.

The public financing to innovation has not been able to attenuate such asymmetries. Data from PINTEC for the industry (IBGE 2008c) shows that the main beneficiaries of all public programmes supporting innovation are the large enterprises located in the southeast of the country.

The programme most accessed by firms in the 2005–08 period was the financing for machinery and equipment provided by the chief governmental banks, especially BNDES, Banco do Brasil, Caixa Econômica Federal, and FINEP. Figure 2.7 shows that from the total government programmes, these resources were the ones more accessible to small enterprise (14.2 per cent). Regarding the financing to research projects, the second most important financing line, the large-scale enterprises presented a participation rate of 4.2 per cent, a number several times higher than the participation of small enterprises (0.8 per cent). This pattern of greater access to large firms to government programmes can be identified in the firms that were benefited by the law of innovation — 1 per cent of small enterprises benefited, compared to 16.2 per cent of large enterprises; this asymmetry is also manifested in the other modalities — Law of Informatics Technology and other programmes — although to a lesser extent.

As already mentioned, an important characteristic of the national production system and, particularly, among the MSEs, is the high informality. According to estimates by SEBRAE, there are approximately 20 million informal small businesses, involving about 60 million people, operating in Brazil. The high degree of informality prevents the access to official financing sources, intensifying these financial limitations and, consequently, hindering the development of innovation activities (Arroio 2009).

The chief policy tools for promoting innovation, adopted in Brazil in the 1990s, were the fiscal incentives to R&D and various financing programmes (both reimbursable and non-reimbursable), among which are research scholarships and grants. The Sectoral Funds comprise the main source of governmental resources and programmes for financing innovation. The Ministry of Science and Technology in association

Figure 2.7: *Participation of Innovative Industrial Firms that Used Governmental Programmes by Bands of Occupied Staff (2008)*

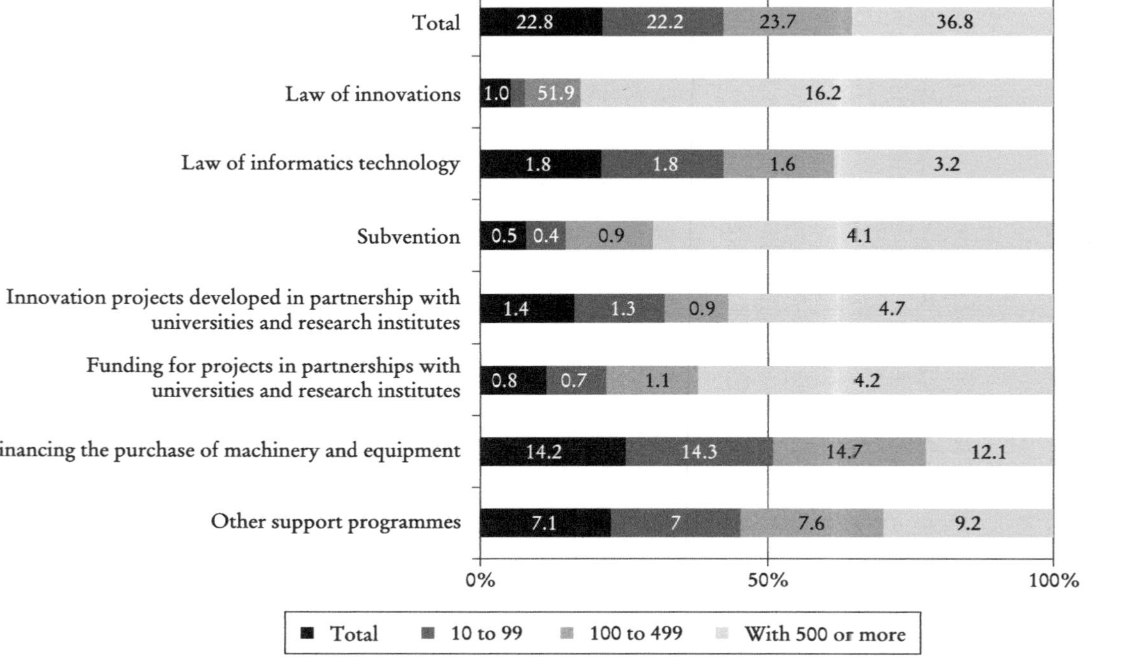

Source: IBGE (2011).

with its agencies — FINEP and CNPq (National Council of Scientific and Technological Development) — is in charge of the coordination and operationalisation of these instruments in the country.

Fiscal incentives for S&T in Brazil were instituted as of 1993, granting the enterprises participating in the programme the possibility of obtaining tax exemptions under the condition of developing R&D projects. The legislation that regulates the concession of fiscal incentives has, since then, undergone changes that influenced the greater or lesser use of these instruments by the firms.[22] In 2007, the participation of real benefits of the firm's investments in R&D in relation to the GDP was 0.03 per cent. Data reveals that the southeastern region concentrated, in the same year, 81 per cent of earned benefits. It is worth mentioning that, insofar as fiscal incentives are granted on the basis of firms' real profits, larger firms stand to concentrate most of the benefits.[23]

The analysis of the evolution of sectoral funds' resources as a percentage of GDP, in the period from 1999 to 2006, reveals a substantial progress in the amount of resources used for the area of STI, starting from 0.03 per cent in 1999 to 0.042 per cent of GDP in 2006. From 2007 to 2009, Sectoral Fund increased by 60 per cent, from R$ 1476.5 million to R$ 2357 million. It is worth highlighting that the legislation that governs the use of sectoral funds establishes as mandatory the application of 30 per cent of the resources in the regions center-west, north and northeast. Nevertheless, recent studies point out that this obligation, in the absence of complementary actions that take into account the specificities of these regions, may lead to the inefficacy of that distributive tool. According to FINEP, disbursements to the southeastern region concentrated nearly 50 per cent of resources during 2003–05. In 2007, the concentration of resources in the southeast increased to nearly 63 per cent, declining to 58 per cent in 2008 (FINEP 2011).

The modalities of financial support involving reimbursable resources comprise credit to R&D and innovation, and risk capital. On the federal level, these supporting modalities are conferred especially by FINEP and BNDES. In 2006, FINEP expended a total of 915 million US$ with financial support, 60 per cent of which comprised non-reimbursable resources and 40 per cent reimbursable resources.[24] As to reimbursable resources, the main instruments used were interest rates equalisation and financing of projects of enterprises. Additionally, FINEP makes investments through funds of risk capital, although the participation of this instrument in the whole of its actions is still quite small. Unfortunately, there is no disaggregated data available showing the participation of disbursements accomplished either by region or by size of the firms. As of 2003, however, FINEP has sought to expand the participation of micro and small enterprises in its actions, and fixed, as its policy, a minimum of resources to be allocated in micro and small enterprises, and also created some new products focused on this kind of enterprises. Yet, there is no information available for the evaluation of the results of this new guideline.

Non-reimbursable resources aimed at fostering and supporting innovation activities in Brazil may be classified according to two modalities: (*a*) the concession of resources for scholarships and grants aimed at research institutions and universities; and (*b*) economic subvention conferred directly to the enterprises.

The first modality aims at supporting universities and research institutions in the development of partnership projects, services and consultancies aimed at the solution of technological problems in enterprises, as well as in the development of new products and production processes. Scholarships and grants for R&D and innovation activities are conferred, mostly, by the federal government, especially through CNPq, and by state governments, through the Foundations of Support to Research (FSRs). The CNPq investments are still extremely concentrated in the southeastern region, although the participation of this region has been reducing during the latter years, declining from 66.7 per cent to 53.1 per cent in the period from 1996 to 2010. Northeastern and northern regions presented greater relative growth, rising from 10 per cent and 2 per cent to 17 per cent and 5 per cent, respectively (CNPq 2010b).

The economic subvention, legally established since 2001, started to effectively operate in the country in 2006. This modality of financial support allows the application of non-reimbursable public resources directly in the firms, so as to reduce costs and risks inherent in innovation. Preliminary estimates indicated that the governmental expenditures with economic subventions in 2007 corresponded to 0.013 per cent of GDP. As in the case of the sectoral funds, the legislation on economic subvention establishes mandatory proportions for the north, northeast and centre-west regions, and goes beyond also adopting minimum percentages for micro and small enterprises. Nevertheless, given the quite recent implementation of this instrument, it is not possible yet to assess the distributive aim targeted by the legislation.

Finally, it should be mentioned that in 2003 the Science and Technology Secretariat for Social Inclusion (SECIS) was created at the Ministry of Science and Technology (MCT) with the aim of proposing policies, programmes and actions that could allow the economic, social and regional development, besides disseminating appropriate knowledge and technologies in poor communities in rural and urban areas.[25] From 2003 to 2008, the SECIS, together with other MCT agencies (especially FINEP and CNPq), provided 727.6 million US$ for social development initiatives (Uderman and Rocha 2009). The creation of the secretariat followed the emergence in the 1990s of diverse interest groups articulated around concerns about the social dimension of STI in Brazil. These groups share a common view that scientific and technological progress has not been able to attend to the basic needs of a large part of Brazilian population (Cassiolato et al. 2008).[26]

Despite representing a step towards the democratisation of S&T in the country, governmental policies in this area are still of limited scope and capacity to influence other public policies. Actions directed at social development accounted for only 2.6 per cent of the budget set by the Plan of Action for Science, Technology and Innovation for National Development 2007–10.[27] An evaluation developed in 2009 by the Center for Strategic Studies and Management in Science, Technology and Innovation (CGEE) — a governmental organisation responsible among others for assessing economic and social impacts of policies, programmes and projects in S&T — still points to the 'absence of mechanisms to coordinate the efforts of STI directed to the purposes of social inclusion, which maximize results and minimize the dispersion of efforts by different government levels' (Uderman and Rocha 2009: 100). In addition, it's worth mentioning that the creation of specific instances inside public administration oriented towards dealing with social gaps and demands for technologies have limited effectiveness if a systemic view is not adopted to articulate these demands with other STI and development policies.

Concluding Remarks

The interest of scholars of innovation in the themes of inequality and distributive effects of innovation is relatively new. Given its complexity, the understanding of the inter-relations between innovation and inequality still constitutes a huge challenge. But despite the magnitude of the task, a better understanding of this issue allows for evaluating different options for configuring the technological change, opening room for policies that may promote changes towards greater equality and social cohesion.

The aim of this study was to contribute to a better understanding of this question, by analysing the relations between inequality and the NSI in Brazil. This work showed that innovation and inequality have been co-evolving in a detrimental way in the country, and pointed out systemic changes that need to be made to ensure a better future.

As shown, in spite of the improvements achieved in the 2000s, Brazil is still one of the most unequal countries in the world. The structural, heterogeneous and broad character of inequality in the country has various impacts on the process of innovation and on the development of the NSI.

Inequality has been affecting the innovation process in the country, limiting learning and the cumulative building of competencies, jeopardising the generation, dissemination and use of innovation, aggravating the heterogeneity of the innovation and production system, restricting the process of endogenisation of technological progress, among other aspects. Understanding inequality as a constitutive part of both the context and the institutional structure that permeated the NIS in Brazil, since its design until its recent development, becomes, therefore, a key point as much from the analytical point of view as from the normative one.

If, on the one hand, inequality affects the NSI, on the other hand, the current dynamic of the Brazilian innovation system contributes to the reproduction and perpetuation of the vicious cycle of inequality.

The historical roots of NSI in the country, as well as the innovation policies implemented were not aimed at building a production structure able to provide social equity or to satisfy either basic or consumption needs of the low income population. Consequently, it hasn't been able to revert or ameliorate extreme inequality in the country. On the contrary, NSI institutional structure has served the current pattern of accumulation, both reflecting and contributing to the reproduction of inequalities.

The asymmetries of Brazilian NSI can be observed in its different dimensions and sub-systems.

A clear example is the infrastructure of S&T, which is characterised by strong disparities. Perhaps the most evident of them is the inequity in the access to quality education (in its diverse levels). The limitations faced by the poorest people in access to a quality public education restrict their opportunities in the labour market, reinforcing inequality. On the other hand, the low quality of education provided to the great majority of the population has a negative impact on the building of human capabilities and of internal capacities for learning and incorporating, disseminating and generating innovations. It also limits the development of important sources of diversity of social agents and institutions, jeopardising the NSI. Another example is the spatial concentration of centres of excellence and of technological services in the richest regions of the country, which similarly reflects and reinforces socio-regional inequality.

A similar pattern can be observed in the production and innovation sub-system. The major parts of the capacities are concentrated in the southern and southeastern regions of the country, where the strength of the national economy is characterised by the hegemony of the state of Sao Paulo and its surroundings. In addition, investments in innovation are concentrated in the hands of large companies and involve a very small segment of the workforce in the country. The great economic density of the south and southeast regions is strengthened by the broad network of higher education and research centres, which also attract the leader companies. These imbalanced spatial dynamics of the Brazilian production and innovation structure reinforce unequal development.

Furthermore, the institutional framework that comprises the current policies and mechanisms for engaging firms in the processes of capabilities building has reinforced existing asymmetries. Public financing and stimulus to innovation are examples of how policy mechanisms also tend to concentrate on large enterprises and in the richest regions of the country. The other pole comprises micro and small enterprises, cooperatives of production, and family farmers, among others — especially those located in regions north and northeast — with major participation of poor people, a precarious insertion in the labour world, high level of informality and tendency to stay marginalised if not excluded from the necessary support to the innovation process. The 'invisibility' of these less structured actors, regions and activities has prevented their inclusion on the police agenda, reinforcing the unequal distribution of capabilities and opportunities.

Innovation and technological progress in Brazil are extremely unfairly distributed between capital and labour. Innovations in process, accomplished with intensive capital influx and imported technology, resulted in the replacement of industrial employments for capital goods in the labour process, generally without the compensation of multiplier effects. In other words, the higher labour productivity of these new production processes had a negative redistributive impact. The precarious social organisation and the workforce surplus existing in the country reinforce the low appropriation of innovation benefits by workers. Additionally, with the emergence of the new technological paradigm, the trend to introduce knowledge-intensive innovations requires increasing qualification on the part of the workers. In a country characterised by quite unequal opportunities of access to the labour market, the differences of remuneration generated between qualified and unqualified job are significant.

Among restrictions observed in the industrialisation model adopted in the country until the end of the 1970s (through imports substitution), the inadequacy of the technological progress stands out. On the supply side, such inadequacy was manifested through intense import of technology, saving workforce in a country with high unemployment rates, without the concomitant process for incorporation and generation of the capabilities required for an endogenous techno-innovative dynamic. On the demand side, it reinforced a concentrative consumption pattern unable to imprint a greater dynamism on the domestic market, generating restrictions to economies of scale, feeding back the production of heterogeneity and the associated pattern of technical progress.

Since the 1990s, Brazil's model of growth is characterised by gradual predominance of a pattern of specialisation of Brazilian production based on commodities and products with low value added, creating a development model with a relatively low technological dynamism. Despite some exceptions — in which the coordinated efforts of the Brazilian government in terms of policies and investments were able to consolidate 'excellence isles' of technological development — we've observed increasing production and export of commodities, as compared to imports, and of knowledge-intensive products. This pattern of specialisation strongly restricts the possibility of a positive structural change, besides relying on intensive use of non-renewable natural resources and being associated with an unfair distributive profile.

There is a relative consensus that the main generators of increase in productivity are technological learning, and innovation and its dissemination in the economy as a whole. In the same way, increasing importance has been attributed to technological disparities as an explanatory factor for the profile of comparative advantages and productivity differences between countries, which have direct impacts on employment and on the distributive profile. Investments in the endogenous generation of knowledge and in the cumulative and systemic building of capacities are considered by some authors to be crucial elements, not only for growth, but also for distributive reasons.

The pattern of growth in Brazil should, therefore, be revised.[28] A development strategy able to overcome the current limitations requires significant qualitative changes. The interactive construction of both innovation systems and systems that meet the priorities of social development may be one important policy instrument to simultaneously reduce inequality and foster innovation, thus leading to a pattern of technological development which would be less unequal and more consistent with a national project of long-term development.

Brazil started to implement policies of distributive character, which had reducing effects on inequality. The improvement in the income of the poorest families has expanded the domestic market, encouraging both the aggregate demand and consumption. The entry into the consumption market by millions of Brazilians who stepped out of poverty should be considered by industrial and technological policies as an opportunity to foster endogenous technological development and innovation. Particular attention should be given to spatial deconcentration privileging less developed territories in the country.

Additionally, the overcoming of historical deficiencies in terms of basic needs of the population may be seen as a chance for exploring the national specificities and seeking to reconcile technological development and social inclusion. As it has been shown, a large part of Brazil's population has precarious or no access to water, sanitation, health, and other social services due to the high levels of inequality. Integrating excluded and precariously included population in adequate consumption conditions, together with the search for improvement in the generation and access of social services infrastructure, could present a huge challenge for innovation policies.

Yet, there is an urgent need for changing the deeply rooted institutional structure that serves the dominant sectors and social classes, perpetuating inequalities. Albuquerque (2007) compares this institutional structure to the 'lock-in' phenomenon brought by evolutionary tradition. Albuquerque points out that in Brazil the inclusive development depends upon breaking this 'lock-in' and suggests that the challenge to be faced implies not only the improvement of democracy in the country, but also the identification of a pattern of technological development, which would allow Brazil to escape the structural polarity.

In contrast to the mainstream belief that market mechanisms would trickle down the economic benefits from the advancements of science, technology and innovation, we argue that deliberate policy efforts are essential to allow social-equality positive correlated innovation. The state, in this context, is vitally important because of its ability to adopt active policies that would enable it to counteract the concentrative and excluding trends, and to dismantle the archaic structures of underdevelopment. The implementation of policies aimed at re-orienting technological progress and the creation of an efficient system of production based on a relative technological autonomy in connection with the objective of social inclusion, constitutes, in this context, a fundamental part of this arrangement.

Public procurement and other public policy instruments (anti-trust actions, health and safety regulations, etc.) should be used to stimulate demand for social innovation, assure the generation and diffusion of the solutions, and promote the accumulation of knowledge and production capabilities in a wide range of production sectors supportive to fulfilling social needs. Academic research incentives and university reward systems could also be valuable instruments to foster problem-solving inventiveness. Additionally, innovation efforts oriented by social policy demands might be an important instrument to stimulate research in areas without market interest but critical for social well-being, such as tropical diseases and other under-researched issues. Similarly, new low-cost solutions could be fostered in order to broaden coverage and access by the poor population, together reducing the gaps and enhancing innovation capabilities.

Besides addressing social needs, innovation policies should help to enhance the stakeholders' capacities to do new things, integrate new technologies into everyday life, and solve problems by making the most extensive use of knowledge. Improvements due to innovation should also generate a broader dynamic process of societal change, including the generation of local learning processes and capabilities for problem resolution as well as taking advantage of opportunities to increase country competitiveness. National policies should be articulated together with local policies as the local dimension is essential to assure the contribution of local actors to find solutions to problems that directly affect them.

The heritage of social injustice that hinders the access of a significant part of the Brazilian population to minimum conditions of dignity and citizenship brings on the challenge of pursuing development strategies that combine economic growth and social inclusion. We believe that promoting the interlinking between social goals (and policies) and innovation policies through the interactive construction of socially oriented innovation systems is an important component of any strategy consistent with a national project of long-term development.

Notes

1. The lines of extreme poverty presented by Ipeadata (one of the main governmental databases on Brazilian economy) are estimated based on the methodology developed by the committee IBGE-ECLAC-IPEA to define a basic food basket that meets the nutritional requirements in each Brazilian region. From the information on total calories per day, the amount consumed and the unit price the expenditure for each product and the sum of expenditure resulting in extreme poverty line per person was estimated. The poverty line is defined as twice the extreme poverty line.
2. For further details on this issue see Medeiros (2003).
3. The concept of 'inadequate technology' developed by the Latin American structuralist school aimed at characterising the persistent barrier to endogenisation of technological progress that was created by the modernisation-marginalisation polarity. The use of intensive technologies in industry without correspondence with degrees of domestic accumulation, and the generation of productivity gains concomitant to high rates of unemployment have both contributed to the reproduction of the structural inequity and led to a pattern of restricted growth. For further details see Prebisch (1951).
4. Although the accelerated industrialisation headed by the state has allowed for an ascending occupational mobility, expanded the modern waged employment and unionism, expanded medium classes and reduced the absolute poverty, it was unable to fully absorb the huge contingent of workers that left the poor rural areas, particularly the northeastern region, towards the urban peripheries.
5. Besides the rise in purchasing power of the real minimum wage due to the economic stabilisation, another factor that contributed to the reduction

of absolute poverty in the 1990s was the extension of retirement pension benefits to the rural workers and the benefits guaranteed by the 1988 Constitution to elderly and disabled poor people.

6. The regressive structure of taxes and the high concentration of public bonds made the Brazilian interest rate a factor of fundamental importance for income concentration as of the 1980s.
7. The workforce surplus and structural unemployment are fundamental traits of the Brazilian economy. There is no job with a socially adequate remuneration for most of those who want work. Given the survival needs of broad segments of the Brazilian population, a huge diversity of low income activities (both legal and illegal) emerges, as much in the countryside as in the cities, which constitute the bottom of the Brazilian economic pyramid. In periods of industrial employment contraction, as happened in Brazil in the 1990s, there is a trend to a significant expansion of those activities, which makes considerable segments of Brazilian population more vulnerable regarding employment and income.
8. The Continuous Cash Benefit (BPC) is an unconditional cash transfer programme for the elderly or extremely poor individuals with disabilities. It was created by the 1988 Federal Constitution, but it was only implemented in 1996. The transfers are made to the elderly (above 65 years) or people with severe disability, whose family per capita income is less than one-fourth of the minimum wage. The value of the transfer is equivalent to a monthly minimum wage. For further details see UNDP (2006).
9. Salm (2006) notes that the personal distribution and the functional distribution of income are two complementary perspectives in the analysis of income distribution, although not necessarily convergent. It is possible to obtain an improvement in the personal income distribution (labour remuneration) without having improvements in the total income distribution due to deterioration in the functional distribution of income. This is the case, when the incomes from property (land and capital) are elevated vis-à-vis the labour income (workforce). Therefore, nothing can be implied about the total distribution of income based only on the analysis of personal income distribution.
10. Specially, from 1994 the real rate of interest set on public goods achieved a very high level pushing up the opportunity cost of capital and depressing the real public spending. The regressive tax structure and the high concentration of public bonds in the hands of a few make the Brazilian interest rate a detrimental determinant of the income distribution in the country. For further details see Medeiros (2006).
11. The same manufacturing unit may present a technologically modern line of production, aimed at manufacturing products directed to the higher income groups of the population, along with another production line, of low technological complexity, aimed at supplying the demand of the low income population.

12. Distinguished from the dynamic and sustained competitiveness, the spurious competition depends mainly on the low cost of traded goods due to low wages and precarious work conditions, the intensive use of natural resources without a long-term perspective, as well as the use of foreign exchange rates and interest rates for short-term commercial purposes. For further details see Fajnzylber (1988).
13. Considering all Brazilian households with incomes ranging between 779 US$ and 3,361 US$ per year (calculated on the basis of 2007 PPP assessment), the study uses the definition of middle class in absolute terms. According to this definition, class 'C', or the middle class, is placed between those immediately above the poorest 50 per cent and the richest 10 per cent, in the turn of the century. That is, class 'C', according to this definition, earns on average the average income of the society in statistical terms.
14. For further details, see '*No ritmo do país*', (2008).
15. In 2005, Pintec included the services sectors in the data base. We, however, excluded services sectors in Table 2.6 so that it would be possible to compare the results of 2000, 2003 with 2005 and 2008.
16. For further details see Cassiolato et al. (2008).
17. Despite the cooperation activities being acknowledged as essential to information flows, learning and diffusion of technologies, in 2003 the MSEs presented a cooperation rate of only 2 per cent (IBGE 2003).
18. However, it is well known that in most of the production segments with predominance of micro and small enterprises, innovative activities do not happen through R&D departments. Generally in these segments innovative activities are related to informal elements, such as improvements in design and quality of the products, changes in the organisational routines, marketing and, remarkably, in the optimisation of the capacity for managing a great variety of links and relationships. Furthermore, the informal relations of cooperation that characterise MSEs are also not captured by the traditional indicators of PINTEC.
19. See, among others, Cohen and Levinthal (1989).
20. The greater decentralisation in S&T activities is part of a general trend towards decentralisation of policy action towards states and municipalities, in accordance with guidelines defined in the 1988 Federal Constitution.
21. BNDES is Brazil's largest bank and the main source of long-term public credit in the country. It has a disbursement volume exceeding those of many multilateral bodies, including the World Bank and IDB. BNDES achieved a record performance in 2010, with disbursements amounting to 95 billion US$. See http://www.bndes.gov.br/SiteBNDES/bndes/bndes_pt/Institucional/Relacao_Com_Investidores/Desempenho/ (accessed 6 March 2013).

22. For further details see de Melo and Rapini (forthcoming).
23. More than 90 per cent of Brazilian enterprises adopt the presumed profits regime instead of that on real profits, which excludes them from the possibility of enjoying fiscal incentives offered by *Lei do Bem*.
24. Calculated on the basis of 2006 PPP assessment.
25. Available at http://www.mct.gov.br (accessed 12 July 2013).
26. Recognising that relationships between STI and society are complex and unequal, especially in a heterogeneous country such as Brazil, groups such as Redes de Economia Solidária (Solidarity Economic Networks), Rede de Tecnologia Social (Social Technology Network) and Incubadoras Tecnológicas de Cooperativas Populares (Technological Incubators of Popular Cooperatives) claim that the benefits from S&T advances must be more equally distributed. Additionally, they argue on behalf of the recognition and valorisation of traditional knowledge and the orientation of STI policies for social inclusion and sustainable development.
27. Available at http://mct.gov.br (accessed 12 July 2013).
28. Besides being inadequate to meet the challenges of a new techno-production paradigm, it would be a mistake to base the pattern of future development on a mode of production that is intensive in non-renewable natural resources and is tied to an extremely unfair distributive profile. The emerging paradigm is that of an economy of resources, greater intensity of knowledge and greater sustainability. Some changes boosted by the emergence of the international crisis corroborate this trend. The North American anti-cyclic package includes among its priorities the investment in the health system that is of high technological content and high social impact. China has been taking advantage of the growth of its domestic market for developing innovations and domestic entrepreneurial capacity based on the specificities of its consumers; and its anti-cyclic package, just like South Korea's, includes expressive participation of investments aimed at an economy low in carbon generation and intensive in innovations.

References

Albuquerque, E., 2007. 'Inadequacy of Technology and Innovation Systems at the Periphery', *Cambridge Journal of Economics*, 31(5), 669–90.

Arroio, A. C., 2009. 'The Role of SME in the National Innovation System of Brazil'. BRICS project report, Rede de Pesquisa em Sistemas e Arranjos Produtivos e Inovativos Locais (RedeSist), Federal University of Rio de Janeiro, Rio de Janeiro.

Arroio, Ana and Mario Scerri, forthcoming. 'Local Productive Systems and SME Development in Brazil', in Ana Arroio and Mario Scerri (eds), *The Promise of Small and Medium Enterprises*. New Delhi: Routledge.

Barros, Ricardo, Mirela Carvalho, Samuel Franco, and Rosane Mendonça, 2010. 'Determinantes da queda na desigualdade de renda no Brasil', IPEA, Texto para discussão, no. 1460, Rio de Janeiro, January, 2010. http://www.ipea.gov.br/sites/000/2/publicacoes/tds/td_1460.pdf (accessed 5 March 2013).

Cassiolato, J. E., 2008. 'The Brazilian System of Innovation: Policy Challenges'. Position Paper prepared for the InterAmerican Development Bank, Rio de Janeiro, February.

Cassiolato, J. E. and H. M. M. Lastres, 2008. 'Discussing Innovation and Development: Converging Points between the Latin American School and the Innovation Systems Perspective', Working Paper no. 08-02, Globelics Working Paper Series, The Global Network for Economics of Learning, Innovation, and Competence Building System.

Cassiolato, J. E., M. C. C. Soares and H. M. M. Lastres, 2008. 'Innovation in Unequal Societies: How Can it Contribute to Improve Equality?' Seminario Internacional Ciencia, Tecnología, Innovación e Inclusión Social, United Nations Educational, Scientific and Cultural Organisation, Montevideo, mayo.

Cassiolato, J. E., Maria Gabriela Podcameni, M. C. C. Soares, Marina Szapiro, Priscila Koeller, Fabio Stalivieri, and Fabiano Geremia, 2008. 'Description and Dynamics of the Brazilian Innovation System'. BRICS project report, Rede de Pesquisa em Sistemas e Arranjos Produtivos e Inovativos Locais (RedeSist), Institute of Economics, Federal University of Rio de Janeiro, Rio de Janeiro.

Chen, J., X. Jin, Y. Bing He, and W. Yao, 2006. *TIM Based Indigenous Innovation: Experiences from Haier Group*. Hangzhou: Research Centre for Innovation & Development, College of Public Administration, Zhejiang University.

Cimoli, Mario, 2005. *Heterogeneidad estructural, asimetrías tecnológicas y crecimiento en América Latina.* ECLAC's Publication No. LC/W.35, November 2005, 1–162. http://mpra.ub.uni-muenchen.de/3832/1/MPRA_paper_3832.pdf (accessed 11 November 2010).

Cohen, W. and D. Levinthal, 1989. 'Innovation and Learning: The Two Faces of R&D', *Economic Journal*, 99(397), 569–96.

Coutinho, L., 2003. 'Macroeconomic Regimes and Business Strategies: An Alternative Industrial Policy for Brazil in the Wake of the 21st Century', in J. E. Cassiolato, H. M. M. Lastres and M. L. Maciel, *Systems of Innovation and Development: Evidence from Brazil.* Cheltenham: Edward Elgar, 311–28.

Cozzens, S. E. and R. Kaplinsky, 2009. 'Innovation, Poverty and Inequality: Cause, Coincidence, or Co-evolution', in B.-Å. Lundvall, K. J. Joseph, C. Chaminade, and J. Vang (eds), *Handbook on Innovation Systems in Developing Countries*. Cheltenham: Edward Elgar, 57–82.

Dalum, B. and B.-Å.Lundvall, 1992. 'Public Policy in the Learning Economy', in B.-Å. Lundvall (ed.), *National Systems of Innovation*. London: Pinter, 293–314.

de Melo, L. M., 1994. 'O Financiamento da Inovação Industrial'. Ph.D. Thesis, Economics Institute, Federal University of Rio de Janeiro.

de Melo. L. M. and M. Rapini, 2009. *Innovation, Finance and Funding in the National System of Innovation: The Brazilian Case*, BRICS Project Report, Rede de Pesquisa em Sistemas e Arranjos Produtivos e Inovativos Locais (RedeSist), Institute of Economics, Federal University of Rio de Janeiro, Rio de Janeiro.

Fajnzylber, F., 1988. 'International Competitiveness: Agreed Goal, Hard Task', *Revista de la CEPAL*, No. 36 (LC/G.1537-P), Santiago de Chile, Comisión Económica para América Latina y el Caribe (CEPAL), diciembre, 7–23.

Freeman, C., 1987. *Technology Policy and Economic Performance: Lessons from Japan*. London: Pinter Publishers.

Furtado, Celso, 1961. *Desenvolvimento e Subdesenvolvimento*. Rio de Janeiro: Fundo de Cultura. Reprinted in 1964 as *Development and Underdevelopment*, trans. Ricardo W. de Aguiar and Eric Charles Drysdale. Los Angeles: University of California Press.

——, 1968. *Um Projeto para o Brasil*. Rio de Janeiro: Ed. Saga.

——, 1986. *Teoría y política del desarrollo económico*, trans. F. de Oliveira and M. Soler. México: Siglo XXI.

——, 2003. 'O Brasil do século XX: uma entrevista', in Instituto Brasileiro de Geografia e Estatística (IBGE), *Estatísticas do século XX*, Rio de Janeiro: IBGE, 11–24.

Institute of Applied Economic Research (IPEA), 2007. 'Social Data on Brazil'. http://www.ipeadata.gov.br (accessed 4 August 2010).

——, (IPEA), 2008a. 'Pesquisa Nacional por Amostra de Domicílios. PNAD 2007: Primeiras Análises. Comunicados da Presidência', 9 (Pobreza e Mudança Social, DF, 22 de setembro de 2008), 10 (Mercado de Trabalho, Trabalho Infantil e Previdência, DF, 30 de setembro de 2008), 11 (Demografia e Gênero, DF, 07 de outubro de 2008), 12 (Educação, Juventude, Raça e Cor, DF, 14 de outubro de 2008) e 13 (Saneamento Básico e Educação, DF, 21 de outubro de 2008). Brasília: Instituto de Pesquisa Econômica Aplicada.

——, 2008b. 'Distribuição Funcional da Renda: situação recente'. Comunicado da Presidência 14, Brasília, DF, 12 de novembro de 2008.

——, 2009a. 'Pobreza e Crise Econômica: o que há de novo no Brasil Metropolitano'. Nota Técnica. Rio de Janeiro, maio 2009. http://www.ipea.gov.br/portal/images/stories/PDFs/livros/notastecnicas211.pdf (accessed 4 September 2011).

Institute of Applied Economic Research (IPEA), 2009b. 'PNAD 2008: Primeiras Análises', Brasília, DF, 24 de setembro de 2009. http://www.ipea.gov.br/portal/images/stories/PDFs/comunicado/090924_comunicadoipea30.pdf (accessed 15 October 2010).

Institute of Applied Economic Research (IPEA), 2009c.' Social Data on Brazil'. http://www.ipeadata.gov.br (accessed 15 November 2010).

——, 2009d. 'Pesquisa Nacional por Amostra de Domicílios. PNAD 2008: Primeiras Análises. Comunicado da Presidência'. 31, 1 de outubro de 2009. http://www.ipea.gov.br/portal/images/stories/PDFs/comunicado/091001_comunicadoipea31.pdf (accessed 10 December 2010).

——, 2010a. 'Evolução das Despesas com habitação e transporte público nos pesquisas de orçamentos familiares (POF): análise preliminar 2002–2009'. Comunicado da Presidência no. 69, Brasília, DF, 1 de dezembro de 2010. http://www.ipea.gov.br/portal/images/stories/PDFs/comunicado/101201_comunicadoipea69.pdf (accessed 28 February 2011).

——, 2010b. 'Social Data on Brazil'. http://www.ipeadata.gov.br (accessed 1 November 2010).

——, 2011a. 'Nature and Dynamics of the Recent Changes in Brazilian Income and Occupational Structure', Announcements of the IPEA, no. 104, August 4, 2011. Brasília, DF.

——, 2011b. IPEADATA Database, 'Educação'. http://www.ipeadata.gov.br (accessed 10 January 2011).

Koeller, P., 2009. 'Política Nacional de Inovação no Brasil: Releitura das estratégias do período1995–2006'. Thesis, Universidade Federal do Rio de Janeiro (UFRJ), Brasil.

Lazonick, W., 2004. 'Indigenous Innovation and Economic Development: Lessons from China's Leap into the Information Age', *Industry and Innovation*, 11(4), 273–98.

Lundvall, B.-Å. (ed.), 1992. *National Innovation Systems: Towards a Theory of Innovation and Interactive Learning.* London: Pinter Publishers.

Medeiros, C., 2003. 'Desenvolvimento Econômico e Estratégias de Redução da Pobreza e das Desigualdades no Brasil', *Ensaios FEE*, Porto Alegre, 24(2), 323–50.

——, 2006. 'Growth Patterns, Income Distribution and Poverty: Lessons from the Latin American Experience'. Paper prepared for the IDEAS Conference on 'International Money and the Macroeconomic Policies of Developing Countries', 16–19 December, Muttukadu, Tamil Nadu.

Melo, H. P., 2005. 'Gênero e Pobreza no Brasil'. Relatório Final do Projeto Gobernabilidad Democrática de Genero en América Latina y el Caribe, Comisión Económica para América Latina (CEPAL), Brasília.

Melo, H. P., forthcoming. 'Innovation, Finance and Funding in the National System of Innovation: The Brazilian Case', in Michael Kahn & Luiz Martins de Melo (eds), *Financing Innovation.* New Delhi: Routledge.

Ministry of Science and Technology (MCT), 2006. 'Coordenação Geral de Indicadores — ASCAV/SECEX'. http://ftp.mct.gov.br/estat/ascavpp (accessed 21 January 2011).

——, 2008. 'Relatório anual da utilização dos incentivos fiscais — ano base 2007', Novembro 2008. http://www.inovacao.usp.br/images/pdf/Relatorio%20MCT%20Incentivos%20Lei%20do%20Bem%202007.pdf (accessed 20 April 2011).

Ministry of Planning, Budgeting and Management, 2007. 'School Census 2007'. http://dados.gov.br/dataset/microdados-do-censo-escolar/resource/64b4b862-8498-44f7-b16e-eec4da126055 (accessed 4 August 2010).

——, 2009. 'Microdados Censo Escolar 2009'. http://dados.gov.br/dataset/microdados-do-censo-escolar/resource/4a67e113-b6b7-4003-820a-8c8a3f162d17 (accessed 12 April 2011).

——, 2010. 'School Census 2010'. http://dados.gov.br/dataset/microdados-do-censo-escolar/resource/f31050aa-bd4b-4687-a947-7423fe216dec (accessed 24 February 2011).

Ministry of Labour and Employment, 2009. 'Relação Anual de Informações Sociais (RAIS)'. http://www.mte.gov.br/rais/default.asp (accessed 3 November 2010).

Moreira, M. and F. Puga, 2000. 'Como a Indústria Financia seu Crescimento: uma análise do Brasil pós-plano real'. Texto para discussão BNDES (84). http://www.bndes.gov.br. (accessed 10 October 2000).

National Confederation of Industry, Brazil (CNI), 2009. 'Sondagem Industrial', ano 12(2), abril/junho. http://www.portaldaindustria.com.br/cni/publicacoes-e-estatisticas/publicacoes/2012/10/1,3990/sondagem-industrial.html (accessed 13 November 2010).

National Council for Scientific and Technological Development (CNPq), 2009. 'Diretório dos Grupos de Pesquisa no Brasil'. http://www.cnpq.br/web/guest/programas (accessed 3 November 2010).

——, 2010a. 'Diretório dos Grupos de Pesquisa no Brasil'. http://dgp.cnpq.br/buscaoperacional/ (accessed 12 April 2011).

——, 2010b. 'Investimentos do CNPQ em CT&I'. http://fomentonacional.cnpq.br/dmfomento/home/fmthome.jsp? (accessed 11 October 2011).

National Institute for Studies and Research on Education (INEP), 2011. 'Censo da Educação Superior'. http://portal.inep.gov.br/web/censo-da-educacao-superior (accessed 24 February 2011).

Neri, M. C. (coord.), 2009. *Consumidores, Produtores e a Nova Classe Média: Miséria Desigualdade e Determinantes das Classes.* Rio de Janeiro: Getúlio Vargas Foundation/Instituto Brasileiro de Economia, Centre for Social Policies.

Neri, M. C. and L. Carvalhaes (coords), 2008. *Miséria e a Nova Classe Média na Década da Igualdade*. Rio de Janeiro: Instituto Brasileiro de Economia (IBRE), Centre for Social Policies (CPS) — Fundação Getúlio Vargas. http://www.fgv.br/cps/desigualdade (accessed 13 September 2008).

'No ritmo do país', *Revista Carta Capital*, ed. 499, 6 jun 2008. http://www.cartacapital.com.br/edicao-da-semana (accessed 10 August 2010).

Pochmann, M., 2005. *Ciclos do Valor do Salário Mínimo e seus Efeitos Redistributivos no Brasil.* Campinas: Instituto de Economia da Unicamp e Centro de Estudos Sindicais e de Economia do Trabalho.

——, 2007a. *Desenvolvimento e Processo de Exclusão Social: a experiência brasileira recente*, mimeo.

——, 2007b. 'Política Social na Periferia do Capitalismo: a situação recente no Brasil', *Ciência & Saúde Coletiva*, 12(6), 1477–489.

——, 2008. 'Progresso Técnico e Subdesenvolvimento', apresentação no XX Fórum Nacional BRASIL 'Um Novo Mundo nos Trópicos' 200 Anos de Independência Econômica e 20 Anos de Fórum Nacional, 26 a 30 de maio de 2008.

Prebisch, R., 1951. 'Theoretical and Practical Problems of Economic Growth', E/CN.12/221, D.F. Comisión Económica para América Latina (CEPAL), México.

Rogers, E. M., 1995. *Diffusion of Innovations.* New York: Free Press.

Saboia, J., 2007. 'Efeitos do Salário Mínimo sobre a Distribuição de Renda no Brasil no Período 1995/2005 — Resultados de Simulações'. Presented at the II Seminar for the Analysis of the Results of the National Research for Sample Survey (PNAD). Organised by Centro de Gestão e Estudos Estratégicos (CGEE)/*Instituto de Pesquisa Econômica Aplicada* (IPEA)/ Ministério da Educação (MEC)/Ministério do Trabalho e Emprego (MTE), 7 March, Brasília.

Salm, C., 2006. Sobre a Recente Queda da Desigualdade de Renda no Brasil: Uma Leitura Crítica. Instituto de Economia (IE), Universidade Federal do Rio de Janeiro (UFRJ), mimeo.

Sen, A., 2000. 'Social Exclusion: Concept, Application and Scrutiny', Social Development Papers no. 1, Office of Environmental and Social Development, Asian Development Bank. Manila.

Soares, M. C. C. and J. E. Cassiolato, 2008. 'Innovation Systems and Inequality: the Experience of Brazil'. Paper presented at The Global Network for Economics of Learning, Innovation, and Competence Building System (Globelics) Conference, Mexico, 22–24 September.

Studart, R., 1995. *Investment Finance in Economic Development.* London: Routledge.

Studies and Projects Finance Organization (FINEP), 2011. http://www.finep.gov.br/pagina.asp?pag=fundos_o_que_sao (accessed 15 January 2012).

Sutz, J., 2008. *Ciencia, Tecnología, Innovación e Inclusión Social: una agenda urgente para universidades y políticas.* Ottawa, Canada: Unidad Académica de la Comisión Sectoral de Investigación Científica, Universidad de la República.

Sutz, J. and R. Arocena, 2006. 'Integrating Innovation Policies with Social Policies: A Strategy to Embed Science and Technology into Development Process', Strategic Commissioned Paper, Policy and Science Program Area, IDRC Innovation, International Development Research Centre, April.

The Brazilian Institute of Geography and Statistics (IBGE), 2003. 'Pesquisa Industrial de Inovação Tecnológica (PINTEC) 2003'. http://www.ibge.gov.br/home/estatistica/economia/industria/pintec/2003/default.shtm (accessed 4 July 2010).

———, 2005. 'IBGE. Pesquisa de Inovação Tecnológica 2005, Análise dos Resultados'. www.ibge.gov.br/home/estatistica/.../pintec/2005/comentario.pdf (accessed 10 September 2007).

———, 2006a. 'National Household Sample Survey 2006'. http://www.ibge.gov.br/home/estatistica/populacao/trabalhoerendimento/pnad2006/tabbrasil.shtm (accessed 13 February 2010).

———, 2007. 'National Household Sample Survey (PNAD) 2007'. http://www.ibge.gov.br/home/estatistica/populacao/trabalhoeren dimento/pnad2007/default.shtm (accessed 4 August 2010).

———, 2008a. 'National Household Sample Survey (PNAD) 2008'. http://www.ibge.gov.br/home/estatistica/populacao/trabalhoerendimento/pnad2008/default.shtm (accessed 3 November 2010).

———, 2008b. 'IBGE divulga as Contas Regionais 2003–2006'. http://www.ibge.gov.br (accessed 14 November 2008).

———, 2008c. 'Pesquisa Industrial de Inovação Tecnológica (PINTEC) 2008'. http://www.ibge.gov.br/home/estatistica/economia/industria/pintec/2008/default.shtm (accessed 10 July 2010).

———, 2008–09a. 'Consumer Expenditure Survey 2008–2009, Social Communication, June 23, 2010'. http://www.ibge.gov.br/english/presidencia/noticias/noticia_impressao.php?id_noticia=1648 (accessed 15 November 2010).

———, 2008–09b. 'Consumer Expenditure Survey (POF) 2008–2009'. http://www.ibge.gov.br/home/estatistica/populacao/condicaodevida/pof/2008_2009_perfil_despesas/default.shtm (accessed 15 November 2010).

———, 2008–09c. 'Consumer Expenditure Survey (POF) 2008–2009'. http://www.ibge.gov.br/home/xml/pof_2008_2009.shtm (accessed 6 October 2010).

———, 2009. 'National Household Sample Survey (PNAD), 2009'. http://www.ibge.gov.br/home/estatistica/populacao/trabalhoerendimento/pnad2009/ (accessed 24 February 2011).

The Brazilian Institute of Geography and Statistics (IBGE), 2010a. 'Census 2010'. http://www.ibge.gov.br/home/presidencia/noticias/noticia_visualiza.php?id_noticia=2194&id_pagina=1 (accessed 4 July 2011).

The Brazilian Institute of Geography and Statistics (IBGE), 2010b. 'Síntese de Indicadores Sociais: Uma Análise das Condições de Vida da População Brasileira 2010, Estudos e Pesquisas — Informação Demográfica e Socioeconômica', no. 27, Rio de Janeiro. http://www.ibge.gov.br/home/estatistica/populacao/condicaodevida/indicadoresminimos/sinteseindicsociais2010/SIS_2010.pdf (accessed 3 November 2010).

——, 2011. 'Pesquisa de Inovação nas Empresas Estatais Federais 2008', Rio de Janeiro. http://www.ibge.gov.br/home/estatistica/economia/inovacao/pieef/2008/pieef_2008.pdf (accessed 5 March 2013).

Uderman, S. and G. Rocha, 2009. 'Convergência de Políticas Públicas: uma metodologia para a construção de agendas de ações de CT&I para inclusão social'. *Parcerias Estratégicas, CGEE,* 14(29), 99–128.

United Nations Development Programme, 2006. 'Cash Transfer Programmes in Brazil: Impacts on Inequality and Poverty', International Poverty Centre, United Nations Development Programme. Working paper no. 21, June, International Poverty Centre, Brasilia DF.

Velho, L., 2007. 'Formação de mestres e doutores e sistema de inovação'. Research Paper 05/07. Rede de Pesquisa em Sistemas e Arranjos Produtivos e Inovativos Locais (RedeSist), Institute of Economics, Federal University of Rio de Janeiro.

World Bank, 2009. World Development Indicators Database. http://web.worldbank.org/WBSITE/EXTERNAL/DATASTATISTICS (accessed 5 March 2012).

——, 2011, World Development Indicators Database. http://web.worldbank.org/WBSITE/EXTERNAL/DATASTATISTICS (accessed 21 December 2011).

3

National Innovation System and Inequality in Russia

Stanislav Zaichenko

Trends and Patterns in Inequality

The historical roots

Russia has a long history but initially it became a powerful empire under Peter I the Great. Peter's reforms brought European cultural influences to Russia, providing grounds for further transition of the Russian feudal setup towards more liberal society. In 1724 Peter founded the Russian Academy of Sciences and Arts — the first official entity in Russia performing R&D on a regular basis. A system of professional schools and academies in engineering, medicine, navigation, military science, etc. was also created. At the same time Peter I established primary schools and declared compulsory primary education for the nobles. The spread of knowledge was accompanied by rapid development of printing houses (including private ones), creation of official education programmes and manuals, and the establishment of public museums and academic libraries. In 1755 the Moscow State University (the first university in Russia) was founded. These reforms were the first step towards wide access to knowledge and competences.

Catherine II (Catherine the Great), reigning from 1762 to 1796, continued the efforts to establish Russia as one of the most progressive counties in Europe. During this period public schools and public libraries became widespread and open for all classes of society. The unified official standards for general education were created.

In the mid-19th century the historical roots of Russia were affected by the conservative policies of Tsar Nicolas I. However, at the next stage his successor Alexander II (1855–81) declared critical reforms. In 1861 serfdom was abolished, and the industrial development of the country went forward at a steady gait.

Alexander II also carried out significant reforms in science and education. He established free access to professional and higher education for all social classes and for women. As a result, by the end of his reign about 40,000 people obtained higher education degrees and more than 200,000, secondary education degrees. New technologies were rapidly spreading in Russia: electric spark lamps, wire telegraph, etc. The most significant reform of that period was the abolition of serfdom. It was the turning point, opening freedom guarantees for all strata. But it did not affect the inequality proportions as such.

Later on, Alexander III and his son Nicholas II faced severe socio-economic conflicts in the country. It was the period of the beginning of the revolutionary socialist movement. Eventually, Nicholas II was forced to introduce political parties' regulation, suffrage and freedom of assembly. The Duma was established as an elected legislative assembly institution. The next critical point was reached when Russia entered World War I in 1914. The costs were painful (3.3 million deaths including civilians). At the same time the population was displeased by the inability of the regime to minimise the casualties and overcome corruption and treason in administration. This situation became a background for the Russian Revolution of 1917.

The October Revolution of 1917 headed by Vladimir Lenin was followed by a civil war between the tsarist regime and the socialist revolutionaries. In 1922 the Russian Soviet Federative Socialist Republic (RSFSR) and three other Soviet republics were proclaimed. Together they formed the Soviet Union (Union of Soviet Socialist Republics, USSR). After Lenin's death in 1924, Joseph Stalin took power. He launched a centralised command economic system, rapid industrialisation processes and collectivisation of agriculture. During a short period the Soviet Union was transformed from an agrarian society to a powerful industrial economy. However, millions of Soviet people died as a consequence of Stalin's harsh policies. It was the time of the violation of all civil liberties and total fear. After Stalin's death, the subsequent leader Nikita Khrushchev condemned Stalin's regime and stopped the repressions. The next period of Soviet history was characterised by slow economic stagnation. It was the time of Leonid Brezhnev's leadership.

The Soviet Constitution of 1936 abolished private ownership of means of production and proclaimed equal rights for citizens (to elections, labour and remuneration, freedom of speech, etc.).[1] The Constitution guaranteed equality by income, access to knowledge, skills and political activities. For example, higher education institutions responded to political directives aimed at tailoring higher education for the masses and the training of 'proletarian specialists', particularly engineers.

However, this equality was mostly illusory. The Soviet agrarian sector was based on collective farms (Laird 1958). The farmers could not have passports (until 1974) and were bound to the farms like slaves. Another example is that of population transfer in 1920–51 represented by about 50 forcible ethnic cleansing actions (Martin 1998). These and many other evidences of glaring social and economic inequality (concerning social mobility, access to schooling, careers, management, etc., see Yanowitch [1977]) explain the 'decorative' nature of the Soviet Constitution and propaganda declarations.

In 1985 the first Soviet president Mikhail Gorbachev (the previous Soviet chiefs were recognised as 'Secretary Generals') announced a new course of development. His new policies were based on the 'glasnost' (openness) principle and 'perestroika' (restructuring) reforms. Soviet people were given a hope for the natural balance between equality and liberty. Even in stagnation the Soviet economy was the second largest in the world and still could provide free equal access to wealth, education and health until the USSR collapse. But during its last years, the economy was afflicted by shortages of goods in shops, huge budget deficits and explosive growth in money supply leading to inflation. The slump in oil prices together with an extremely inflexible command system was the grounds for a deep systemic decline of the Soviet economy. At the same time the ethnic tensions in various Soviet republics and their struggle for independence led to the final Dissolution of the Soviet Union. In August 1991, an unsuccessful military coup against Gorbachev aimed at preserving the Soviet Union led to its definitive collapse instead.

In Russia, Boris Yeltsin came to power and declared the end of the Communist regime. The USSR was separated into 15 independent republics and was officially dissolved in December 1991. During and after the disintegration of the USSR when wide ranging reforms including privatisation and market and trade liberalisation were being undertaken, the Russian economy went through a major crisis. This period was characterised by deep contraction of output, with Gross Domestic Product (GDP) declining by roughly 50 per cent between 1990 and the end of 1995 and industrial output declining by over 50 per cent.

In October 1991 a radical market-oriented reform was officially announced (the so-called 'shock therapy') as it was recommended by the United States and the International Monetary Fund (Fagen 1992). Price controls were abolished, privatisation was started. By the end of 1991 inflation reached 301.5 per cent, and 34 per cent of the population were plunged into poverty (in Russia poverty bounds are statistically determined by minimum of subsistence — a minimal basket of goods value, set by law for particular period of time and region). According to the World Bank (Milanovic 1998), in the late Soviet era 1.5 per cent of the population were living in poverty, but by mid-1993 this value increased up to 39–49 per cent, so the situation changed drastically. Delays in wage payment became regular (with millions of employees being paid their salaries months and even years later). The deep economic depression was followed by social decay. Social services collapsed and the birth rate plummeted while the death rate considerably increased.

One more shock occurred in 1993 when a constitutional crisis took place, and Moscow was enveloped in civil strife. Military forces were involved to resolve the political conflict between the Russian president and the Russian parliament. According to official estimates, 187 people were killed and 437 wounded (Andrews 2002). And in 1994 the first Chechen war started. It led to a death toll of 5500 in the Russian military during two years, thousands of Chechen militants killed (no reliable estimations by now), and provided grounds for the second Chechen war (German 2003). All these cataclysms led to a deep socio-economic crisis. In the late 1990s high budget deficits and the 1997 Asian Financial Crisis caused the financial crisis of 1998 and resulted in further GDP decline. It was the last economic shock in Russia till the end of 2008.

In terms of inequality the Russian history includes six evolutionary stages. The first one starts from the reforms of Peter I and lasts until the serfdom abolition in 1861. It was the period of slow adaptation of basic equality and freedom concepts to the feudal system (from the first public education institutions, professional mobility mechanisms, free media, etc., towards the abolition of serfdom). However, this task was impossible both on grounds of feudalism and the following political crisis. The liberty and equity principles transformed into revolt. Therefore, it was a very short and unstable second stage. The third period began with the socialist revolution and the new Soviet regime. Total freedom and equality were proclaimed, however, these declarations were rather just a cover for exploitation and totalitarian power (mostly under Stalin's regime — including political repressions, collective farms system, ethnic cleansing, etc.). The inflexible Soviet system started collapsing by the mid-1980s. In 1985 the first (and the last) Soviet president Gorbachev took a shot at a new Europe-like system based on a combination of liberalism and high social guarantees of the state. However, the stagnant Soviet economy could not bear such a load. Gorbachev's reforms were aimed at a gradual liberal transition, while the actual situation required immediate economic mobilisation. The USSR collapsed finally by the early 1990s; this was the end of the fourth stage. The fifth period was characterised by severe socio-economic crisis following the transition to the market economy. The 1990s were the time of not just an inequality burst, but rather a total pauperisation of the whole population. Only in the early 2000s did the Russian economy become stable and showed some growth. However, this fifth stage may be already finished by the current world economic crisis. It is not clear until now to what extent the Russian economy will change because of the shock.

Interpersonal inequalities

The Gini Coefficient (GC) indicates income disparity floating from zero (a perfect income distribution) to one (the richest obtain all the income). It is quite an 'aggregate' indicator but still informative enough to take a look at dynamics and international comparisons. When the Soviet Union collapsed, Russia had a GC of 0.29. Income disparity exploded in Russia in the beginning of the 1990s, but even in the 2000s, when the ecomomy became stable, Russia's GC did not change. It reached 0.4 in 2000 and has increased only a bit during the next years (Figure 3.1).

This level is close to the BRICS countries' average (0.479) as well as to the US' value (Table 3.1). However the GC value does not reflect the inequality structure as such. A deeper analysis shows that GC calculated for households (instead of individuals) and corrected by

Figure 3.1: *Gini Coefficient Dynamics in Russia (1992–2009)*

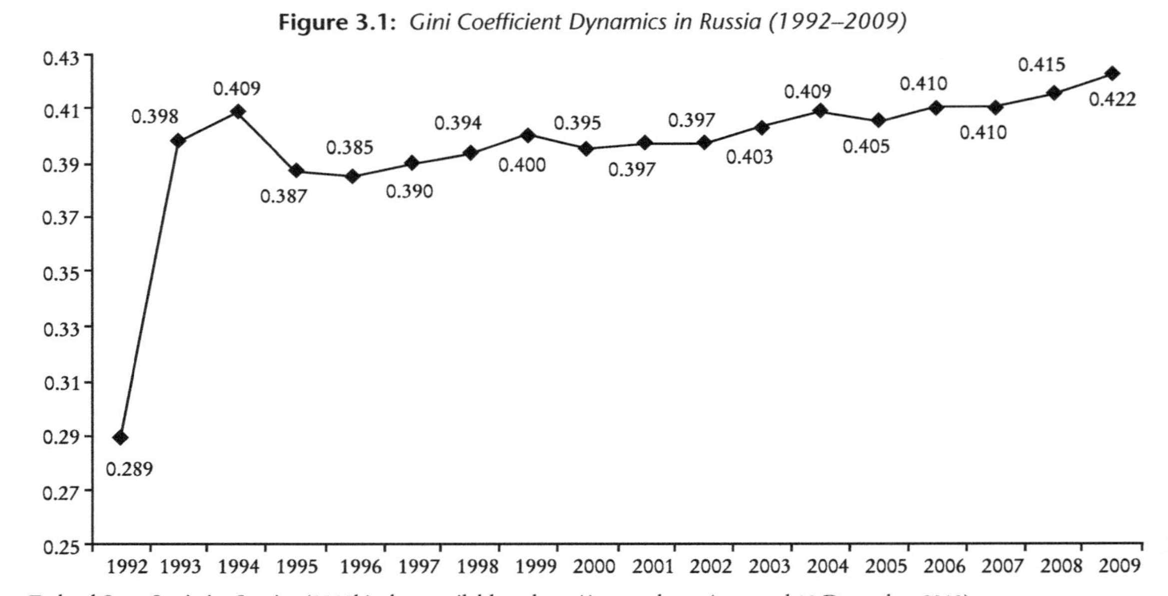

Source: Federal State Statistics Service (2010b); data available at http://www.gks.ru (accessed 10 December 2010).

Table 3.1: *Gini Coefficient International Comparison*

BRICS	
Brazil	0.539 (2009)
Russia	0.422 (2009)
India	0.368 (2004)
China	0.415 (2007)
South Africa	0.650 (2005)
EU (25)	0.304 (2009) – est.
USA	0.450 (2007)

Source: CIA (2010).

the regional purchasing power is usually lower by 15–17 per cent than official values in Russia (Besstremyannaya et al. 2005).

The main income shock in Russia took place in 1991–92. It was the time when the real income fell dramatically after transition from fixed prices to market-based ones, and the price index grew up to 26. As a result, by the end of 1992 about 80 per cent of households in Russia appeared below the minimal consumer basket price level (or the poverty level).[2] As already mentioned, this level in Russia is set quarterly by law for each region. In 1993 it was corrected, and the poor population accounted for 33.5 per cent. To compare, in 2007 the poor population share did not exceed 13.3 per cent (subsistence minimum in Russia was $293 by purchasing power parity [PPP], and minimal wage, also determined by law, accounted for $153 PPP). In 1993–98 the income level did not improve significantly for two reasons: economic decline (the 1997 GDP amounted to 63 per cent of the 1990 value) and huge wage debt (as well as social payments debt). The second shock occurred in 1998 as a result of the financial crisis. However, it did not contribute to inequality growth as in 1991–92. By that time the households already had abilities necessary for survival in the 'wild market' environment (see later) including informal employment, income and time budget redistribution, new wealth saving forms, etc. This mechanism is mainly reflected by the 15.2-point dynamic gap (1998) between the real income and the real wages (Figure 3.2). In 2007 the difference reached 33 points. The third crisis started in the end of 2008. It caused a certain drop of real wages, but did not affect income(s) and pension(s).

The income structure has changed significantly after the market reforms (Figure 3.3). First of all, the 'other income' share grew 8.6 times. This income source can be defined as 'hidden wages'

Figure 3.2: *Real Income, Real Wages and Real Pension per capita (percentage) (1991 = 100 per cent) (1991–2004)*

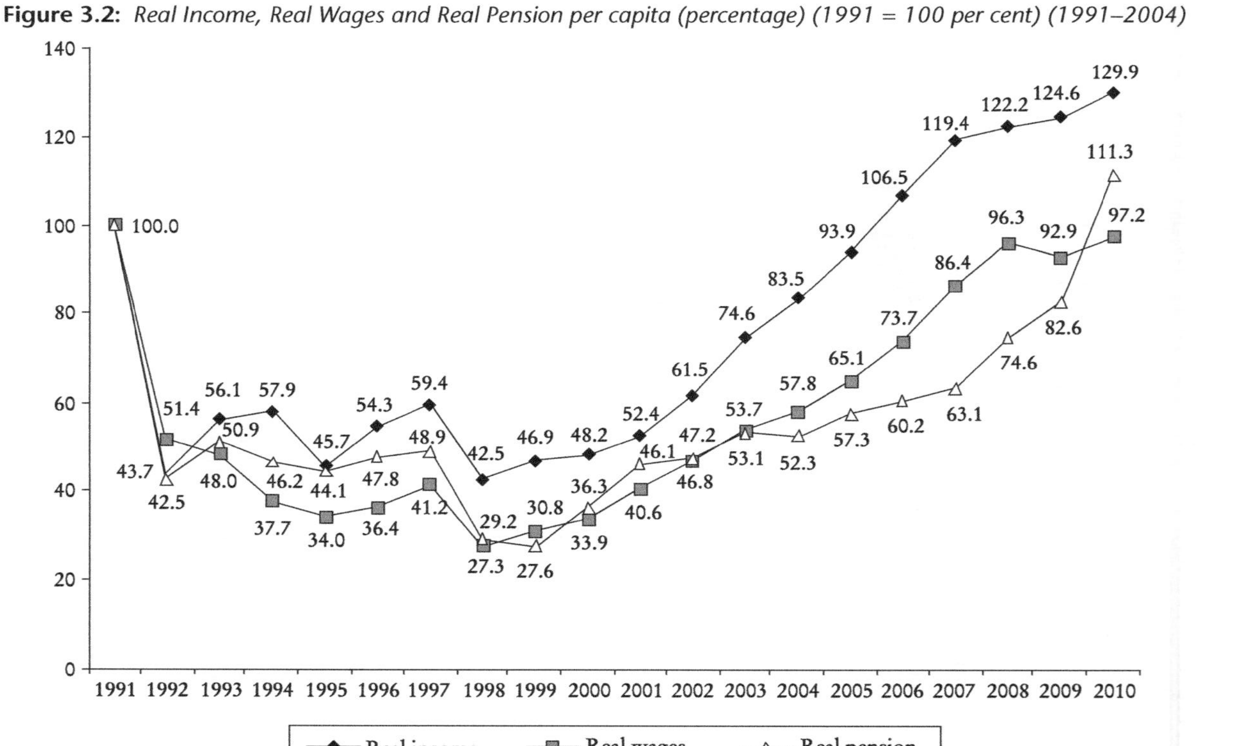

Source: Besstremyannaya et al. (2005); Federal State Statistics Service (2011).

(undocumented labour earnings — the shadow economy [or informal economy] sector). The self-employment activities in 2003 took 3.2-fold higher share compared with 1990. The buffer composed by these two sources and the rent income (46.4 per cent in total) provides not only a mechanism for survival facing the economic instability, but also a strong motivation for labour mobility, developing new competences and lifelong learning.

Figure 3.3: *Income Structure Transformation (1990–2003)*

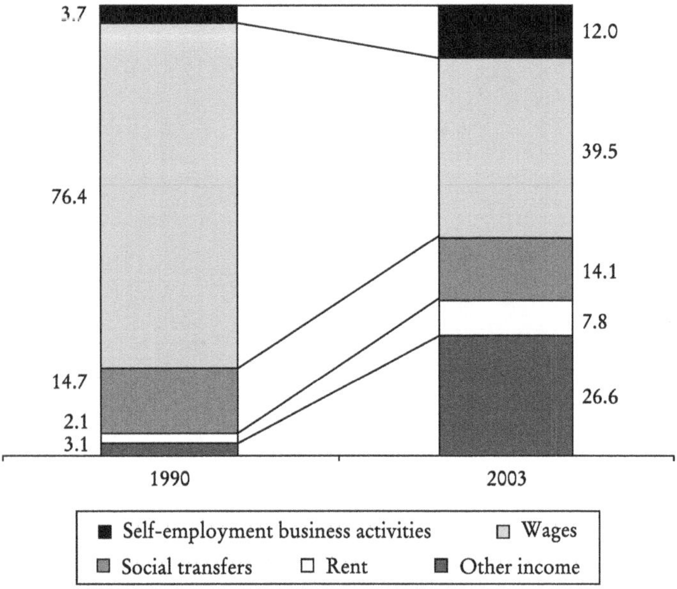

Source: Besstremyannaya et al. (2005).

Though the Russian households utilise some adaptation mechanisms, they still have little capacity for the income base expansion (as will be shown in further discussion) as a result of moderate income level, insufficient access to skills advancement, qualified medical services, actual and 'hidden' unemployment, etc. Typically about 70 per cent of their spending is allocated for basic current needs like food, transport, clothes, housing bills, etc. (Figure 3.4). At the same time demand for potentially innovation-intensive goods and services is supported by only 16 per cent of spending (marked with the red line).

Figure 3.4: *Spending Structure of Russian Households (2002–07)*

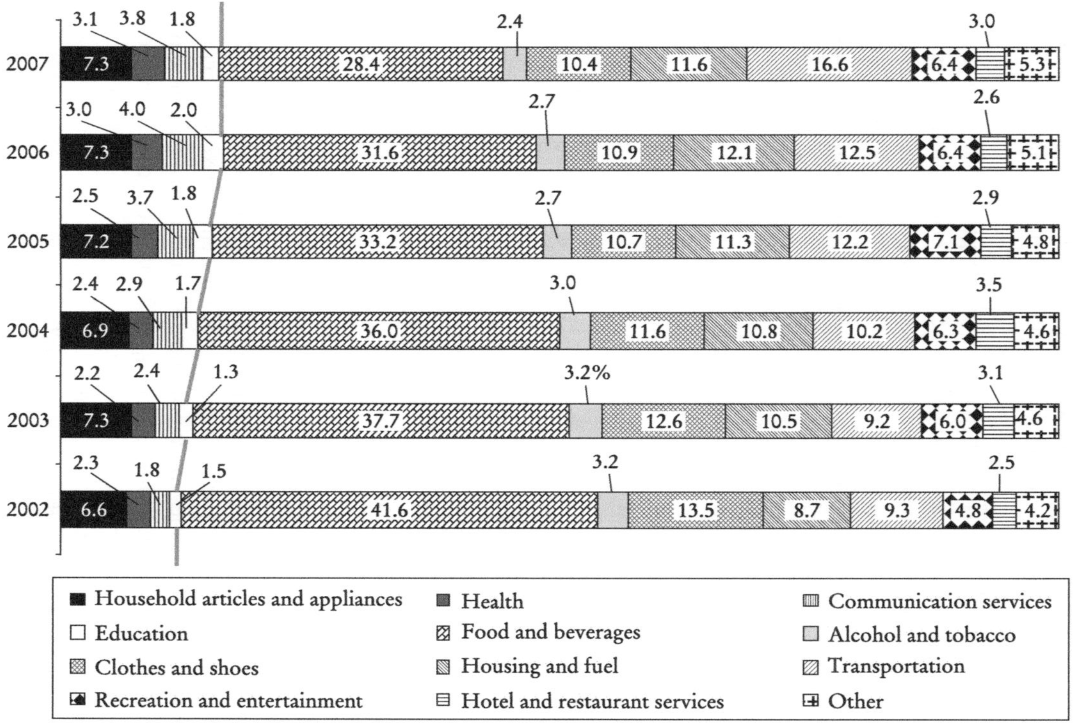

Source: Calculated using Federal State Statistics Service (2010b) data.
Notes: Figures in percentage.

This set includes household articles and appliances (7 per cent), communication (4 per cent), health (3 per cent), and education services (2 per cent). The first two items potentially include high-tech products while the latter two provide grounds for innovative adaptation and self-development. However, in 2002 even this share was four points less.

Household purchasing capacity and receptivity to innovation (willingness to purchase innovative or new products) influences the consumption of innovative goods and services inside the previously mentioned 16 per cent segment. According to the national survey in 2006 only 7 per cent of the population were ready to purchase innovative products (Figure 3.5). Another group (16 per cent) were willing to buy, but their income level did not allow experiments with new products. It is worth noting that 60 per cent of the population were definitely not willing to deal with innovation.

Figure 3.5: *Innovation Behaviour Survey 2006: Public Opinion on Innovative Products (percentage)*

Ready to try a new product	Would like to buy an innovative product but can not afford it	Prefer to by time-proved products only	I am against any innovation	No answer
7	16	43	17	17

Source: National Research University–Higher School of Economics (2008).

While 16 per cent of respondents were convinced they couldn't afford new products for the moment, 50 per cent were ready to purchase them only if they were not more expensive (or just a bit more expensive) than other products (Figure 3.6). Therefore, apart from 17–20 per cent of the population ignoring any innovation, other groups were ready to have a demand for innovative products if their income allowed it or if innovative products were more economically attractive.

Just to illustrate the situation, one can compare potential and real demand for some high-tech products. More than one-third of Russians wished to use a personal computer (PC) at home in 2003, but only 9 per cent could afford it (Figure 3.7). A close proportion

Figure 3.6: *Innovation Behaviour Survey 2006: 'In What Case Could you Buy an Innovative Product?' (percentage)*

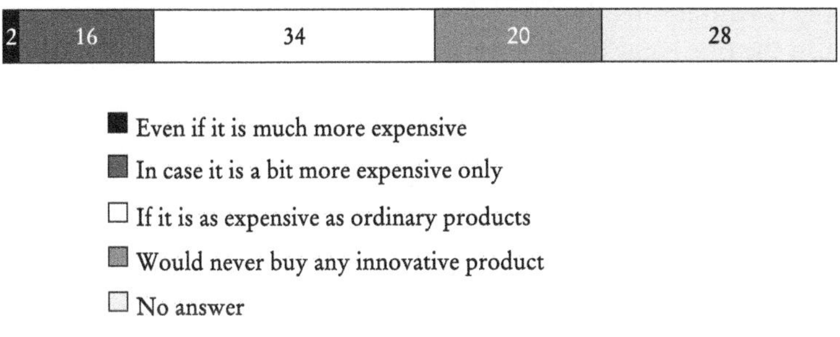

Source: National Research University–Higher School of Economics (2008).

Figure 3.7: *Potential and Real Demand for High-tech Products in Russia: Some Examples (2003) (percentage)*

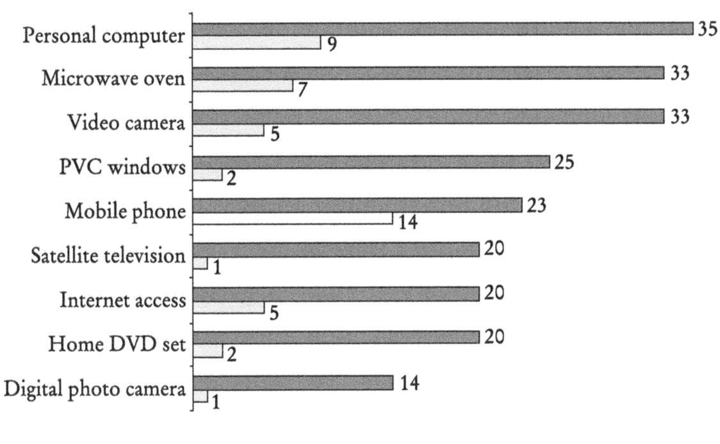

Source: Gokhberg and Shuvalova (2004); Shuvalova (2007).

could be found with Internet access (20 per cent vs 5 per cent), video cameras (33 per cent vs 5 per cent), etc. For some high-tech products this ratio reached 14-fold (digital photo cameras) and even 20-fold (satellite television).

The demand problem seems to be defined not by inequality as such but rather by the total income level, related in turn to the national economy productivity. As it was earlier mentioned, the GC in Russia is comparable with the USA level as well as with some other countries (Israel, Japan, etc.). However, the GDP per capita levels in Russia and the US differ three-fold ($15.900 PPP and $47.200 PPP respectively). On the one hand this difference does not affect basic products like food ('Big Mac index' in Russia is three-fold lower than in US).[3] On the other hand, in 2000-2010 about a half (41–44 per cent) of consumer goods sales in Russia were represented by imported consumer goods at significantly higher prices than domestic basic products (Federal State Statistics Service 2011). Therefore the income level definitely affects the aggregate demand in Russia. But the next question is the role of inequality in this context (Figure 3.8).

Figure 3.8: *Distribution of GC and GDP per capita (PPP) by Country (2009)*

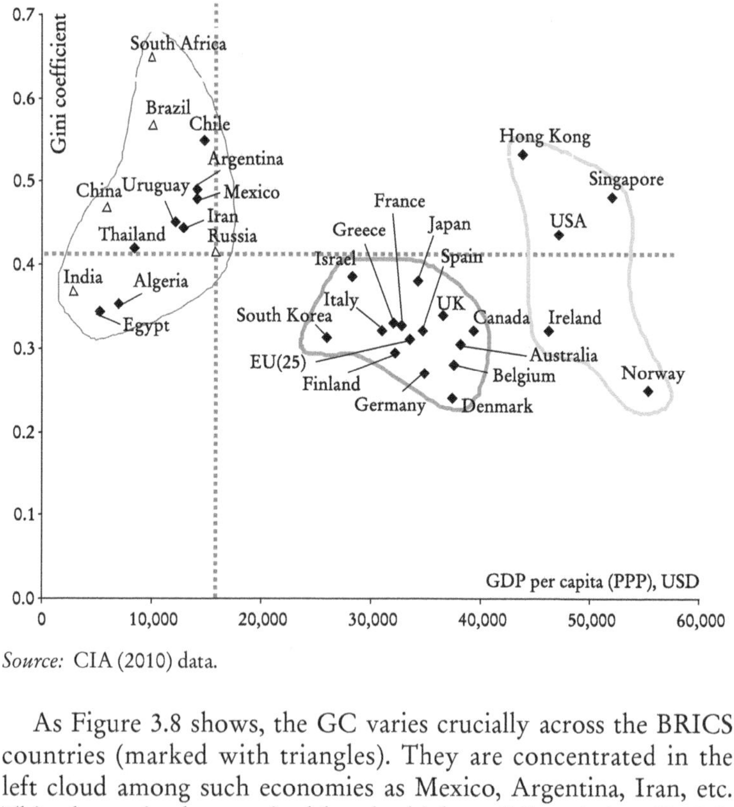

Source: CIA (2010) data.

As Figure 3.8 shows, the GC varies crucially across the BRICS countries (marked with triangles). They are concentrated in the left cloud among such economies as Mexico, Argentina, Iran, etc. This cluster is characterised by the highest GC variation (0.306).

To compare, the central cloud of 'Europe-like' economies performs GC variation of 0.146. For the BRICS countries the spread amounts to 0.282. It is almost the same as in the 'US-like' cloud on the right (0.283). However, in the latter economies the GDP per capita level is five times higher, so even the poorest strata have much more resources for access to education and innovative products there.

As mentioned before, India and Russia perform inequality levels comparable with Japan, Israel, and some European economies. Their reduction to Norway or Denmark levels is hard to imagine, so any probable GC shifts in India and Russia are not likely to improve the access to innovation and education significantly. A more powerful lever here could be a stable economic growth (however, the growth task itself requires increasing demand for innovation and education, so we have a bi-directional process in this case). South Africa and Brazil, on the contrary, are significantly more saturated with interpersonal inequality, so GC reduction could have a tangible effect there.

It is worth noting that these outcomes concern an aggregate interpersonal income level inequality. However, the following discussion shows that such assumptions are not accurate for some particular dimensions of inequality.

The other two outcomes refer to the position of the Russian economy itself. First, it fits perfectly into the BRICS cluster and cannot be described in inequality and poverty terms and norms typical of European economies. Second, the clusters described in this section can be used as perfect comparison values for the inter-regional indicators for Russia (see the next section).

The analysis shows that the inequality growth in Russia was an effect of transition from the socialist economic model to the free market economy in the early 1990s. It was also the time of crucial decline in the households' income. The market reforms provided the Russian households with new adaptation mechanisms (first of all, new sources of income). However, this buffer was sufficient for survival, not for development. The share of innovative products, education and health services in the households' consumption structure remains low and inferior to the basic needs. Russians are psychologically ready for innovative behaviour, but mainly cannot afford it. The cross-country comparison in this section shows that the income inequality level in India and Russia is comparable with a number of industrially developed countries, but the GDP per capita value is much lower. Significantly higher inequality rates are typical for South Africa and

Brazil. Therefore, the interpersonal income inequality reduction policies could have an influence on the innovation demand in South Africa or Brazil rather than in India or Russia. The latter two should mainly rely upon the overall national economic growth and cross-regional equalisation.

Inter-regional inequalities

In spacious countries like Russia it is extremely important to avoid regional distortions in social and economic development. Otherwise depressive regions, absorbing federal resources without any significant output (see the following sections on output and productivity), would hamper the economic growth. The Russian Federation is divided into 12 economic regions and eight federal districts (see Figure 3.9), which, in turn, are separated into smaller administrative territories. They are notably different in all possible characteristics including area, population, economy, climate, etc. In the Soviet Union the regional division was suited for the particular structure of the Soviet centralised economy (leading to regional specialisation), and after the breakdown of USSR some of the regions actually failed the economic transformation. Therefore today some territories perform steady economic growth while others remain in deep stagnation.

The cross-regional comparison shows a significant inequality in income per capita, business activity and economic productivity (Table 3.2). The financial flows are concentrated just in a few key regions and cities, causing severe inequality.

The regional disproportions in Russia are evident with a simple comparison between, e.g. Moscow city and the Far Eastern Federal District (the largest federal district with an area of 6.2 million sq km): Moscow is 1.6-fold greater in population, 2.2-fold in income per capita, 5.5-fold in gross regional product (GRP) and six-fold in number of enterprises. In the Russian statistics enterprise is defined as an institution recognised as a separate legal entity producing value (goods and services), generating income and covering the requirements of society. The classification of enterprises by size is based on the number of employees including small (up to 100 employees), medium (101–250 employees) and large (251 and more employees) enterprises and other criteria.[4] Actually Moscow with population of 10.4 million people is an atypical region of the country, covering one-fifth of the total GRP and one-fourth of the total enterprises (Table 3.3).

Figure 3.9: *Federal Districts and Economic Regions of Russia*

Federal Districts
Central
Far Eastern
North Caucasian
Northwestern
Siberian
Southern
Ural
Volga

Economic Regions and Federal Subjects

Central
1. Bryansk Oblast
2. Ivanovo Oblast
3. Kaluga Oblast
4. Kostroma Oblast
5. federal city of Moscow
6. Moscow Oblast
7. Oryol Oblast
8. Ryazan Oblast
9. Smolensk Oblast
10. Tula Oblast
11. Tver Oblast
12. Vladimir Oblast
13. Yaroslavl Oblast Central

Black Earth
1. Belgorod Oblast
2. Kursk Oblast
3. Lipetsk Oblast
4. Tambov Oblast
5. Voronezh Oblast

East Siberian
1. Buryat Republic
2. Irkutsk Oblast
3. Republic of Khakassia
4. Krasnoyarsk Krai
5. Tuva Republic
6. ZabaykalskyKrai

Far Eastern
1. Amur Oblast
2. Chukotka Autonomous Okrug
3. Jewish Autonomous Oblast
4. Kamchatka Krai
5. Khabarovsk Krai
6. Magadan Oblast
7. PrimorskyKrai
8. Sakha Republic
9. Sakhalin Oblast

Kaliningrad
1. Kaliningrad Oblast

North Caucasus
1. Republic of Adygea
2. Chechen Republic
3. Republic of Dagestan
4. Republic of Ingushetia
5. Kabardino-Balkar Republic
6. Karachay–Cherkess Republic
7. Krasnodar Krai
8. Republic of North Ossetia–Alania
9. Rostov Oblast
10. Stavropol Krai

Northern
1. Arkhangelsk Oblast
2. Republic of Karelia
3. Komi Republic
4. Murmansk Oblast
5. Nenets Autonomous Okrug
6. Vologda Oblast

Northwestern
1. Leningrad Oblast
2. Novgorod Oblast
3. Pskov Oblast
4. Federal City of St. Petersburg

Urals
1. Republic of Bashkortostan
2. Chelyabinsk Oblast
3. Kurgan Oblast
4. Orenburg Oblast
5. Perm Krai
6. Sverdlovsk Oblast
7. Udmurt Republic

Volga
1. Astrakhan Oblast
2. Republic of Kalmykia
3. Penza Oblast
4. Samara Oblast
5. Saratov Oblast
6. Republic of Tatarstan
7. Ulyanovsk Oblast
8. Volgograd Oblast

Volga-Vyatka
1. Chuvash Republic
2. Kirov Oblast
3. Mari El Republic
4. Republic of Mordovia
5. Nizhny Novgorod Oblast

West Siberian
1. Altai Krai
2. Altai Republic
3. Kemerovo Oblast
4. Khanty–Mansi Autonomous Okrug
5. Novosibirsk Oblast
6. Omsk Oblast
7. Tomsk Oblast
8. Tyumen Oblast
9. Yamalo-Nenets Autonomous Okrug

Source: Prepared by the author.

Table 3.2: *Key Regional Indicators (2009 or nearest available)*

	Area, %	*Population, %*	*Income Per capita, $ PPP*	*Gross Regional Product, %*	*Enterprises, %*	*Small Enterprises, %*
Central Federal District	3.8	26.2	1,533.8	37.7	39.4	34.5
Moscow (as a part of the Central Federal District)	0.01	7.4	2,892.2	24.6	25.6	20.4
Northwestern Federal District	9.8	9.5	1,204.5	9.9	12.8	16.8
Southern Federal District	3.5	16.2	858.6	8.0	10.6	11.1
Volga Federal District	6.1	21.2	957.4	15.5	14.6	16.4
Urals Federal District	10.5	8.7	1,370.4	14.2	7.7	6.7
Siberian Federal District	30.0	13.7	931.4	10.2	10.9	10.6
Far Eastern Federal District	36.4	4.5	1,260.8	4.5	4.0	3.9

Source: Calculated using Federal State Statistics Service (2010a) data.

Table 3.3: *Regional Distribution of Innovation Indicators in Russia (2009)*

	Technological Innovation Activity of Industrial Enterprises, %	*Production of Innovative Goods and Services, Million $ PPP*	*Technology Transfer Activity of Industrial Enterprises, %*	*Expenditure for Technological Innovation, Million $ PPP*
Central Federal District	9.0	14,996	4.6	5,357
Moscow (as a part of the Central Federal District)	13.9	1,427	8.7	726
Northwestern Federal District	9.1	4,908	3.8	1,942
Southern Federal District	7.4	4,455	2.1	565
Volga Federal District	13.0	26,691	2.4	5,222
Urals Federal District	10.1	5,754	4.8	5,507
Siberian Federal District	7.3	1,963	3.9	1,698
Far Eastern Federal District	6.7	690	1.6	4,299

Source: National Research University–Higher School of Economics (2011).

A simple comparison shows that there is no correlation between regional innovation activity and regional welfare in this environment. The Volga Federal District is one of the leading regions by innovation activity and technology transfer, however, it shows three-fold lower income per capita than Moscow. This fact can be easily explained by the current structure of the Russian economy. The export orientation of the natural resources creates the background where innovation is not a key factor of competitiveness. Much more important priorities are: (*a*) administrative resources, (*b*) relationships with large corporations and (*c*) proximity to the biggest nodes of financial flows (Gokhberg 2003).

Just following the logic of the previous paragraph one can easily develop the cross-regional comparisons of income structure, consumption structure (including innovative consumption), and GC-to-income distributions (Figure 3.10). The income structure disproportions are explained by multiple local factors. For example, the Southeastern Federal District has the lowest share of wages because of

Figure 3.10: *Income Structure by Region (percentage) (2007)*

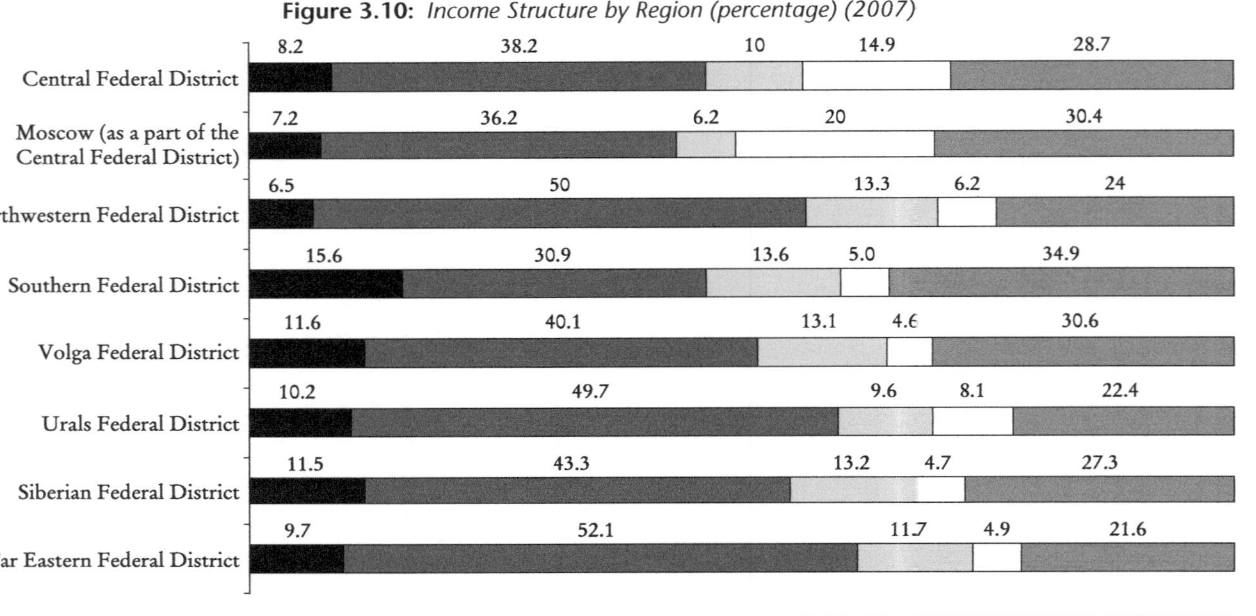

Source: Calculations based on Federal State Statistics Service (2010b) data.

an extremely high local unemployment rate (11.7 per cent in 2007 or twice higher than the national level). In Moscow wages also occupy a relatively moderate part of income, because of being replaced by developed business activities (including informal economy) and rent income (the real estate is extremely expensive in Moscow). Therefore, the first example demonstrates a rather depressive nature of the income disproportion, while the latter one describes a variety of possible sources of income.

A more notable fact is that despite different local income per capita levels, the consumption structure does not vary as it could be expected (Figure 3.11). This likeness is determined mainly by the difference in purchasing power by region. Perhaps the most interesting issue here is the difference in expenditure on education. In Moscow, one of the most developed local economies, households allocate just 0.8 per cent of their income for this purpose. To compare, in the Volga Federal District this share is three-fold higher. This trend is determined by easier access to education in Moscow (more competition, higher quantity and quality of education institutions at lower prices) on the one hand, and a higher overall income per capita on the other.

It was discussed earlier that regions in Russia differ by gross regional product and nominal income per capita. At the same time the spending structure remains relatively stable by region. The compensation mechanism consists of purchase power adjustment and adaptation by quality. The regional purchasing power correlates positively with the local income per capita. However, the slope is not high enough to assure a compensation effect (Figure 3.12) (Government of Russian Federation 2007).[5] A more powerful tool is adjustment by quality (the consumption varies not by structure, but rather by quality of products). Unfortunately the official statistics do not take into account the quality of goods and services.

The access to some products like computers, automobiles or advanced drugs can be rather complicated in more depressive regions. For example, a home computer is a usual tool for most Moscow families, while in the Southern Federal District only a quarter of households can afford it (Figure 3.13). In a more detailed view the situation is much worse for some particular areas (e.g. in the Chechen Republic a home PC can be found only in one household per 100).

To conclude, one can compare GC and income per capita by region (Figure 3.14). The distribution shows that interpersonal inequality does not vary significantly (from about 0.35 to 0.45) while difference

Figure 3.11: *Russian Households' Spending Structure by Region (percentage) (2007)*

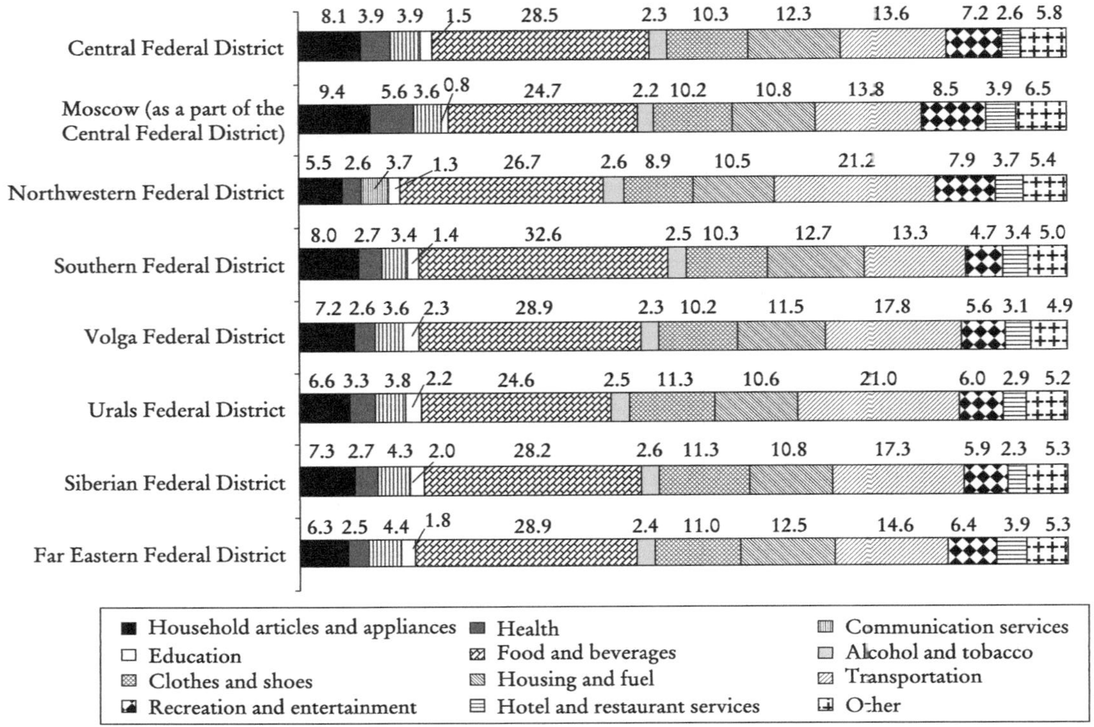

Central Federal District
8.1 3.9 3.9 1.5 28.5 2.3 10.3 12.3 13.6 7.2 2.6 5.8

Moscow (as a part of the Central Federal District)
9.4 5.6 3.6 0.8 24.7 2.2 10.2 10.8 13.8 8.5 3.9 6.5

Northwestern Federal District
5.5 2.6 3.7 1.3 26.7 2.6 8.9 10.5 21.2 7.9 3.7 5.4

Southern Federal District
8.0 2.7 3.4 1.4 32.6 2.5 10.3 12.7 13.3 4.7 3.4 5.0

Volga Federal District
7.2 2.6 3.6 2.3 28.9 2.3 10.2 11.5 17.8 5.6 3.1 4.9

Urals Federal District
6.6 3.3 3.8 2.2 24.6 2.5 11.3 10.6 21.0 6.0 2.9 5.2

Siberian Federal District
7.3 2.7 4.3 2.0 28.2 2.6 11.3 10.8 17.3 5.9 2.3 5.3

Far Eastern Federal District
6.3 2.5 4.4 1.8 28.9 2.4 11.0 12.5 14.6 6.4 3.9 5.3

Household articles and appliances
Health
Communication services
Education
Food and beverages
Alcohol and tobacco
Clothes and shoes
Housing and fuel
Transportation
Recreation and entertainment
Hotel and restaurant services
Other

Source: Calculations based on Federal State Statistics Service (2010b) data.

Figure 3.12: *Correlation between Consumer Basket Price and Income per capita by Region (2007)*

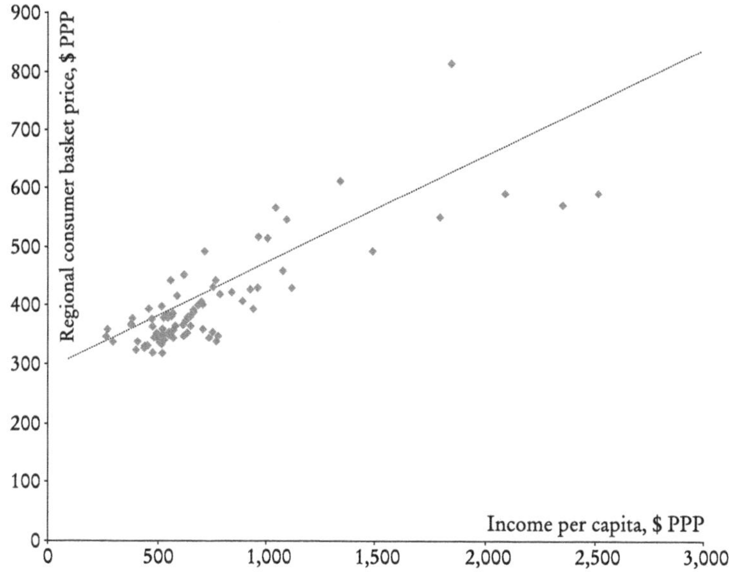

Source: Calculations based on Federal State Statistics Service (2010b) data.

Figure 3.13: *Personal Computers per 100 Households by Region (2007)*

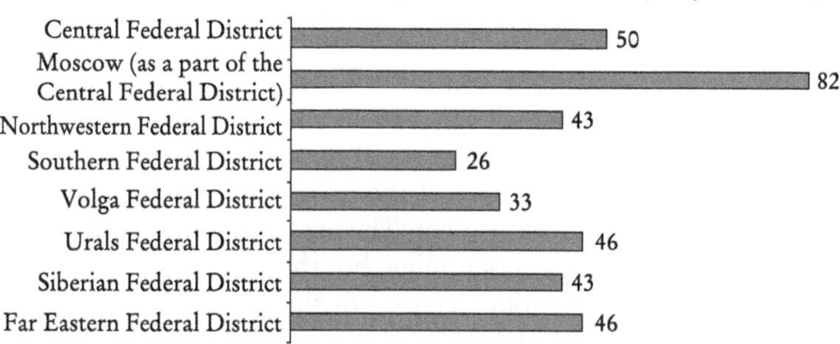

Source: Calculations based on Federal State Statistics Service (2010b) data.

by income is three-fold (eight-fold including 'deviants'). The interpersonal inequality inside any particular region is moderate while the inter-regional inequality by income level is significant. The regional consumer baskets structure is preserved (mainly by difference in quality of products), but access to other products (including high-tech, education, advanced drugs, and medical services) is uneven.

Figure 3.14: *Distribution of GC and Income per capita by Region (2007)*

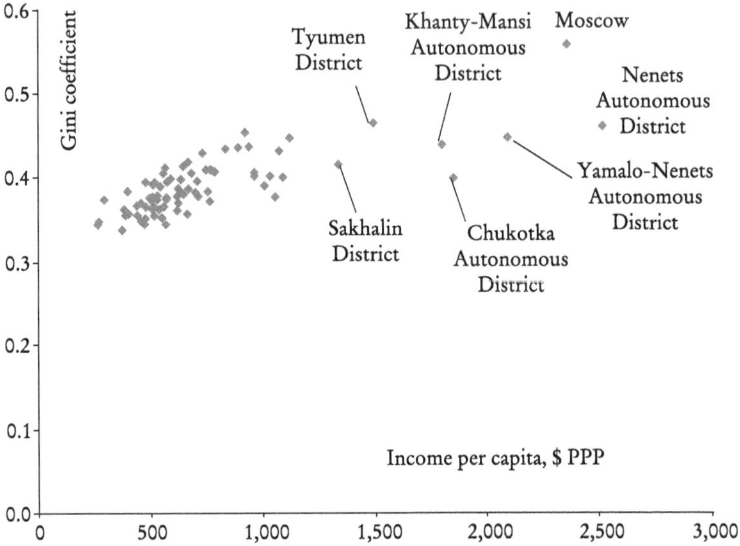

Source: Calculations based on Federal State Statistics Service (2010b) data.

The deviating regions are considered to be the richest. Moscow city is the key financial hub of the country. It is characterised by the highest inequality level (which is compensated by high overall quality of life). Other 'deviants' are known by the enormous output of the natural resources industries like oil and natural gas, diamonds, gold, etc. However, compared with Figure 3.8, these regions are still in the 'BRICS-like' economies cloud.

As of today the main share of the Russian regions do not show successful economic development. The best performers ensure their success by natural resources mining, but this advantage may vanish during the current economic crisis. On the contrary, learning and innovation could be regarded as a general-purpose tool for regional development irrespective of geographical position or natural resources. Today the poorest Russian regions are behind the BRICS economies in terms of income per capita (PPP) and could be compared with such countries as Kenya, Zambia or Nigeria (about $300 PPP).

According to these facts and figures, regions of the Russian Federation differ a lot with regard to many characteristics; first of all, in terms of economic productivity and income per capita. This variation is mainly characterised by different abilities of adapting to the economic transition. The difference of regional economic profiles is reflected in the income structure by region. However, the consumption structure does not vary a lot. A deeper analysis shows that such 'equality' concerns mainly the unified consumer products set, but the access to advanced goods and services (like information and communication technologies [ICT], high-tech, education, advanced medical services) is uneven from region to region. Inside the regions the inequality level is rather low (GC is about 0.38 in average), while the inter-regional income per capita level varies three-fold. Therefore the most effective policy trajectory deals with the 'reanimation' of particular depressive regional economies.

Inequality across social groups

Russia is traditionally regarded as a multinational secular country. It does not have any sort of caste system as well. However, one can discuss the gender inequality problem in Russia. There are also some other inequality groups, but they are statistical ones rather than 'culturally defined' strata: disabled persons, one-parent families, retirees, etc. It is also complicated to analyse inequality by ethnic group or religion insofar as such indicators are not reflected in official Russian statistics on quality of life, education and employment.

The male-to-female ratio in Russia is 46 per cent to 54 per cent respectively while the life expectancy is 61 and 74 years respectively. This balance remained stable for decades (in 1960 the same statistics accounted for 45 per cent to 55 per cent and 63 to 71 years respectively). Some basic indicators are enough to demonstrate the gender inequality in Russia (Table 3.4). The main trend is that Russian women are involved in higher education tot the same extent as men and earn a bit less income. It needs to be admitted that female labour

Table 3.4: *Some Gender Inequality Indicators (2006)*

	Males	*Females*
Income distribution, %	52	48
Unemployment rate, %	7.0	6.5
Illiteracy rate, %	0.3	0.8
Distribution of students (higher education), %	44	56

Source: Calculations based on Federal State Statistics Service (2010b) data.

is slightly underestimated as compared to male. The main reason is difference in position structure by gender (in 2005 the proportion of higher position holders among females and males was 41 per cent to 59 per cent; the same proportion by wages accounted for 39 per cent to 61 per cent (Federal State Statistics Service 2006).

However, statistics show much more alarming inequalities in some social groups. In 2003 the Committee for Statistics of the Russian Federation started the 'National Survey of the Households Welfare and Participation in the Social Programmes' (the NOBUS programme).[6] The outcomes of the survey clarify the structure and factors of the income inequality and poverty in Russia. The analysis of the poverty factors shows that households with children represent the most risky group (Figure 3.15). In households without children the income deficit is still rather high, but the risk of falling below the poverty level is much less than in families with one or more children. As already discussed, salaries are often just a part of the total household income in Russia. Families with two, three or more undergage children need more space and free time, so such income sources as rent or supplementary informal employment are excluded in this case. The social transfer system is rather imperfect, so there is not much help from transfers. At the same time the expenditure on children (including not only food and wearing, but healthcare and education) is much higher compared to childless households or families with adult children.

The most worrying outcome is decreasing motivation for childbearing. During the last decades the fertility decline in Russia is getting more and more crucial. According to projections by the United Nations Population Division, Russia's population, which was around 143 million four years ago, might be as high as 136 million or as low as 121 million in 2025, and as low as 115 million in 2030 (United Nations 2008).

According to the NOBUS survey, households of the disabled represent another risky group. Disability followed by absence of any career record is an especially dangerous factor (Figure 3.16). It is determined mainly by two reasons: education access barriers and employment barriers. The access to education (for all levels starting from the primary education) for the disabled is a big problem affecting the possibility of obtaining any professional skills. The employment barriers for the disabled arise from this problem as well as from imperfect labour regulation lacking efficient mechanisms for disabled employment stimulation.

Figure 3.15: *Income Deficit and Poverty Risk by Different Household Types (2003)*

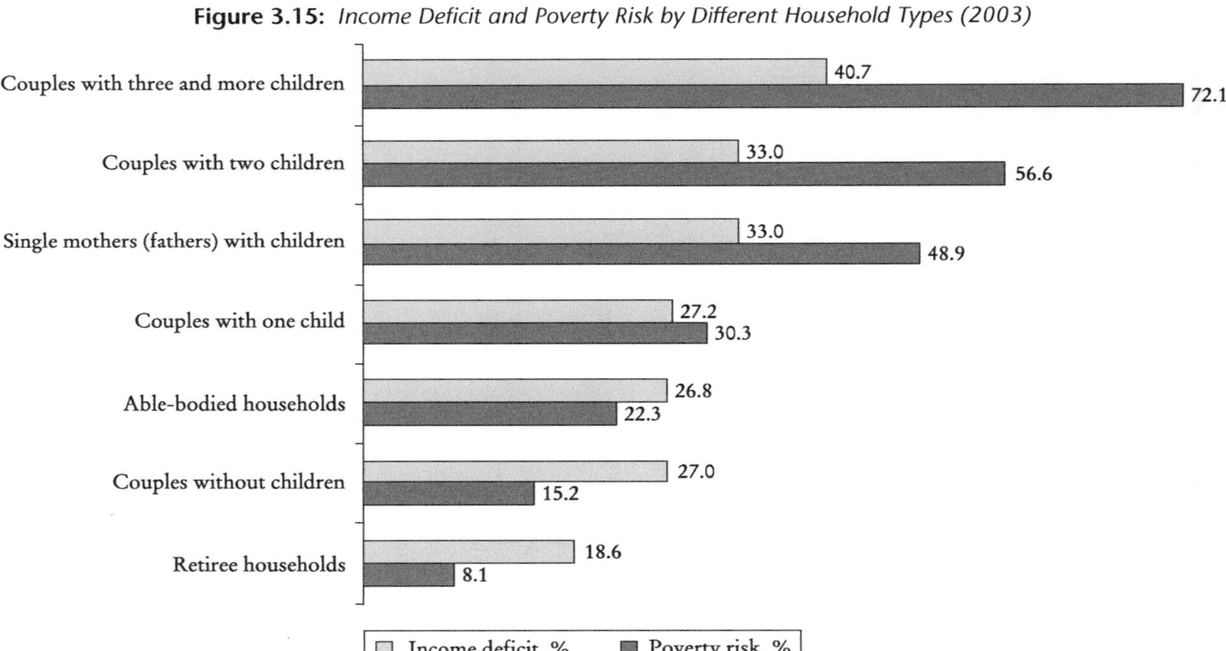

Source: National Survey of Household Welfare and Program Participation (NOBUS) data published in Besstremyannaya et al. (2005).

Figure 3.16: *Households with Disabled: Poverty Risk (percentage) (2003)*

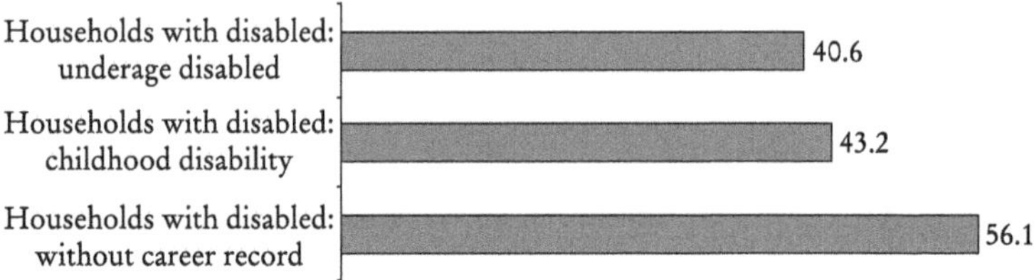

Source: National Survey of Household Welfare and Program Participation (NOBUS) data published in Besstremyannaya et al. (2005).

The Federal State Statistics Service data shows that disability decreases the chances for higher education enrolment almost three-fold (Figure 3.17). Though the share of the disabled population is about 1 per cent in Russia, this problem remains painful and difficult to solve.

Figure 3.17: *Comparison of Students-to-Population Ratio (higher education) in Disabled and Total Population (2006)*

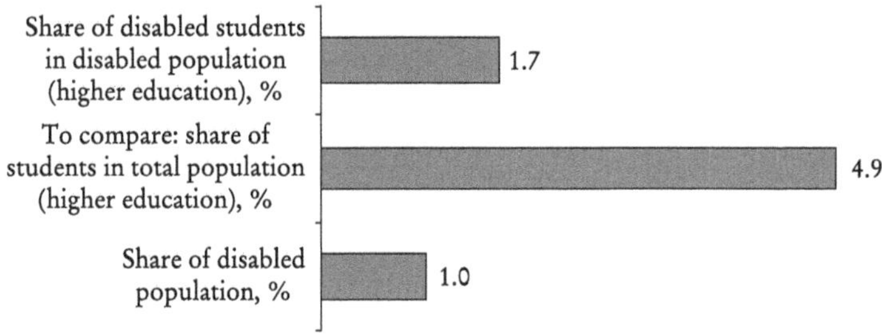

Source: Calculations based on the Federal State Statistics Service (2010b) data.

In 2005 Besstremyannaya et al. (2005) developed a statistical model showing that additional changes in the labour regulation could increase minimal salaries up to the poverty level, but this effect would decrease productivity (because of labour motivation decline and transfer of employers to the shadow economy schemes) and would not improve the inequality as such. The latter two risky groups discussed earlier would not enjoy such innovation at all, just because of employment barriers.

A more elegant solution could be related to the introduction of new forms of employment and education. First of all, e-employment and e-learning must become a powerful tool for the disabled population and households with children (Zaichenko 2002). This transition would require large-scale federal programmes for spreading access to ICT as well as the services sector expansion (Zaichenko 2007).

In conclusion, facts and figures show that traditional inequality zones like castes, races, religions, or gender are not common for Russia. However, there exist other social groups with high poverty risks. Households with children and/or the disabled perform extremely high poverty risks in Russia. They have considerably less access to sources of income and education. Direct assistance policies are still not efficient for the latter two categories. However, new innovative mechanisms (flexible forms of employment and education) could improve the situation.

Co-evolution of Innovation System and Inequality

Changing context of national system of innovation and production

As already discussed, the inter-regional inequality in Russia is defined by the ability of the regions to adapt to a new economic environment. However, the most flourishing districts are related to petroleum and natural gas industries only (except Moscow, the key financial hub). It seems like the whole Russian economy is biased towards these industries and all other economic activities stay in more or less deep stagnation.

Actually the bias towards hydrocarbons trade is a predictable phenomenon for the Russian economy. The Russian Federation has the largest known natural gas reserves of any state on earth, along with the second largest coal reserves; it is the world's second largest oil producer and possesses the eighth largest oil reserves. In 2009 more than 12 per cent of the world's gas and oil exports came from Russia (Figure 3.18).

The world demand for natural resources is the main factor of the current Russian economic profile (Figure 3.19). Its gas and oil specialisation index (proportion of the national and the world exports share for particular product groups) amounted to 5.04 in 2009.

Figure 3.18: *Petroleum, Petroleum Products and Related Materials, Gas, Natural and Manufactured: World Exports by Country (percentage) (2009)*

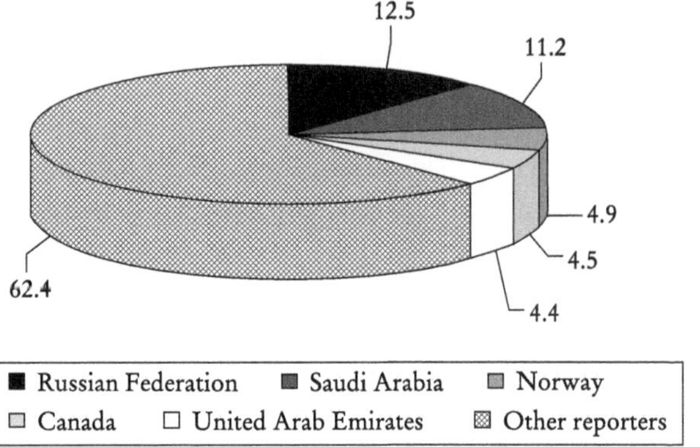

Source: Calculations based on United Nations Commodity Trade Statistics Database (UN COMTRADE), http://comtrade.un.org/db/ (accessed 10 December 2010).

Figure 3.19: *Russia's Economy Specialisation Factor (2009)*

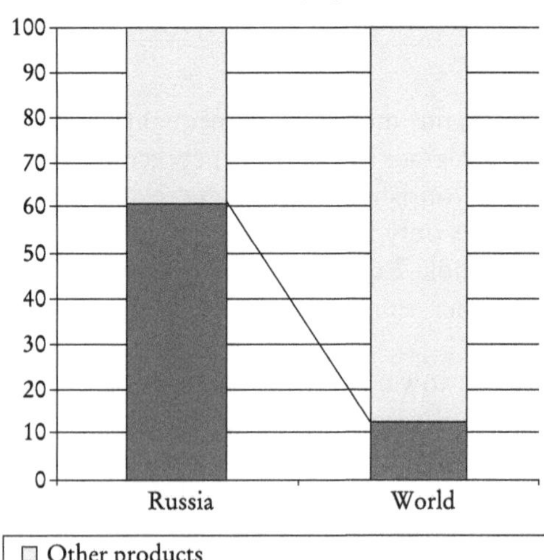

Source: Calculations based on United Nations Commodity Trade Statistics Database (UN COMTRADE), http://comtrade.un.org/db/ (accessed 10 December 2010).

However, the oil and natural gas sector in Russia is characterised by strong state participation and control as well as by high monopolisation. For example, Gazprom, controlled by the state (50 per cent plus 1 holding of stock), performed capitalisation of $347.6 billion (the world's third position) by May 2008 (Walters and Mauldin 2008). It acquires 93 per cent of all gas-extraction in Russia. The second corporation after Gazprom is Rosneft, also controlled by the state.

During the last years these corporations became a strong instrument of the state's foreign policy (needless to say, also the general income source for the federal budget). This explains the strong reluctance of authorities to change the orientation of the national economy towards diversification (taking in consideration the overall poor performance of manufacturing and other economic sectors). Nevertheless the new international economic crisis has broken the status quo. During the period from 8 May to 9 September of 2008, the Gazprom capitalisation fell from $347.6 billion to $191.8 billion and continues to decrease (Tutushkin 2009). In 2009 the government started an initiative for economic diversification with a focus on private sector support and particularly on innovation activities.

There exist a number of barriers for diversification, including imperfect competition, lack of public control and performance evaluation mechanisms, high administration costs, system resistance, etc. (ibid.). However, the main barrier in the innovation sphere refers to atrophied mechanisms of the whole NIS (remember the lack of correlation between regional innovation activity and welfare). Just to illustrate this trend one can compare the high-tech products export indicators (Figure 3.20) according to the EUROSTAT classification (EUROSTAT 2005).

According to estimations of the Institute of Statistical Studies and Economics of Knowledge the output share of the high-tech manufacturing in Russia was about 10.4 per cent in 2006. At the same time the national exports share was just 1.5 per cent. This difference may characterise not only the export orientation of the national economy, but also the international competitiveness of the Russian civil high-tech products. Its position on the global high-tech markets is less than moderate: compared to countries like Brazil or China, Russia's civil high-tech products exports are two-fold and 70-fold lower respectively (Figure 3.21).

Figure 3.20: *Share of Civil High-tech Products Exports in the Total National Products Exports by Country (2006) (percentage)*

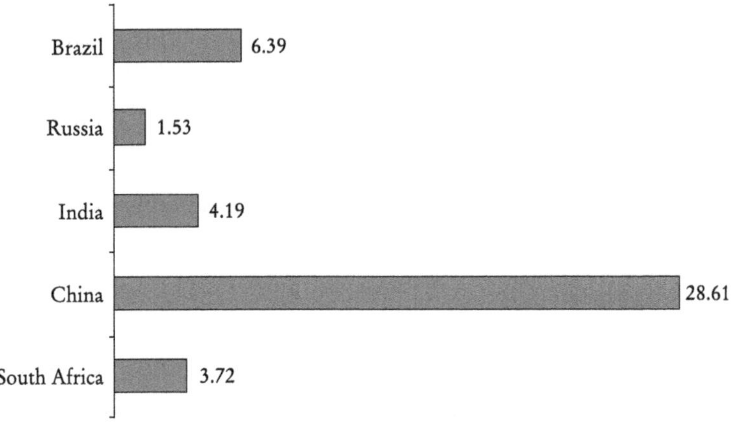

Source: Calculations based on United Nations Commodity Trade Statistics Database (UN COMTRADE), http://comtrade.un.org/db (accessed 10 December 2010).

Figure 3.21: *Civil High-tech Products Exports by Country, percentage of the World Civil High-tech Products Exports (2006)*

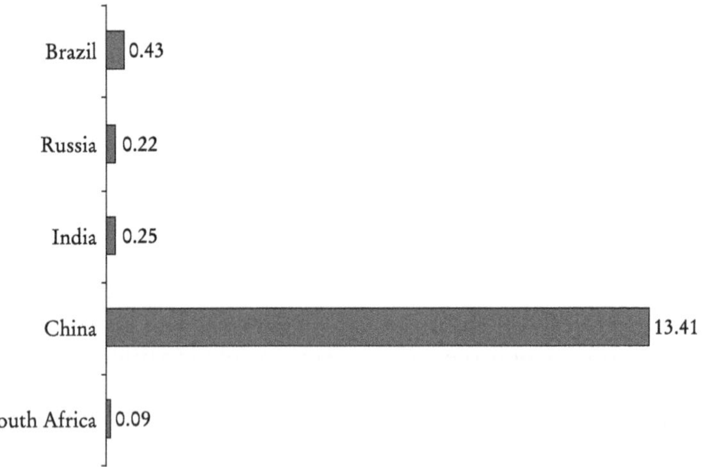

Source: Calculations based on United Nations Commodity Trade Statistics Database (UN COMTRADE), http://comtrade.un.org/db (accessed 10 December 2010).

There do exist certain fields of possible excellence (Figure 3.22). Mainly, chemicals, power generating machinery and aerospace — priority areas of the former Soviet manufacturing system. However, these products are not oriented towards an ultimate consumer. Therefore the demand is rather limited. Russian high-tech consumer products like pharmaceuticals or computers cannot gain even 1 per cent of the global markets. It is also to be noted that other BRICS countries perform more demarcated high-tech export specialisation like aerospace-electronics (Brazil), pharmacy-chemistry (India), computers-electronics (China), etc.

Another worrying trend is acquisition of high-tech manufacturing by the state corporations, as happened with natural gas and oil industries. The aerospace monopoly belongs to Roskosmos (Russian Federal Space Agency) and Joint Aircraft Building Corporation (state corporation). The Russian Corporation for Nanotechnology (state corporation) acquires the front-end R&D in chemicals, materials, electronics, etc.

The state corporations do not carry out R&D, innovation or manufacturing activities themselves, but provide funding and access to national/international projects on competitive basis for R&D institutions and companies. Therefore the key development factor for the Russian innovative businesses is not competitiveness, but rather relationships with the state corporations and willingness to follow the state priorities instead of the market trends. This system also creates barriers for small innovative companies.

During the last decade natural gas and oil industries were the only drivers for economic growth (as also, only regions disposing of these resources could show high quality of life). They remained under control of the state, and neither public nor private sectors had any motivations to develop other activities including innovation. Such a strategy was attractive while Russia, the world's second largest natural gas exporter, could enjoy demand for oil and gas at high prices. However, the contemporary global economic crisis has broken the status quo and provided motivation for economic diversification and innovation. The export positions of the Russian high-tech manufacturing are comparatively inferior. Some high-tech industries where Russia still keeps an advantage do not refer to the ultimate consumer markets. Therefore a considerable effort is required to return to the innovation-driven economy vis-à-vis the global economy trends. The latter government initiatives reflect the intention of urgent structural

Figure 3.22: *Structure of Civil High-tech Products Exports: Shares of the Global Markets (percentage) (2006)*

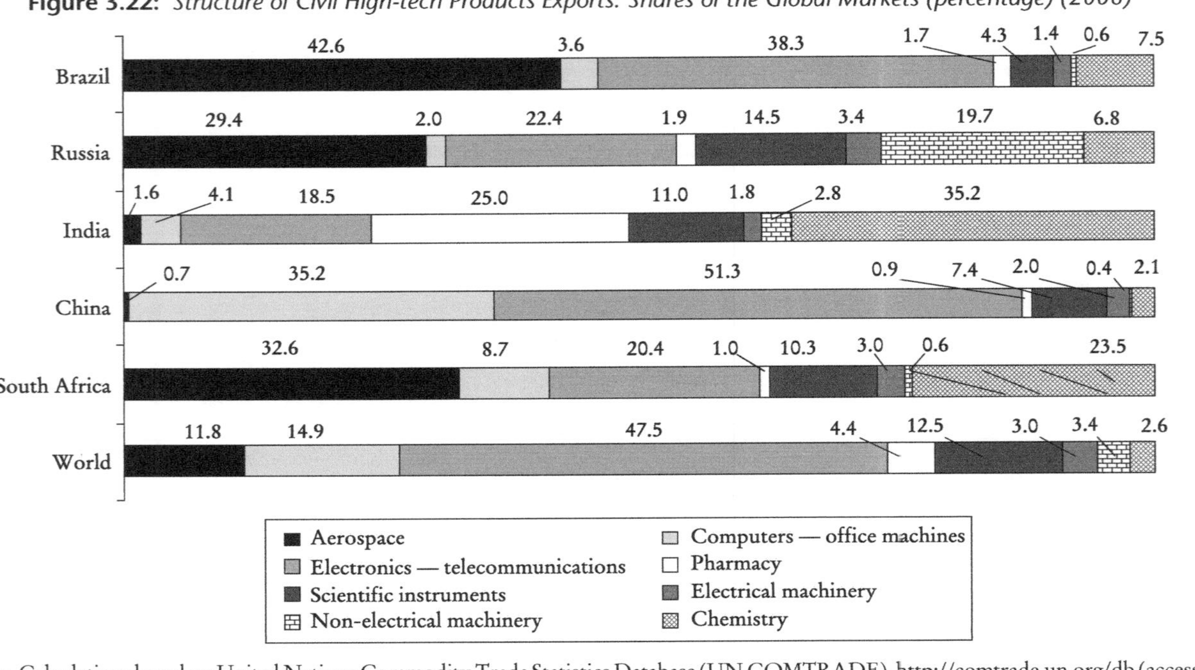

Source: Calculations based on United Nations Commodity Trade Statistics Database (UN COMTRADE), http://comtrade.un.org/db (accessed 10 December 2010).

economic diversification and NIS development policies. However, there are signs of transition from the 'state gas and oil monopoly' to the 'state innovation monopoly'. The future reforms are likely to preserve state control over promising economic activities, threatening with barriers for small and medium enterprises (SMEs) and lack of market competition.

Access to health and education

Trends in inequalities by social groups discussed in the first part of the chapter inevitably affect accessibility of the key social services like health and education. The second factor is driven by historical roots: a dramatic transition from free public services towards a paid service market. In the former Soviet Union all citizens were provided free health and education services. After the USSR collapsed in 1991 the government tried to keep these guarantees, but not quite successfully. The economic crisis and budget deficit entailed shrinking of state support; the quality of free health and education decreased. At the same time the market economy provided supply for paid quality services.

As a result, the share of the population's expenses in the total medical services expenditure grew three-fold in 1994–2004 (from 11 per cent to 35 per cent). But the real income level of the population started to grow only after 1998 as earlier discussed. Therefore the period 1993–98 was especially complicated for households. By 2005 the obligatory medical insurance covered 23 per cent of the total expenditure, and 42 per cent was allocated from the federal budget (Figure 3.23).

More detailed cross-sections (Table 3.5) show that retirees spend the most for health — 8 per cent of available resources (including the household resources). Almost all this expenditure is used to buy drugs. About 3 per cent is allocated for children and able-bodied men, and able-bodied women spend about 6 per cent. It is to be noted that able-bodied men and women have almost the same sickness rate (745–60 per 1,000 population), but males prefer to spend less than half of women for health services. Probably this fact affects the difference in their life expectancy (61 and 74 years respectively, a 13-year difference).

Specialised surveys carried out by the Federal State Statistics Service can give much more information on the access to medical services and medicines. They show that the main barriers are lack of qualified

Figure 3.23: *Expenditure on Medical Services by Source of Funds (percentage) (1993–2004)*

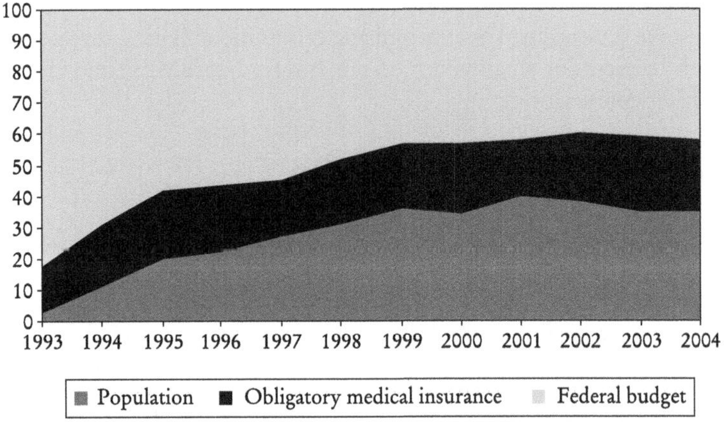

Source: National Survey of Household Welfare and Program Participation (NOBUS) data published in Besstremyannaya et al. (2005).

Table 3.5: *The Structure of the Monthly Health Care Expenditure by Type of Expenditure and Group of Population (US$ PPP) (2004)*

	Children		*Able-bodied*		*Retirees*	
	Males	*Females*	*Males*	*Females*	*Males*	*Females*
Available resources	228.5	235.7	300.5	284.9	248.4	250.5
Total health care expenditure	7.0	6.0	8.4	16.4	19.0	21.7
Clinic services	0.3	0.2	0.4	0.7	1.0	0.7
Hospital services	1.4	1.6	1.6	3.0	1.7	1.9
Medicines	5.3	5.2	6.5	12.7	16.3	19.1

Source: National Survey of Household Welfare and Program Participation (NOBUS) data published in Besstremyannaya et al. (2005).

medical personnel in rural areas and lack of resources to spend for healthcare. The distribution by place reflects clearly that more than a half of the rural population cannot find qualified medical specialists in their place of residence (Figure 3.24). In urban places one can find qualified doctors easier, but very probably the population cannot afford their services. The large cities are the most favourable for overcoming these two problems, but the health infrastructure cannot handle such a high density of population.

Figure 3.24: *Survey Results: 'What were the Reasons to Refuse the Health Care Services Recently?' (2007)*

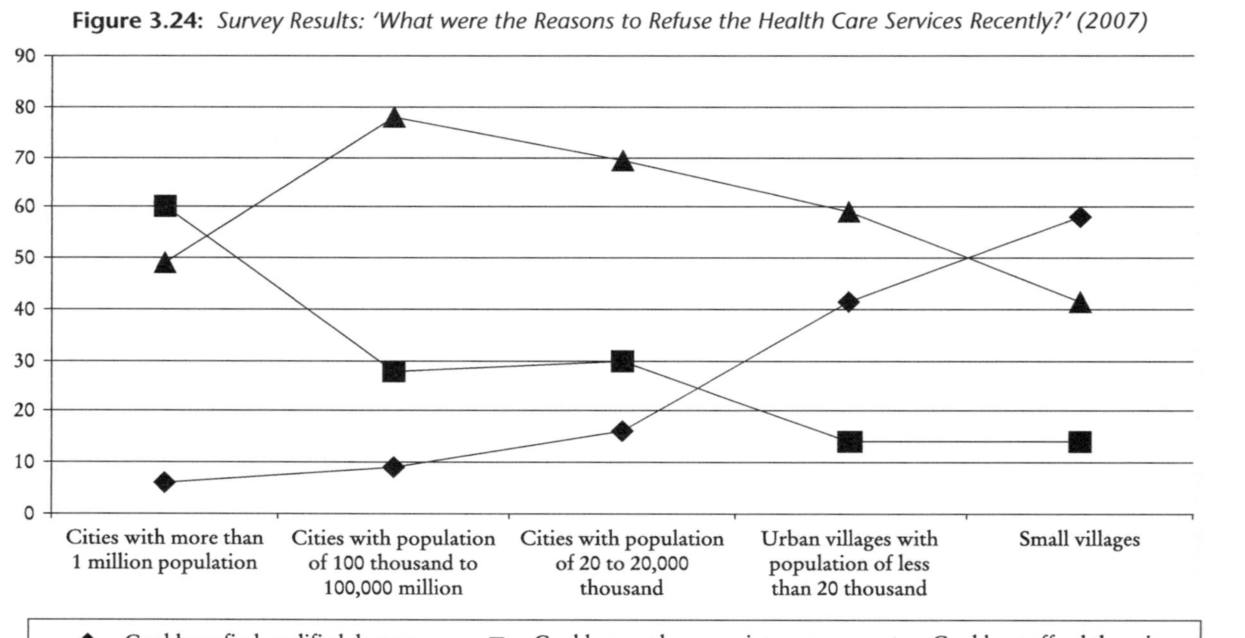

Source: Federal State Statistics Service (2008b).

Nevertheless, the lack of resources remains the main barrier for healthcare (Figure 3.25). Almost a half of the population does not have access to the necessary healthcare services. Taking into consideration the higher poverty risks for households with children (discussed earlier), the situation should be regarded as really alarming.

Figure 3.25: *Survey Results: 'Are you Going to Purchase Health Care Services?' (2005–07)*

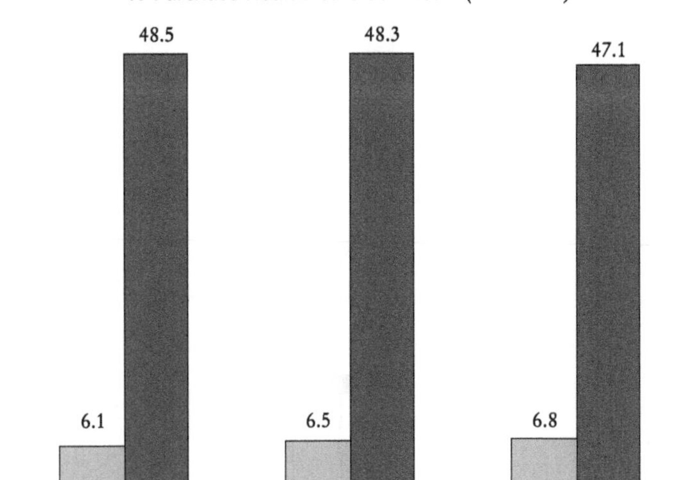

Source: Federal State Statistics Service (2008b).

Free education is guaranteed by the Constitution for all Russian citizens. Nevertheless the state does not have enough resources to provide free and quality education for everyone. Free enrolment is limited even in state education institutions (budgetary funded). The average monthly expenditure per student for secondary, professional and higher education is $21.8, $47.5 and $105.1 PPP respectively (Table 3.6).

Comparing this expenditure with an average monthly income of $835.6 PPP, it is evident that the average household still has access to all levels of education. However, obtaining higher education often means loosing alternative wages for the period of learning. The situation

Table 3.6: *Monthly Average Expenditure on Education Services per Student by Type of Expenditure and Level of Education (US$ PPP) (2007)*

	Secondary Education	*Professional Education*	*Higher Education*
Total expenditure	21.76	47.51	105.11
Core education expenditure	13.67	45.17	100.52
Contract payment	1.36	35.51	86.77
Textbooks, stationery, etc.	5.44	2.99	3.85
Uniform	1.40	0.24	0.07
Penalties for repeating examinations	0.25	0.72	1.26
'Informal' payments	1.50	1.03	2.98
Supplementary education expenditure	6.02	2.09	4.03
Contracts for supplementary classes	3.49	1.30	2.66
Private tutor fees	2.30	0.69	1.07
Enrolment expenditure	2.07	0.25	0.56
Contracts for preliminary courses	0.96	0.15	0.50
Private tutor fees	1.05	0.07	0.05

Source: Federal State Statistics Service (2008b).

is much more complicated for households with several children. Therefore it is not surprising that a quarter of the population cannot afford education services (Figure 3.26).

The main outcome of this discussion is that the low income level entailed severe barriers for human capital development. Almost a half of the population has no access to necessary medical care and about a quarter cannot afford education they need. Children are a strategically important group requiring especially simplified access to health and education. However, households with two, three or more children have the highest probability of appearing below the poverty level, facing extremely high barriers for human capital development.

As shown, the access to health and education in Russia is complicated (mostly for the risk groups). These barriers seriously affect the human capital level of the future generations. In the last decade the situation has also sharpened due to the current demographic decline in Russia.

Access to knowledge, R&D and innovation infrastructure

About one-quarter of the population in Russia cannot afford the education they need, as discussed earlier. A more detailed view could

Figure 3.26: *Survey Results: 'Are You Going to Purchase Education Services?' (2005–07)*

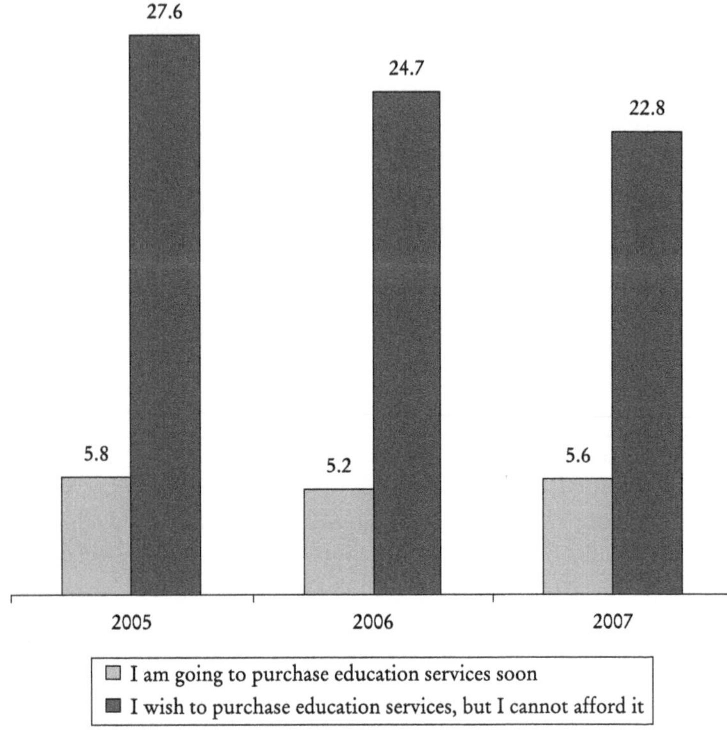

Source: Federal State Statistics Service (2008b).

explain this barrier in terms of social group inequality. Table 3.6 shows that every stage of education definitely requires more resources than the previous one. The basic outcome is that barriers for education must be in correlation with the income level. This was already illustrated in the first part of the chapter by the household consumption structure. Actually the difference in expenditure on education by income level (between first and last deciles) is 17-fold (Table 3.7). The number of children in the family is also significant as well as geographic location.

The poverty risk statistics could describe the cut-off education level for the average population (Figure 3.27). This level concerns both access to education and effect of education level on poverty. The poverty risk index equals poverty risk in a group divided by the

Table 3.7: *Monthly Average Expenditure on Education Services of Households (2008)*

	Monthly Average Expenditure on Education of Households	
	US$ (PPP) Per One Person at a Household	*as % of Total Consumption of a Household*
Total	8.37	1.5
By location:		
Urban households	9.72	1.6
Rural households	4.69	1.3
By income level (deciles):		
1 (lower)	0.94	0.6
2	1.90	0.8
3	2.91	1.0
4	4.47	1.3
5	6.57	1.7
6	8.72	1.9
7	13.45	2.3
8	15.60	2.2
9	13.35	1.5
10 (higher)	15.86	1.1
By number of children(<16 year old)		
1	8.42	1.7
2	5.98	1.6
3	2.93	1.3
4 and more	0.96	0.8

Sources: Federal State Statistics Service (2008a, 2009b).

average poverty risk. The cut-off point is situated above the initial vocational education, and the higher education levels are rather atypical for a population with average poverty risk.

Access to knowledge and innovation infrastructure provides resources for individual self-development, SMEs' innovation activities and the national innovation-driven economic growth. One of the most important factors of the human resources efficiency is rapid learning and capability to adapt quickly to changes on the labour markets vis-à-vis global trends. This is the way the 'learning economy' concept considers prosperity potential for individuals, firms, regions, and national systems (Lundvall and Johnson 1994; Lundvall and Borrás 1997; Archibugi and Lundvall 2001).

Figure 3.27: *Poverty Risk Index by Level of Education (2008)*

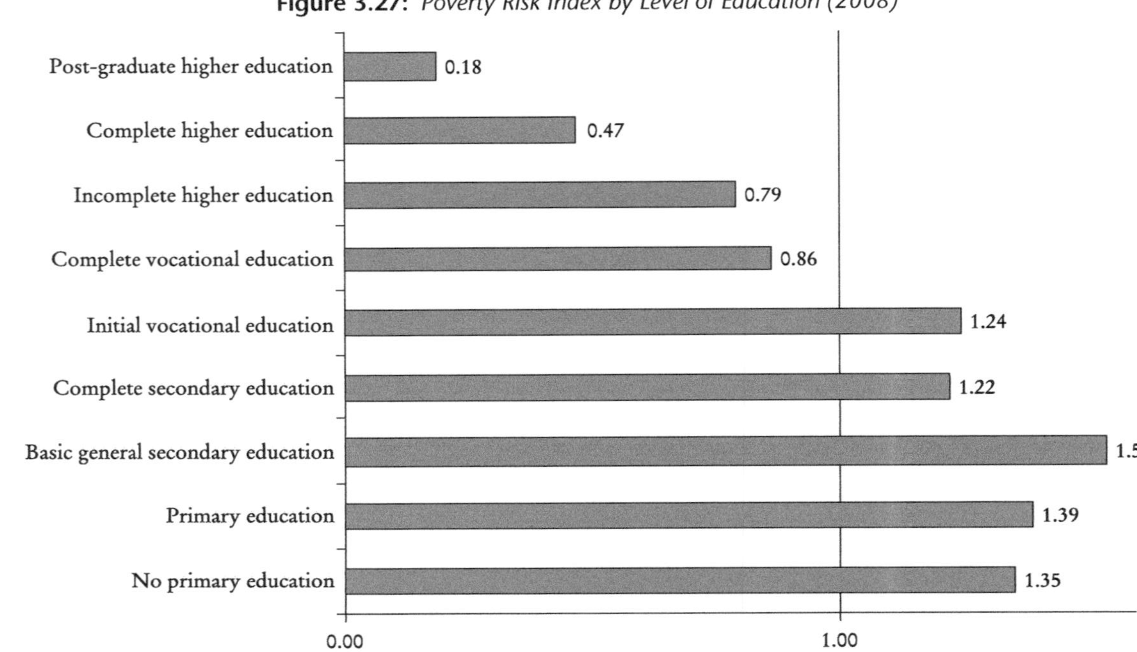

Source: Federal State Statistics Service (2009a).

Nowadays e-learning and lifelong learning (LLL) are the front-end tools for individual competence building. E-learning is considered to be a powerful tool for access to knowledge; e-learning services are inexpensive or even free. However, it still requires expenses for PC and Internet access. As discussed later, in 2003 25 per cent of the population was willing to purchase Internet access, but only 5 per cent admitted they could afford it. For home PCs this proportion was 35 per cent and 9 per cent respectively. The regional disparities are also very high here. In 2007 the regional shares of households having PCs varied from 82 per cent in Moscow to 1 per cent in the Chechen Republic (discussed earlier).

The first natural step to improve the situation and overcome the disparities is to spread e-learning practices via primary school and further levels of education. By 2005 almost all Russian schools were equipped with computer classes with 10–13 PCs on average (Table 3.8). However, it means that an average school can provide just one computer class a week with one PC per two students.

Table 3.8: *Personal Computers at Primary School in Russia (1992–2004)*

	Schools with PC Classes, %	*Number of PCs Per One School with PC Classes*
1992	51.1	12
1994	65.1	13
1996	68.6	13
1998	68.7	13
2000	68.4	13
2002	74.5	11
2004	90.6	10

Source: Gaslikova et al. (2005).

The second problem is that local governments allocate miserable funding for Internet access at schools. For example, in January 2009 the total online traffic of the Russian schools did not reach 22.5 TB (less than 40 MB per one school). The third barrier is that an average schoolteacher still does not have necessary PC skills. And one more problem is that many PCs at schools are outdated or even not functional. Therefore almost all Russian schools are equipped with computers with Internet connection, but are still unable to provide access to e-learning, and often, minimal computer skills.

While the e-learning access problems still remain unsolved, the e-learning content issue is rather positive. First of all, the international content is always available for all online users. However, the Russian resources volume is also growing from year to year. They can be separated into two groups — transit portals and content portals. The first group is represented by portals providing access for selected organisations or individuals to non-free learning or scientific content. For example, the Russian Foundation for Basic Research handles the scientific e-library project providing web-access to online resources of the world's leading scientific journals and publishers (11 sources, several thousand journals). Free access to these resources is provided for research organisations after registration (without any competition). The programme was approved in 1997 with a starting fund of $1 million. By 2000 its budget grew by several multiples; the number of subscribed research organisations reached 300 and continues to grow till today. The second group is represented by portals providing their own content. There exist 15 official Russian scientific and education portals as of now.

Lifelong learning encompasses all purposeful learning activities, whether formal or informal, undertaken on an ongoing basis with the aim of improving knowledge, skills and competence. In international practice the indicator of population participation in the LLL used takes into account the share of persons who participated during the previous 12 months in three forms of the goal-oriented educational activity (formal education, non-formal education and informal learning) in the population aged 25–64.

Formal professional education is the less popular form of LLL in Russia as well as in many other countries. In 2006 only 4.5 per cent of the population aged 25–64 chose this form (State University–Higher School of Economics 2007). It is the same level as an average for EU-25.

Non-formal education in LLL includes refresher courses, master of business administration (MBA) courses, second higher education, vocational courses, etc. Being more flexible and short-term oriented, this form is much more popular. In Russia its share is nearly twice higher than the formal education. However, in other countries this gap is even higher (e.g. nearly four-fold in EU). At the same time the non-formal form in Russia is not as widespread as abroad. Its share is half than that in EU-25. But on the other hand it is balanced by high average education hours — 90 hours a year in Russia. Higher values can be noticed only in Portugal, Spain and Hungary (96, 102 and 126 hours a year respectively). The EU average is just 66 hours a year (State University–Higher School of Economics 2007).

The structure of non-formal education and training is biased towards refresher courses, vocational courses and regular training events (Table 3.9).

Table 3.9: *Structure of Non-formal Education and Training Activities, Reasons and Place of Training (lifelong learning): percentage of 25–64-year-old Respondents (2006)*

(i) Types of Taught Activities	
Refresher courses	4.6
Regularly conducted professional conferences, seminars, training events (weekly, monthly, annually)	1.5
One-time (single) vocational lectures, conferences, seminars, training events	1.1
Second higher education	0.1
MBA studies	0.0
Vocational courses	1.6
Training for unemployed	0.0
Amateur (hobby) courses (driving, dress-making, housekeeping, etc.)	0.9
Preliminary courses for colleges, universities	0.0
Other	0.1

Main Reasons for Participating in Non-formal Education/Training		*(ii) Place of Training*	
To do my job better	3.1	At specialised training centre	2.7
To advance vocational knowledge and skills	2.8	At work	1.9
To earn more money	0.8	At a HEI/affiliate	1.2
To change the nature of job	0.5	At a secondary vocational institution/affiliate	0.8
To find another job	0.5	At a general educational institution/affiliate	0.3
For self-development (nothing to do with work)	0.3	At a lower vocational institute/ affiliate	0.2
To enter a college or university	0.0	At private employment/ recruiting agencies	0.2
		At governmental employment agencies	0.1
		At the army	0.1
		At a hotel, holiday home, pension, etc.	0.1
		At distant learning courses	0.0
		Other	0.5

Source: State University–Higher School of Economics (2007).

Usually these forms are used to upgrade the current qualification (for the further professional promotion in the same field) without breaking the current professional activities. Very often this training is related with learning foreign language (English). The less popular forms are second higher education, MBA, training for unemployed and preliminary courses. Almost zero share of training for the unemployed is a very significant trend coming up as a result of low quality of these courses as well as inappropriate structure of proposed professions.

The structure or reasons for non-formal education in Russia are biased towards promotion on the current job. However, the innovation economy is based more on capability for job diversifying. The most typical places of non-formal training are specialised centres, offices and higher education institutions (HEIs). Other institutions are less in number.

In the discussion on lifelong learning one should mention such important issues as courses fees and time budgets. They allow one to find out who is interested in lifelong learning and to what extent. Surveys show that in the case of refresher courses and regular training events the employer usually pays for training and these courses typically take place during paid working hours (Table 3.10). This trend, however, is not seen in the case of vocational courses. That means that employers are more interested in the advancement of existing skills of their personnel while individuals are more often motivated for acquiring a new vocation.

As opposed to non-formal education discussed earlier, informal learning is not related to any institutional origin. It includes such activities as self-learning via Internet, informal novice office learning, using educational TV and radio broadcasts, etc. In Russia, this form is less popular than in EU (17.4 per cent, twice lower than EU-25 average), mainly because of lack of free time and of access to appropriate sources of information (Internet, broadcasts, etc.).

As Table 3.11 shows, the main difference between Russia and EU is in the low share of e-learning and TV/radio educational broadcasts. Unfortunately today a very small fraction of the population has daily Internet access. As for the practice of learning broadcasts, it almost disappeared after the breakup of USSR.

The next step of the discussion is corporative access to the innovation infrastructure. The most common form of such access is technoparks. There exist several tens of technoparks in Russia, however, only

Table 3.10: *Non-formal Education/Training (lifelong learning) Indicators of Interest: percentage of Participants of Learning Activity (2006)*

	Groups by type of activity				
	Refresher Courses	*Professional Training Events, Lectures, Conferences*		*Vocational Courses (to Acquire New Vocation)*	*Amateur (Hobby) Courses*
		Regular	*One-time*		
(iii) Who pays for training?					
Total in the group	100	100	100	100	100
Myself (family, friends, etc.)	18	19	40	40	83
Partially myself, partially employer	7	7	–	6	17
Employer	49	74	49	42	–
Governmental employment agency	23	–	11	12	–
Other sources of funding	3	–	–	–	–
(iv) Does the training take place during paid working hours?					
Total in the group	100	100	100	100	100
Only during paid working hours	46	31	30	13	–
Mostly during paid working hours	17	20	44	20	–
Mostly out of the paid working hours	22	22	26	25	34
Only out of the paid working hours	13	14	–	42	66
Education/training while unemployed	2	13	–	–	–

Source: State University–Higher School of Economics (2007).

Table 3.11: *Forms of Informal Learning in Russia and EU: 2006 or Nearest Available, percentage of 25–64-year-old Respondents*

	Russia	*EU (25)*
Total	17.4	32.5
Self-studying with printed materials	12.7	24.0
Studying in libraries or learning centres	6.3	12.2
Computer based learning (e-learning)	3.6	19.2
TV/radio educational broadcasting	2.0	15.1

Source: State University–Higher School of Economics (2007).

some of them have official licenses. Technopark policies are full of hidden problems. First of all, multiple 'white spots' in the legislation dramatically weaken the technology commercialisation capabilities of universities and R&D institutions. For example, state universities or R&D institutions are not allowed to support other entities created on their base. That means that a state university can create a start-up, but cannot provide any funding or facilities for it. That is why technoparks do not operate independently in Russia as in other countries but are a part of the 'host organisation's' (university or R&D institution) structure. In addition to the organisational inflexibility Russian technoparks lack performance monitoring and best practices diffusion mechanisms. They also suffer from underdeveloped business consulting system.

Conceptually the Russian technoparks aspired to become an essential class of centres of excellence performing all their unique features (Zaichenko 2008). As a response to these negative factors some new trends of state policy for technoparks in Russia appear. A condensed development of technoparks started in 'industry and manufacturing special economic zones' (disscussed in the subsequent section). It makes it possible to significantly reduce the tax pressure and to attract investors. There also exist other solutions like particular mechanisms of business incubators and start-up financial support mechanisms within technoparks; providing conversion and commercialisation mechanisms for defence 'dual-purpose' technologies, etc.

Currently a number of legal mechanisms for technopark development and support are under construction. They are mostly related to one of three directions: (*a*) federal lands provision for technoparks on a competitive basis (both for ownership and for long lease), (*b*) technopark infrastructure direct investments by federal executive bodies and (*c*) creation of favourable conditions for sharing technoparks investment (including construction sites, transport and living infrastructure funding) expenditures between federal and regional authorities.

The access to the knowledge, R&D and innovation infrastructure in Russia can be discussed via the following issues: (*a*) school e-learning; (*b*) online learning and scientific portals; (*c*) lifelong learning activities and (*d*) business access to innovation infrastructure. The access to e-learning is limited mainly by expenses for computers and Internet access. The average accessibility of these products is still very low in Russia. However, almost all Russian schools are equipped with PCs and Internet connection. It could be a great starting point for e-learning, but due to many reasons discussed earlier e-learning is not available at schools. At the same time the Russian e-learning content is developed enough both in terms of transit portals and content portals. Perhaps the most convenient framework for such resources is lifelong learning activities. However, the LLL is not widespread due to lack of infrastructure as such. Russians prefer to attend informal LLL activities. Usually it is a form of professional skills advancement initiated for employees by managers and paid for by companies. The small business access to innovation is provided mainly via technoparks. However, the technoparks' infrastructure does not function properly in Russia due to legal and administrative barriers and lack of infrastructure services. The main problem of Russian technoparks is low overall demand for innovation and consequently underdeveloped innovation activity in the economy.

Access to financial infrastructure

The financial infrastructure for R&D and innovation in Russia is represented both by foundations providing project funding for individuals and institutions providing corporate project funding. To illustrate both categories one can discuss the activities of two leading budgetary foundations.

The Russian Foundation for Basic Research (RFBR) is a self-governing non-commercial public organisation (a federal institution under the jurisdiction of the government of the Russian Federation). Its main goal is to provide assistance to activities in all areas of basic research on a competitive basis. The RFBR enables scientists to focus on the most promising research topics and to set up research teams. The main goal of the foundation is to identify the most promising projects among submitted proposals for convenient organisational and financial support. The RFBR performs over 70,000 merit reviews annually. The total number of peer reviews by the Foundation exceeds 1 million. Currently the RFBR provides expert panels in all supported areas of knowledge and in targeted initiative-based fundamental research as well. There's also a coordination council for regional competitions.

In 2005–09 the federal budget appropriations for the RFBR amounted to 11.4–11.7 per cent of the total budgetary funding for basic research. For 2009 it is $577 million PPP (4.1 per cent of the total budgetary funding for civil R&D). The main part of the funds (over 70 per cent) is directed to support approved research projects carried out by small research teams (up to 10 members) or by individuals (Figure 3.28). The foundation also supports a set of programmes including free e-library, assistance to mobility of young researchers, equipment support grants, etc.

Figure 3.28: *RFBR: Distribution of Funding by Knowledge Area in the Initiative-based Research Projects and Other Competitions (2008)*

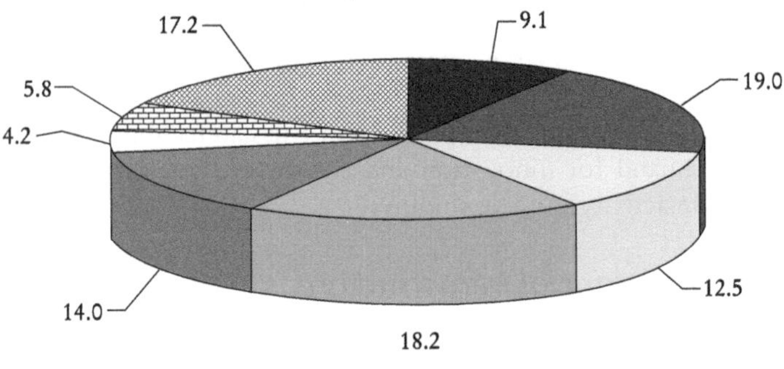

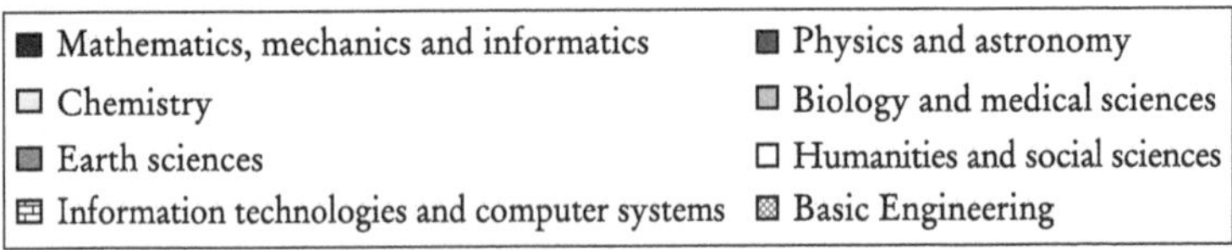

Source: RFBR funding reports, http://www.rfbr.ru/rffi/portal/funding (accessed 10 December 2010).

The other example is Foundation for Assistance to Small Innovational Enterprises (FASIE). This federal institution was founded in 1994 to assist small innovative firms in commercialisation of R&D

results, to reduce investment risks and to ensure start-up development. The FASIE activities are funded by the federal budget (1.5 per cent of the total budgetary appropriations for civil R&D). In 2007 the foundation disposed of 1.35 billion RUR ($89.5 million PPP), and the 2011 budget amounts to 4 billion RUR.

Along its history the foundation received more than 24,000 applications and approved more than 8,000 projects. An average supported small innovational company shows a turnover of $1 million PPP with growth rate of about 20 per cent. The overall number of such companies created with the assistance of the foundation exceeds 1,500; the number of patents is about 3,500.

The FASIE programmes (about 20 programmes) are focused on five key activities: creation of new small innovational companies, involving external investors, development of innovation infrastructure, technology transfer, and assistance to human capital development. The creation of new small innovational companies is the main activity. It requires a considerable effort to attract all the necessary partners and actors (Figure 3.29).

Figure 3.29: *FASIE, the Initial Stage Chart: Creation of New Small Innovational Companies*

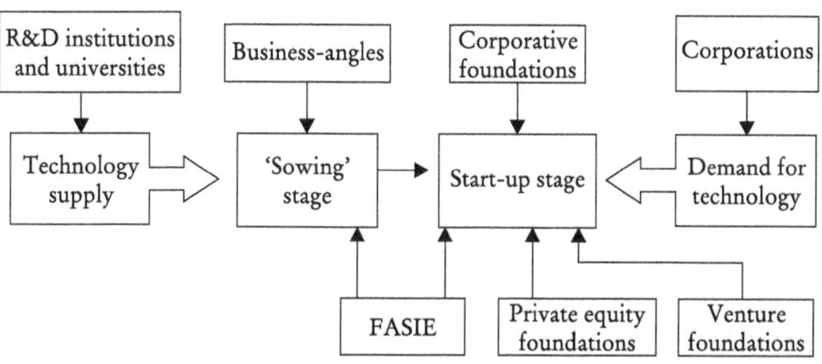

Source: Chart designed using information from the FASIE official web site http://www.fasie.ru (accessed 10 December 2010).

A totally opposite approach was developed under the 'special economic zones' (SEZs) infrastructure concept. It provides the innovational companies with financial incentives and ready-to-use infrastructure and a chance to develop independently. This instrument was introduced in Russia in 2005 by the special federal law (Government of Russian Federation 2005). Special zones are the Russian Federation territories defined by the government, where a special regime for entrepreneurial activity applies. The SEZs were intended to promote high-technology industries.

There are three types of such zones — industrial (special tax preferences, favourable investment regime); technology and innovation (out of the customs zone, favourable for imports/exports) and recreational zones (special conditions for tourism). The first two types today include six zones (Table 3.12). Special economic areas can be created on land owned by the government and/or municipalities. However, official initiatives aimed for innovation infrastructure development (as well as other mechanisms discussed earlier) do not guarantee growth in demand for and/or supply of innovation.

Table 3.12: *Industrial and Technological SEZs in Russia*

Type	*Location*	*Description*
Industry and manufacturing special economic zones	Elabuga	Automobile and oil industries
	Lipetsk	Home appliances, building materials, chemical products
Technology and innovation special economic zones	Dubna	Nuclear physics
	Zelenograd	Microelectronics
	Strelna	Electrolux, BSH Bosch und Siemens Hausgeräte GmbH
	Tomsk	Chemicals, pharmaceuticals, mechanical engineering

Source: Based on information from the RUSSEZ official web site, http://www.russez.ru/oez (accessed 10 December 2010).

However, the Russian high-tech sector is still unable to absorb enough investment and to find demand for innovation as well. This problem was the reason behind launching the state intervention activities in the form of the Russian Venture Company and state corporations like Russian Corporation for Nanotechnology, State Corporation for Nuclear Energy, etc.

The role of the Russian Venture Company is to promote venture investment and financial support for S&T all over the country. The company invests in regional and sectoral closed end investment funds (established under the Russian legislation and regulated by the Federal Service on Financial Markets). Each fund is controlled by a special management company. The management companies compete for the right to sell fund investment shares to the Russian Venture Company. Funding can be accepted for the projects corresponding with the critical technologies only.

After complete formation of the venture fund (i.e. filling with monetary funds), the fund management company can start investment activities (launch innovation companies in areas of microelectronics, information technologies, telecommunication technologies, biotechnologies, medical technologies, environment-friendly energy, and nanotechnologies). The resources for the Russian Venture Company capitalisation are allocated from the Investment Fund of the Russian Federation. Initially it was planned to allocate up to \$350 million PPP in 2006 and \$660 million PPP in 2007. However, in 2008 the authorised capital stock amounted for \$1.8 billion PPP.

State corporations play the role of financial instruments for resources concentration and distribution in the areas corresponding with the state interests and priorities. For example, Russian Corporation for Nanotechnology (Rosnano) was founded in 2007 by special federal law to address the growing challenge that arises with the rapid development of new technologies on the nanoscale.[10]

Rosnano, one of seven Russian state corporations, enjoys direct budgetary support. Its five-year budget accounts for \$8.6 billion PPP. Due to its special status, the corporation is not part of government property and out of the control of regulating bodies. The director is appointed by the Russian president only. In 2011 there were 439 projects applied to Rosnano (about \$117 billion PPP in total).

Flexibility of operation and stable support for the projects should considerably boost their efficiency. However such 'freedom' may also cause an unforeseen abuse. The need for creating such corporations was formulated in 2007 by the Russian president in his annual message to the Federation Council of the Federal Assembly of the Russian Federation. In this law the legislative basis, organisation principles, creation, and activity goals of the Russian Corporation for Nanotechnologies were stated. Three key directions of Rosnano activities are related to assistance to the state policies in the sphere of nanotechnology, development of innovative infrastructure for nanotechnologies and achievement of projects aimed at creating innovative nanotechnologies and nanoindustries.

In order to achieve its goals, three main functions are carried out: R&D, nanotechnology education and financial support for innovative projects. The first two functions are provided by financial support of the R&D and nanotechnology education projects. The third function includes support of the entire innovation cycle, from project evaluation, financing and provision for commercialisation and production to supervision of the projects after commercialisation.

Generally the financial infrastructure for R&D and innovation in Russia is open for different actors including individuals, research teams and start-ups, as well as for a wide range of activities (from basic research to innovation projects and initial public offerings [IPOs]). There also exist two different approaches to the funding. The first one is focused on the total assistance to individuals or small businesses winning the competition (foundation). The other approach provides the small innovational companies with financial incentives and total freedom in the market environment (SEZs). But practically the capacities of the two sources mentioned are not as high as required, covering just about 14 per cent of the expenditures on technological innovation. The rest comes from organisations. However, the access to this funding flow is more complicated. Access to credits and loans for innovation is considerably limited (especially for SMEs). Therefore the private sector actors are being gradually replaced by the large structures closely linked with the state (like state corporations), and the whole innovation activity rates of organisations in Russia remain low (in 2008 expenditure on technological innovation accounted for 1.2 per cent of the industrial output value).

Output & employment

The two main sectors — industry and services — provide employment for 40 per cent of the labour force in Russia (Figure 3.30). However, most of the available statistics concern the industrial sector. The third sphere by employment scale is education, health and social care. And the forth one (11.2 per cent) includes employees with undocumented sphere of activities (mostly self-employed and informally employed).

The last decade was characterised by two controversial processes in the industrial sector: declining employment together with increasing industrial output (Figure 3.31). A possible reason for such transformation could be moderate reorganisation of many industrial companies. It was the period of the 'equity reallocation' when many medium and large businesses changed their owners or were incorporated into

Figure 3.30: *Distribution of Labour Force by Sector (percentage) (2003)*

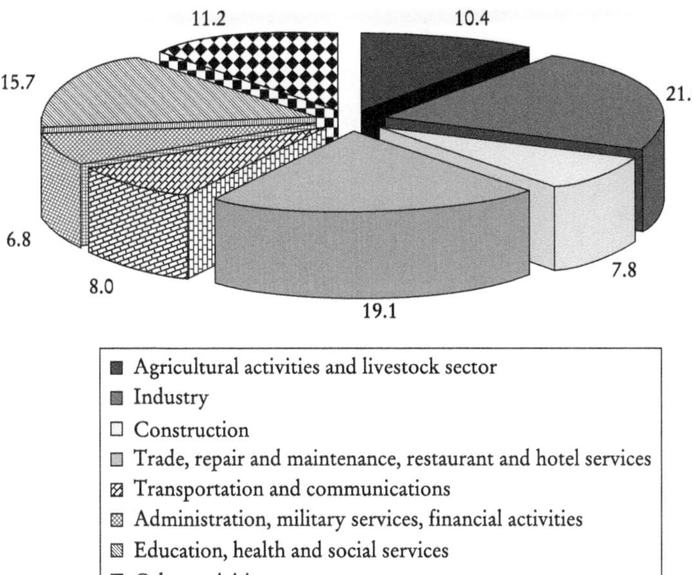

Source: Calculated using the Federal State Statistics Service (2010b) data.

larger structures. The reorganisation revealed the inefficiency of many enterprises and became an instrument for their modernisation.

The difference in distributions of output and labour force by industry (Figure 3.32) indicates that about three-quarters (74 per cent) of industrial personnel is concentrated in industries performing 46 per cent of the output while the rest 26 per cent employees ensure more than half of the industrial production. The latter group is represented by natural resources (mainly gas and oil) extraction and medium low-tech manufacturing. The natural resources extraction industries are characterised by relatively low labour intensity accompanied by relatively high capital intensity. For high-tech enterprises (which perform the opposite proportion) any reorganisation process should be more painful and complicated.

However, in the section on inter-sectoral wages/productivity differential the productivity issue is discussed in more detail. Particularly, it is illustrated, that the main factor of the natural resources extraction sector productivity is rather gas and oil prices dynamics than any other reason.

Figure 3.31: *Employment and Output Dynamics in Industry (percentage) (1995–2007)*

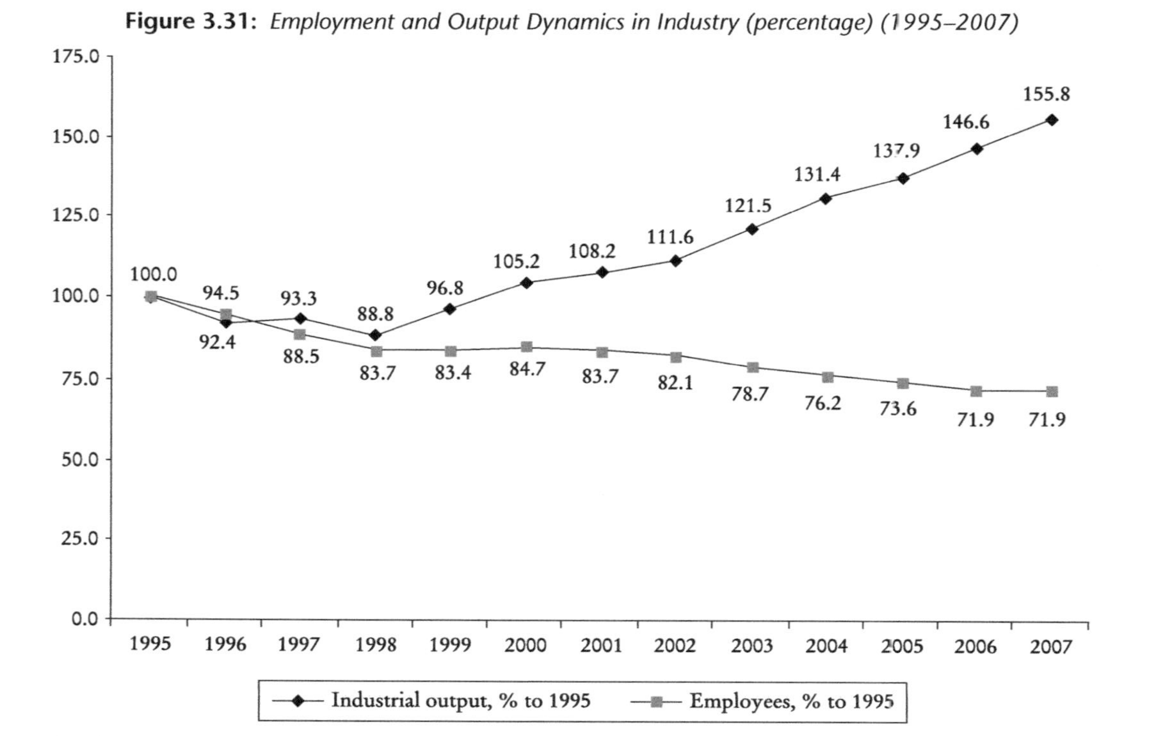

Source: Calculated using Federal State Statistics Service (2010b) data.

Figure 3.32: *Structure of Output and Employment by Industry (percentage) (2007)*

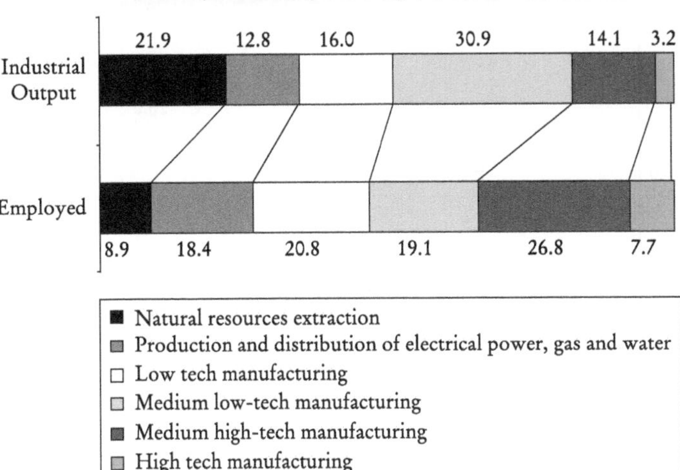

Source: Calculated using Federal State Statistics Service (2010b) data.

Nature of employment

The next three sections are focused mostly on different aspects of the inter-regional inequalities discussed in the first part of the chapter. The main feature of employment in Russia is high risks vis-à-vis stagnating local economies and whole industries. Therefore from the early 1990s a new set of adaptation mechanisms was developed. They were related to the informal or 'shadow' economic activities, part-time employment, 'hidden' employment (to avoid taxation), etc. It is extremely difficult to separate these activities from each other statistically, but the whole informal segment can be found by excluding all the 'official' activities documented in figures.

The beginning of informal employment takes place even before the collapse of the USSR. In 1990 it composed an inferior but still calculable part of the population's income of 3 per cent (Figure 3.33). The market reforms provided freedom and, more importantly, a tangible necessity (especially for the poorer population) for such activities. As a result, by 2000 their share in income exceeded 27 per cent. This steady-state level of 27–28 per cent remained almost unchanged for the next seven years.

Figure 3.33: *Share of Informal Employment in Total Income (percentage) (1990–2007)*

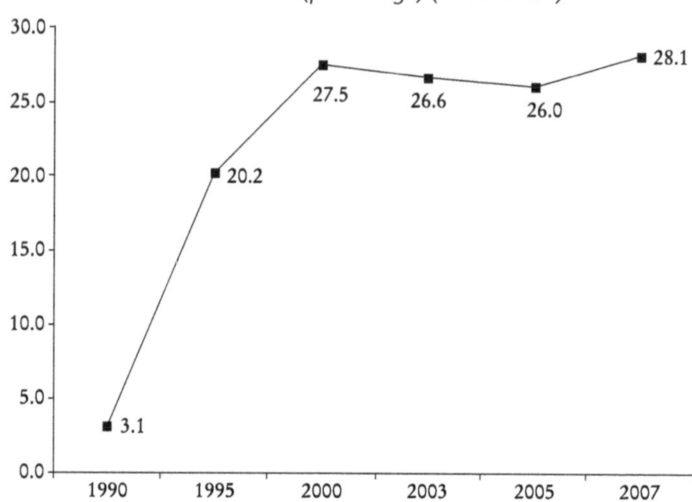

Source: Calculated using Federal State Statistics Service (2010b) data.

However, the aggregate average level hides huge local disparities. The distribution on the detailed regional sample shows that locally this share varies from 0.6 (Nenets Autonomous District) to 51.1 (Dagestan Republic) (Figure 3.34). The positive correlation with the local poverty level indicates the nature of the informal employment mechanism.

At the same time a considerable dispersion of the informal employment income share at higher poverty rates reveals a alarming trend. It means that in some depressive regions this adaptation mechanism is inefficient and unable to cover the income deficit. These are regions with extremely low economic activity, where most of the population cannot find a demand for their labour even informally and have to survive by, for example, subsistence farming.

The Soviet state guaranteed employment for all citizens. However, after its collapse Russian households faced severe poverty and unemployment risks, and from the early 1990s informal employment has became a new mechanism for survival in the market economy environment. During the last seven years the informal employment share in income per capita remains constant at the level of about a quarter. Nevertheless, the regional values spread from zero to more than a

Figure 3.34: *Distribution of Regions (Detailed Sample) by Regional Poverty Level and Share of Informal Employment in Income per capita (2007)*

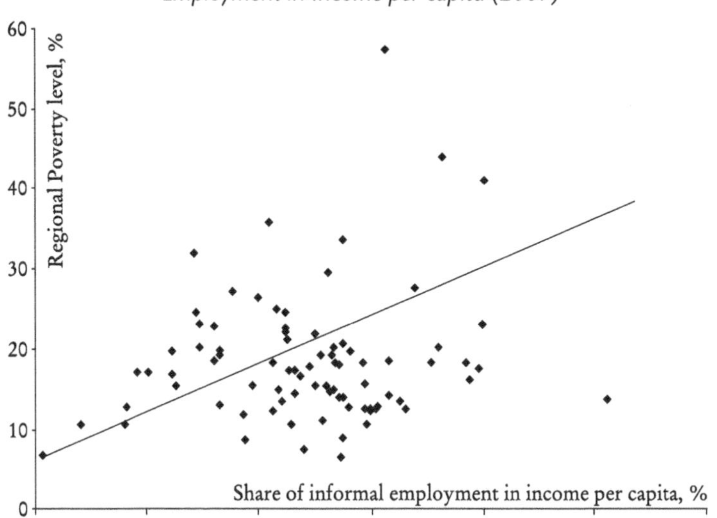

Source: Calculated using Federal State Statistics Service (2010b) data.

half. There exists a positive correlation between the regional poverty level and this share, but in some regions the economic activity level is too low even for informal employment.

Inter-sectoral wages/productivity differential and their bearing on inequality

Defining productivity as value added per employee one can compare disparities in workers' remuneration by industry. By 2007 the lowest productivity level could be found in high-tech manufacturing (Figure 3.35). The medium low-tech manufacturing shows a three-fold higher productivity at much higher growth rates (three-fold growth in five years). However, the leader is the natural resource extraction sector. Producing 78.2 per cent of the total industrial value-added, it performs 10 times higher productivity than high-tech and the highest productivity growth (4.4-fold in five years).

Comparative dynamics of gas and oil prices and the oil/gas sector productivity could explain the inter-sectoral misbalances (Figure 3.36).

Figure 3.35: *Productivity: Value Added per One Employee by Industry (Thousands US$ PPP) (2002–06)*

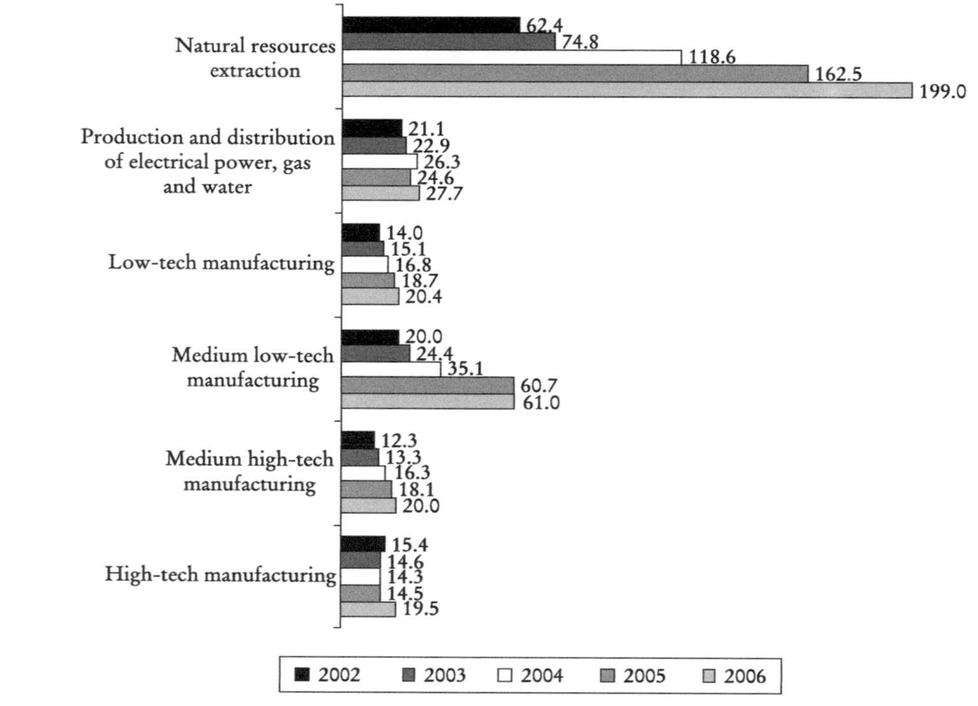

Source: Calculation by the Institute for Statistical Studies and Economy of Knowledge, Moscow.

Figure 3.36: *Productivity Factors in the Natural Resources Extraction Sector: Gas and Oil Prices Dynamics (2002–06)*

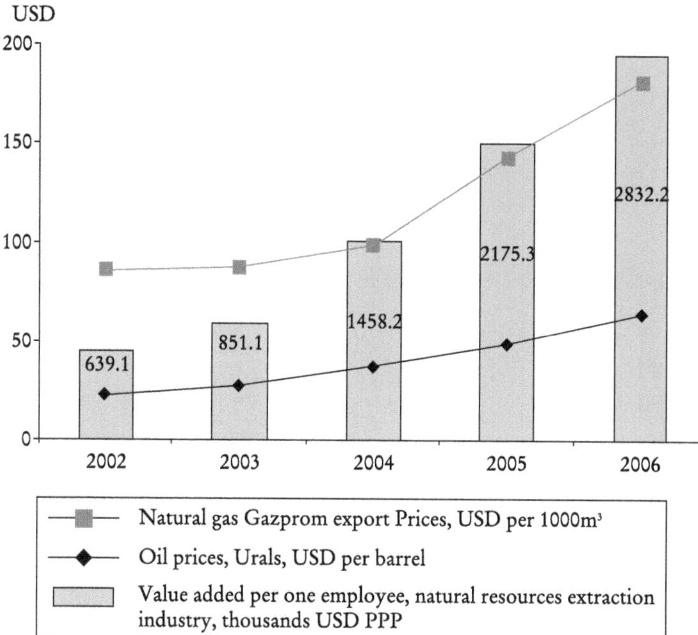

Source: Federal State Statistics Service (2010b) data.

Actually the speculative nature of the sector output subordinates the whole economy to the gas/oil prices behaviour to a great extent. Inside the high-tech manufacturing segment industries differ not by productivity scale, but rather by its changes (Figure 3.37). By 2007 almost all of them showed stable growth except aerospace.

The wages disparity configuration strictly follows the difference in productivity by sectors (compare Figures 3.38 and 3.35). However, this inequality is smoother than the productivity spread. For example, the natural resources extracting industries perform 3.4-fold higher labour productivity than the average value, but the wages difference here is just 1.7-fold. Therefore the equalisation mechanisms provide moderate smoothing of the income disparities.

However, the effect of these mechanisms is not single-valued. On the one hand the inter-regional inequality caused mainly by the regional economic specialisation is being softened. On the other, the

Figure 3.37: *Productivity: Value Added per One Employee by High-tech Manufacturing Industry (Thousands US$ PPP) (2002–06)*

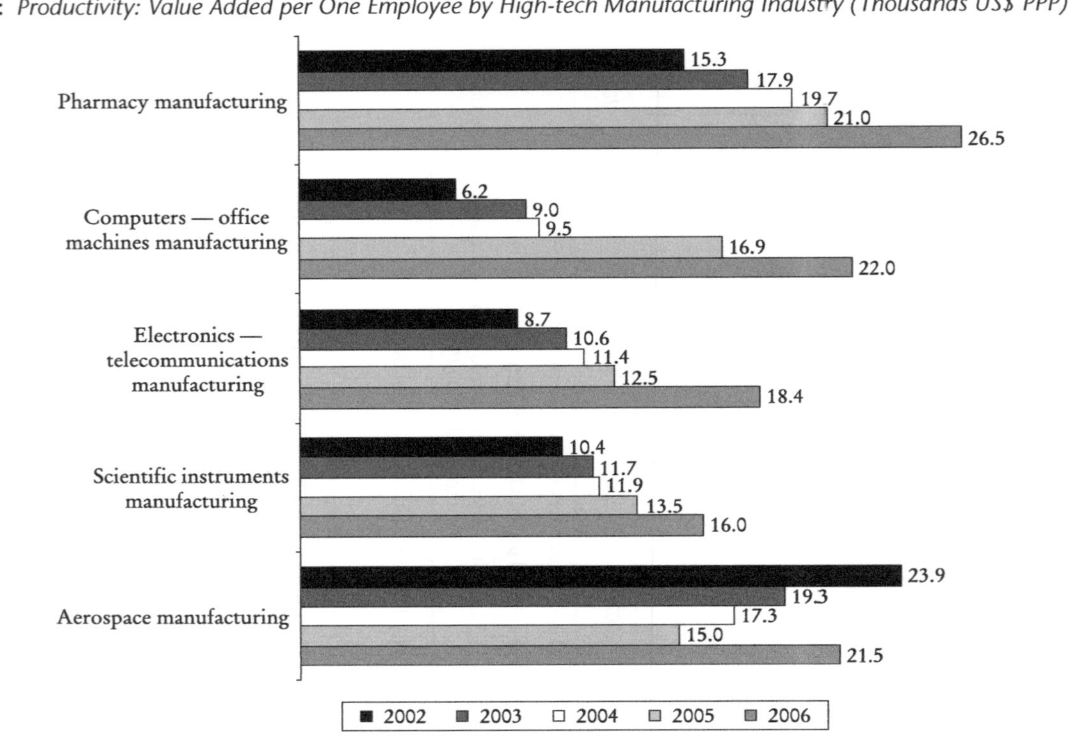

Source: Calculation by the Institute for Statistical Studies and Economy of Knowledge, Moscow.

Figure 3.38: *Monthly Wages Distribution by Industry (US$ PPP) (2000–07)*

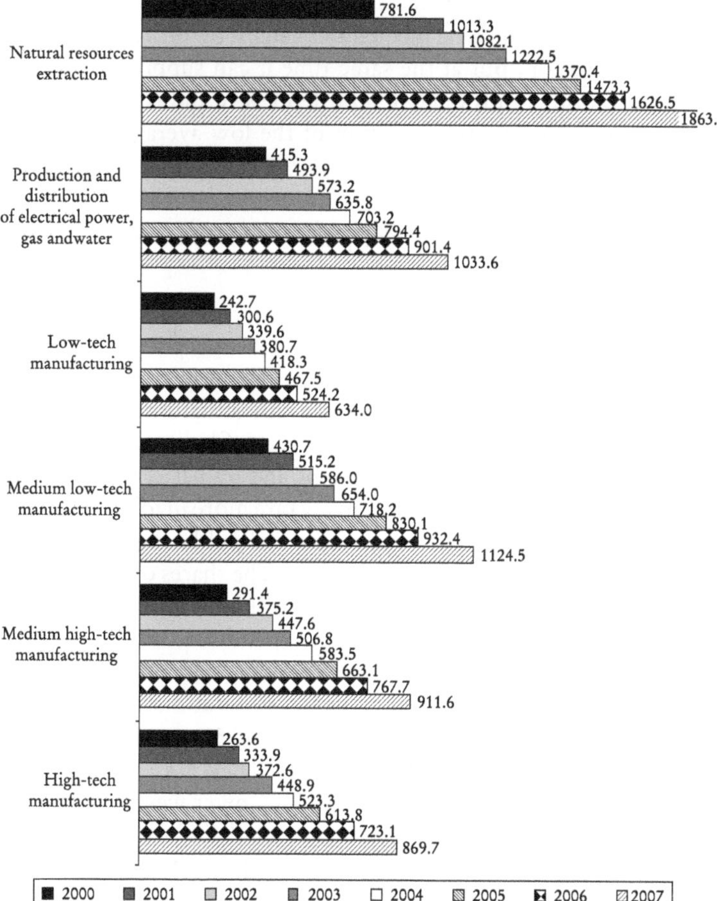

Source: Calculated using Federal State Statistics Service (2010b) data.

wage-to-productivity discrepancy can affect the labour motivation and the whole economy's productivity.

The labour productivity in Russia is evidently unevenly biased towards the natural resources extraction industries following gas and oil prices dynamics. The manufacturing sectors (especially high-tech) perform 10-fold lower productivity. The wages structure follows these disparities, but to a lesser extent. The difference in average wages between natural resources extraction and manufacturing sectors is just about two-fold. Such a balancing mechanism restrains the inter-regional income level inequalities caused by the regional industries specialisation. But at the same time it can suppress the labour motivation both in productive and depressive industries. Anyway it does not contribute to a solution of the low average income per capita problem.

Regional disparities in competence building institutions and production

As was discussed earlier, the inter-regional income per capita inequality is influenced mainly by the regional economies specialisation. The indicators in Table 3.13 describe this situation more clearly. The regions with evident manufacturing profile like Northwestern or Volga Federal Districts (75 per cent and 69 per cent of the total industrial output per capita respectively) are more involved in science and education. They dispose of a wide set of public higher education institutions as well as R&D organisations. The shares of public higher education students and R&D staff are also close to the national value. Volga District is also known for high expenditure on technological innovation.

To compare, Urals and Far Eastern Federal districts are more advanced in natural resources (51 per cent and 57 per cent of the total industrial output per capita respectively). They have lower number of HEIs and R&D institutions as well as a lower weight of students and scientists in the population. However their income per capita above average and, for Urals, the highest (after Moscow) level of GRP per capita.

Moscow is the most deviating territory here. This single city acquires 25 per cent and 22 per cent of all national public HEIs and R&D organisations respectively. The density of university students is two-fold higher and the density of scientists is four-fold higher compared to the national levels, while GRP and income per capita are three times higher. However, these disparities are defined rather by the political and financial status of the capital than by its industrial profile.

Table 3.13: *Competence Building Institutions and Production Output Compared to GRP and Income per capita (2009)*

		Public Higher Education Institutions	*Organisations Performing R&D Activities*	*Public Higher Education Students Per 1000 Population*	*R&D Personnel Per 1,000 Population*	*Industrial output Per Capita, Thousand $ PPP*				*Gross Regional Product Per Capita, Thousand $ PPP*	*Monthly Income Per Capita, Thousand $ PPP*
						Total	*Natural Resources Extraction*	*Production and Distribution Of Electric Power, Gas and Water*	*Manufacturing*		
	Total	430	3,536	43.2	5.2	10.94	2.48	1.48	6.98	16.70	1.16
	Central Federal District	206	1,383	47.4	10.4	11.07	1.02	1.71	8.34	24.05	1.53
→	Moscow (as a part of the Central Federal District)	**107**	759	**83.5**	**22.7**	16.09	3.09	2.30	**10.71**	**55.17**	**2.89**
	Northwestern Federal District	77	518	47.5	7.3	14.13	1.83	1.70	**10.60**	17.47	1.20
	Southern Federal District	80	316	35.9	1.5	4.18	0.25	0.80	3.13	8.25	0.86
	Volga Federal District	121	532	41.6	3.9	10.39	1.86	1.32	7.20	12.27	0.96
→	Urals Federal District	52	211	43.3	3.4	24.85	**12.63**	2.18	**10.04**	**27.32**	**1.37**
	Siberian Federal District	86	410	42.9	2.7	9.10	1.94	1.40	5.76	12.32	0.93
→	Far Eastern Federal District	38	166	44.9	2.0	9.34	5.30	1.85	2.19	16.59	**1.26**

Source: Calculated using Federal State Statistics Service 2010a data.

The Russian regions differ significantly by their production specialisation. The most common typology by production power could include manufacturing-oriented regional economies and ones specialised on the natural resources (gas and oil) extraction. As can be expected, the manufacturing-oriented regions contain the main share of competence-building institutions including universities and R&D organisations. They also perform higher expenditure for technological innovation. The opposite trend is typical for the 'mining regions'. However, the latter group is more progressive in the regional value added as well as in income per capita while the manufacturing regions are often near or below the average.

Concluding Remarks

Russia's experience in the nature of inequality and its dynamics is strongly affected by the sudden and quick breakthrough from the command administration system towards a market economy in 1990–91. The chronological scope here is rather short and includes mainly two key stages. The first one is the period of socio-economic transition from the early 1990s to about 2000. The second one lasts from the early 2000s to the end of 2008. From the latter point a new stage begins, the period of structural reorganisation vis-à-vis the world economic crisis. The Soviet system was too different from the contemporary market economy by all characteristics and may be regarded rather as a 'starting point'. There also exists a practical barrier caused by the incompatibility of many key standards in the Soviet statistics and the Russian Federal State Statistics Service practices.

This analysis shows that the aggregate interpersonal inequality by income is not a valid issue for the Russian case. Statistically Russia holds the same position by this indicator as many industrially developed economies. Nevertheless the Russian inequality takes on an alarming scale when discussed in three particular dimensions: inter-regional disparities, inequalities by social groups and the overall income level. The inter-regional disparities are grounded at the natural resource-based profile of the Russian economy. The regions specialised in natural gas and oil extraction enjoy high economic productivity and higher income per capita level. The other local economies (the majority) have inferior grounds for development, lacking demand for their output. Besides, the resources-based economy eliminates demand for innovation as such. The regional economies' stagnation entails unemployment growth, welfare level decrease, infrastructure collapse, etc. The Russian example shows that as against the concept of innovation-driven inequality (e.g. Cozzens and Kaplinsky 2008), a pathological lack of innovation also remains a crucial inequality factor.

The inter-regional inequality is elicited as a 'solid residual' of the discussion. It explains the key imbalances of the social structure in Russia as well as main barriers for the socio-economic development. The income redistribution system (mainly represented by transfers) is regarded to be a protection mechanism worked out by the state. However, it does not provide motivation for independent growth in depressed regions. On the contrary, it contributes to conservation of depression. However, some other initiatives aimed at promotion of innovative learning and education/labour mobility could break the status-quo.

During the last two decades the Russian households have cultivated their own adaptation instruments to overcome the shocks of a free economy (consumption and time budgets redistribution, informal employment, etc.). These mechanisms as a 'bottom-up initiative' are efficient enough to survive under conditions of low income and high inter-regional inequality. They are also supported by the 'top-down' initiative of the state (income redistribution under the centralised federal budget system). However, this 'emergency' strategy can be regarded as a temporary measure only; it does not contribute much to socio-economic development in the long run.

The discussion shows that Russia still possesses enough resources and infrastructure capacities to provide access to innovation for all key NIS actors. The next step required is to revise the current strategic priorities towards a diversified economy based on multiple growth points. A single policy framework could enable the positive factors towards social development. The key function of this package is to combine already existing policies (risk social groups assistance, mobility and infrastructure development, etc.) under an integrated system of strategies and instruments. The contemporary social policies in Russia still lack direct relationships with each other, with economic, learning, S&T, and innovation initiatives. However, it could be a worthy challenge for the future.

Notes

1. The English translation of the 1936 Constitution is available online: http://www.departments.bucknell.edu/russian/const/1936toc.html (accessed 10 December 2010).
2. However, this fact forced the government to review the minimal consumer basket price level. But even after that about one-third of Russians had income below the poverty line.
3. The 'Big Mac' index table is available at http://www.nationmaster.com/graph/eco_big_mac_ind-economy-big-mac-index (accessed 10 December 2010).
4. For example, small enterprises are also limited by share of federal, regional and municipal property in the authorised capital stock, as well as share of property of foundations, public and religious organisations (should not exceed 25 per cent); by share in the authorised capital stock of other legal entities except other small enterprises (also should not exceed 25 per cent); by type (consumer's co-operation entities cannot be regarded as small enterprises).
5. The graph includes a more detailed regional list.
6. The programme website is http://nobus.worldbank.org.ru (accessed 10 December 2010).

References

Andrews, J. T., 2002. *When Majorities Fail: The Russian Parliament 1990–1993*. Cambridge: Cambridge University Press.

Archibugi, D. and B.-Å. Lundvall (eds), 2001. *The Globalising Learning Economy: Major Socio-economic Trends and European Innovation Policy*. Oxford: Oxford University Press.

Besstremyannaya, G., L. Ovcharova, A. Burdyak, D. Ibragimova, A. Zaborovskaya, and N. Zubarevich, 2005. *Incomes and Social Services: Inequality, Vulnerability, Poverty*. Moscow: State University–Higher School of Economics (in Russian).

Central Intelligence Agency (CIA), 2010. *The CIA World Factbook 2011*. New York: Skyhorse Publishing.

Cozzens, S. E. and R. Kaplinsky, 2009. 'Innovation, Poverty and Inequality: Cause, Coincidence, or Co-evolution', in B.-Å. Lundvall, K. J. Joseph, C. Chaminade, and J. Vang (eds), *Handbook on Innovation Systems in Developing Countries*. Cheltenham: Edward Elgar, 57–82.

EUROSTAT, 2005. *What is High-Tech Trade? Definition Based on the SITC Nomenclature*. Luxembourg: Office for Official Publications of the European Communities, March.

Fagen, M., 1992. 'Russia: Shock Therapy Isn't the Way to Promote Democracy'. *International Herald Tribune*, Tuesday, 12 May.

Federal State Unitary Enterprise, State Research and Innovation Center for Geographic Information Systems and Technologies, 'National Atlas of Russia', http://national-atlas.ru (accessed 10 December 2010).

Gaslikova, I., L. Gokhberg and G. Kovalyova, 2005. *ICT in the Russian Economy*. Moscow: State University–Higher School of Economics (in Russian).

German, T. C., 2003. *Russia's Chechen War*. London: Routledge.

Gokhberg, L. 2003. 'Russia: A New Innovation System for the New Economy'. Background material for a presentation at the First Globelics Conference, 'Innovation Systems and Development Strategies for the Third Millennium', Rio de Janeiro, 2–6 November.

Gokhberg, L. and O. Shuvalova, 2004. *Russian Public Opinion of the Knowledge Economy: Science, Innovation, Information Technology and Education as Drivers of Economic Growth and Quality of Life*. Moscow: The British Council, Russia.

Federal State Statistics Service, 2006. *Women and Men in Russia*. Moscow: Federal State Statistics Service (in Russian).

———, 2008a. 'Family in Russia: 2008'. *Statistical Handbook*. Moscow: Federal State Statistics Service (in Russian).

———, 2008b. *Social Level and Life Quality of the Russian Population*. Moscow: Federal State Statistics Service (in Russian).

———, 2008c. *The Russian Statistical Yearbook*. Moscow: Federal State Statistics Service (in Russian).

———, 2009a. 'Poverty Indicators'. *Data Book*. Moscow: Federal State Statistics Service (in Russian).

———, 2009b. 'Income, Spending, and Consumption of Households in 2008'. *Data Book*. Moscow: Federal State Statistics Service (in Russian).

———, 2010a. 'Regions of Russia: Socio-Economic Indicators'. *Statistical Handbook*. Moscow: Federal State Statistics Service.

———, 2010b. 'Russian Statistical Yearbook 2010'. *Statistical Handbook*. Moscow: Federal State Statistics Service (in Russian).

———, 2011. 'Russia in Figures'. *Statistical Handbook*. Moscow: Federal State Statistics Service.

Government of Russian Federation, 2005. Federal Law of the Russian Federation, 'On Special Economic Zones in the Russian Federation'. (116) FZ (22.07.2005) (in Russian).

———, 2007. 'On the Russian Corporation for Nanotechnology', (139) FZ (12.07.2007) (in Russian).

Laird, R. D., 1958. *Collective Farming in Russia: A Political Study of the Soviet Kolkhozy*. Lawrence: University of Kansas.

Lundvall, B.-Å. and S. Borrás, 1997. *The Globalising Learning Economy: Implications for Innovation Policy*. Luxembourg: European Communities.

Lundvall, B.-Å. and B. Johnson, 1994. 'The Learning Economy', *Journal of Industry Studies*, 1(2) (December), 23–42.

Martin, T., 1998. 'The Origins of Soviet Ethnic Cleansing', *Journal of Modern History*, 70 (December), 813–61.

Milanovic, B., 1998. 'Income, Inequality, and Poverty during the Transformation from Planned to Market Economy'. Washington DC: World Bank.

National Research University–Higher School of Economics, 2011. 'Innovation Activity Indicators: 2011'. *Data Book*. Moscow: National Research University–Higher School of Economics (in Russian).

Shuvalova, O. 2007. 'The Image of Science: Public Opinion on the Scientific Activities Results', *Foresight*, 2(2), 50–59 (in Russian).

State University–Higher School of Economics, 2007. 'Indicators of Education in the Russian Federation. *Data Book*. Moscow: State University–Higher School of Economics.

State University–Higher School of Economics, 2008. 'Innovation Activity Indicators: 2008'. *Data Book*. Moscow: State University–Higher School of Economics (in Russian).

Tutushkin, A., 2009. 'The Gazprom's Fall', *Vedomosti*, 170(2192), 10 September 2009, B2 (in Russian).

United Nations, 2008. 'World Fertility Patterns 2007'. Wall Chart Edition. New York: United Nations Publications.

Walters, G. and W. Mauldin, 2008. 'Gazprom Passes GE, China Mobile, Becomes World No. 3', *Bloomberg*, 8 May 2008. http://www.bloomberg.com/apps/news?pid=newsarchive&sid=aZomK8T5CtUs (accessed 30 January 2013).

Yanowitch, M., 1977. *Social and Economic Inequality in the Soviet Union: Six Studies*. White Plains NY: M.E. Sharpe.

Zaichenko, S., 2002. 'E-employment: Atypical Features and New Analytic Approaches', *Economic Sociology*, 3(5), November, 93–110 (in Russian).

——, 2007. 'Innovation Development in the Services Sector', *Foresight*, 1(1), 30–33 (in Russian).

——, 2008. 'Centers of Excellence in the Contemporary S&T Policy System', *Foresight*, 2(1), 42–50 (in Russian).

4

Dealing with the Innovation–Inequality Conundrum: The Indian Experience

K. J. Joseph, Lakhwinder Singh and *Vinoj Abraham*

At the time of independence, India inherited an extremely backward economy with asymmetric social and economic structures from the colonial rulers. Hence, the core concern of India's innovation system that was built over the strong edifice laid down by the first prime minister, Jawaharlal Nehru, has been faster economic growth and development with equitable distribution of wealth by harnessing, amongst other things, the power of science and technology. While the constitution ensured equality and social justice, various institutional arrangements built up under the planned development consistently aimed at inclusive growth. This incorporated the enactment of various policies that exclusively aimed at altering the structure of economy and society (Srinivasan 1974). Apart from policies relating to redistribution of productive assets and control of monopoly capital in the industrial sector, there were policies and programmes that aimed at addressing poverty indicating that the Indian state adopted an institutional approach to tackle various issues arising out of the institutional architecture that it inherited.

However, given the lower rate of economic growth under the development strategy with focus on equity and social justice along with disenchantment with the controlled regime in general, there has been a shift away from a planned economy to a market-based economy. The shift in development strategy notwithstanding, being a democratic society, concern for equity continued with much vigour as is evident from various institutional interventions under the liberalised regime. Under the liberalised regime, apart from policies that directly addressed poverty, there were a number of institutional interventions to facilitate innovation as a process that entails accumulation of technological capabilities within the system (Nelson 1994) and measures to facilitate technological learning and innovation given its role in productivity expansion (Soares and Cassiolato 2008) in a context of heightened competition. Nonetheless, while the emerging innovation system in India that evolved to address the bottlenecks in achieving faster growth of the economy also reinforced inequalities of certain form, the vast influence of the actors and institutions of the innovation system of the pre-liberalised era kept inequalities at low levels in the new regime. Hence, India, with the lowest Human Development Index in the BRICS, also has the lowest levels of income inequality in terms of the Gini Index and one of the lowest income shares of the richest 10 per cent of the population. It is remarkable that compared to the rest of the BRICS countries India has been able to achieve a fairly high economic growth without worsening inequality in the economy. This relative equality in India has been the product of a unique set of institutions that discouraged and mitigated inequality.

This chapter unravels the Indian story on innovation and inequality. The remainder of this chapter is organised as follows: the second section presents the trends in inequality in its different dimensions in an evolutionary perspective. An outline of different sets of institutions that helped contain inequality forms the focus of the third section. The fourth section makes an attempt at portraying the co-evolution of the innovation system and inequality followed by the concluding observations.

Inequality in India: Trends and Patterns

Inequality in the Indian society, as elsewhere, has multiple dimensions. Income and wealth inequality manifests the underlying inequalities in the capabilities and choices, which in turn are tempered by the institutions that make or mar disparities in society. Here we draw the multiple dimensions of inequality outcomes, and their related latent factors. We look at inequality from three perspectives, namely personal, regional and social. First we look at the trends in interpersonal inequality in consumption and income. Then we trace the trends in regional disparities in per capita income and finally the social disparities are captured in terms of caste-, religion- and gender-based discriminations.

Trends and patterns of interpersonal inequality in consumption

While it has been argued that the Indian economy was highly unequal at the time of independence, there are serious problems in presenting a credible time series analysis on account of the availability of reliable and comparable data. Nonetheless, different scholars have attempted an estimate of interpersonal inequality using different indicators like inequality in consumption (Dastidar 2004; Himanshu 2007), income (Ahmed and Bhattacharya 1974; Ojha and Bhatt 1974) and wealth (Subramanian and Jayaraj 2006). Since there has been broad trend synchronisation in terms of different indicators, we shall focus on inequality in terms of consumption.

A systematic analysis of economic inequality based on per capita consumption expenditure since 1951 has been undertaken by Dastidar (2004) and Himanshu (2007). The gini coefficient based on per capita monthly consumption expenditure was of the order of 0.33 and 0.40 in 1951 for rural and urban population respectively. This evidence shows that there did exist substantial economic inequality across rural and urban households in India and the urban population witnessed dramatically higher levels of inequality compared with the rural population. The values of gini coefficient showed an upward trend in consumption inequality across rural and urban households of India from 1951 to 1954. The gini coefficient for rural households was 0.36 in 1954 and it was 0.48 for urban households indicating widening rural–urban inequality. Thereafter, inequality started declining and continued to decline up to the year 1963 except some reversals in urban inequality.

The interpersonal inequality in rural India was largely determined by the green revolution technology (since the mid-1960s) that has raised production and productivity of the agricultural sector. The early green revolution technology was labour intensive in nature and therefore it increased the gains of generated income both to the small and medium farmers as well as to the landless agriculture labour (Hanumantha Rao 1975). Thus, the income distribution across households in the countryside marginally improved due to the expansion of farm employment. Hanumantha Rao asserted that 'the net impact of technological changes and the changes in the distribution of area operated is a decline in the relative share of large incomes and in income disparities in the rural sector' (Hanumantha Rao 1975: 149–50).

Apart from this, there were several policy measures taken by the state to reduce the disparities ranging from asset redistribution, control over the industrial monopoly capital, subsidised food items, education, employment to price control (Srinivasan 1974). These measures generated a sizable middle class population both in the rural and urban areas of India at a very early stage of economic development. The organised participation of the middle class in the process of economic development and political processes allowed it to secure substantial advantages. As a consequence, inequality remained relatively under control. The decades of 1970s and 1980s broadly observed a stabilisation of inequality. It further declined in the late 1980s and early 1990s. But in the latter half of the 1990s, inequality increased as is indicated by the trends recorded by the gini coefficient except for the year 1999.[1] However, the corrected estimates of inequality have actually shown a rising trend since the period 1993–94 and 1999–2000 (Deaton and Dreze 2002; Sundaram and Tendulkar 2003; Sen and Himanshu 2005).

To ascertain the extent of inequality, it is pertinent to examine the extent of poverty that prevailed in the country. Sen (1974) argued that poverty and inequality are intimately correlated. He postulated that higher levels of inequality tend to be positively correlated with a higher level of poverty. Thus, the poverty estimates can unravel the aspects of relative income inequality. An early attempt was made to provide estimates on poverty by Ahluwalia (1978) and Minhas (1974). Both the studies provided estimates for the population living below poverty line for the year 1956–57 that was as high as 54.1 per cent according to Ahluwalia and 65 per cent according to Minhas. The poverty estimates started declining at a sharp rate between the period 1956–57 and 1960–61 and reversed thereafter showing a U-shape relationship (Ahluwalia 1978). Minhas's estimates showed a consistently declining trend from 1956–57 to 1967–68. It is significant that the proportion of population below the poverty line was 56.5 per cent in 1967–68 according to Ahluwalia's estimates and it was 50.5 per cent according to Minhas's estimates. Table 4.1 presents the distribution of a large sample of Indian population across different levels of income groups, keeping the official poverty line as the point of reference.

The sample households are divided into 'extremely poor', 'poor', 'marginal', 'vulnerable', 'middle income' and 'high income' groups if the monthly per capita expenditure (MPCE) of their households was below or above a specified multiple of the poverty line (PL).

Table 4.1 brings out very clearly the skewed distribution of income in the population. A very large share of the population of the economy can be described as poor and vulnerable. The percentage of population classified as 'poor and vulnerable', that had an average daily per capita consumption of ₹16 or US$ 1.8 in PPP or less was 836 million, accounting for 76.7 per cent of the population during 2004–05. The middle-income group consisted of 210 million people, accounting for 19.3 per cent of the population and the high-income group consists of 43.7 million people accounting for 4 per cent of the population. Over the period from 1993–94 to 2004–05 the share of population in the poor and vulnerable group had declined from 81.8 per cent to the current level of 76.7 per cent. On the other hand the middle- and high-income groups increased from 18.2 per cent to 23.3 per cent of the population.

Table 4.1: *Distribution of Population According to Levels of Poverty*

		Population Percentage Distribution		
	Poverty Status	*1993–94*	*1999–2000*	*2004–05*
1	Extremely poor	11.5	8.7	6.4
2	Poor	19.2	17.3	15.4
3	Marginal	18.8	19.9	19
4	Vulnerable	32.4	34.8	36
5	Middle income	15.5	16.7	19.3
6	High income	2.7	2.6	4
7	Extremely poor and poor (1+2)	30.7	26.1	21.8
8	Marginal and vulnerable (3+4)	51.2	54.7	55
9	Poor and vulnerable (7+8)	81.8	80.7	76.7
10	Middle and high income (5+6)	18.2	19.3	23.3
11	All	100	100	100

Source: Sengupta et al. (2008).

Inter-regional inequality

Being a large country of continental size and more diverse than most continents, balanced regional development has been upheld as a major aspect of India's innovation system. Hence, soon after independence there was narrowing down of regional disparities in per capita income till the mid-1960s (Nair 1982; Mathur 1983). The interstate variations in the per capita Net State Domestic Product (NSDP) declined during the period 1950–51 to 1964–65 (Table 4.1). The coefficient of variation of per capita NSDP declined from 26.7 to 19.6. This decline in the regional variation occurred mainly due to the extension of agriculture to all regions of the country. Moreover, the regions that gained their growth impetus from the colonial relations lost their prominence. This was also a period of slow economic growth in the country.

However, there is a rising trend of regional disparities from the mid-1960s till date. The Coefficient of Variation (CV) of per capita NSDP increased from 19.6 in 1964–65 to 30.2 in 1980–81 (Table 4.2). One of the important reasons for this trend of rising regional disparity could be attributed to the regionally concentrated agricultural growth under the green revolution. High-yielding variety seeds, intensive cultivation, technological upgradation, and land consolidation in the northwestern regions of India, namely, Punjab, Haryana and Western Uttar Pradesh led to a higher growth of agriculture in the region in the 1960s and 1970s. Green revolution technology and the agricultural innovation system governed interstate income disparities since

Table 4.2: *Inter-state Variations in per capita SDP: Coefficient of Variation*

	CV at 1960-61 Prices	*CV at 1970–71 Prices*	*CV at 1980–81 Prices*
1950–51	26.7		
1955–56	23.5		
1960–61	24.2		
1964–65	19.6		
1965–66	24.6		
1970–71	24.7		
1975–76	27.2	28.23	
1980–81	30.2	31.35	
1980–81 to 1982–83			30.66
1985–86 to 1987–88			32.59
1990–91 to 1992–93			34.62
1995–96 to 1997–98			36.59
1998–99 to 2000–2001			37.99
2009–10*			39.74

Source: Mathur (1994, 2005).
Notes: *Own estimate based on National Accounts statistics.

the mid-1960s to the late 1980s (Hanumantha Rao 1975; Banerjee and Ghosh 1988). The rise in the production and productivity in the northern Indian states was the contribution of the research and extension system developed by the state and union government along with supporting institutional infrastructure such as minimum support price, procurement system of food grains by the central government agencies and agricultural credit system.

By the mid-1980s the regional disparity in agricultural productivity and growth declined. However, by the time the service sector became the harbinger of national economic growth, the regional disparities in economic growth got reflected through the changes in the growth patterns in services sector. The information technology sector and the allied sectors, trade and transportation, business services, construction, etc. became the prime growing sectors. Much of these growth sectors were regionally concentrated in the southern states of the country and the large metropolitan and mega cities. These factors furthered the regional divide in the country. Along with it came the investment and trade liberalisation, privatisation and delicensing of industrial activity. Even Foreign Direct Investment (FDI) was concentrated in economically more advanced regions and thus aggravated regional inequality. As most of the regulatory provisions that worked for regional balance were done away with, regional divides got accentuated. These factors led to the unabated rise in regional disparity after the 1980s till date. The CV increased from 30.6 in the triennium 1980–83 to 38 in triennium 1998–01 and the available evidence suggests that the trend continued thereafter (see Table 4.2).

Social disparity

The traditional institutions of social stratification and discrimination, which had been passed on through many millennia still continue to hold sway despite varied social sector innovations. In India the socially challenged and oppressed groups have been identified in the constitution into three different groups. These groups are the Scheduled Castes (SC), Scheduled Tribes (ST) and Other Backward Castes (OBC). The Scheduled Castes and Tribes were to enjoy protected political representation as envisaged in the constitution drafted in 1947 for a period of 10 years, led by Dr B. R. Ambedkar. Subsequently the 'reservation' policy in political representation has continued till now and it has been extended to the spheres of public education and public employment. The OBCs consisting of socially and economically backward groups have also been awarded reservation through constitutional provision.

As per the latest census (Government of India 2001a) for which detailed data is available, the share of Scheduled Castes in the population is 16.2 per cent (166 million people), while that of Scheduled Tribes is 8.2 per cent (84 million). However, there are wide variations in the regional distribution of the SC and ST population. For instance, Punjab has an ST population of 29 per cent, while Mizoram has only less than 0.05 per cent. The Indian population is also stratified on the basis of religion. The distribution of population on the basis of major religious groups is as follows: Hindus 80.5, Muslims 13.4, Christians 2.3, Sikhs 1.9, others 1.9 per cent. A substantial share of these ST and SC groups were previously accounted for as part of the Hindu religion. But subsequently the discriminatory practices in the religion have persuaded many to convert to other religious orders. However, many studies show that most practices and rituals associated with caste hierarchy continue to be practiced in other religious groups even after conversion.

Disparity in capacity building

Mohanty (2006) shows that in the rural areas, among the Scheduled Tribes, nearly 58 per cent were illiterates, among SCs this number was 53 per cent, and among OBCs it was 45 per cent. On the other hand, in the rest of the population the rate of illiteracy was much lower at 32 per cent, and if we take only upper-caste Hindus it came further down to 18 per cent. In the urban areas the illiteracy rates in general are lower than the rural areas yet the disparity in illiteracy rates are very visible in the urban areas as well. While among the STs the illiteracy rate was 30 per cent, this rate was 39 per cent among the SC population. Among OBCs, the illiteracy rate was less at 25 per cent and among others it was only 14 per cent. The upper-caste Hindus, on the other hand, had a substantially lower illiteracy rate at 3 per cent. This disparity in literacy rates is visible in the case of educational completion and educational dropout rates as well. The rate of educational dropouts is much higher for SC, STs and OBCs in comparison to the other groups both in the rural and urban areas.

The caste-based discrimination manifests not only at the lower levels of education, but in the highest levels of education. The share of graduates of SCs, STs and OBCs in all disciplines is found to be much smaller as a proportion to their population share (Table 4.3), whereas

Table 4.3: *Sample Number and Proportion of Persons with Graduate Degrees, National Sample Survey Organisation (1999–2000)*

Castes and Communities	*Number and Percentage Share of Graduates in Various Disciplines in the Sample*								*Caste/Community Share of Total Urban Population%*
	Agriculture		*Engineering*		*Medicine*		*Other Subjects*		
Hindu ST	26	2.4	18	1.3	10	1.8	229	1.3	2.6
Hindu SC	41	3.8	30	2.2	10	1.8	629	3.6	12.9
All Muslim	101	9.4	68	5.0	54	10.0	1,006	5.7	17.0
Hindu OBC	108	10.0	202	14.9	56	10.4	2,402	13.7	24.2
Hindu UC	669	62.1	908	66.8	350	65.3	11,529	65.9	36.9
All Christian	90	8.4	70	5.2	35	6.6	707	4.0	2.8
All Sikh	18	1.7	30	2.2	11	2.1	419	2.4	1.6
All others	25	2.4	33	2.4	10	1.9	581	3.3	2.0
Total	1,078	100.0	1,359	100.0	535	100.0	17,501	100.0	100.0

Source: Deshpande (2006).

the Hindu upper castes have a much higher share of graduates as a proportion to their population share. Similarly, among various communities the Muslim community has a much lower share of graduates as a proportion to their population share, while all other minority communities such as Christians, Sikhs and others have a higher share of graduates than their population share. The observed social inequity shows up even after a long history of social sector innovations in terms of job reservations, academic entry reservations, educational subsidies, etc. to support the SC and ST groups since the early 1950s.

The discrimination in educational attainment manifests in the returns to skill as well. Madheswaran and Attwell (2007) estimated the Mincerian earnings function and showed that the rates of return to investment in education for SC/STs is considerably lower than for others. They conclude that a major share of the earnings differential between SC/ST and others is due to differences in human capital endowments, while about 15 per cent is due also to discrimination in the marketplace. It is a well-acknowledged fact that caste-based discrimination is occurring even after education has been attained from elite educational institutions. Chakravarty and Somanathan (2008) find that graduates belonging to Scheduled Castes or Scheduled Tribes get significantly lower wages (19 per cent lower in domestic jobs and 35 per cent lower when foreign jobs are included) than those in the general category. This difference seems to be mainly propelled by the weaker academic performance of SC and ST candidates.

Gender-based discrimination

The entrenchment of traditional institutions of patriarchy has created deeply rooted discriminatory practices towards women and girls in India. Similar to the disadvantaged communities and castes, women are a disadvantaged group in India. Gender-based discrimination is visible in every aspects of life in India. The gender ratio in India as per the latest census in 2001 was 933 per thousand males. This was 971 in 1901. The decline in the gender ratio is also attributed mostly to discriminatory practices such as female infanticide, female foeticide and practices of dowry. The new innovations both in diagnostic system and medicines have adversely affected the gender ratio due to gender-related selected abortions.

The literacy rate among women increased from 30 per cent in 1981 to 54 per cent in 2001 and further to 64.5 per cent in 2011. However, even in 2011, the gender gap was of the order of 0.79, i.e. the female literacy rate was only 79 per cent that of the male literacy rate. Nevertheless, on the optimistic side, the gender gap in literacy rates declined during the period 1981 to 2011.

The gender gap in school enrolment especially at the upper primary level is considerable though it has been declining. In 1980–81 the enrolment of girls (28.6) at the upper primary level was only a little over half of that of boys (see Table 4.4) As we move to the terminal year (2005–06) for which data is available, the enrolment of girls increased to over 66 per cent but remains lower than that of boys which is also at a lower level of 75 per cent.

Table 4.4: *Gross Enrolment Ratios (GER) of All Categories of Students*

	Primary (I–V)		*Upper Primary (VI–VIII)*	
Year	*Male*	*Female*	*Male*	*Female*
1980–81	95.8	64.1	54.3	28.6
1990–91	94.8	71.9	80.1	51.9
2000–01	104.9	85.9	66.7	49.9
2005–06	112.8	105.8	75.2	66.4

Source: Government of India, Ministry of Human Resource Development, Selected Educational Statistics, http://www.education.nic.in/stats/Timeseries0506.pdf (accessed 16 November 2009).

The disparities in literacy and educational opportunities are also reflected in the earnings. The gender gap in wages is substantially high in both regular and casual employment, and also in rural and urban areas. In 2004–05 the wage level of females was only 62 per cent that of males for regular employment in rural areas while it was 71 per cent in the urban areas (Table 4.5). For casual employment the wage differential was worse than for regular employment. The female wage was only 59 per cent that of males in rural casual employment and the worst disparity was for urban casual workers, the female wage being only 58 per cent that of the male wages. However, among regular workers the wage disparity seems to be widening over the years.

Institutions, Innovations and Inequality

India's development experience in the post-colonial period has remained quite unique and challenging. In a context of multiple challenges of transforming a rural agrarian economy with low saving and investment capacity plagued by social and economic inequities, a

Table 4.5: *Female Real Wage Level and Disparity, Regular and Casual Employees (1983 prices)*

	Regular						*Casual*	
	Rural		*Urban*		*Rural*		*Urban*	
	Female	*Gender Wage Differential*	*Female*	*Gender Wage Differential*	*Female*	*Gender Wage Differential*	*Female*	*Gender Wage Differential*
1983	10.44	0.68	17.02	0.70	4.89	0.63	5.62	0.51
1993–94	18.9	0.67	27.2	0.81	7.31	0.68	7.78	0.57
1999–2000	24.88	0.67	35.1	0.84	8.39	0.64	9.27	0.58
2004–05	25.7	0.62	28.37	0.71	9.04	0.59	8.98	0.58

Source: Abraham (2007).

plethora of institutional interventions were taken up to address these challenges. These interventions broadly characterised the emerging innovation system in India. The innovation system that emerged was characterised by the focus on the state-sponsored development of an industrial base, especially the heavy industries and generation of technological capabilities by promoting R&D and transfer of technology for raising productivity and welfare with a greater role for the state. Such an innovation system driven by the state was expected to increase capital intensity and productivity in certain sectors and thus aggravate inequality by widening the gap between the traditional and modern economic activities. Therefore, in a democratic polity, it was realised by the political leadership at the conception stage that it will be difficult to sustain a heterogeneous social and economic structure. In what follows we highlight some of the key aspects of India's innovation system that helped address inequality under the early phase of state-driven innovation system and in the later phase of globalisation.

Phase I: State-driven innovation system for growth with equity

As already noted, at the time of independence India inherited a highly unequal society. The land revenue system in the country was aimed at creating and sustaining inequalities in asset ownership and revenue extraction.[2] Soon after independence of the country in 1947 the prevailing political climate was one that supported anti-colonial, anti-west and pro-socialist ideas, which had their roots in the bitter experiences of colonial exploitation during the pre-independence period. The rise of the erstwhile USSR and the communist/socialist bloc on the world map, being based on central planning and principles of self-sufficiency was seen as a viable alternative to the colonial model of dependent growth trajectories based on international trade. The elements of an innovation system formed within this broad rubric of the early period after independence are demarked in the following sections.

Industrial Technology Policies

Being a country that stood for establishing a socialistic pattern of society as laid down in the preamble of the Indian constitution, the various policy measures from time to time towards development of various sectors of economy underscored the need for ensuring that the growth does not aggravate, but instead mitigates inequality. While the genesis of India's innovation system could be traced to the pre-independence period, an innovation system in a narrow and national perspective could be considered as having its origin with the Science Policy Resolution (SPR) of 1958. Pundit Jawaharlal Nehru, the first prime minister of India, at whose instance the SPR was formulated, believed in the paramount nature of the state, distrusted business, had an abiding concern for the poor, and admired Soviet-style planning, which led to the establishment of Planning Commission and to its subsequent primacy in the Indian economic development.[3] Finally he had full faith in the capability of science and technology as a key to development.[4] Under Nehru, India embarked upon a journey of freedom with the avowed objectives of growth, prosperity, economic development, and equitable distribution of wealth (Nehru 1951), by harnessing, amongst others, the power of S&T. The firm belief in the role that science and technology could play to improve productivity, to generate employment for the growing population, for long-term economic growth and his unbending commitment to self-reliance led to a strategy of heavy industries-led industrialisation. The Industrial Policy Resolution (IPR 1948) thus explicitly stated that, 'meagre redistribution of existing wealth would make no difference, and a dynamic policy must therefore be directed to continuous increase in production'.

Though the issue of land reform remained a subject only for discussion, a number of policies were evolved over the years with a view to mitigate inequities at all levels, especially personal and regional. There was hardly any five-year plan that did not have a series of programmes designed to address the welfare of weaker sections. The concerted effort by the state towards achieving an equitable growth notwithstanding, prominent committees (Mahalanobis 1964; Hazari 1967) came out with disturbing evidence with respect to achieving equitable growth. While Mahalanobis pointed towards growing interpersonal inequalities, the Hazari Committee revealed that the licensing system as it existed in the country, though inadvertently, had been acting as an instrument of promoting industrial concentration and monopoly power. Responding to the findings of the Industrial Licensing Policy Inquiry Committee, the government, among others, appointed the Monopoly Enquiry Commission and its recommendations *inter alia* leading to the passing of Monopolies and Restrictive Trade Practices (MRTP) Act (1970). The MRTP was instrumental in regulating competition and restricting predatory market behaviour in the economy. Together, the MRTP and the licensing regime were able to restrain the growth of monopoly capital, while they also ensured balanced regional distribution and balanced size distribution of the Indian manufacturing sector.

FDI with Domestic Controls

The policy towards FDI, beginning with 1948 to the mid-1960s, was marked by 'cautious welcome' as evident from the Industrial Policy Resolution of 1948. Such an approach was further reinforced in the Prime Minister's Statement of 1949 on foreign investment that acknowledged the importance of foreign capital as a source of industrial technology for the rapid industrialisation of the country but called for carefully regulating the conditions under which they may participate in the national interest. As FDI was considered important, foreign investors were assured of treatment on par with the local enterprises, provided the repatriation of profits and compensation in the event of compulsory acquisition. But it was also laid down that as a rule, the controlling interest and ownership should be with the Indian hands. At that time the market for technology was not developed, therefore, foreign direct investment with majority Indian control was envisaged as a source of technology transfer from the developed countries. Foreign investment was in fact used as a strategic tool to fill the technology gap in the deficit areas.

From the mid-1960s to almost the late 1970s the policy stance was more restrictive. This needs to be viewed against the fact that by the mid-1960s the external balance of the country became highly unfavourable and FDI acted as a catalyst in the outflows from the economy *inter alia* in the form of transfer payments. It was to contain this outflow that the Foreign Exchange Regulation Act (FERA) came to being in 1973. FERA became the key to guiding controlled FDI inflows. FERA in effect discouraged many large transnational corporations (TNCs) to continue operations in India. This period thus witnessed the winding up of the operations of leading TNCs like IBM and Coca Cola in the country. These policies, needless to say, have had their effect on the size distribution of firms in the country. Moreover, these inequities were caused by the differences in the salary structure of domestic and foreign firms that resulted from public policy that has regulated the entry and operation of these foreign firms.

Promotion of the Public Sector

Given that the private sector was in its infancy and the commitment to prevent the concentration of income and wealth was given the highest priority, the innovation system envisaged the state as the prime mover of industrialisation. The Industrial Policy Resolution of 1948 reserved major sectors of the industry exclusively for the state, and reserved the right 'to intervene whenever the progress of the private sector is unsatisfactory' which the state seldom did. The underpinning of an equity-oriented import substitution strategy for technology development implied that while dependence on imported technology and capital was accepted, the policy made it clear that ownership and control, as a rule, would lie in the Indian hands as per the statement made by the prime minister in Parliament in 1949. The outcome of such a technology strategy was the establishment of a large industrial or capital goods sector dominated by the public sector. However, based on the sectoral studies by D'Mello (1985) on steel, Khanna (1984) on petrochemicals, Taybji (2000) concluded that though the public sector achieved a certain degree of innovation capacity, they were severely constrained by state support and consequently subjected to political vagaries. While the public sector achieved production capabilities, sometimes comparable to some of the developed countries, and helped to achieve a regionally balanced development, there was evidence to suggest that they were dependent substantially on foreign technological assistance, as shown by Joseph (1997) in the case of electronics, Mani (1989) with respect to telecom and Menon (1980) in the case of the fertiliser industry. This in turn undermined their ability not only to play the commanding role in industrial development but also to help foster an equitable society.

IPR Regime

The innovation policy is the home of one particular and specialised form of ownership, namely, ownership of intellectual property (Granstrand 2006). Based on a principle first established as part of the US Constitution, patent and copyright laws are one of the oldest forms of innovation policy, designed specifically to provide incentives for invention. As corporations have become the homes for most inventors, intellectual property has also become an important set of assets for firms. As the new technology remains under the control of the firm that invented it, the firm can charge monopoly prices for its product or services. These high prices or monopoly rents are considered as incentives for firms to innovate.

The Indian Patent act passed by the Indian Parliament in 1970 was one of the cornerstones of India's innovations system that facilitated indigenous technology development. Comprehensive and extensive, the Act aimed at protecting the nascent domestic industry, and was a role model for many developing countries. In the case of food, pharmaceuticals, pesticides, and other agrochemical products, the term of patents was shortened to five years from the date of sealing the patent or seven years from date of filing whichever was earlier. The Act had many interesting features, like adoption of process instead of product patenting, reduction in the number of years of patent protection, powerful compulsory licensing provisions, enabling state intervention in pricing of patented products and other features having their implications on the system of reward distribution and inequality. The mechanism of process patenting proved very effective for the development of pharmaceuticals which in turn had its direct bearing on the price of medicines and its access to poor, light engineering, industrial components and even chemical process equipment industry which has had its effect in terms of promoting the development of these industries even in the small-scale sector. Process patenting not only allowed the development of a unique competitive advantage for these industries but enabled the country to develop essential medicines and a medical care system that enabled the state to provide a healthcare system either at low cost or free of cost to the poor and deprived sections of society. Also, it prevented concentration of market power and profiteering by monopolists on the basis of their patent power.

Labour Market Institutions

Unlike most of the East Asian countries, since independence, India enacted and implemented a variety of legislations for protecting the labour of the organised sector from exploitation and ensuring their well-being. The traditional view of such legislation is that it protects labour welfare, but has an adverse effect of making the Indian labour market less flexible (Basu 1995). Employers prefer regulation-free labour markets to have flexibility in employing people, in paying them and in getting work out of them, solely with a view to cutting labour costs and enhancing profits. These aspects of labour market flexibility are bound to have their bearing on the distribution of income and earning by the workers.

In India employment flexibility is mainly circumscribed by the Industrial Dispute Act and the Contract Labour (Regulation and Abolition) Act; wage flexibility by legislations such as Minimum Wage Act, the Payment of Wage Act, the Bonus Act, and the Equal Remuneration Act; and work process flexibility by the Industrial Dispute Act and the Contract Labour (Regulation and Abolition) Act. Working conditions on the other hand are regulated by a host of labour laws like the Factories Act. In all, it is said that there are 52 central laws in operation dealing with some aspect of labour or the other. Labour market institutions facilitated the workers in terms of security of job and social security system very much required for the middle-class people, which have certainly influenced to some extent the reduction of inequalities and poverty.

Promotion of Small-scale Sector

Given the perceived role of the small-scale sector in creating large-scale employment and helping in promoting a regionally balanced development, small-sector development has been high on the agenda since the first Industrial Policy Resolution of 1948. The Industrial Policy Statement (1977) was epochal in the sense that it understood the fact that 'a technique of production not only generates certain incomes' but also determines the pattern of production. So the IPS (1977) recognised the relationship between technological choices and overall development. This policy is breathtaking in the range of areas covered from small-scale sector to pricing policy to appropriate technologies. It acknowledges that in terms of generation of employment, bridging of the rural–urban divide, growth of rate of investment and industrial output, the polices have performed well below expectations. The policy correctly diagnosed the problem that there was very little interaction between the agricultural and industrial sectors, which is important since only by a such a process of reinforcing interaction can employment be found for large numbers of the rural population who cannot be absorbed in the agricultural sector. The Statement on

Industrial Policy of 1978 was also important in the sense that it gave for the first time, adequate attention to the small (almost 25 per cent of the report was focusing on it), cottage, tiny industries considered very crucial in facilitating an equity-based growth.

Education and Capacity Building

The most important pillar of modern economic development and the national innovation system is the capability building of the workforce. The education system not only provides capable human capital for the demand generated in the productive activities but also acts as a tool of promoting equitable social structure. To fulfil the cherished goal of providing adequate trained manpower for the industrialisation of the Indian economy, the governments, both at the central and state level, made concerted efforts and generated educational infrastructure both in the rural and urban areas with a view to provide universal access to education. Education was provided free of cost at primary level and highly subsidised beyond primary level. However, the institutions of higher learning were instituted in the urban centres and that has impinged on the access to higher education for the weaker sections of society. But the state-led educational system at subsidised rates has facilitated the development of a middle class because of the absorption of the educated manpower in gainful employment opportunities created by the public sector and also in the organised private sector. It is important to note that elite institutions related to science and technology are mainly in the metropolis cities and low-quality education in the smaller towns and rural areas, creating a wedge between educational attainments of the workforce and consequently earnings differentials. This can be one of the major factors that allowed the inequalities to persist.

Yet another institutional intervention with bearing on inequality related to the establishment of a public distribution system for the provision of essential commodities both in the urban and rural areas. The public distribution system was developed to meet the challenge of scarcity of essential commodities which was mainly generated by the traders. The public distribution system not only helped in controlling food-related inflationary pressures but also proved quite useful in providing adequate nutrition and ensuring regular supply of food grains to the population. Inflation of essential items transfers income from the poor to rich usually generating inequitable distribution of income. Therefore, the public distribution system of essential commodities came as a handy tool for ensuring equity within the system. Apart from this, there were numerous institutional interventions like the progressive taxation system, nationalisation of banks that led to the ownership of major banks by the state, provision of priority sector lending, a variety of subsidies and welfare schemes that were used by the state to reduce poverty and inequality.

Phase II: Market-driven innovation system — growth for equity

In the context of the heightened euphoria created by the South East Asian tigers and the downfall of the Soviet Union leading to an erosion of confidence in central planning and state intervention in conjunction with a number of government committees calling for dilution of bureaucratic controls and regulations that stifled the economy, there were a series of initiatives that marked a move towards an innovation system driven by market forces. This involved, during the early phase, an internal liberalisation that aimed at making the industrial sector more competitive and efficient. The focus shifted from growth with equity to growth for equity wherein the emphasis was more on the creation of the cake rather than its distribution. The result was the series of economic reforms in the 1980s involving internal liberalisation and globalisation in the 1990s.

The reforms in the 1980s involved the removal of entry barriers through industrial delicensing, removal of restrictions on capacity expansion along with regularisation of the excess capacities created earlier, dismantling of price controls and expansionary fiscal policies to expand the domestic demand base. The 1983 Technology Policy Statement (TPS) aimed to step up the pace of technological change by developing new policy instruments. The basic objective set in the Policy Statement was to develop indigenous technology and ensure efficient adaptation and upgrading of imported technology appropriate to national priorities and resources. The policy highlighted the importance of building up human capital and of providing maximum gainful and satisfying employment to all strata of society, especially to women and the weaker sections of society, while harnessing their traditional skills and capabilities and making them commercially competitive. Given the context of increasing international competition and concern for the environment, the policy also underscored, among other things, the need to develop technologies which are internationally competitive, particularly those with export potential, and to reduce demand for energy, particularly from non-renewable sources, and ensure harmony with the environment (Joseph and Abrol 2009).

Some of the initiatives under the Technology Policy Statement of 1983 included the Programme Aimed at Technological Self-reliance (PASTER), now known as the Technology Development and Demonstration Programme (TDDP), which aims at technology adaptation by means of research, design and development work carried out by industry and overseen by experts from labouratories/universities, the Technology Absorption and Adaptation Scheme, the National Register on Foreign Collabouration, S&T for Weaker Sections, S&T for Rural Development and the Science & Technology Entrepreneurship Park (1984), along with financial institutions, state government bodies and academic institutions. Added incentives for in-house R&D and technology development were offered to industry, apart from setting up the Technology Development Fund (1987), by introducing a levy on all technology import payments (Gupta and Dutta 2005). Finally, a full-fledged Ministry of Science and Technology was set up in 1985, incorporating the earlier Department of Science and Technology (DST) and a new Department of Scientific and Industrial Research (DSIR) (Richardson 2002). During this period the DSIR also launched the scheme for granting recognition to scientific and industrial research organisations (SIROs) in the private sector.

One major innovation during this period was the introduction of technology missions to promote civil development of technological applications and dissemination thereof in society. Significant positive outcomes were obtained from these missions in terms of technology development and dissemination in the fields of telecommunications, oilseeds and literacy. Successful establishment of the rural telephone exchanges developed by C-DOT and improvements of almost 10 per cent in literacy are examples of what was achieved by technology missions. However, technology missions for societal development were no longer pursued consistently by the implementing agencies appointed by the government after 1991. India soon lost the momentum built up by these missions. The government failed to institutionalise this connection between S&T and development, particularly considering the need to consolidate the mission orientation emerging for societal development in the S&T agencies on the one hand and in the government line departments on the other. Therefore, after 1991 the policymakers in these agencies were also free to shift to projects that they believed to be far more consistent with the new goals of external liberalisation (Joseph and Abrol 2009).

During the early 1990s, in the context of an unprecedented crisis in the external sector, India embarked on a series of stabilisation cum structural adjustment policies heralding the beginning of an era of globalisation. The New Industrial policy 1991, abolished industrial licensing for industries, but for some select sectors, thereby signalling the end of planned development of the economy and placing its trust on the market to govern the phase and direction of industrialisation. The policy permitted automatic approval for foreign investment up to 51 per cent in a wide range of industries. With respect to the MRTP Act, the thrust shifted from governing the size, nature and direction of investments by business houses, to taking appropriate action in respect of monopolistic, restrictive and unfair trade practices.

Reforms in the trade sector included the progressive reduction in the customs tariff rates from peak rates of 150 per cent in 1991–92 to 45 per cent by 1997–98 to 25 per cent in 2003–04. In January 2008 these were further brought down to 10 per cent for most non-agricultural goods. The import licensing system has been dismantled and quantitative restrictions on imports have been phased out two years ahead of schedule. India has bound over 3,298 of the 4,701 (i.e. 70 per cent) of her tariff lines (at six-digit level HS classification). Of these 99 per cent of the bound lines have been bound at rates 40 per cent or lower. The applied rates are much lower than the binding rates for most of the products. All these policies have had the effect of heightened international competition, which had an adverse effect on the small-scale sector wherein the reservation and protection have been phased out over the years.

In the labour market, the reforms appeared far-reaching with its likely implications on inequality. The Factories (Amendment) Bill 2005, proposed to provide flexibility and safety to the employed women, and Amendment of Labour Laws (Exemption from Furnishing Returns and Maintaining Registers by Certain Establishments) in 1988 to simplify the procedure for maintaining registers and filing returns are under active consideration (Government of India 2006).

Routine inspection by labour officials has been curtailed in many states. The first step towards this direction was taken in 1994, which called for limiting the number of inspections of factories and establishments under various laws. Relaxations of various kinds have been allowed in the use of contract labour and in the hours of work in export oriented units and IT establishments (Anant et al. 2006). It is shown in some of the latest studies that contract labour as a percentage of employment in manufacturing increased from 7 per cent in 1984 to 21.6 per cent in 1998 (Bhandari et al. 2006). The Act bars use of contract labour in 'core' and perennial activities and regulates employment of contract labour in other activities. But in the wake of globalisation the nature of 'core' and 'perennial' activities has changed and greater flexibility in the use of contract labour is deemed to be necessary. It seems illogical not to allow an enterprise to employ workers on a non-regular, contract basis if the work that it carries out is not of a regular nature and varies in volume from time to time (Papola 2006).

Needless to say, the series of institutional interventions undertaken to influence technology, trade, industry, labour, finance, investment, and other sectors has had significant bearing, either explicitly or implicitly, on inequality. Their actual outcomes, however, need to be seen against the fact that the new policies were initiated over the fairly strong edifice built during the import substitution phase and being a democracy, the need for reforms with a human face continues to be the guiding principle in policy making. This in turn gets manifested *inter alia* in the National Rural employment guarantee act that ensured 100 days of paid employment to all the family below the poverty line in the country.

Co-Evolution of Innovation System and Inequality: Implications of a Shift from a State-driven to Market-driven Innovation System

Growth and distribution

During the first phase of India's development programme the innovation system was mostly driven by the state and fundamentally strived to achieve self-reliant growth under the import substitution regime like many other newly independent countries. This process allowed the Indian economy to initiate modern economic growth and as was expected, to face numerous problems. In terms of the driving force behind the innovation system, we could divide the period since development planning into two sub-periods, that is, 1950–51 to 1979–80 and the post-1980–81 period. During the first period marked by active state intervention in different spheres of the economy relating to production and distribution, including science and technology for fostering self-reliant development, the rate of GDP growth was 3.5 per cent (which is typically known as the *Hindu rate of growth* associated with the name of the late Raj Krishna). Per capita income increased at a rate of growth of 1.22 per cent during the first sub-period. This growth of GDP and per capita income has been regarded as meagre when viewed from the perspective of high-performing Asian economies, but quite respectable compared with India's colonial period growth. The low rate of growth notwithstanding, as we have noted in the previous sections, achievements in terms of reducing interpersonal and inter-regional inequality were commendable.

As we move to the second phase marked by a market-driven innovation system with greater role for the market, the recorded growth rate was amazingly high which can very easily be regarded as a departure from the Hindu rate of growth. The rates of growth of GDP and per capita income during 1980–81 to 2004–05 were 5.7 and 3.50 per cent per annum respectively (Table 4.6). As is evident from Table 4.6 the growth rate recorded since 2004–06 was still

Table 4.6: *Growth in GDP and Different Sectors of the Indian Economy (1950–51 to 2009–10) (1993–94 prices)*

Year	*Gross Domestic Product*	*Per Capita Income*	*Sectors*		
			Primary	*Secondary*	*Tertiary*
1950–51 to 2004–05	4.36	2.02	2.50	5.30	5.40
1950–51 to 1979–80	3.50	1.22	2.20	5.30	4.50
1980–81 to 2004–05	5.70	3.50	2.90	6.10	7.10
2005–06 to 2009–10	8.66*	6.94*	3.20**	9.30**	10.31**

Source: Estimates are based on Government of India (2007, 2011) and sectoral growth rates are taken from Nayyar (2008).

Notes: *stands for growth rates at 1999–2000 prices and **for growth rates at 2004 prices.

higher than what was recorded during 1980–81 to 2004–05. This high growth rate of both GDP and per capita income compared with the previous period has been essentially attributed to the success of the pro-market-oriented policies adopted by the Union Government of India since July 1991.

An important fact that needs to be noted here with regard to the long-term growth rate in the second half of the 20th century is that the structural break in the growth has occurred at the year 1980–81 and not at 1991–92. The stepping up of the rate of growth in the 1980s has been essentially attributed to the expansionary macroeconomic policies of the late 1970s and the 1980s and resulted into expansion of aggregate demand. These policies also stepped up the investment — GDP ratio rose from 18.7 per cent in the 1980–81 to 24.1 per cent in 1990–91.

While there are debates around the exact period of structural break in economic growth for India there is a broad consensus on the argument that the two broad periods of economic growth had taken place in the context of two different and contending regimes of institutional arrangements. While the earlier phase of state-driven innovation system characterised by command control and physical planning largely focussed on the question of distributional correction, with growth as a tool to achieve this distributional correction in the economy, the second phase of market driven innovation system that intensified free and open market orientation mainly remained focused on achieving a higher rate of economic growth, however, the issue of distributive justice was put on the back burner.

In the first phase of state-driven innovation system the choice of products, location and technology was aimed at enhancing growth in sectors and regions such that the overall distributional inequality was minimised. Moreover, the input and output markets were either monopolised by state-run enterprises or closely regulated by the state such that equity was maintained. On the other hand, in the second phase of market-driven innovation system the product basket, location and technology was largely determined by the signals from the market such that economic growth was maximised. Such a shift in the broad economic philosophy of the country was instrumental in altering the existing institutional arrangements or developing new ones that bolstered growth. The capital labour intensity in the organised industrial sector had grown during the period 1992–2001 at 4.39 per cent, much higher than the growth rate at 2.01 per cent (Virmani and Hashim 2009). The rise in the capital intensity had shifted the employment elasticity of output such that employment growth slowed down.

Even when the growth rates in the economy had been robust during the last two decades the growth rates in the employment had been weak. The employment growth during the period after liberalisation had been at the rate of –1.57 per cent per annum, while in the pre-liberalisation period it was 0.12 per cent per annum (Guha 2008). The slowdown in the employment and wage growth of the economy, as argued later, during times of high growth rates in output, is perpetuating class divides further, with the entrepreneurial capitalists garnering a large and increasing share of the value added, while the share of the workers has been declining substantially.

This decline in the share of the value added due to the declining wages and the number of workers in the production process has led to a tilting of the bargaining power of the workers. For instance, the number of workers in the registered trade unions in the country declined from a high of 7.4 million in 1997–98 to 6.9 million in 2001–02 (Government of India 2009). This has created substantial changes in the production relations and has embarked on an impoverishment of the working class. These changing dynamics of the political bargaining power of the workers vis-à-vis the employer, have led to newer modes of production, with greater subcontracting of work and contractualisation of existing jobs within the organised sectors.

Structural heterogeneity and inter-sectoral inequality

As the innovation system became increasingly integrated with the rest of the world, the high growth rate of the economy has been associated with a much skewed structural transformation. In 1950–51 the primary sector was predominant with 59.2 per cent of the GDP. But by 2004–05, it has been reduced to a marginal sector with a relative share of 22.14 per cent. The tertiary sector has emerged as a leading sector of the Indian economy and improved its relative share in GDP from mere 27.5 per cent in 1950–51 to 55.3 per cent in 2009–10 (see Table 4.7). The structural change that has occurred during the second half of the 20th century provides credence to the view that the engine of growth of the Indian economy is the 'service sector'. While there has been a structural transition from the primary sector to the tertiary sector, the secondary sector has remained at relatively low

Table 4.7: *Distribution of Gross National Product across Sectors*

Year	*Primary Sector*	*Secondary Sector*	*Tertiary Sector*
1950–51	59.20	13.29	27.51
1960–61	54.75	16.61	28.64
1970–71	48.12	19.91	31.97
1980–81	41.82	21.59	36.59
1990–91	34.93	24.49	40.58
2000–01	26.55	23.62	49.83
2004–05	22.14	25.24	52.62
2009–10	20.27	24.45	55.28

Source: Estimated from Government of India (2011).

levels. The manufacturing sector grew from 13 per cent in 1950–51 to 24 per cent in 2009–10. Thus the growth of the service sector in India occurred without strong forward and backward interlinkages with the domestic industrial sector. Similarly, the interlinkage between the agricultural sector and industrial sector had been very weak (Shand and Kaliarajan 1994). This is counter-intuitive to the traditional demand side (Fisher 1939; Clark 1940) or supply side structural change theories (Baumol 1967). The ongoing boom in the service sector mostly driven by external linkages (Joseph et al. 2009) is bound to widen the class divide within economies.

This becomes more evident when we analyse the sectoral distribution of the workforce using the census data which is available only up the year 2001. The primary sector of the Indian economy has been continuously absorbing the largest size of workforce. The workforce engaged in the primary sector was 72 per cent in the 1951 and has been declining thereafter at a very slow rate compared with income decline. The workforce engaged in the primary sector in the 2001 was nearly 57 per cent against the income share of 26.55 per cent. The secondary and tertiary sectors absorbed more of the workforce during the second half of the 20th century but their combined share remained below 50 per cent against the income share of 74 per cent (Table 4.8). The elasticity of factor substitution has clearly indicated the decline in the capacity of primary and secondary sectors to absorb more workers. While the service sector has been providing gainful employment to high skilled urban work force, the semi-skilled and low skilled workforce has been facing adverse employment conditions.

This inter-sectoral divide in the economy is creating a rural–urban schism wherein the rural agrarian sector remains stagnant without

Table 4.8: *Distribution of India's Workforce across Sectors*

Year	*Primary Sector*	*Secondary Sector*	*Tertiary Sector*
1951	72.10	10.70	17.20
1961	71.80	12.20	16.00
1971	72.10	11.20	16.70
1981	68.80	13.50	17.70
1991	66.80	12.70	20.50
2000–01	56.70	17.50	25.80

Source: Census of India (various years).

much interaction with the urban industrial sector. This in turn has increased the gap between the rural economy and urban economy. As shown by Himanshu (2010) the ratio of the urban to rural monthly per capita expenditure has increased from 1.50 in 1983 to 1.91 in 2004–05 implying a widening of the rural–urban per capita expenditure. This is also corroborated by the rural to urban ratio of the Net Domestic Product, which increased from 2.45 in 1970–71 to 2.89 in 1999–2000 as shown by Himanshu (ibid.).

Analysis of inter-sectoral wage differences indicated that while the wage differentials between the agriculture and manufacturing sectors have been declining over the years, the wage differential of these two sectors relative to the service sector is widening. Thus it may be argued that there was some evidence for widening inter-sectoral wage differentials, supporting the hypothesis that wage inequality in India is related to differential sectoral growth patterns.

The widening trends in wage inequality are mostly concentrated within the service sector, while wage inequality has declined between manufacturing and agricultural sectors. The widening wage differential between the manufacturing and service sector is probably a reflection of the service-oriented economic growth de-linked from the manufacturing sector. The emergence of export-oriented new technology sectors such as software industries within the service sector whose wage rates are probably the highest across all industries is crucial in pushing up the upper limit of the range of wage rate across industries. At the same time, distress in the agricultural sector due to declining productivity continue to push workers into the informal segments of the service sector widening the wage gap within the service sector.

This dichotomy in the development path of the Indian economy has generated another set of consequences, namely the rise of a large informal sector in the economy, engaged in diverse economic activities at very low levels of productivity and hence poor remuneration. The National Commission for Enterprises in the Unorganised Sector (NCEUS) estimated that nearly 85 per cent of the Indian establishments and more than 92 per cent of the workers are informal in nature. Moreover, the share of the informal sector is only expanding, rather than declining. A large share of the workers in the informal sector consists of agricultural workers. More than 50 per cent of the workers in the agriculture sector are self-employed workers working in their own farms, at subsistence level generating no marketable surplus.

Regional disparities in competence building institutions and production

During the last six decades, more than 1,300 science and technology institutions of varied size, scope and specialisations and 1,470 private and public sector R&D units have been established (DST 2006). These institutions and R&D units, which were established to provide necessary technological impetus, are mainly located in eight states, namely Andhra Pradesh, Karnataka, Kerala, Tamil Nadu, Maharashtra, Delhi, Uttar Pradesh, and West Bengal (Shukla et al. 2009). These institutions can be broadly classified on the basis of the sources of finance and come under the umbrella organisations such as central government, state government, non-governmental organisations, and university centres. The dominant form of science and technology institutions has been created and funded by the central government. The central government has been funding institutions that come under the Department of Atomic Energy, Council of Scientific and Industrial Research, Defence Research and Development Organisation, Indian Council of Agricultural Research, Department of Electronics, Department of Environment, Department of Science and Technology, Indian Council of Medical Research, Department of Space, and others. These institutions are being mainly housed by six major Indian states, that is, Andhra Pradesh, Delhi, Karnataka, Maharashtra Tamil Nadu, and Uttar Pradesh. The state of Maharashtra remained predominant so far as the location of centrally-funded institutions in the areas of basic sciences, medical science research, engineering research and agriculture research are concerned. The above analysis of science and technological infrastructure location by the central government agencies clearly brings out the fact that considerations other than equity seem to have played a dominant role in the establishment of institutions for capacity building in innovations.

The state governments have also made efforts to establish institutional infrastructure for innovation keeping in view the state-specific developmental priorities. It is important to point out here that agriculture is in the state list and therefore remained under the purview of the state government. However, some state governments have made substantial efforts to expend resources for making the appropriate institutional arrangements. It is important to note that five states — Tamil Nadu, West Bengal, Gujarat, Kerala, and Maharashtra — accounted for 60 per cent of the institutions established by all the states of India.

Another indicator of unequal distribution of state-wise support to extramural R&D projects sponsored by various funding agencies shows that out of the total number of projects (that is 2,718 in the year 2002–03) 70 per cent were allocated to institutions located in seven states (Maharashtra, Uttar Pradesh, West Bengal, Tamil Nadu, Karnataka, Delhi, and Andhra Pradesh). So far as project cost of these projects is concerned, these seven states have received 72 per cent of the total funds allocated by the various funding agencies (DST 2006). It can safely be argued here that institutional concentration appropriated a higher number of projects and finances and set the ball rolling for the operation of the cumulative causation process that perpetuated the concentration and centralisation of institutional infrastructure as well as economic outcomes.

The relationship between resources devoted for innovation activities are not only positively linked with the innovation outcomes but also highly correlated with generation of wealth and prosperity. Therefore, it is pertinent to analyse the extent of resources expended for development of science and technology infrastructure during the period 1958–59 to 2004–05. R&D intensity in India was 0.17 per cent in the year 1958–59. It steadily increased thereafter and touched 0.89 per cent in the year 1985–86. After achieving nearly 0.9 per cent, the R&D intensity dwindled to 0.85 per cent of GNP in the year 1990–91. In the post-liberalisation phase, the intensity of R&D declined sharply to reach a level of 0.71 per cent in the mid-1990s mainly because of the decline in public sector R&D expenditure (Joseph and Abrol 2009). Thus R&D expenditure could not keep pace with the fast rate of growth of the gross domestic product during the same period. Towards the late 1990s, the Government of India realised that over the four decades efforts of capability building in innovations suffered due to reduction of public sector knowledge power.

After six decades of independence, India could not reach the 1 per cent threshold level of R&D intensity, whereas the East Asian countries have surpassed even most of the European R&D intensity levels (Singh and Shergill 2009). An important feature of India's R&D expenditure is that the share of public sector R&D expenditure, which was more than 99 per cent in 1958–59, has continuously declined and was 79.19 per cent in the year 2004–05. However, the share of R&D expenditure of the state sector (by regional governments) and the private sector has increased steadily during the period under examination. These changes indicate that the R&D expenditure of India underwent profound structural transformation especially in the late 1980s and the decade of the 1990s.

The structure of R&D expenditure by fields of science is presented in Table 4.9. The relative priority of the public sector and private sector is evident from the field-wise allocation of expenditure by the public and private sectors and the changes therein over time. Public sector expenditure distribution shows that natural sciences were the first priority and expended 43.07 per cent of the total expenditure incurred in the year 1980–81. As per the distribution of R&D expenditure in 1980–81 it is evident that engineering and technology and agricultural sciences with 30.11 per cent and 24.48 per cent of the total expenditure were the second and third priority fields. It is important to note that medical sciences received meagre resources (2.34 per cent) in the year 1980–81 and subsequently medical sciences received somewhat similar proportion of resources but showed an upward trend in 2005–06. The private sector's priorities were different from the public sector. This can be ascertained from the higher proportion of resources that has been allocated to applied sciences, that is, engineering and technology, in the year 1980–81. The natural sciences and medical sciences received second and third priority. However, the agricultural sciences received least consideration in terms of allocation of R&D expenditure by the private sector. It is significant to note that both public and private sectors accorded priority to the engineering and technology in terms of allocation of R&D and consequently fast progress of information and communication technology industry both in terms of export performance and employment generation. The foregoing analysis of distribution of R&D expenditure across various fields of science over time enables us to argue that there has occurred a high degree of

Table 4.9: *Distribution of R&D Expenditure by Field of Science (percentage)*

Year	*1980–81*		*1990–91*		*2000–01*		*2005–06*	
Field of Science	*Public*	*Private*	*Public*	*Private*	*Public*	*Private*	*Public*	*Private*
Natural sciences	43.07	27.75	29.27	30.98	21.72	39.31	22.74	30.60
Engineering and technology	30.11	58.21	51.66	56.27	55.39	49.14	54.79	49.46
Medical sciences	2.34	12.40	2.24	8.20	2.97	7.95	5.06	14.80
Agricultural sciences	24.48	1.65	16.83	4.55	20.93	3.59	19.41	5.14
Total	100.00	100.00	100.00	100.00	100.00	100.00	100.00	100.00

Source: Department of Science and Technology (various years).

concentration of capability building efforts in the area of engineering and technology. Thus, the capabilities in the area of engineering and technology have been reflected in the high economic performance of the ICT industry, which recently re-articulate inequality across households and regions.

Concluding Observations

Our analysis of India's experience with inequality and the innovation system, as it evolved over the years, tends to provide credence to the observation by Cozzens and Kaplinski (2009) that the relationship between innovation and inequality is multidimensional and they co-evolve with innovation sometimes reinforcing inequalities and sometimes undermining them. The study observed different trends in different dimensions of inequality. While interpersonal inequality over the years has not aggravated, it has not mitigated to a satisfactory level; inequality across different regions and that between different social groups has increased. Nonetheless India appeared to be more equal today than its counterparts in BRICS countries, providing credence to the constitutional assurance for equity and social justice.

Analysis of the Indian experience further suggests that the extent to which the innovation system reinforced or undermined inequality was governed to a great extent by the forces that drive the innovation system. Thus, during the first phase of the evolution of India's innovation system, driven by the state with the declared objective of 'growth with equity', there were a number of institutional arrangements that helped to mitigate inequality. Achievements in the sphere of equality, however, turned out to be at the cost of growth. During the second phase of its evolution, wherein the innovation system was driven by market forces with a view to facilitate 'growth for equity', there appears to have been a tendency towards the weakening of institutions working for equity. Indeed there has been a remarkable turnaround in growth but at the cost of equity. This is not to argue that equity considerations are done away with, as there are fresh institutional interventions like the (now known as) Mahatma Gandhi National Rural Employment Guarantee Act to ensure 100 days of employment to at least one person in those families under the poverty line and a series of regulatory agencies in different spheres of economic activity. Moreover, the 11th five year plan (2007–12) and 12th five-year plan (2012–17) have been driven by the prime objective of inclusive growth.

However, a Commission appointed by the Government of India observed that about 76.7 per cent of the population in 2004 are 'poor and vulnerable' (with an average daily per capita consumption of ₹16 or US$ 1.8 in PPP or less). Under the globalised innovation system with greater play of market forces, the country has witnessed agrarian distress and farmers' suicides at a rate unheard of in history. The operation of the *free market forces* and non-delivery of essential services to the weaker sections of society have added to the misery and deprivation of these underprivileged people. It is important to note that in the year 2005–06 more than 40 per cent children were suffering from severe malnutrition, more than 46 per cent children remained unvaccinated, more than half of the births took place without the benefit of a skilled attendant and more than 52 per cent children dropped out before completing primary education. These statistics are just the tip of the iceberg. At the same time, India has the fourth largest number of billionaires in the Forbes magazine list after US, Germany and Japan. The challenge, therefore with the innovation system is to harness the market forces in such away as to facilitate growth while catering to the needs of the underprivileged section of society and generate essential capabilities that reduce inequitable outcomes in the society. How India's innovation system manages to ensure the delicate balance of growth with equity under a system that is driven by market forces is to be seen.

Notes

1. The estimate of gini coefficient for the year 1999 was based on a thin sample and consequently reduced inequality and poverty ratios substantially. This has led to the questioning of estimates based on thin samples.
2. In Bengal, for instance, despite rising prices the *zamindars* (land-owning classes) were able to hold the colonial government to the permanence of settlement. Correspondingly the zamindari incomes grew while the income of the cultivators remained stagnant. The additional income that the zamindars received were used for further securing the rights to collect revenues from the tillers (Sabharwal 1979).
3. Correspondence between Pundit Nehru and T. T. Krishnamachari, Pvt. Papers, NMML, New Delhi.

4. It also needs to be mentioned here that but for Pundit Nehru, the majority of the Indian political establishment was at best indifferent to science or at worst even anti-science. This led to the development of an axis between Pundit Nehru and a selected group of scientists, and the consequent development of Indian science in a particular direction. An examination of the rich and political relevant discourse regarding this period has been done by a bevy of scholars (for instance, see Krishna 1991; Babbar 1996; Osborne and Kumar 1999).

References

Abraham, V., 2007. 'Growth and Inequality of Wages in India: Recent Trends and Patterns', *Indian Journal of Labour Economics*, 50(4): 927–41.

———, 2009. *The Effect of Information Technology on Wage Inequality: Evidence from Indian Manufacturing Sector*. Centre for Development Studies, Trivandrum: Mimeo.

Acharya, M. and G. Puspa, 2005. 'Gender Indicators of Equality, Inclusion and Poverty Reduction Measuring Programme/Project Effectiveness', *Economic and Political Weekly*, 40(44–45), 29 October, 4719–28.

Aghion, P., E. Carli and C. G. Penalosa, 1999. 'Inequality and Economic Growth: The Perspective of the New Growth Theories', *Journal of Economic Literature*, 34(4), 1615–60.

Ahluwalia, M. S., 1978. 'Poverty and Agricultural Performance in India', *Journal of Development Studies*, 14(3), 298–323.

———, 2009. 'Growth, Distribution and Inclusiveness: Reflection on India's Experience', in K. Basu and R. Kanbur (eds), *Arguments for a Better World: Essays in Honor of Amartya Sen, Society, Institutions, and Development*, vol. 2. Oxford: Oxford University Press, 327–49.

Ahmed, M. and N. Bhattacharya, 1974. 'Size Distribution of Per Capita Personal Income in India: 1955–56, 1960–61 and 1963–64,' in T. N. Srinivasan and P. K. Bardhan(eds), *Poverty and Income Distribution in India*. Calcutta: Statistical Publishing Society, 167–82.

Anant, T. C. A., R. Hasan, P. Mohapatra, R. Nagaraj, and S. K. Sasikumar, 2006.'Labor Markets in India: Issues and Perspectives', in J. Felipe, J. and R. Hasan(ed.), *Labor Markets in Asia: Issues and Perspectives*. London: Palgrave Macmillan for the Asian Development Bank, 205–300.

Arvind V. and D. A. Hashim, 2009. 'Factor Employment, Sources and Sustainability of Output Growth: Analysis of Indian Manufacturing'. Working Paper (3)/2009-DEA, Ministry of Finance, Government of India, New Delhi.

Babbar, Z., 1996. *The Science of the Empire: Scientific Knowledge, Civilization and Colonial Rule in India*. Albany: State University of New York Press.

Bairoch, P., 1981. 'The Main Trends in National Income Distribution since Industrial Revolution', in P. *Bairoch* and M. Lévy-Leboyer (eds), *Disparities in Economic Development Since the Industrial Revolution.* London: Palgrave Macmillan, 3–17.

Banerjee, D. and A. Ghosh, 1988. 'Indian Planning and Regional Disparity in Growth', in A. K. Bagchi (ed.), *Economy, Society and Polity: Essays in the Political Economy of Indian Planning in Honour of Professor Bhabatosh Datta*, Perspectives in Social Sciences 3. Calcutta: Oxford University Press, 104–65.

Basu, K., 1995. 'Do India's Labor Laws Hurt Indian Laborers? A Theoretical Investigation', Working Paper #95-12, Center for Analytical Economics (CAE), Cornell University, Ithaca, NY.

Baumol, W. J., 1967. 'Macro-economics of Unbalanced Growth: The Anatomy of Urban Crisis', *American Economic Review*, 57(3), 415–26.

Bhandari, A. K. and A. Heshmati, 2006. 'Wage Inequality and Job Insecurity among Permanent and Contract Workers in India: Evidence from Organized Manufacturing Industries', Discussion Papers 2097, Institute for the Study of Labor, Bonn, Germany.

Chakravarty, S. and E. Somanathan, 2008. 'Discrimination in an Elite Labour Market? Job Placements at IIM-Ahmedabad', *Economic and Political Weekly*, 43(44), 1 November, 45–50.

Clark, C., 1940. *The Conditions of Economic Progress.* London: Macmillan.

Cozzens, S. E. and R. Kaplinsky, 2009. 'Innovation, Poverty and Inequality: Cause, Coincidence, or Co-evolution', in B.-Å. Lundvall, K. J. Joseph, C. Chaminade, and J. Vang (eds), *Handbook on Innovation Systems in Developing Countries*. Cheltenham: Edward Elgar, 57–82.

D'Mello, B., 1985. 'Jettisoning Indigenous Technology', *Economic and Political Weekly*, 20(8), 313–14.

Dasgupta, S. and A. Singh, 2007. 'Manufacturing, Services and Premature Deindustrialization in Developing Countries: A Kaldorian Analysis', in G. Mavrotas and Anthony Shorrocks (eds), *Advancing Development: Core Themes in Global Economics.* Hampshire: Palgrave Macmillan, 435–54.

Dastidar, A. G., 2004. 'Structural Change and Income Distribution in Developing Economies: Evidence from a Group of Asian and Latin American Countries', Working Paper (121), Centre for Development Economics, Delhi School of Economics, University of Delhi, New Delhi.

Deaton, A. and J. Dreaze, 2002. 'Poverty and Inequality in India: A Re-examination', *Economic and Political Weekly*, 37(36), 3729–48.

Department of Science and Technology, 2006. *Research and Development Statistics*. Department of Science and Technology, Government of India, New Delhi.

———, various years. *Research and Development Statistics*. Department of Science and Technology, Government of India, New Delhi.

Deshpande, S., 2006. 'Exclusive Inequalities: Merit, Caste and Discrimination in Indian Higher Education Today', *Economic and Political Weekly*, 41(24), 2438–44.

Fisher, A. G. B., 1939. 'Primary, Secondary, Tertiary Production', *The Economic Records*, 15(1), 24–38.

Government of India, 2001a. 'Census of India: Primary Census Abstracts', New Delhi: Registrar General of India.

———, 2001b. 'Census of India, General Economic Tables'. New Delhi: Registrar General of India.

———, 2002. *National Human Development Report 2001*. New Delhi: Planning Commission

———, 2006. *Economic Survey 2005–6*. New Delhi: Ministry of Finance.

———, 2007. *National Accounts Statistics*. New Delhi: Central Statistical Organisation.

———, 2008. *National Accounts Statistics*. New Delhi: Central Statistical Organisation.

———, 2009. *Statistics on Industrial Disputes, Closures, Retrenchments and Lay-Offs in India during the Year, 2007*. Shimla: Labour Bureau.

———, 2011. *Economic Survey*. New Delhi, Ministry of Finance: Government of India.

Granstrand, O., 2006. 'Intellectual Property Rights for Governance in and of Innovation Systems', in B. Andersen (ed.), *Intellectual Property Rights: Innovation, Governance and the Institutional Environment*. Cheltenham: Edward Elgar Publishers, Chapter 10, 311–43.

Guha, A., 2008. 'Evolution of Indian Organised Manufacturing Industrial Structure: A Comparison between Liberalised and Pre-liberalised Regimes', National Conference on Industrial Development and Economic Policy Issues, Institute for Studies in Industrial Development, 27–28 June, New Delhi.

Gupta, A. and P. K. Dutta, 2005. 'Indian Innovation System: Perspective and Challenges', *Technology Exports*, 7(4), April–June, 1–12.

Hanumantha Rao, C. H., 1975. *Technological Change and Distribution of Gains in Indian Agriculture*. Delhi: Macmillan.

Hazari, R. K., 1967. *Industrial Planning and Licensing Policy: Final Report*. New Delhi, Planning Commission.

Himanshu, 2007. 'Recent Trends in Poverty and Inequality: Some Preliminary Results', *Economic and Political Weekly*, 42(6), 497–508.

———, 2010. 'Urban Poverty in India by Size-Class of Towns: Level, Trends and Characteristics', mimeo, Centre de Sciences Humanes, New Delhi. http://www.csh-delhi.com/team.php?idstaff=111 (accessed 29 January 2010).

Jha, R., 2000. 'Reducing Poverty and Inequality in India: Has Liberalization Helped?' Research Paper 204, World Institute for Development Economics Research, Helsinki.

Joseph K. J., 1997. *Industry under Economic Liberalisation: Case of Indian Electronics*. New Delhi: Sage Publications.

Joseph, K. J. and D. Abrol, 2009. 'Science Technology and Innovation Policies in India', in J. E. Cassiolato and V. Vitorino (eds), *BRICS and Development Alternatives: Innovation Systems and Policies*. London: Anthem Press, 101–32.

Joseph, K. J., A. Vinoj and M. Hrushikesh, 2009. 'The Role of Service Sector in India's Economic Growth'. Paper presented at the 17th Seoul Journal of Economics Symposium, Department of Economics, Seoul National University, 16 October, Seoul.

Khanna, S., 1984. 'Transnational Corporation and Technology Transfer; Indian Petrochemical Industry', *Economic and Political Weekly*, 19 (31), 1319–40.

Krishna, V. V., 1991. 'The "Colonial Model" and the Emergence of National Science in India, 1876–1920', in P. Petteitecin, J. Catherine and A. M. Moulin (eds), *Sciences and Empires*. Dordrecht: Kluver Academic Press, 57–72.

Madheswaran, S. and P. Attwell, 2007. 'Caste Discrimination in Indian Urban Labour Market', *Economic and Political Weekly*, 41(41), 4146–53.

Mahalanobis, P. C., 1963. *The Approach of the Operational Research to Planning in India.* Bombay: Asia Publishing House.

———, 1964. 'Report of the Committee on Distribution of Income and Levels of Living'. New Delhi: Planning Commission.

Mani, S., 1989. 'Technology Acquisition and Development: Case of Telecom Switching Equipment', *Economic and Political Weekly*, 24(47), 25 November, M-181–M-191.

Mathur, A., 1983. 'Regional Development and Income Disparities in India: A Sectoral Analysis', *Economic Development and Cultural Change*, 31(2), April, 167–99.

———, 1994. 'Regional Development Disparities and Economic Reforms in India', in K. S. Dhindsa and Anju Sharma (eds), *Economic Reforms and Development*. New Delhi: Concept Publishing Company, 475–505.

———, 2005. 'Spatial Income Inequality and Economic Development', Paper presented at the National Seminar on Accelerated Economic Growth and Regional Imbalance, IEA, ISID and IHD, 16–18 September, New Delhi.

Menon, U., 1980. 'World Bank and Transfer of Technology', *Economic and Political Weekly*, 15(34), 1437–43.

Minhas, B. S., 1974. *Planning and the Poor*. New Delhi: S. Chand and Company Ltd.

Mohanty, M., 2006. 'Social Inequality, Labour Market Dynamics and Reservation', *Economic and Political Weekly*, 41(35), 3777–89.

Mutatkar, R., 2005. 'Social Group Disparities and Poverty in India', Working Paper Series No. WP-2005-004, Indira Gandhi Institute of Development Research, Mumbai.

Nair, K. R. G., 1982. *Regional Experience in a Developing Economy*. New Delhi: Wiley Eastern.

Nayar, B. R., 1983. *India'a Quest for Technological Independence: Policy Foundation and Policy Change I*. New Delhi: Lancers Publishers.

Nayyar, D., 2008. 'India's Unfinished Journey: Transforming Growth into Development', in *Liberalization and Development*. Delhi: Oxford University Press.

Nehru, J., 1951. *An Autobiography*. Moscow: Raduka Publications.

Nelson, R. R., 1994. 'The Co-evolution of Technology, Industrial Structure, and Supporting Institutions', *Industrial and Corporate Change*, 3(1), 47–63.

Ojha, P. D. and V. V. Bhatt, 1974. 'Patterns of Income Distribution in India: 1953–55 to 1963–65' in T. N. Srinivasan and P. K. Bardhan (eds), *Poverty and Income Distribution in India*. Calcutta: Statistical Publishing Society, 163–66.

Osborne, M. and D. Kumar, 1999. 'Social History of Science', *Science, Technology and Society*, 42, 161–70.

Pal, P. and J. Ghosh, 2007. 'Inequality in India: A Survey of Recent Trends', DESA Working Paper (45), United Nations Department of Economic and Social Affairs, New York.

Papola, T. S., 2006. 'Emerging Structure of Indian Economy: Implications of Growing Intersectoral Imbalance', *The Indian Economic Journal*, 54(1), 5–25.

Pradhan, J. and V. Abraham, 2005. 'Women's Status and Economic Growth', in S K. Thorat, J. P. Pradhan and V. Abraham (eds), *Industrialisation, Economic Reforms and Regional Development: Essays in Honour of Professor Ashok Mathur*. New Delhi: Shipra Publications, 295–312.

Rahman, A. and P. N. Chowdhury (eds), 1980. *Science and Society*. New Delhi: Council for Scientific and Industrial Research.

Rani, U., 2008. *Impact of Changing Work Patterns on Income Inequality*, Discussion Paper (193), Geneva: International Institute of Labour Studies.

Richardson, P., 2002. *New Science, Technology and Innovation Development in India*. Brussels: European Commission Directorate-General for Research.

Sabharwal, S., 1979. 'Inequality in Colonial India', *Contributions to Indian Sociology*, 13(2), 241–64.

Sen, A. K., 1974. 'Poverty, Inequality and Unemployment: Some Conceptual Issues in Measurment', in T. N. Srinivasan and P. K. Bardhan (eds), *Poverty and Income Distribution in India*. Calcutta: Statistical Publishing Society, 67–83.

Sen, A. K., 2005. *The Argumentative Indian: Writings on Indian History, Culture and Identity*. London: Allen Lane.

Sen, A. and Himanshu, 2005. 'Poverty and Inequality in India: Getting Closer to Truth', in A. Deaton and V. Kozel (eds), *Data and Dogma: The Great Indian Poverty Debate*. New Delhi: Macmillan, 306–70.

Sengupta, A., K. P. Kannan and G. Raveendran, 2008. 'India's Common People: Who Are They, How Many Are They and How Do They Live?' *Economic and Political Weekly*, 43(11), 15–21 March, 49–63.

Shand, R. and Kaliarajan, 1994. 'India's Economic Reform: Towards a New Paradigm', Economic Division Working Paper South Asia (1), Research School of Pacific and Asian Studies, The Australian National University, Canberra.

Shukla, R., N. G. Satish and P. R. Rao, 2009. 'Asymmetry in the Science and Technology Base and Its Bearing on Regional Development', *Margin-The Journal of Economic Research*, 3(1), 63–96.

Singh, L. and B. S. Shergill, 2009. 'National Innovation System in the Era of Liberalisation: Implications for Science and Technology Policy for the Developing Economies', MPRA Paper 15432, Munich University Library, Germany.

Sivasubramonian, S., 2000. *The National Income of India in the Twentieth Century*. New Delhi: Oxford University.

Soares, M. C. C. and J. E. Cassiolato, 2008. 'Innovation Systems and Inequality: The Experience of Brazil'. Paper presented at The Global Network for Economics of Learning, Innovation, and Competence Building System (Globelics), 6th Globelics Conference, 22–24 September, Mexico City.

Srinivasan, T. N., 1974. 'Income Distribution: A Survey of Policy Aspects', in T. N. Srinivasan and P. K. Bardhan (eds), *Poverty and Income Distribution in India*. Calcutta, Statistical Publishing Society, 369–96.

Srivastava, R. and S. Richa, 2006. 'Rural Wages During the 1990s: A Re-estimation', *Economic and Political Weekly*, 41(38), 23 September, 4053–62.

Subramanian, S. and D. Jayaraj, 2006. 'The Distribution of Household Wealth in India', Research Paper RP2006/116, UNU-WIDER, Helsinki.

Sukhadeo T. and K. S. Newman, 2007. 'Caste and Economic Discrimination: Causes, Consequences and Remedies', *Economic and Political Weekly*, 42(41), 13 October, 4121–24.

Sundaram, K. and S. D. Tendulkar, 2003. 'Poverty Has Declined in 1990s: A Resolution of Comparability Problems in NSS Consumer Expenditure Data', *Economic and Political Weekly*, 38(4), 25 January, 327–37.

Sutz, J. and R. Arocena, 2006. 'Integrating Innovation Policies with Social Policies: A Strategy to Embed Science and Technology into Development Process', Strategic Commissioned Paper, Policy and Science Program Area, IDRC Innovation, International Development Research Centre, April.

Tyabji, N., 2000. *Industrialization and Innovation: The Indian Experience*. New Delhi: Sage Publications.

United Nations Development Programme (UNDP), 2009. *Human Development Report 2009 – Overcoming Barriers: Human Mobility and Development*. New York: United Nations Development Programme.

Vaid, D., 2004. 'Gendered Inequality in Educational Transitions', *Economic and Political Weekly*, 39(35), 3927–38.

Virmani, Arvind and Danish A. Hashim, 2009. '*Factor Employment, Sources and Sustainability of Output Growth: Analysis of Indian Manufacturing*', Working Paper No. 3/2009-DEA, Ministry of Finance, Government of India.

5

Innovation System and Inequality Reduction in China

Xielin Liu, Shucheng Han and *Ao Chen*

China has made great progress in economic development and innovation in the last 30 years. But as social and economic inequality followed development, coping with them became a difficult and sensitive issue. By 2011, the Chinese government called upon its administration system to learn the capability of 'social management' in order to deal with the ever increasing social problems. In this regard, China has valuable experiences it can share with other developing countries.

This chapter explores the relationship between innovation and inequality in China. It analyses the patterns and trends of inequality, and shows that, in China, inequality increased as the country's economic development and social transition intensified. Taking into account the changing context of China's economic development, this study discusses the co-evolution of the national system of innovation (NSI) and inequality. It also reviews the process of economic development and emerging inequality, analyses why equality cannot be taking place in parallel with innovation, and tries to forecast the impact of innovation and inequality on harmonious society building in China.

Trends and Patterns of Inequality

China has experienced fast economic development and fast technological progress since the 1980s. It was considered a third-world country in terms of GDP size in 2008. The GDP per capita has increased from 100 US$ in 1978 to 3,000 US$ in 2008 (by PPP, this is about 6,000 US$) (Figure 5.1). While for a socialist regime equality is usually a key socio-economic goal, in China, after the country entered a transition to market economy, inequality quickly followed economic development. Since 1997, the seriousness of inequality in China has been increasingly recognised by the Chinese government. The government started to make great efforts to overcome inequality by, for example, promoting the so-called 'harmonious society' a society with more democracy, equality and stability, as one of the development goals defined in 2007 by the 17th political bureau of the Chinese Communist Party.

Figure 5.1: *GDP per capita (1978–2008) (US$ PPP)*

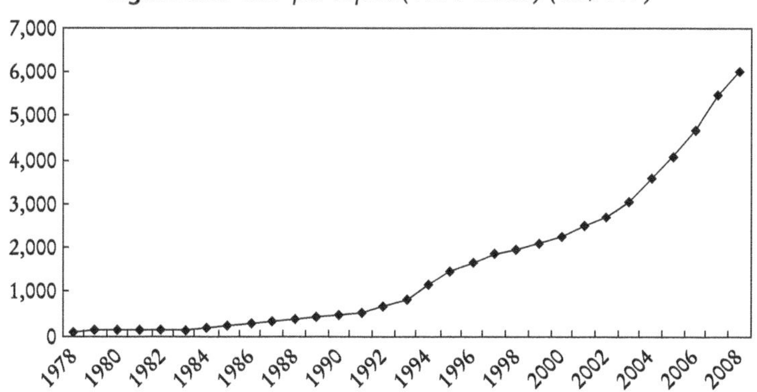

Source: National Statistical Bureau of China, *China's Statistical Yearbook* (various years).

History of Inequality in China

It is expected that China, as a socialist country, should establish more ways to balance development, innovation and inequality. Equality was the goal of socialism in China under Chairman Mao (Yang et al. 2009), but the planned economy did not bring to China the hoped-for welfare and competitiveness. Instead, China had been on the road to collapse politically and economically before 1978 (Chinese Communist Party Congress 1981). The breakthrough was made by Deng Xiaoping, the leader of the Chinese Communist Party since 1978, when he told China and the world that a market economy can be integrated with socialist ideology.

Through an open and market-based[1] reform over the last three decades, China has witnessed the finest period of economic growth and catch-up in modern Chinese history in terms of speed and stability. Economic growth continuously improves people's standard of living and increases consumption spending. China's per capita income has grown at an average annual rate of more than 8 per cent over the last three decades (Figure 5.2 and Figure 5.3).

Figure 5.2: *Per capita Consumption of Rural Households (1987–2006) (US$ PPP)*

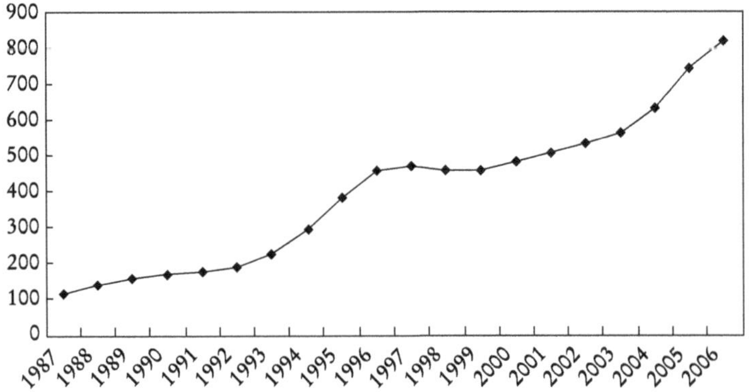

900
800
700
600
500
400
300
200
100
0
1987
1988
1989
1990
1991
1992
1993
1994
1995
1996
1997
1998
1999
2000
2001
2002
2003
2004
2005
2006

Source: National Statistical Bureau of China, *China's Statistical Yearbook* (various years).

Figure 5.3: *Per capita Consumption of Urban Households (1987–2006) (US$ PPP)*

3,000
2,500
2,000
1,500
1,000
500
0
1987
1988
1989
1990
1991
1992
1993
1994
1995
1996
1997
1998
1999
2000
2001
2002
2003
2004
2005
2006

Source: National Statistical Bureau of China, *China's Statistical Yearbook* (various years).

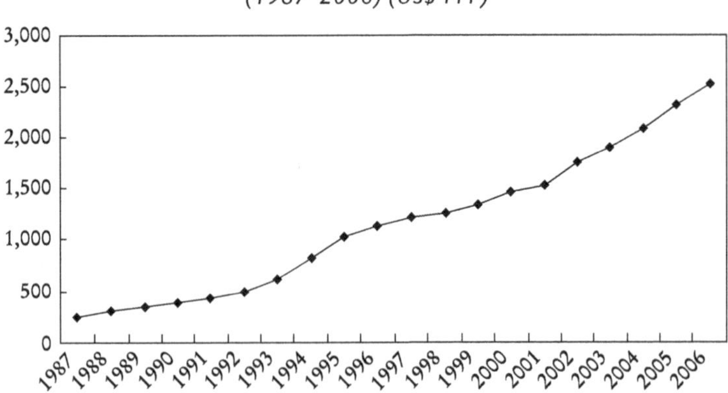

Rapid economic growth has been accompanied by sharp structural changes in the economy. Whereas the agriculture sector accounted for more than 30 per cent of Gross Domestic Product (GDP) prior to the economic reforms of 1979, by 2008 the share of agriculture in GDP had fallen to 11.3 per cent (Table 5.1). Industrial share in the national GDP started to decline after the early 1980s, but rose again to about 50 per cent in the late 1990s with nearly 58.6 per cent in 2008. In contrast to the agriculture sector, the service sector has expanded rapidly. The share of the service sector in the national GDP has increased from 13 per cent in 1970 to 22 per cent in 1980, and 40 per cent in 2008 (Table 5.1).

Table 5.1: *Changes in Structure of China's Economy (1970–2008) (percentage)*

	1970	*1980*	*1985*	*1990*	*1995*	*2000*	*2005*	*2008*
Share in GDP								
Primary industry	40.2	30.2	28.4	27.1	19.9	15.1	12.2	11.3
Secondary industry	56.7	48.2	42.9	41.3	47.2	45.9	47.7	58.6
Tertiary industry	13.1	21.6	28.7	31.6	32.9	39.0	40.1	40.1
Share in employment								
Primary industry	80.8	68.7	62.4	60.1	52.2	50.0	44.8	–
Secondary industry	10.2	18.2	20.8	21.4	23.0	22.5	23.8	–
Tertiary industry	9.0	13.1	16.8	18.5	24.8	27.5	31.4	–
Share of rural population	83.0	80.6	76.3	73.6	71.0	64.8	57.0	–

Source: National Statistical Bureau of China, *China's Statistical Yearbook* (various years).

The fast economic growth has dramatically reduced the absolute poverty level in China but relative inequality has been increasing since the 1980s. There are many reasons for inequality expanding in Chinese society, but the most important are the following three:

First, there is a large income gap between those employed in monopoly industries such as energy, electricity, financing, telecommunication, and those in competitive industries. Those industries usually were controlled by large state-owned enterprises (SOE) and their employees were paid much higher than that of other industries.

Second, Foreign Direct Investment (FDI) played an important role in the inequality process in China. Trade liberalisation and foreign investment have played important roles in shaping China's economy for the entire period of reforms. During the past two decades, China has attracted huge amounts of FDI inflows, and FDI firms have become an important element of the Chinese economy. The inflow of FDI created massive employment opportunities, which helped urban population growth, but also opened the gap between those employed by multinationals and those in other kinds of enterprises. For example, as most of FDI is located in east of China, it expanded the income gap between the eastern and western region.

Third, there are institutional inequality factors in China that have been set since 1948. One is the difference between urban citizens and rural farmers with the opportunity of development. In China, successive generations of farmers have been fixed to their land and have found it hard to transfer their jobs. The other differnce is between the eastern and western regions as having different resource endowment; this reduces development opportunities in the western part of China.

In reality, the inequality is increasing rather than slowing down in China, which in many ways is typical for a transition country. When entering market reform, the transition country aims to have better innovation capability, but in the process it often does not escape the trap of a widening inequality gap among various layers of society. Since China is a socialist country, it will be very interesting for policy makers to see how it balances innovation and the reduction of inequality.

Interpersonal inequalities

In China, the rapid economic growth parallels fast growing income inequality. China's Gini coefficient for household income was 0.21 in 1978, and reached 0.465 in 2005 (NBS 2006). The trend of widening income inequality is reflected in the increase of within-urban and within-rural inequalities, and the inequality between urban and rural sectors.

Between 1990 and 2008, urban income inequality increased by 10.5 points (from 0.175 to 0.280). While the share of income of top quintile in total income rose from 26.6 per cent to 32.6 per cent, the bottom quintile's share dropped from 14.4 per cent to 10.8 per cent. The middle class (middle three quintiles) also slightly suffered with the lapse, with its claim dropping by 2.3 per cent (from 58.9 per cent to 56.6 per cent). Figure 5.4 presents the trend of the official Gini coefficient for urban China from 1988 to 2005.

Figure 5.4: *GINI Indexes in Urban China*

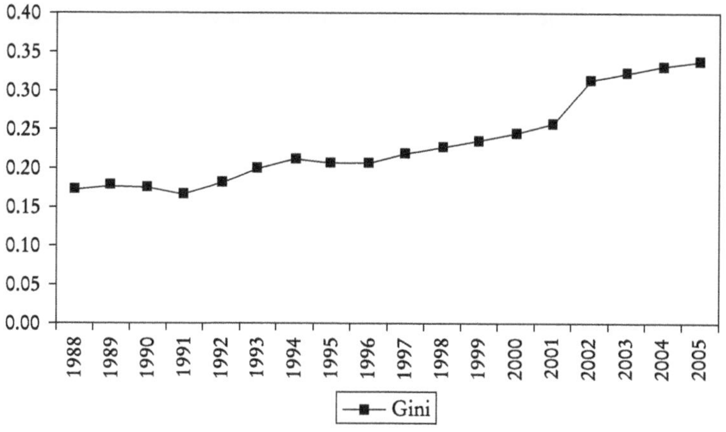

Source: Jin (2008).

Increasing income inequality does not occur only at the urban level, but also between the urban and rural sectors, which is the largest contributor to China's overall income inequality. Since the beginning of reform and the country's opening up, there has been rapid growth in the incomes of both urban and rural residents. In 1957, the population in China was 646.53 million, with 15.39 per cent living in the urban area. In 2008, the population is about 1.32 billion with 44.94 per cent living in urban areas. From 1978 to 2007, both urban and rural per capita incomes increased more than six-fold (NBS 2007). Figure 5.5 indicates that the growth rate of income of rural households since 1987 has clearly been lower than that of urban residents, and that the gap in absolute income between the two has been widening year after year. The difference in the absolute income between urban and rural residents rose nearly twelve-fold over the past 20 years. Because of the income inequality between urban and rural residents, the consumption gap between urban and rural residents also has been widening year after year (Figure 5.6).

Along with the income difference between rural and urban regions, the consumption difference is in evidence (Table 5.2 to Table 5.5). This consumption gap provides an indication of the huge latent market and product innovation potential that would become possible if the income level of the rural population is highly enhanced.

Figure 5.5: *Trends in per capita Annual Income: Urban and Rural Residents (1990–2007) (at variable prices, US$ PPP)*

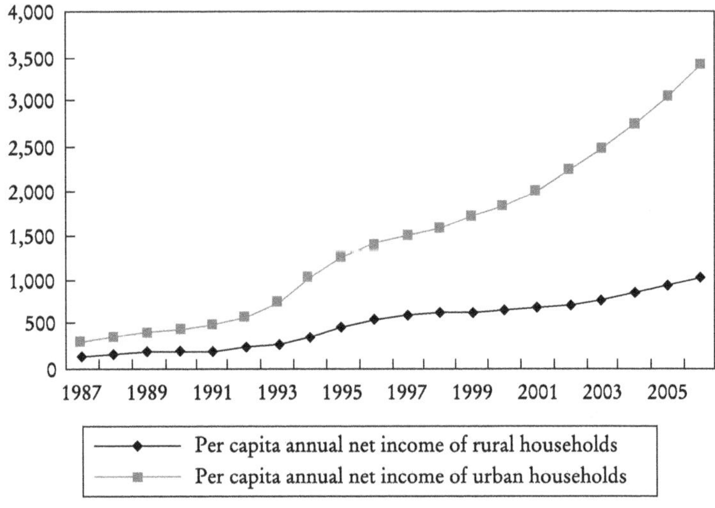

Source: Based on data of National Bureau of Statistics of China (2007).

Figure 5.6: *Trends in per capita Consumption of Urban and Rural Households (1990–2007) (at variable prices, US$ PPP)*

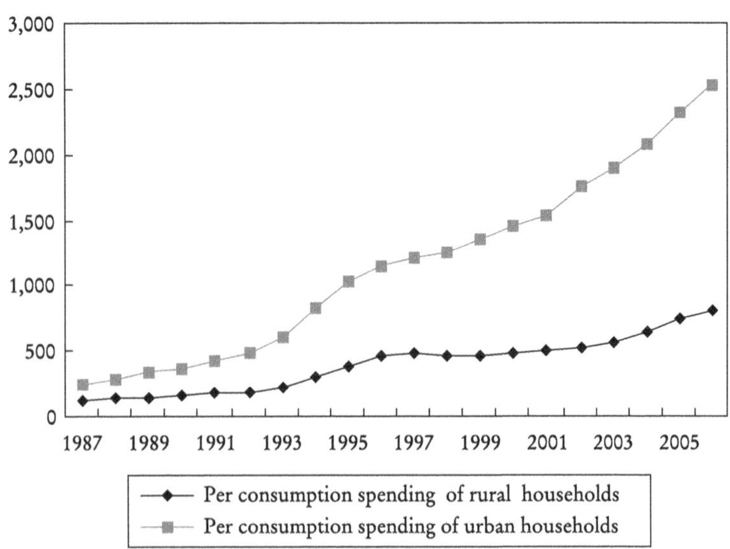

Source: Based on data of National Bureau of Statistics of China (2007).

Table 5.2: *Number of Durable Consumer Goods Owned per 100 Rural Households at Year-end*

Items	*1990*	*1995*	*2000*	*2005*	*2006*
Washing machine (unit)	9.12	16.90	28.58	40.20	42.98
Electric fan (unit)	41.36	88.96	122.62	146.35	152.08
Refrigerator (unit)	1.22	5.15	12.31	20.10	22.48
Air conditioner (unit)	–	0.18	1.32	6.40	7.28
Exhaust fan (unit)	–	0.61	2.75	5.98	7.027
Bicycle (unit)	118.33	147.02	120.48	98.37	98.74
Motorcycle (unit)	0.89	4.91	21.94	40.7	44.59
Telephone (set)	–	–	26.38	58.37	64.09
Mobile telephone (set)	–	–	4.32	50.24	62.05
Hi-fi stereo component system (unit)	–	–	7.76	13.00	14.29
Beep-pager (unit)	–	–	7.74	0.36	0.29
Black and white TV set (unit)	39.72	63.81	52.97	21.77	17.45
Colour TV set (unit)	4.72	16.92	48.74	84.08	89.43
Video-recorder (unit)	–	1.12	3.30	3.00	2.97
Radio cassette player (unit)	17.83	28.25	21.58	10.99	10.28
Camera (set)	0.70	1.42	3.12	4.048	4.18
Computer (set)	–	–	0.47	2.10	2.73

Source: National Statistical Bureau of China, *China's Statistical Yearbook* (various years).

Table 5.3: *Ownership of Major Durable Consumer Goods per 100 Urban Households*

Items	*1990*	*1995*	*2000*	*2005*	*2006*
Washing machine (set)	78.41	88.97	90.5	95.51	96.77
Refrigerator (set)	42.33	66.22	80.1	90.72	91.75
Air conditioner (unit)	0.34	8.09	30.8	80.67	87.79
Exhaust fan (unit)	–	34.47	54.1	67.93	69.78
Motorcycle (unit)	1.94	6.29	18.8	25	25.3
Telephone (set)	–	–	–	94.4	93.3
Mobile telephone (unit)	–	–	19.5	137	152.88
Colour television set (set)	59.04	89.79	116.6	134.8	137.43
Video-recorder (set)	–	18.19	20.1	15.49	15.08
System (set)	–	10.52	22.2	28.79	29.05
Camera (set)	19.22	30.56	38.4	46.94	47.99
Video camera (set)	–	–	1.3	4.32	5.11
Video disc player (set)	–	–	37.5	68.07	70.15
Water heater for shower (unit)	–	30.05	49.1	72.65	75.13
Computer (set)	–	–	9.7	41.52	47.2
Microwave oven (unit)	–	–	17.6	47.61	50.61
Health equipment (set)	–	–	3.5	4.68	5
Automobile (unit)	–	–	0.5	3.37	4.32

Source: National Statistical Bureau of China, *China's Statistical Yearbook* (various years).

The continuous widening of the urban–rural income gap was also manifested in the concentration of high-income residents in urban areas and poor people in rural areas. According to the data from an income survey conducted in 2002 by the Institute of Economics under the Chinese Academy of Social Sciences, urban and rural residents accounted for 93 per cent and 7 per cent respectively of the highest income decile nationwide, and 1.3 per cent and 98.7 per cent respectively of the lowest income decile. This is an exceptionally sharp contrast.

Comparing Tables 5.2 and 5.3, one can find that several goods, such as washing machines, refrigerators and colour TVs, have a higher diffusion rate in urban than in rural households.

Comparing Table 5.4 with 5.5, we can see that there is no significant difference in the daily needs between rural and urban households. The big gap lies in nutrition-related products, such as milk, aquatic products (including fish and sea food) and fruits.

Table 5.4: *Per capita Consumption of Major Foods by Rural Households (kg)*

Items	*1990*	*1995*	*2000*	*2005*	*2006*
Grain (unprocessed)	262.08	256.07	250.23	208.85	205.62
Wheat	80.03	81.11	80.27	68.44	66.11
Rice	134.99	129.19	126.82	113.36	111.93
Soybeans	–	2.28	2.53	1.91	2.09
Fresh vegetables	134.00	104.62	106.74	102.28	100.53
Edible oil	5.17	5.80	7.06	6.01	5.84
Vegetable oil	3.54	4.25	5.45	4.90	4.72
Meats, poultry and processed products	12.59	13.42	18.30	22.42	22.31
Pork	10.54	10.58	13.28	15.62	15.46
Beef	0.40	0.36	0.52	0.64	0.67
Mutton	0.40	0.35	0.61	0.83	0.90
Poultry	1.25	1.83	2.81	3.67	3.51
Eggs and processed products	2.41	3.22	4.77	4.71	5.00
Milk and processed products	1.10	0.60	1.06	2.86	3.15
Aquatic products	2.13	3.36	3.92	4.94	5.01
Sugar	1.50	1.28	1.28	1.13	1.09
Liquor	6.14	6.53	7.02	9.59	9.97
Fruits and processed products	5.89	13.01	18.31	17.18	19.09
Nuts and processed products	–	0.13	0.74	0.81	0.89

Source: National Statistical Bureau of China, *China's Statistical Yearbook* (various years).

Table 5.5: *Per capita Annual Purchases of Major Commodities of Urban Households (kg)*

Items	*1990*	*1995*	*2000*	*2005*	*2006*
Grain	130.72	97.00	82.31	76.98	75.92
Fresh vegetables	138.70	116.47	114.74	118.58	117.56
Edible vegetable Oil	6.40	7.11	8.16	9.25	9.38
Pork	18.46	17.24	16.73	20.15	20.00
Beef and mutton	3.28	2.44	3.33	3.71	3.78
Poultry	3.42	3.97	5.44	8.97	8.34
Fresh eggs	7.25	9.74	11.21	10.40	10.41
Aquatic products	7.69	9.20	11.74	12.55	12.95
Milk	4.63	4.62	9.94	17.92	18.32
Fresh melons and fruits	41.11	44.96	57.48	56.69	60.17
Nuts and kernels	3.21	3.04	3.30	2.97	3.03
Liquor	9.25	9.93	10.01	8.85	9.12
Coal	206.04	129.52	128.07	84.01	70.91

Source: National Statistical Bureau of China, *China's Statistical Yearbook* (various years).

The widening income gap between urban and rural areas depends to a large extent on the growth of rural household income. This is because the income growth in urban households has always been high, largely in step with the macroeconomic growth rate, while the growth of rural household income is basically fixed to sales of farm products and farmers' opportunity to work outside their place of origin. As the 'world's factory', the manufacturing and service industries in China have a much higher growth rate than that of the primary sectors. At the same time, the income of rural households depends on the price of primary goods. When the price of farm products goes up, rural income increases and the urban–rural income gap becomes smaller. If the prices of farm products remain unchanged or decline, the urban–rural income gap will widen. In addition, if farmers receive less income from farming, they can make up for the loss by taking up non-farm occupations; but if farmers face restrictions on working elsewhere, or if alternative occupations are insufficient to cover the decline in the income from farming, rural incomes inevitably drop.

The income distribution among different groups was polarized during the 1985–2000 period. The highest income group was earning a higher and higher share of the total national income, and the lowest income group's income was declining. In Table 5.6, we can find that income gap between the poor and the rich became larger during the 1985–2000 period.

Table 5.6: *Income Distribution in China during 1985–2000*

	Household Group by Income Level							
	Bottom 10%	*Second 10%*	*Third 20%*	*Middle 20%*	*Fifth 20%*	*10% Next to Top 10%*	*Top 10%*	*Ratio of Top 10% to Bottom 10%*
1985	5.65	7.07	16.37	19.05	22.29	13.08	16.49	2.92
1986	5.51	7.04	16.37	19.09	22.35	13.02	16.63	3.02
1987	5.59	6.98	16.34	19.04	22.26	13.03	16.77	3.00
1988	5.41	6.83	16.09	19.00	22.35	13.22	17.10	3.16
1989	5.32	6.76	15.96	18.90	22.36	13.21	17.50	3.29
1990	5.34	6.80	16.05	18.97	22.42	13.26	17.17	3.22
1991	5.60	6.97	16.28	19.02	22.25	13.03	16.85	3.01
1992	5.18	6.67	15.89	18.89	22.41	13.30	17.66	3.41
1993	4.91	6.36	15.31	18.48	22.52	13.71	18.72	3.82
1994	4.66	6.15	15.05	18.38	22.66	13.95	19.14	4.11
1995	4.81	6.27	15.21	18.50	22.57	13.77	18.86	3.92
1996	4.81	6.27	15.16	18.50	22.64	13.81	18.81	3.91
1997	4.57	6.06	14.92	18.41	22.74	14.03	19.27	4.22
1998	4.44	5.92	14.72	18.34	22.83	14.11	19.64	4.43
1999	4.33	5.78	14.45	18.26	22.87	14.29	20.01	4.60
2000	4.08	5.59	14.21	18.13	23.02	14.50	20.46	5.02

Source: Zeng and Hu (2008).

According to the Social Blue Book 2006 (Ru et al. 2005), the average per capita disposable income of the top 10 per cent of the population is more than eight times that of the bottom 10 per cent. Besides, the total wealth of the top 10 per cent accounts for half of the total wealth owned by urban and rural residents, while that of the poorest 10 per cent accounts for only 1 per cent.

Table 5.7 gives a group of income sampling data by the National Statistics Bureau. In 1995, the annual disposable income of China's 10 per cent of households with the highest income per capita was 3.92 times of that of the 10 per cent of households with the lowest income per capita. It rose to 5.39 times in 2001, and 9.18 times in 2005 (NBS 2006).

Inter-regional inequalities

Economic progress has also been accompanied by growing inter-regional inequality in China. During 1979–2008, China's real per capita GDP increased more than eight-fold, registering an average

Table 5.7: *Income and Expenditure per capita for the Highest Income Group and the Lowest Income Group in Urban Unit: RMB*

Items	*1995*	*1998*	*2001*	*2003*	*2005*
Income per capita for the highest income group	7,537.98	10,962.16	15,114.85	21,837.32	28,773.11
Expenditure per capita for the highest income group	6,033.10	7,593.95	9,834.20	14,515.68	19,153.73
Income per capita for the lowest income group	1,923.80	2,476.75	2,802.83	2,590.17	3,134.88
Expenditure per capita for the lowest income group	2,060.96	2,397.60	2,690.98	2,562.36	3,111.47

Source: National Statistical Bureau of China, *China's Statistical Yearbook* (various years).

annual growth of 9.41 per cent, while that of the east, central and west were 10.17 per cent, 8.5 per cent and 8.05 per cent, respectively. The ratio of east-central-west per capita real GDP was 1.71:1.23:1 in 1979; 2.03:1.15:1 in 1992; rising to 2.98:1.56:1 in 2005. Figure 5.7 shows that the gap of real GDP per capita between the east, central and west region has widened dramatically since 1992. Per capita incomes

Figure 5.7: *Real GDP per capita between the East, Central and West Region*

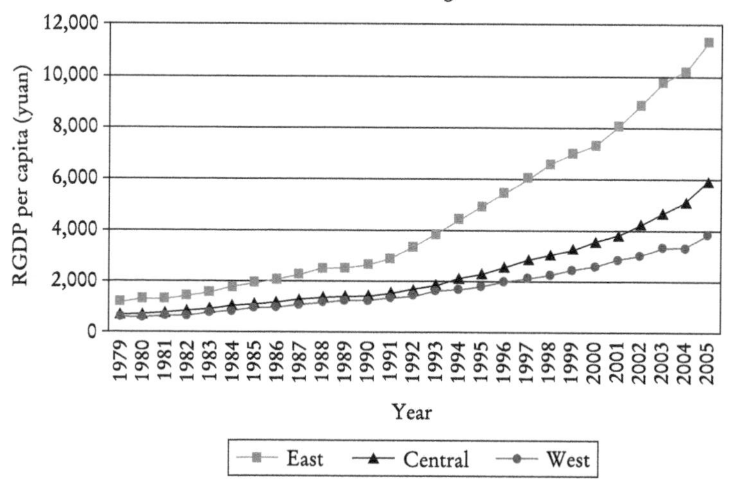

Source: National Statistical Bureau of China, *China's Statistical Yearbook* (various years).

Note: Per capita GDP measured in 1990s prices.

between the central and the west used to be very close but started to change gradually in the following years as well.

There are extremely imbalanced R&D investments in different regions. R&D resources are intensively located in eastern regions (Table 5.8), especially in some well-established areas, as for example, in Pearl River Delta, Yangtze River Delta and Bohai Rim Region.

Table 5.8: *Unequal S&T and Education Investment*

	Expenditure for R&D, Billion RMB	*Patents Application for Invention, Piece*	*Invention Patents Granted, Piece*	*Revenues from the Sale of New Products, Billion RMB*
Eastern region	218.63	86,040	15,882	23,810.1
Middle region	45.93	15,117	3,643	4,352.37
Western region	35.75	10,189	2,711	3,070.34

Source: NBS and MOST (2007).
Note: The revenues are from the large and medium enterprises.

Although the relation between the S&T investment level and innovation capacity in a region is not linear, they're closely linked (RTCSTD 2008). In 2006, the funding for science and technology activities increased by 11.32 per cent compared with that in 2005, and the majority of local governments have increased S&T funding. The S&T investments in Beijing, Shanghai, Guangdong, Jiangsu, Zhejiang, Shandong, and other regions with advanced innovation capacity are far higher than that of other regions (Figure 5.8).

In 2006, the S&T investments of enterprises and governments accounted for 56.95 per cent of the total investment in S&T throughout the country. Beijing is the region with the highest investment in S&T. The total government investment in S&T in 2006 amounted to 37.422 billion RMB, accounting for 27.36 per cent of that in the whole country (RTCSTD 2007).

Looking at the high-tech parks in China, we can find that there are 56 high-tech parks across China, but only 10 of them are located in the west. At the same time, the high-tech parks in the eastern region were established much earlier than those in the middle or western region. There is an inequality effect of China's extremely rapid development of innovation systems in the eastern regions, which are the most advanced regions in the country. First, China will in the future have a number of mega-cities located in its eastern areas, where

Figure 5.8: *Regional Distribution of R&D Expenditure of China (2007)*

Region	R&D expenditure (100 million yuan)	R&D/GDP (%)
Beijing	256,3	7,00
Guangdong	179,8	1,32
Jiangsu	150,5	1,21
Shanghai	128,9	2,06
Shandong	103,8	0,84
Liaoning	83,0	1,38
Sichuan	79,4	1,46
Zhejiang	75,2	0,80
Shaanxi	68,0	2,83
Hubei	54,8	1,01
Tianjin	40,4	1,65
Hebei	38,1	0,54
Fujian	37,5	0,72
Henan	34,2	0,49
Heilongjiang	32,7	0,74
Anhui	32,4	0,82
Hunan	30,1	0,65
Jilin	27,8	1,10
Chongqi	17,4	0,77
Jiangxi	17,0	0,60
Shanxi	15,8	0,64
Gansu	12,8	0,98
Guangxi	11,2	0,41
Yunnan	11,0	0,45
Guizhou	7,9	0,58
Inner Mongolia	6,4	0,30
Xinjiang	3,8	0,20
Ningxia	2,4	0,62
Qinghai	2,4	0,62
Hainan	1,2	0,18
Tibet	0,3	0,17

Source: NBS and MOST (2007).

vigorous industrialisation has already started. These mega-cities will not only remain centres of continued development but also become captivating magnets for people and activities from the middle and the western regions.

Second, partly as a consequence, people who are now referred to as floaters will become residents in eastern regions and will be joined by many more from the middle and eastern regions. Third, also as a consequence, a substantial shift of China's population will be away from the inland regions. Thus, the emerging industrial and economic structure in the middle and eastern regions is more difficult to predict. If this is the trend, the regional inequality will significantly rise in the future.

Some other indicators on inter-regional inequalities, including employment, investment in fixed assets, education and healthcare, are shown in Table 5.9.

Table 5.9: *Main Indicators of National Economic and Social Development by Eastern, Central and Western Provinces (2007)*

Items	*Eastern*	*Central*	*Western*
Employment			
Number of staff and workers (10,000 persons)	5,098.92	2,517.96	2,622.79
Registered unemployment rate in urban area (%)	3.30	3.90	4.10
Investment in fixed assets			
Total investment in fixed assets (100 million RMB)	64,875.99	27,746.16	28,250.93
Real estate development	14,153.81	3,901.86	4,863.13
Government finance			
Local governments revenue (100 million RMB)	14,052.85	3,590.42	4,085.49
Local governments expenditure (100 million RMB)	16,949.93	7,703.79	9,850.26
Education			
Institutions of higher education			
Number of institutions (unit)	769.00	481.00	467.00
New student enrolment (10,000 persons)	231.24	154.59	124.84
Student enrolment (10,000 persons)	779.28	515.42	401.90
Number of graduates (10,000 persons)	180.94	128.53	95.60
Health care			
Number of health care institutions (unit)	104,076.00	65,240.00	96,126.00
Hospitals and health centres	16,797.00	15,556.00	22,943.00
Medical technical personnel (10,000 persons)	191.06	119.20	118.50
Licensed doctors	79.34	48.63	51.87
Number of beds of medical organisations (10,000 beds)	133.15	85.88	91.26
Hospitals and health centres	129.54	84.64	92.47
People's livelihood			
Per capita disposable income of urban households (RMB)	16,974.22	11,634.37	11,309.45
Per capita net income of rural households (RMB)	5,854.98	3,844.37	3,028.38

Source: National Statistical Bureau of China, *China's Statistical Yearbook* (2008).

Historical Background of Inequality

Market competition is the mother of innovation, but competition can widen the gap as there are unequal resources, capabilities and opportunities (Liu 2008). Deng Xiaoping knew that very well and had made a famous statement: 'Let a few get rich first, and the others will follow',[2] but once China started market reforms, the widening gap of inequality followed.

Scholars still have not reached a consensus on the impacts of innovation on inequality. Cozzens (2006) said that innovation sometimes reinforces inequalities and sometimes undermines them. Castells (1996) argues that the increased use of digital communication technologies to tailor goods and services to smaller markets supports a trend toward more flexible workplaces, more skilled work, and more autonomous workers.

Why can equality not go in parallel with innovation in China? We have summarised the factors in the following sections.

The outcome of transition to market economy

From the 1980s on, China entered a transition stage. As China moved away from traditional socialist ideology and adopted the new ideology of a socialist market economy, China's economic growth was increasingly driven by profits and personal wealth accumulation.[1]

The market-oriented reform allowed some people to get rich. In 1980s, those who were not hired by the government or by the state-owned enterprises and institutions became the first rich group in China. They set up their venture in trade and small products that the large SOEs never paid attention to. Some of them are farmers with little education; some of them left their jobs with the government or SOEs, although at that time, most people preferred to find a job with low but stable wage in state-owned enterprises. Those who dedicated themselves to the market economy became rich, such as the founder of Lenovo, Chuanzhi Liu, who resigned from the Chinese Academy of Sciences to start his company. Lenovo's first business was to sell foreign computer products in China. Later on, the company became the largest domestic PC maker in China and Asia.

After the 1990s, various elite groups, some of them well-educated businessmen of SOEs or private enterprises, got more chances to become rich, and today they influence important economic and political resources.

Intervention of government

Another reason for rising inequality is the government's intervention in the economy. The inter-regional inequalities in China can be attributed to many factors such as different natural resources, human capital endowments, infrastructure and transportation, geographical location, proximity to foreign markets and investors, economic structures, and coast-oriented regional policy. Among these factors, uneven distribution of resources and preferential policies given to the east by the government are widely regarded as the dominant causes of regional inequality.

Since 1978, the focus of government policies in China has been on opening up to the outside world, decentralisation in economic decision-making and market-oriented reforms. These policies promoted rapid growth in the coastal areas, but had far less impacts on the inland provinces. The eastern coast possesses advantages of geography, endowments, and preferential policies, such as the establishment of the special economic zones (SEZs) and open coastal cities, as well as other incentive policies aimed at attracting foreign investments. At the same time, the industrialisation policies towards the central and western regions were tightened. As a result the gap between the inland and coastal regions widened continuously, and rose sharply in the 1990s, causing overall inter-provincial inequality to increase. In other words, China's regional inequalities are to a great extent due to the regional development policies established by the government.

In order to control rising regional inequality, China has shifted its focus from the coast onto the interior regions. The central government put the 'western development strategy' into practice in 1998, with the 'northeast revival strategy' following in 2003. Most recently, the 'rise of central China' strategy has been implemented.

In addition, in some industries, governmental franchise is required for a firm to produce or distribute a product. This is a monopoly created by the government. The monopoly creates higher profit in some industries than in others. In industries such as tobacco, oil and telecommunication. employees and employers earn much higher income than in other industries.

Inequality of education

Better education in the eastern regions gives people more opportunities to attract the investment of multinationals and well-paid jobs.

Skilled people can work in knowledge-intensive activities, such as university, hospitals, financing, etc. Therefore, the eastern regions have better human resources than western regions.

China is characterised by substantial regional and urban–rural inequalities that are evident in both economic and human development indicators (Zhang and Kanbur 2005). In education, data through the early 1980s shows substantial urban–rural differences in both the provision of basic and secondary education and in educational attainments (Hannum 1999). More recent data shows that economically advantaged provinces continue to enjoy substantial advantages in educational provision (Zhang and Kanbur 2005) (see Table 5.10). For example, many of the more urbanised and coastal provinces have achieved an important benchmark on the way to universalising nine years of compulsory education; nearly all primary graduates can go to the secondary school. In contrast, in many of the impoverished western provinces, roughly one in 10 primary school graduates fail to continue; in Guizhou, the figure is close to 21 per cent, and in Tibet a full 45 per cent (see Table 5.10).

Inequality between SOE and SME

As the concentration ratio of the financial assets of four major state-owned commercial banks has reached nearly 70 per cent (Li and Long 2006), the majority of these financial resources were allocated to the state-owned enterprises, and thus the financing needs of numerous SMEs could not be met. At the same time, financial controls are too stringent, and state intervention in the financial activities and financial system restricts the development of direct financing. The development of the capital market seriously lags behind, which leads to excessive dependence on banks.

The main issues that China's corporate finance stakeholders have been facing are the following:

First, the financing of large SOEs and SMEs is unequal. SMEs play an important role in the national economy of China. SMEs are main channels of employment growth. Most of them are labour-intensive enterprises, which can provide a good number of job opportunities. According to the national statistics, SMEs provided about 75 per cent of the urban employment opportunities in recent years. They are also major financial resources for local government. However, the financing status of SMEs is difficult. Although SMEs are playing

Table 5.10: *Percentage of Primary School Graduates Entering Secondary School by Year and Province*

Province	*1990*	*1991*	*1992*	*1993*	*1994*	*1995*	*1996*	*1997*	*1998*	*1999*	*2000*
Beijing	99	99	100	99	99	100	99	99	99	98	99
Tianjin	97	97	96	96	96	97	97	97	96	–	–
Hebei	80	82	84	86	88	90	94	99	98	98	98
Shanxi	81	83	85	84	85	89	92	95	93	–	–
Inner Mongolia	82	84	88	86	87	90	90	94	94	–	–
Liaoning	92	93	93	90	93	93	96	96	96	95	94
Jilin	86	90	91	91	95	96	95	–	–	–	–
Heilongjiang	83	86	84	83	84	93	95	94	94	94	96
Shanghai	100	100	100	100	100	100	99	100	100	–	–
Jiangsu	82	84	86	88	94	97	97	97	98	97	97
Zhejiang	85	89	92	92	95	99	99	99	99	–	–
Anhui	69	70	72	77	91	99	98	98	97	97	98
Fujian	65	71	76	81	83	92	98	99	98	97	97
Jiangxi	66	67	72	81	86	90	93	94	94	94	95
Shandong	76	79	82	83	88	94	96	97	98	98	98
Henan	66	68	68	71	79	86	91	93	95	96	95

Hubei	74	78	78	81	85	89	93	94	93	91	94
Hunan	71	77	78	84	87	91	94	96	95	95	97
Guangdong	86	87	86	88	92	95	96	96	96	96	96
Guangxi	64	65	67	70	78	86	90	91	94	–	–
Hainan	79	81	82	82	73	74	77	79	84	–	–
Chongqing	–	–	–	–	–	–	87	90	93	91	94
Sichuan											
Guizhou	61	60	60	64	70	73	72	76	75	78	79
Yunnan	61	63	67	68	71	74	75	76	83	–	–
Tibet	62	68	63	74	87	68	67	62	65	45	55
Shaanxi	86	86	86	85	88	90	91	91	90	90	92
Gansu	81	83	83	82	84	86	87	88	87	–	–
Qinghai	89	91	90	87	86	87	88	87	91	91	89
Ningxia	86	85	88	83	89	86	90	88	88	–	–
Xinjiang	82	88	78	80	82	84	86	91		–	–

Source: Calculated from All China Marketing Research Co., LTD (ACMR). N. D. *China Statistical Data Compilation 1949–2000* (CD-ROM). Beijing: All China Marketing Research Co., LTD., Table C-25. Cited in Zhang and Kanbur (2005).

an important part in China's national economy, accounting for 99 per cent of total enterprises, the loan resources available to them don't exceed 20 per cent of the total (Sun 2009), and other sources of financing are almost inaccessible to them. Regarding indirect financing, the state-owned commercial bank credit favours the large-scale enterprises, so it is quite difficult for the SMEs to get state-owned bank credit.

Second, state-owned enterprises and private enterprises are not treated equally. On the one hand, policy bias causes banks to privilege the SOEs and use lenient clauses for their credit guarantee when providing credit. For the private enterprises, on the other hand, the banks require strict and detailed guarantee, and the credit limit is quite low, which cannot meet their need for long-term capital. For instance, the private enterprises that created 70 per cent of GDP can only get 30 per cent of the credit capital. On the other hand, the public enterprises are mostly state-owned large- and medium-sized, and with strong capital scale and profitability, especially the key ones in the pillar industries. As for private enterprises, only those that are large in scale have mature technology or products, and good developing prospects and brand, can access market financing.

Third, the financing of traditional enterprises and high-tech ones is not harmonised. Traditional enterprises have the advantages of mature products, steady cash flow, low risk, easy-mortgage assets because they mainly engage in real industries; therefore, it's easy for them to succeed when applying for bank loans. Whereas high-tech enterprises, when applying for loans, face disadvantages — more intangible assets, intellectual property included, unsteady cash flow, high risk in developing costly and immature products. Although China supports the loans for high-tech enterprises all the time, loans for science and technology are declining year by year (from 15.19 per cent in 1991 to 7.7 per cent; in 2006 there was a decrease of 7.49 per cent). At the same time, while bank loans alone cannot meet the high-tech enterprises' huge demand for capital in the R&D process, equity financing also faces many problems. It is especially difficult for start-ups to obtain the trust of investors: they are unable to pass the threshold into a higher equity market because of their smaller scale and uncertainty in the market demand for their products. As a result of financing difficulties, innovation without capital support faces a large obstacle.

Co-evolution of the Innovation System and Inequality

Changing context of NSI and inequality

China's NSI has developed alongside the transition from a planned economy into a market economy, and from an agriculture-based country into a manufactures-based country. China also has the potential to develop a national system of innovation that will be a powerful engine for sustainable growth and facilitate the smooth integration of China's expanding economy into the global trading and knowledge system (OECD 2008). As China is a socialist country, there is more government intervention in the innovation process than other countries.

The Chinese innovation system is firstly characterised by strong government intervention. The first type of tool for intervention is national S&T programmes. In other words, government bodies control lots of resources required for innovation. Second, in China's innovation system FDI plays a very important role. Third, both SOEs and SMEs can find their market niche in their operation. But as there is a large pool of labour supply, people employed in manufacturing sectors, most of whom are farmers, still get limited pay. Therefore, the market economy established two layers: one is the capitalist class, which controls resources and the other is non-skilled labourers. The income gap between these two layers has been growing continuously. Though China has made great social progress and enjoyed rapid economic development, inequality is also rising. China's inequality is mainly reflected in the increasing gap between rural and urban, skilled and non-skilled labour. As previously mentioned, the fast technological progress in the agricultural sector increased labour productivity continuously (Table 5.11), though the increased income of farmers

Table 5.11: *Labour Productivity Change*

Year	*Labour Productivity (1952 = 100)*
1952	100.00
1978	181.62
1988	599.94
1998	2,089.23
2003	2,361.92

Sources: Calculated from National Statistical Bureau of China, *China's Statistical Yearbook* (various years).

cannot help narrow the gap between rural and urban labour because urban households' income increased more quickly (see Figure 5.5).

Theoretically, a better innovation system can play an important role in reduction of inequality. Susan E. Cozzens (2006) has pointed out that the traditional innovation system had not paid much attention to another dimension of development, namely, inequalities between individuals, households and groups. Cozzens thinks that in practice, innovation systems are organised in ways that reproduce and even amplify inequalities between individuals, households and groups. She puts forward the theory that innovation policies can help to re-invent innovation practice so that it helps to reduce these inequalities rather than reproducing them (Cozzens 2006).

In general, China's changing innovation system fostered economic development and technology progress, which is helpful to the whole economy and benefits poor people. However, the unbalanced development of the innovation systems can also worsen inequality in China. Recently, the government has issued a more ambitious strategy to deal with inequality and development. The new strategy is called 'building of harmonious society', and aims to narrow the wealth gap, increase employment, improve the government's public service and protect the environment. It redesigned the direction of the national innovation system of China.

All policies mentioned are just a beginning of the building of a harmonious society. With China's economic development and social transition, inequality has deep rooted causes within a complex web of social problems. Therefore, a single policy can never be effective enough to address these concerns; rather, it is necessary to take a comprehensive approach to formulate policies, and actually develop a policy framework that is up to the task of forming a harmonious society. In this framework, innovation policy can play an important role.

To achieve these goals, the government stressed that more efforts shall be made to co-ordinate economic and social development. The government picked rural development, employment, education, medical service, environmental protection, income distribution, and social security systems as key sectors that should be given priority. The strategy promises more S&T work and innovation with regards to healthcare, pollution control, water supply, and food safety. It requires S&T and innovation to serve people, helping to narrow the inequality by regions and groups.

For example, the safety of drinking water has become a great concern in China. Some 64 per cent of the water reaching urban areas is categorised as suitable only for industrial or agricultural purposes, and half of Chinese cities have suffered from groundwater pollution to some degree.[3] Poor water quality is a problem that poor regions are more likely to encounter.

The water programme is one of the 16 key projects listed in the National Mid-term and Long-term Science and Technology Development Plan (2006–20) issued by the State Council in 2006, which provides guidelines for China's science and technology development in the next 15 years. The project, which has an estimated budget of more than 30 billion Chinese RMB (around 4.4 billion US$) over 12 years, aims to improve the deteriorating water quality affecting millions of Chinese people and their livelihoods.

By taking this approach the treatment of the highly polluted Lake Tai, for example, the third-largest freshwater lake in China, will benefit not just Shanghai, but also the eastern provinces like Jiangsu and Zhejiang. The aim of the project is to guarantee the safety of drinking water and improve the overall water environment. A number of demonstration projects will be carried out at major rivers across China, such as Haihe, Huaihe, Liaohe, and Songhuajiang, as well as Lake Tai and the Three Gorges.

Measures against the rural–urban gap and inequality

During the 10th Plan (2001–05) period, government efforts to improve the position of rural areas focused on tax reform. For a long time, rural areas were subject to the same taxes as urban areas. On average, in 2000, these taxes and levies amounted to 13–15 per cent of the average rural income (Lin and Tao 2002). From 1 January 2006, all taxes and fees were abolished.

At the same time, the central government specifically identified poverty-stricken villages and counties (about 20 per cent of the national total of both) and introduced specific programmes to help these areas. The most noticeable programmes since 2000 have been designed to help designated poor villages on a comprehensive basis, to retrain the labour force in poor counties and help people find employment in developed regions, to develop agriculture and industry in poor regions and to improve compulsory education in poor areas. Outlays have been relatively limited, averaging less than 0.1 per cent of GDP per year. However, there is evidence that, between 2000 and 2006, the income of designated poor villages rose 2 per cent per year faster than incomes in all villages (Herd 2010).

At the same time, a new welfare assistance programme, called the minimum living allowance or MLA for urban areas, was introduced. Under this system, the local authority establishes the minimum cost of living (MCL) for purchasing the products needed for a person to survive. This cost varies across the country, depending on local prices and earnings or household incomes. Across provincial capitals, a 1 per cent increase in household income is associated with a 0.7 per cent increase in the level of the MCL. The MCL serves as the threshold income to qualify for the MLA. People with an income less than this level are entitled to a top-up payment equal to the difference between their income and the MLA threshold (Herd 2010).

Access to health and education

Healthcare Service in China

The Chinese healthcare system has a strong mark of planned economy. There are three different healthcare modalities in China. One is called the public healthcare system, aimed at government workers, university and government research institutes' staff, and provides almost 100 per cent coverage. Second is a medical insurance system for employees of business enterprises. Until 2004, only 44.4 per cent of the employees were covered and only 54 per cent of total medical care cost could be reimbursed. The last modality is called collective medical system for rural areas, where only 9.1 per cent of rural farmers are covered; under this modality, only 23 per cent of total medical care cost can be reimbursed (Liang et al. 2005). Therefore it remains difficult in rural areas to set up a health insurance system that is similar to that in urban areas, although the need for healthcare service in rural areas is actually much greater.

In rural China, most business enterprises provide little or no health insurance to their employees. Due to the low income levels in rural areas, rural citizens are not able to pay insurance premiums. Mandatory insurance premiums from rural citizens will only exacerbate the financial hardship they face. So financing the rural healthcare system has to depend mostly on the central government's subsidy. However, the state subsidy is limited since, to a certain degree, it relies on funding collected by the local governments. Moreover, labour mobility from rural to urban areas has become very common. Therefore a unified rural health insurance system will face risks of distortion. Reform in rural areas moves many farmers out of agricultural production and these people are employed temporarily in urban areas. However, farmers working in urban areas are not necessarily entitled to urban health insurance. When they suffer from severe illness, they usually go back to the hospitals in their hometowns for treatment because few of these people can afford the expensive healthcare service in urban hospitals.

This kind of medical care system is not good for innovation in China, especially when there is such a high discrepancy between the public medical care system and the private medical care system, since it in effect inhibits workers' mobility from the public sector to private sector.

Education and Innovation

China educates the world's largest school population, some 300 million children. Key educational policies are formulated by an education commission in Beijing, and implemented in counties, towns and villages. Education in China begins with nine years of universal, compulsory education. Educational reform, instituted after 1976, invigorated education, especially in urban centres. However, in less-developed rural areas, many schools still fail to meet national standards for such basic facilities as chairs, desks and safe drinking water. The pressures on rural children to leave school are huge.

First, there is a large discrepancy between education and employment opportunities — and when there are few jobs requiring education, there is less incentive to get an education. Rural children are ill-prepared for the national competitive examinations they must pass to get access to schooling beyond grade nine, further limiting their opportunities.

During the late 1990s, two key problems intensified in seriousness with respect to the financing of education in poor localities. First, the burden of school fees shouldered by rural households increased, leading to considerable unrest among farmers who faced the imposition of all manner of levies and taxes by cash-strapped local officials.

Under such pressure, children in the poorest families, children with lower grades and female children were vulnerable to being withdrawn from school. Second, there was a shortage of funds to maintain school buildings and facilities and to pay rural teachers' wages. Indeed, wages were commonly delayed by several months or paid only in part (Murphy 2006). This shortage was often exacerbated because unaccountable local governments responded to distorted priorities by diverting funds away from schools, the poor and villagers (Bardhan and Mookherjee 2005).

These circumstances created part of the impetus for a trend towards the re-centralisation of fiscal powers. Since the early 2000s the central government has increasingly claimed a share of the personal and enterprise income taxes that used to belong exclusively to localities. At the same time, in 2002 the central government initiated rural tax reforms to replace those local fees that so crippled and outraged poor farmers, with fiscal transfers from upper administrative levels. Such reforms have deprived local governments of much of their fiscal and administrative autonomy and made them more dependent on transfers. The reforms have also placed more revenue expenditure under the monitoring of upper administrative levels, with the aim of constraining local-level abuses.

During the 2000s, the central government further decided to use its increased fiscal powers to redress the inequalities in educational inputs that had prevailed throughout the 1990s and early 2000s. The most politically pressing was the need to reduce the burden of school fees on rural households and to ensure the payment of teachers' salaries. In 2001, the central government required that the responsibility for funding compulsory education be shifted up from the township government to the county-level government. In 2004, the central government capped school fees, while in 2006–07 it increased transfers to education in rural and western regions, and proclaimed free compulsory education for all. Such measures clearly reduced the economic burden that nine years of compulsory education placed on poor township governments and therefore on rural households. In the case of Gansu, while in 2000 around 70 per cent of compulsory education was paid by the township government (bellow local city level), by 2008 this figure had fallen to 10 per cent. Such measures have helped to stabilise the rural teaching profession and ensure that students can stay in school.

Still, there is inequality between different regions. Students in rich areas can enjoy more opportunity for further study than those in poor regions. For example, 79.5 per cent of high school students in Beijing can access undergraduate education, while only about 58 per cent of high school students can do this in Henan. In this way, innovation is more likely to happen in rich and urban areas.

Access to knowledge infrastructure, R&D infrastructure

S&T for Reducing Urban–Rural Income Inequality

There is a well-established system to diffuse agricultural technology in the rural areas in China, from demonstration, expert-led collectives, to agricultural envoys of S&T (specialists from government research institutes and university were selected to go to rural areas to serve as experts for agricultural, fishing and other industries). For example, up to 2007 about 45,000 agricultural envoys have been sent out and have delivered special service to nine million farmers (Liu et al. 2009).

There are also special S&T policies or programmes to narrow the development gap between the eastern, central and western regions. The central government established major special projects for western development as a part of the national scientific and technological research plan. These projects focus on the ecological environment construction in western China. Officials from Ministry of Science and Technology said,[2] from 2000 to 2010, National S&T programmes have expanded quickly to support the western region since the government's Developing West Plan of 2000. In these years the funds increased from 0.417 billion to 2.62 billion. (The funds for 973 programmes for the western region totalled about 0.95 billion, the S&T breakthrough programme had about 0.35 billion. Innovation funds for the western region stood at about 1.6 billion.) For example, there are more than 400 special aiding projects for Tibet with funds of 0.33 billion. With the support of the Ministry of Science and Technology, more than 20 provinces have established 700 joint projects with Xingjiang region (Han 2010).

Third, there is a system to encourage young scientists and engineers to work as vice directors who specialise in technology transfer in rural regions. This system was established in the 1990s. It required young scientists or engineers in university, government research institutes and state-owned companies to spend some years in poor agricultural regions as vice directors, acting as brokers for technology transfer and helping with decision-making in local technology development. For example, the Chinese Academy of Sciences, sent out many scientists to poor regions as vice ministers on the county level annually (Bai 2013). According to the *Henan Daily*, in 2008, in Henan province, there were more than 3,000 PhD scholars bidding for 128 positions of vice director at the county level.

Grassroot Innovation for Low Income People

There is a good tradition in China in which local companies are taking a grassroot innovation strategy and trying to compete with multinationals. This strategy is focused on a specific niche market or an untapped rural market which may be neglected by competitors. Because of China's rural poverty, rural residents have low income and low purchasing power. However, private businesses do well in developing products or services that specifically address the needs of rural residents. Many outstanding local businesses, such as Huawei, Lenovo, Haier, etc., developed grassroot innovation strategies to compete with multinationals in China. They rely on the vast rural market to develop niche markets, which are usually characterised by good potential for development, specific groups of customers and no competitors. For example, Lenovo developed a kind of computer that costs only 150 US$ (1000 RMB), which is cheap enough for rural residents to afford. Haier designed new washing machines for peasants that can wash sweet potatoes as well as clothes. These cases show that innovation can improve peasants' life quality. Huawei (Figure 5.9) began to do R&D and introduce digital switching solutions in rural areas in 1992. At that time, China's rural markets were just ignored by the giant multinational companies, so rural markets became the niche markets at Huawei's early stage of development. In 1995, the sales of Huawei were 1.5 billion RMB, contributed mainly by China's rural markets. Then in 1997 Huawei introduced the wireless GSM solution and in 1998 they expanded the market to major cities of China. In that year, *Business Weekly* named 'the world's top ten most influential companies', and ranked Huawei third in the world in the area of the mobile device market. They had set up a large-scale commercial UMTS/HSPA network for the first time in North America, and also built the next-generation wireless network for the Canadian operators Telus and Bell. Nowadays, the World Intellectual Property Organisation Statistics show that patent applications of Huawei in 2008 ranked number one and the patent numbers of LTE accounted for more than 10 per cent of LTE patents worldwide.

Although Huawei has become the world's leading communication equipment company, they haven't given up the majority of China's rural markets. Because the rural market has its own characteristics such as a remote location requiring equipment investment, extensive laying of fibre-optic and copper cable, and dealing with a vast territory and far-scattered residents — Huawei developed a tailor-made system for broadband coverage in the rural areas, which includes: high bandwidth, high efficiency, high reliability, low cost, and maintenance-free operation. The system has provided an effective coverage of broadband network to the rural markets.

While, to some extent, multinationals have technological advantage, local companies in developing countries can benefit from their local market knowledge, so grassroot innovation strategy may be a feasible strategy for Chinese companies to compete with multinationals (Liu 2008).

The solar thermal system (STS) is another case of grassroot innovation for low income people in China. The solar thermal system is mainly used for heating water for bathroom use. Unlike the panel-heating system in Europe, the solar thermal system uses a vacuum tube with dark paint-coat to assimilate solar heating and this system can maintain the temperature during the night.

In the early 1980s, when STS was first introduced into the market, it was positioned in the high-end market, competing with electricity-driven and gas-driven thermal systems. The main value proposition at that time was bathing cheaply, instead of being environment friendly. The product was accepted by many users because it was cheap in summer (free hot water). However, the product met bottle-necks in cities. First, when living infrastructures were improved in cities, most families could access electricity- or gas-driven hot water systems. When more and more urban families could afford such service, they discarded the unstable STS (it could not be used on cloudy days, and in winter the solar system would break down due to the cold temperature). Second, the urban families lived in centralised high buildings, which had no room for solar systems.

Figure 5.9: *Huawei's Catching-up by Using Grassroot Innovation Strategy*

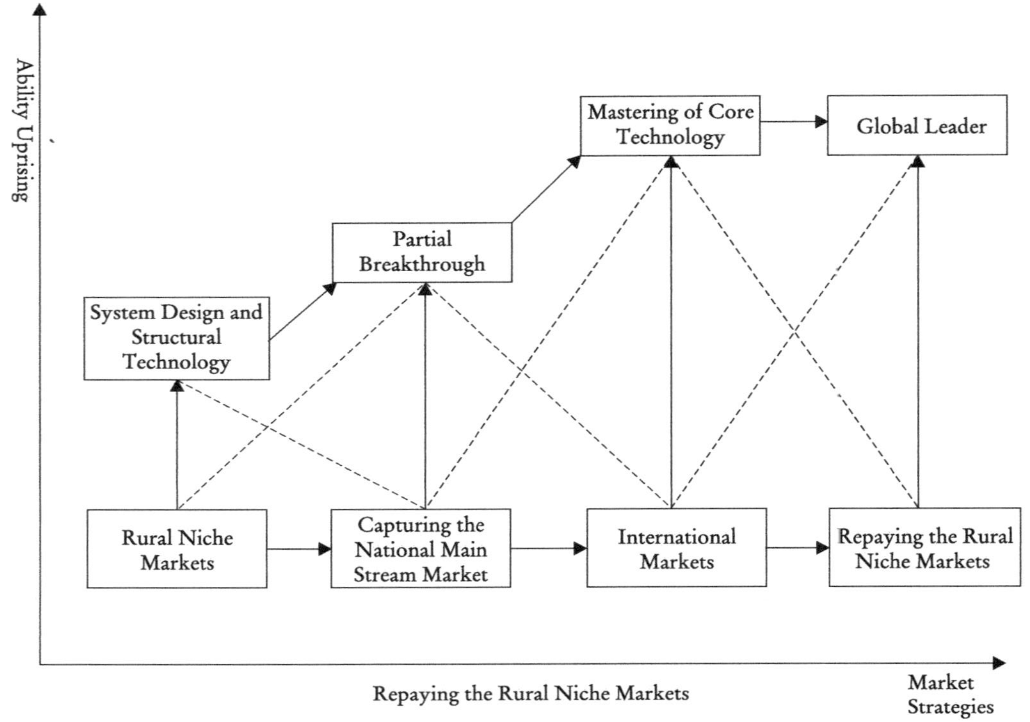

Source: Authors' compilation.

In rural areas, the social infrastructure was poor. Low-income farmers could not get access to convenient bathing facilities, and could only bathe in public bathrooms (which were unclean and crowded) or in nearby company bathrooms (usually the company bathrooms did not permit non-employees to bathe unless one knew some employees within the company). In summer, some families would put a water container on top of the roof of their house, heated the water by sunlight, and took bath before the water cooled down.

There was a demand in rural areas for a convenient bath and decent life. The value proposition of STS met the need of these low-income groups. Seeing that most farmers could not afford expensive STS with many functions, many STS companies de-functioned the product, and only kept the water heating function with low-price. Although the product could not maintain water temperature for a long time, and did not have other functions, it could heat water quickly in sunny summer days, and could be used throughout summer and half of the spring and autumn. Such products sold well in rural markets because they satisfied the farmers' demand.

With rural markets, many STS companies grew into big companies, and more are still small companies but profitable and highly active. The markets are still growing quickly, leaving room for these companies. Rural markets were considered as the major factors for the quick growth in the STS industry. During our interview to Tsinghua Solar, one of the earliest STS companies in China, one manager said,

> The (STS) market accelerated in 2005, thanks to the sudden growth in rural markets. At first, we were technology-driven company, and didn't care for rural market. But all of a sudden, thousands of companies emerged, selling their products to low-end users and getting good return from the market. Some of them started to enter high-end users, giving competition pressure to us; at the same time, they still grow very fast in rural areas (the low-end users). We had to re-think our strategy, and entered rural market in 2008 (Zhou et al. 2010).

From the rural markets, STS technology began its growth and improvement. Now with the improvement of the quality and the government's emphasis on low-carbon technology, STS started to enter and regain the urban market. Some local government agencies have even issued policies requiring that newly built buildings have to leave room for STS. Nowadays some large STS companies have started to export their products to European countries. STS is a good example of innovation moving from the bottom of the pyramid up to top (Zhou et al. 2010).

Access to financial infrastructure

Subsidy to the Agriculture Sector

The government invests large amounts of money into R&D in the agricultural industry. For example, based on the technology of hybrid rice, a famous scientist named Longping Yuan invented Super-Hybrid Rice. The technology increased the rice productivity greatly, from 0.45 kilogram per square metre in the 1970s to 1.35 kilogram per square metre in 2008.

Stressing the 'three rural issues' — agriculture, village and farmer — the government has sought to comprehensively narrow the development gap between urban and rural areas.

Traditional rural industries are becoming increasingly important sources of new innovation. New technologies are being applied in traditional rural industries to spin out new innovations targeting new markets and creating new added value. In traditional rural industries, such as agriculture and food, a growing urban demand for high-quality food is a major source of innovation. Organic farming, the production of high-quality products and regional specialties, on-farm processing and marketing, as well as the creation of new short supply chains, are all driving new waves of innovation. The most common rural-driven innovations are in traditional rural industries: such as farming through new harvesting machinery or tractors; fishing boats, nets or navigation systems; and mining automation or drilling equipment. Incremental innovations in these industries improve productivity. Indeed, even when such innovations are developed outside rural areas, rural businesses (often through farmers or fishermen associations) still play an important role as 'users' in shaping and pushing the development of many such innovations.

Some rural areas urgently need to conquer natural barriers, such as harsh climate, the effects of climate change (including rising sea levels), rugged topography, desertification or sheer remoteness. This demands new types of innovations. Many rural innovations have their origins in basic needs, such as access to critical public services, like education, health and social services, and at a minimum level to commercial services, such as post offices, banks and retail outlets. In this regard, rural areas have benefited from the distance learning over the Internet, the provision of online banking, and e-government services created to lessen the barriers of distance.

Rural regions are comparatively disadvantaged in their ability to be innovative. Most economic geography literature suggests that the low business density and dispersed business population undermine rural businesses' ability to access and benefit from knowledge transfer (tacit or otherwise), the knowledge spillovers and external economies that prevail in cities (Maye et al. 2007). Moreover, a weak business environment does not normally create an environment sufficiently competitive to stimulate innovation. Therefore, in rural areas, financing is a big challenge for SME's innovation and development.

SMEs have already become an essential part of the national economy which contribute 58.5 per cent of GDP, 68 per cent of import and export volume, 48.2 per cent of tax revenue, 75 per cent of urban employment.

Promoting the SMEs is one of the policies for economic development in China, especially the technology-based SMEs. About 3.3 per cent of SMEs are technology-based.[4] To do this, a supporting system has been established, with some parts aiming at innovation and entrepreneurship, some at incubators, some at financing support (see Figure 5.10).

First, we shall talk of the policy for entrepreneurship: China launched the Torch Programme in the 1980s. The major mission of

Figure 5.10: *The Function of Innofund for SMEs Growth*

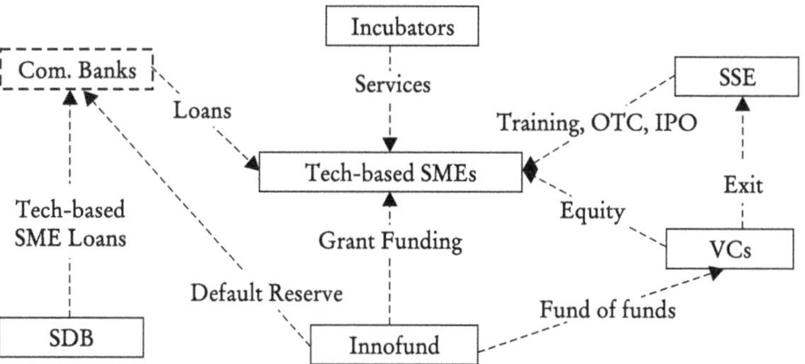

Source: Authors' compilation based on various sources.

the Torch Programme is to nurture technopreneurs and technology-based start-ups. By the end of 2010, there were about 896 technology business incubators, with more than 30 million square meter incubating area. There are about 56,382 tenant companies of which 7,677 are set by returnees.[5]

Second, the Innovation Fund for Tech-based SMEs was established in 1998. The purpose of the fund is to support projects in their early stage of commercialisation, with innovative technology and good market potential but unattractive to commercial capital. It specifically targets areas of 'market failure', where government support is needed to bridge the gap of capital market and incubate innovative start-ups.

Facing the finance crisis, the government pushed forward a special policy for SMEs development. There are six major measures: improve the legal system; effectively alleviate the financing difficulties of SMEs; increase the financial and taxation support for small and medium enterprises; speed up the SMEs' technological progress and structural adjustment; support eligible SMEs involved in home appliances, agricultural machinery, automobile motorcycle countryside; strengthen and improve services to SMEs.

Overall, since 1978, there have been some positive signs of improvement for SMEs, but no dramatic shift occurred on the fundamental level. Large SOEs are the most important for the government, followed by multinationals, and, lastly, private companies. The financing problems of SMEs have not yet been resolved.

Output and employment

China is a country with an apparent dual economic structure — i.e. the modern industrial sector and the traditional agricultural sector — which co-exist and co-develop (see Figure 5.11 and Figure 5.12). The Chinese industrial sector is usually capital-intensive, large-scale and, as with most industrial enterprises, located in urban areas, while the agricultural sector is more labour-intensive and by nature mainly rural. Thus the income levels of rural and urban residents were different before reform.

When reform started, the successful implementation of the household responsibility system (HRS) together with higher procurement

Figure 5.11: *Changes of GDP Composition (1990–2007)*

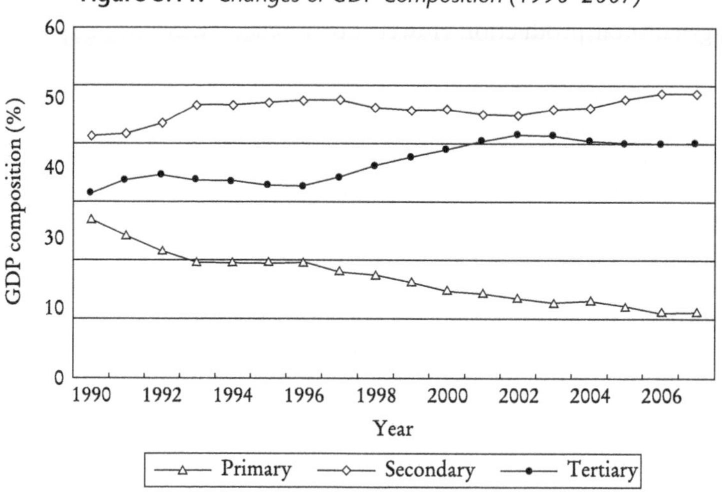

Source: National Statistical Bureau of China, *China's Statistical Yearbook* (1990–2008).

Figure 5.12: *Employment by Economic Sector (1990–2007)*

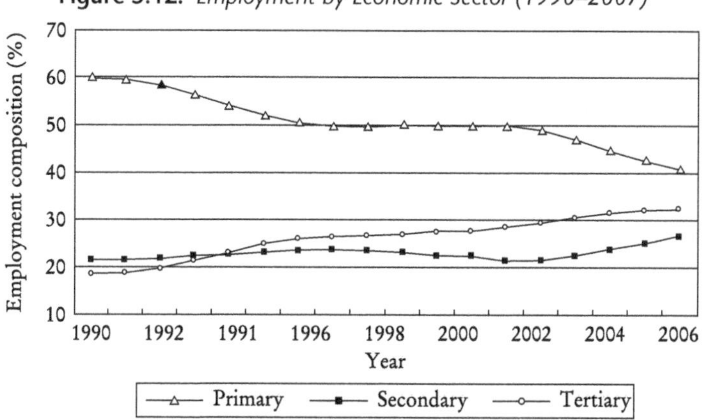

Source: National Statistical Bureau of China, *China's Statistical Yearbook* (1990–2008).

prices greatly increased farmers' productivity in the agricultural sector. Farmers benefited from higher output that was a crucial basis for income increases.

In the late 1980s as reform efforts expanded, not only did rural–urban income inequality gradually expand, but also income differences among rural families appeared. For some, income increases from agricultural production slowed down since HRS only improved productivity by raising farmers' incentives for a short period of time. For others, development of rural industry (TVEs) did help rural non-agricultural workers achieve higher incomes. From 1984, the emphasis of the Chinese economic reform began shifting from rural areas to urban areas. The natural advantages of the existence of a large industrial sector together with the strong government support greatly encouraged urban economic growth and in terms of income increases, urban workers benefited much more than rural workers during that period.

By the 1990s, a number of dimensions exhibited growing income inequality; that is, a rural–urban inequality, a rural only inequality and an urban only inequality. Throughout the whole decade, firms employed less labour as pursuing growth depended on increasing productivity rather than increasing labour input and both the urban industrial sector and TVEs demonstrated strong trends to substitute capital for labour. China is famous for its huge labour endowment. However, although higher productivity resulted in income increases of those who stayed employed, the increases were at the expense of those who lost the opportunity to work. Benefits from rapid economic growth have not been spread across the regions, because preferential regional policies have been adopted. For example, because of concern for political safety the central government for a long time only implemented the open-door policy (open for foreign direct investment) in south and coastal areas. Thus, those open-door regions accumulated capital resources more easily and quickly than other regions. In addition, the open regions used their resources more efficiently, further adding to regional inequality.

China is at the critical stage of reform characterised by a high economic growth rate and high inequality. It is now necessary for the Chinese government to improve the present social security system so as to keep inequality levels within an acceptable range. Higher growth allows people to enjoy a better living standard but growth with widening inequality means that not only will the disadvantaged groups benefit less from the growth, that their situation may get even worse.

Previously, Chinese social security was tied to the firms not to the individuals. Only if people were employed in state firms could they enjoy unemployment insurance, medical care and a retirement pension. If they left, none of these benefits would be provided. Therefore, even those who did not feel satisfied working in state firms and had opportunities to be employed in non-state firms with higher wages chose to stay until retirement when all the benefits could be realised.

Since 1995, China has undertaken reform in its social security system, and in 2002 a basic framework for a social security system was established and successively implemented, covering the vast majority of urban workers and retirees (Government of China 2002). This new system consists of social insurance, social relief, social welfare, social mutual help, and special care for disabled people and family members of revolutionary martyrs, and features the raising of funds through various channels instead of depending on enterprises and institutions only.

However, for the time being, the country's social security system is not able to cover the population of 800 million in rural areas. Broadened coverage still needs to be developed, with security programmes applying to all members of society, not only those with urban employees.

Nature of employment

Employment is the primary channel through which growth translates into better living standards, reduced poverty and welfare improvements. Although informal employment has existed in China since 1949, informal employment as a fully developed concept is new. Until 1978, the ideological emphasis upon state and collective ownership severely limited the scope for other types of ownership of enterprise (for example, by private, self-employed individuals), and back then informal employment existed on a small scale only. In the wake of reforms in 1978, particularly in the 1990s, the share of employment in state-owned enterprise has declined (see Figure 5.13). Growing informal employment in China is a recent phenomenon. With the intensification of state enterprise reform from the mid-1990s onwards, the Chinese government has taken an increasing interest in improving the share of informal employment, as a means of addressing the issue of unemployment.

Figure 5.13: *Declining Share of Employment in SOEs (1993–2007)*

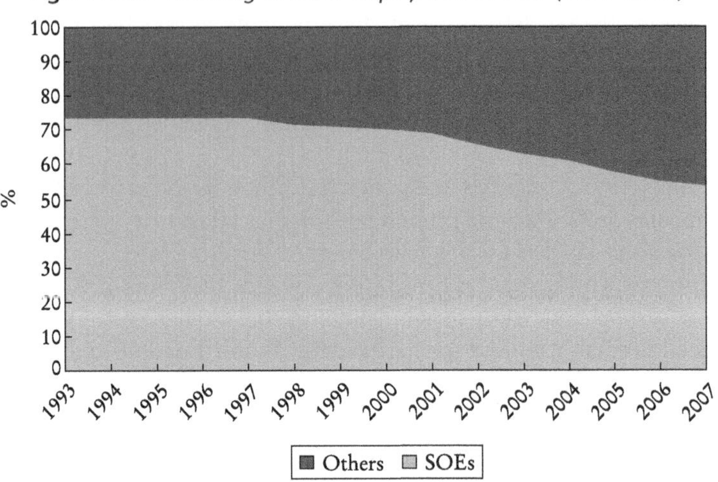

Source: National Statistical Bureau of China, *China's Statistical Yearbook* (various years).

On the other hand, state- and collective-owned enterprises have also made use of informal employment in order to cut costs. From the supply side, without taking mass redundancies by state- and collective-owned enterprises into account, the effect of heavy migrations from rural areas and new entrants into the labour market every year has been sharply increasing informal employment. In the following three ways, some sample surveys of informal employment in urban China will be given (Table 5.12):

1) Chinese Household Income Project Survey (CHIPS) 1988, 1995 and 2002, eight provinces.
2) China Urban Labour Survey (CULS), 2001 and 2005, five cities: Institute of Population and Labour Economics, CASS.
3) Ministry of Human Resources and Social Security of the People's Republic of China (MOHRSS), Labour Force Employment and Social Security in Urban China in 2002, 66 cities.

The share of informal employment in China's urban labour market has been more and more important. Informal employment is not only a means of addressing the issue of unemployment but also a means of relieving poverty.

Table 5.12: *Percentage of Informal Employment Calculated*

	1988	*1995*	*2002*	*2002*	*2005*
Age Group	*CHIP*	*CHIP*	*MOHRSS*	*MOHRSS**	*(CULS)**
16–24	8.1	15.7	59.2	50.5	38.2
25–34	3.1	7.4	45.1	43.2	37.3
35–44	2.9	6.7	42.4	41.8	44.3
45–54	3.9	7.8	42.4	41.2	43
55–64	9.3	16.3	54.7	54.5	44.2

Source: 1988 and 1995, CHIP's data; 2002, MOHRSS's 66 city data; 2005, CULS2. Peng et al. (2007).

Notes: *Large size city (population exceeding 2 million).

Wages and productivity differentials and their bearing on inequality

From Figure 5.14, the real wage growth rate of employed persons in urban areas may be demonstrated; one way to reduce rural–urban inequality is increasing migration flow. As more and more rural migrants come to the city and become urban households, the difference of rural–urban inequality may decline slowly (Table 5.13).

Another way to cope with the inequality is China's improved social protection system, instead of channelling laid-off workers into re-employment service centres. The new Chinese unemployment insurance system is similar to the old-age pension system, i.e. the

Figure 5.14: *Real Wage Growth Rates of Employed Persons in Urban Areas*

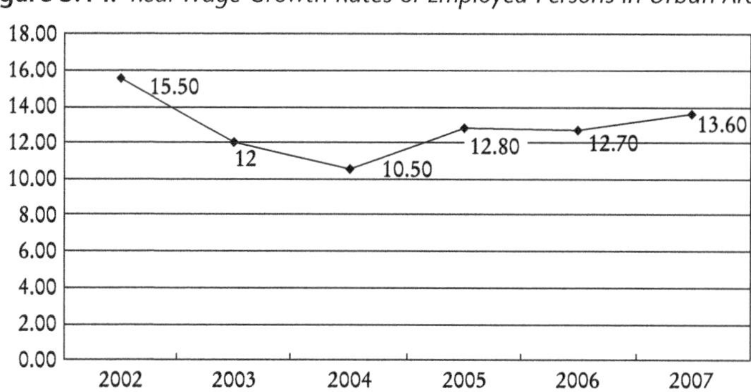

Source: Fang et al. (2007).

Table 5.13: *Numbers and Growth Rates of Rural Migrants*

	Numbers (million)	*Increases (%)*
1997	38.90	–
1998	49.36	26.89
1999	52.04	5.43
2000	61.34	17.89
2001	78.49	27.96
2002	83.99	7.01
2003	98.31	17.05
2004	102.60	4.50

Source: Fang et al. (2007).

joint employer–employee contribution system. The system required a standardised contribution not only from enterprises but also from employees themselves. It is now the responsibility of employees to contribute 1 per cent of their wages to the personal account as premiums, and if they become unemployed they can receive a corresponding insurance payment that is based on their contribution.

Finally, the Employment Contract Law enacted in 2007 is a milestone symbolising China's approach to a more regulated labour market. The new act was effective 1 January 2008. The law adopts a strong action to protect the legal interests of employees, such as mandating that any employee should be protected by the formal contract. Employees enjoy the social insurance and pension plan, but its effect on inequality is not clear so far.

China has made substantial progress in economic development since the economic reform started in 1978. Strong economic growth has been fuelled by rapid productivity growth (Table 5.13), and has been accompanied by impressive declines in the incidence of poverty.

Accompanying the rapid growth of the national economy in China has been an astounding achievement in the reduction of poverty, especially rural poverty. Based on the government's definition of poverty, between 1978 and 2000 the number of poverty-stricken people in rural areas — that is, people without enough food to eat and clothes to wear — decreased from 250 million to 30 million; and the proportion of poverty-stricken people in the total rural population dropped from 30.7 per cent to about 3.4 per cent.

The Centre for the Study of Living Standards (CSLS) Research Report, using official labour productivity and poverty and inequality data from the World Bank, estimates the effect of productivity and inequality on poverty. Productivity is found to have a strong negative effect on poverty in China, although when controlling for different productivity levels across sectors it is found that industrial labour productivity is the key driver of reductions in poverty (Table 5.14). The weak positive relationship observed between agricultural labour productivity and poverty in the 1990s might reflect a terms of trade effect: agricultural prices, when compared with urban industrial prices, are unreasonably low, so that rural people cannot obtain a corresponding benefit from productivity increases. Trends in income inequality appear to have no substantial effect on poverty in China. Despite some statistical weaknesses, the productivity performance has not

Table 5.14: *Relative Labour Productivity by Sector (1978–2001)*

	Relative Labour Productivity (%)		
Year	*Primary* (1)	*Secondary* (2)	*Tertiary* (3)
1978	39.9	278.6	194.3
1979	44.7	269.3	169.8
1980	43.8	266.5	163.4
1981	46.7	253.6	160.3
1982	48.9	244.6	161.9
1983	49.2	238.5	157.7
1984	50.0	217.6	153.4
1985	45.5	207.2	169.6
1986	44.5	200.9	168.0
1987	44.7	197.7	164.6
1988	43.3	196.9	165.0
1989	41.7	199.1	174.9
1990	45.1	194.4	169.2
1991	41.0	196.7	176.7
1992	37.3	202.3	173.2
1993	35.3	211.6	154.2
1994	37.2	211.0	138.7
1995	39.3	212.2	123.8
1996	40.4	210.6	115.8
1997	33.3	211.0	117.0
1998	37.3	209.8	120.2
1999	35.1	214.8	122.7
2000	32.8	223.1	121.5
2001	30.4	229.1	121.3

Source: Centre for the Study of Living Standards (2007).

been uniform across the agricultural and industrial sectors, but both have contributed to aggregate growth and poverty reduction. We still have confidence in the main conclusion that productivity increases have played a key role in reducing poverty in China.

The process of economic growth, besides bringing the benefits of productivity increases, also brings structural adjustments that exacerbate income inequality through displacing workers. The government of China has an important role to play in further developing a social security system that will ensure the gains from productivity are more equally shared, thus maintaining a healthy and equitable society in which further productivity gains can be achieved.

Regional strategy against inequality

Since the 1990s, the government realised the problem of widening inequalities between different regions, so some national strategies have been issued aiming at the relatively poorer regions in China.

Great Western Development

In 1999, the government timely introduced a strategy called the Great Western Development to narrow the gap between eastern and western regions. The strategy covers six provinces (Gansu, Guizhou, Qinghai, Shaanxi, Sichuan, and Yunnan), five autonomous regions (Guangxi, Inner Mongolia, Ningxia, Tibet, and Xinjiang), and one municipality (Chongqing).

Infrastructure development: The strategy includes plans to expand the highway network in the western region. The plan calls for building more railway tracks, airports, and gas trunk pipelines. Electric power grids and telecommunications, radio, and television facilities would be expanded, as they will support infrastructure in large- and medium-sized cities. The plan also calls for 'rational' exploitation of water resources and water conservation in general.

Development of local industry: Rather than forcing a uniform approach to development, the government is encouraging different regions to develop industries that maximise local comparative advantages in geography, climate, resources, and other conditions. Where possible, these regions are also urged to capitalise on high- and new-technology industries.

Revitalize Northeast China

This plan is to rejuvenate the industrial bases in northeastern China. It covers three provinces: Heilongjiang, Jilin and Liaoning. The core of the programme is to revitalise the traditional industry in these regions, while speeding up development in aspects of structural regulation, regional cooperation, economic reform, the construction of an environment-friendly economy, and increased efforts in education, healthcare and cultural projects.

Rise of Central China Plan

This policy is adopted by the People's Republic of China to accelerate the development of its central regions. It was announced by Premier Wen Jiabao on 5 March 2004. It covers six provinces: Shanxi, Henan, Anhui, Hubei, Hunan, and Jiangxi. The six inland provinces lie in the heart of central China. They enjoy a combined geographical advantage, with a combined population and economic volume of more than 28 per cent and 20 per cent of the national total, respectively. The six provinces make up the base of China's grain production, energy and raw materials, and are also the centre of the country's comprehensive transportation network. They play an important role in China's overall economic and social development.

Focus on central China is another strategic decision made by the Chinese government following its earlier decisions to give priority to the development of the eastern region, to implement the western development strategy and to rejuvenate the old industrial bases in the northeast. It is yet another key task in implementing China's overall strategy of promoting a coordinated development of different regions.

In conclusion, through tax breaks, technology upgrades and a trial reform of the social security system, these preferential policies have played a role in promoting regional development.

Conclusion

Under a socialist regime, China was a relatively equal society. After the transition to a market economy, inequality among different regions, urban and rural, groups and even industries, continued to grow.

For a long time, the Chinese innovation system was oriented to fast economic development. But the differences in regional resource endowments, regional entrepreneurship, government intervention and other factors, led to inequalities in regions, among groups and in specific living areas (urban vs rural areas). The inequalities can be seen in access to education, healthcare, access to infrastructure. There are different reasons for these widening inequalities, such as government intervention and capability to access market resources.

At the same time, the government used a variety of policy tools to control the inequality process, such as special programmes for the rural sector and western regions. Some businesses employ the model of grassroot innovation, which helps reduce the absolute poverty in China. For example, the government has rapidly increased its financial support for the medical system and healthcare. In 2009, it spent about 127.7 billion Yuan on healthcare, which is a 49.5 per cent increase from last year (Wen 2010). In addition, the social insurance system will be applied to the whole employed population, with a basic social security system available to all members of society, not only urban employees.

In the new century, the Chinese innovation system has been undergoing some changes; building a harmonious society requires new criteria for resource allocation in the area of S&T and innovation. Chinese Premier Wen Jiabao has said he will reverse the trend of increasing income gap from 2010 onwards (ibid.). But as China is a large country with various levels of development, and although the Chinese government has tried hard to use lots of measures to control inequality, reaching a balance between innovation and inequality reduction will be a tough challenge both for China and other developing countries. We need a new philosophy of development and innovation to address this need.

Notes

1. The socialist market economy was stated by Mr Deng Xiaoping on 26 November 1979, during a meeting with guests from USA and Canada.

2. Available at http://cpc.people.com.cn (accessed 12 July 2013).)
3. Speech made by Mr Liu Yanhua, the vice minister of science and technology, at a conference on national water resources, 19 September 2009.
4. See http://news.xinhuanet.com/fortune/2004-12/25/content_2379784.htm (accessed 12 June 2013).
5. Available at http://www.most.gov.cn/tztg/201301/W020130111527800312678.doc (accessed 12 July 2013).

References

Asian Development Bank, 2007. 'Reducing Inequalities in China Requires Inclusive Growth', Asian Development Bank news release, 9 August.

Bai, Chunli, 2013. http://www.shb.cas.ac.cn/xwzx/tzgg/201302 (accessed 2 February 2013).

Bardhan, P. and D. Mookherjee, 2005. *Decentralization and Local Governments in Developing Countries: A Comparative Perspective*, Cambridge: Massachusetts Institute of Technology Press.

Bound, J. and G. Johnson, 1992. 'Changes in the Structure of Wages in the 1980's: An Evaluation of Alternative Explanations', *American Economic Review*, 82, 371–92.

Braverman, H., 1974. *Labour and Monopoly Capital.* New York: Monthly Review Press.

Centre for the Study of Living Standards, 2003. 'China's Productivity Performance and Its Impact on Poverty in the Transition Period', Final Report, Centre for the Study of Living Standards, Ontario. http://www.csls.ca/res_reports.asp (accessed 12 June 2013).

Castells, M., 1996. *The Rise of the Network Society: The Information Age: Economy, Society and Culture*, vol. 1. Boston: Blackwell.

Chang, G. H. and J. C. Brada, 2006. 'The Paradox of China's Growing Under-Urbanization', *Economic Systems*, 30, 24–40.

China Daily, 2008. 'China's GDP Grows 11.4% in 2007, Fastest in 13 Years', 24 January.

Chinese Communist Party Congress, 1981. 'Some Statements on Historical Events of Chinese Communist Party Since 1949', 27 June, Pamphlet.

Cozzens, S. E., 2006. 'Innovation and Inequality'. http://www.cas.uio.no/research/0708innovation/Cozzens_120208.pdf (accessed 29 March 2013).

David, C. and J. E. DiNardo, 2002. 'Skill Biased Technological Change and Rising Wage Inequality: Some Problems and Puzzles', Working Paper 8769, National Bureau of Economic Research.

Fang, C., Y. Du and C. Zhao, 2007. 'Regional Labour Market Integration since China's World Trade Organization Entry: Evidence from Household-level Data', in G. Ross and L. Song (eds), *China – Linking Markets for Growth*. Canberra: Asia Pacific Press, 133–50.

Galor, O. and D. Tsiddon, 1997. 'Technological Progress, Mobility and Economic Growth', *American Economic Review*, 87, 363–82.

Government of China, 2002. 'White Paper for Labor and Social Security Development of China'. http://news.sohu.com/77/23/news200652377.shtml (accessed 2 March 2013).

Han, Side, 2010. 'Support West Development by MOST', 6 January 2010. http://www.stdaily.com/kjrb/content/2010-01/06/content_142406.htm (accessed 15 April 2012).

Hannum, E., 1999. 'Political Change and the Urban–Rural Gap in Education in China, 1949–1990', *Comparative Education Review*, 43(2), 193–211.

Herd, R., 2010. 'A Pause in the Growth of Inequality in China?' Working Paper 748, Economics Department, Organisation for Economic Co-operation and Development, Paris.

Jin, F. 2008. 'Within-urban Inequality and the Urban-rural Gap in China, CEA (UK)'. Conference Paper. http://www.ceauk.org.uk/2008-conference-papers/Furong-China (accessed 29 March 2013).

Juhn, C., K. M. Murphy and B. Pierce, 1991. 'Accounting for the Slowdown in Black-White Wage Convergence', in M. H. Kostes (ed.), *Workers and Their Wages: Changing Patterns in the United States*. AEI Press: Washington DC, 107–43.

Lewin, C. and M. Orleans, 2000. 'The Class Situation of Information Specialists: A Case Analysis', *Sociological Research Online*, 5. http://www/socresonline/org.uk/5/3/lewin.html (accessed 5 February 2013).

Li, S. and Chenfen Long, 2006. 'Reflections on Perfecting the Financing Structure of Enterprise', *Taxing and Economy* (in Chinese), 3, 33–36.

Lin, J. and R. Tao, 2002. *Urban and Rural Household Taxation in China: Measurement and Stylized Facts*. Beijing: China Centre for Economic Research, Peking University.

Liu, C., J. Wang and X. Lian, 2009. 'Evaluation of Chinese Agricultural S&T Extension Models', *Economic Research Guide* (in Chinese), 10, 27–29.

Liu, Y., 2009. 'Speech at the Conference of National S&T for Water Resources', 19 September. http://yunnan.stis.cn/kjdt/gndt/200804/t20080410_172974.htm (accessed 25 February 2013).

Liu, X., 2008. *Globalization, Catch-up and Innovation* (in Chinese). Beijing: Science Press.

Maye, D., L. Holloway and M. Kneafsey (eds), 2007. *Alternative Food Geographies: Representation and Practice*. Boston/Amsterdam: Elsevier.

Murphy, R., 2006. 'Paying for Education in Rural China', in V. Shue and C. Wong (eds), *Paying for Progress in China: Public Finance, Human Welfare and Changing Patterns of Inequality*. London: Routledge, 69–95.

National Bureau of Statistics of China (NBSC), 2006–08. *China Statistical Yearbook*. Beijing: National Press of Statistics.

National Bureau of Statistics of China and Ministry of Science and Technology (NBSC and MOST), 2007. *China Statistical Yearbook on Science and Technology*. Beijing: National Press of Statistics.

News of the Communist Party of China. http:// cpc. people. com.cn/GB/ 34136/ 2569304.html (accessed 5 February 2013).
Organisation for Economic Co-operation and Development (OECD), 2008. *OECD Reviews of Innovation Policy: China*. Paris: Organisation for Economic Co-operation and Development.
Peng, Xizhe, Yaowu Wu and Jeemol Unni, 2007. 'Data Analysis of Informal Employment in China and India'. http://wiego.org/resources/session-2-data-analysis-informal-employment-china-and-india (accessed 21 June 2013) .
Research Team for Chinese Science and Technology for Development (RTCSTD), 2007. *Annual Report of Regional Innovation Capability of China (2007)*. Beijing: Science Press.
——, 2008. *Annual Report of Regional Innovation Capability of China (2008)*. Beijing: Science Press.
Ru, Xin, et al., 2005. *Social Blue Book (2006)* (in Chinese). Beijing: Press of Chinese Social Sciences Literature.
Saint-Paul, G., 2008. *Innovation and Inequality: How Does Technical Progress Affect Workers?* Princeton: Princeton University Press.
Sun, Xiuping, 2009. 'On SME's Financing in China', *Development (Fazhan)* (in Chinese), 2, 76–77.
Tu, L. and M. Fangzhu, 2005. 'Study on Construction of the Agricultural S&T Extension System and Innovative Model in New Period', *Chinese Agricultural Science Bulletin*, 21(11), 430–32.
USA Today, 2007. 'Chinese Economy Slows to Still Sizzling 11.5% Growth', 25 October.
Veblen, T., 1983 [1921]. *Engineers and the Price System*. New Brunswick, N.J.: Transaction Books.
Wannian, L. et al., 2005. 'On Improvement of Chinese Medical Insurance System', *Chinese General Practice*, 8(9), 13–17.
Wen, J., 2010. 'Government Report to the National People's Congress', 5 March. http://www.gov.cn/2010lh/content_1555767.htm (accessed 29 March 2013).
Weiss, M., 2008. 'Skill-biased Technological Change: Is There Hope for the Unskilled?' *Economics Letters*, Elsevier, 100(3), 439–41.
World Intellectual Property Organization (WIPO). *WIPO Patent Report, 2007*, Geneva: World Intellectual Property Organization.
Yang, H., Yinpin Wu and Lichen Zhang, 2009. 'On Mao's View of Equality', *Marxism Theoretical Study* (in Chinese), May, 36–39.
Zeng, G. and Jingjing Hu, 2008. 'On the Change in Income Gap between Urban and Rural Residents since the End of 1970s and Its Impacts on Urban and Rural Consumption', *Economic Review*, 1, 45–54.
Zhang, X. and Ravi Kanbur, 2005. 'Spatial Inequality in Education and Health Care in China', *China Economic Review*, 16, 189–204.
Zhou, Jianhua, Yunhuan Tong and Jizhen Li, 2010. 'Study of Innovation Models for Low Income People, *Research of Economics and Management (in Chinese)*, 10, 12–17.

6

South Africa: The Need to Disrupt the Co-evolution of the Innovation System and Inequality

Lucienne Abrahams and *Thomas E. Pogue*

Trends and Patterns of Inequality

Inequality has defined South Africa's political economy historically and continues to be an intractable reality, with race, class, gender, and geographic dimensions. This chapter traces trends in interpersonal and inter-regional inequality within South Africa since the establishment of a democratic state in 1994. Since it is a trends study, the data used is from a range of years between 1994 and 2010, rather than only the most recent. The chapter further reviews key aspects of the co-evolution of the innovation system, side by side with current and historical inequality in the science, engineering and technology (SET) workforce and inequality in the benefits of innovation output.

Poverty and inequality can be examined from at least five perspectives, namely income, assets, services, infrastructure, and knowledge (Moser 1998; Angang and Chunbo 2001; Satterthwaite 2004). The examination in this chapter will touch on a few of these perspectives, including patterns of inequality in income, housing assets, health and education services and knowledge and innovation infrastructure.

Historical patterns of inequality

With an estimated population of 50.5 million people living in more than 14 million households (StatsSA 2010a, 2011a), South Africa's economic production is concentrated in six urban centres. These are Johannesburg, the country's financial and services hub, Pretoria, the administrative seat of government, Ekurhuleni, the historical focus of manufacturing, Cape Town, the heart of tourism and the seat of Parliament, Durban, a trade port and base of automotive manufacturing and Port Elizabeth with comparatively smaller industrial and services sectors. The majority of South Africa's urban population, or approximately 11.3 million people, reside in the province of Gauteng where the metropolitan municipalities of Johannesburg, Tshwane and Ekurhuleni are situated. South Africa was ranked 123 out of 187 countries with a Human Development Index (HDI) of 0.619 in 2011, with life expectancy at birth estimated at 52.8 years, adult literacy rate of 88.7 per cent, a combined gross enrolment ratio of only 51.6 per cent and GDP per capita of US$ 9,333 (PPP, constant US$ 2005) (UNDP 2011). HIV/AIDS is a significant factor influencing population trends and it is estimated that 5.3 million people are currently living with HIV (StatsSA 2011a).

More than 65 per cent of South Africa's population, or 34 million, people live outside the six metropolitan areas; in large and small towns and in rural locations, where the predominant economic activity is community services.[1] The Western Cape, Eastern Cape and KwaZulu-Natal provinces have very large rural town and village populations. For example, approximately 6 million people live in the rural municipalities of KwaZulu-Natal and approximately 6 million people in the rural parts of the Eastern Cape, many living on agriculture, subsistence farming, informal tourism ventures, or social grants. The Free State, Mpumalanga, Limpopo, and Northern Cape provinces have smaller populations and are not endowed with valuable economic infrastructure as in the other provinces, nor do they attract significant productive capital investment. Each province has a major city which is the seat of the provincial government, and where business and government services are therefore important contributors to gross geographic product. The estimate for migration of people from one province to another indicates that net migration is positive for the provinces of Gauteng, Western Cape and KwaZulu-Natal and negative for the remaining six provinces (StatsSA 2011a).

Interpersonal inequalities: Income and consumption

The size of the South African economy in 2010 was US$ 534.2 billion and GDP per capita was approximately US$ 10,687 (StatsSA 2010b, 2011b).[1] The mean per capita income for the population as a whole is relatively low at US$ 361.71 per month and income inequality is extremely high at a ratio of 43:1 for the richest quintile as compared to the poorest quintile (RSA 2010: 23). The richest 20 per cent of the population earned 70 per cent of total per capita income, while the poorest 20 per cent of the population earned 1.6 per cent of total per capita income in 2008. The African mean income is little more than half of the total mean per capita income, the Coloured mean is just under the total, and the Indian and White means are significantly greater than the total, reflecting the racial history of income and poverty patterns (ibid.).

While income distribution is a limited indicator because of its exclusion of non-income-based public resources that benefit an individual or a household, it is a relatively tractable indicator that is useful in international comparisons. Figure 6.1 reports South Africa's Lorenz curve on a five-yearly basis between 1995 and 2005 (StatsSA 1995, 2000, 2005).[3]

Income inequality represented by the Lorenz curves has decreased recently among the poorest third of South African households, but inequality has risen among the remaining two-thirds of households. Table 6.1 reports differences between mean and median income per decile in 2005. It illustrates a relatively large number of households near the decile average for the poorest third of households, as well as increasing inequality amongst the higher income deciles, with the top decile reporting a median income per household of US$ 74.424 compared to that decile's mean income of US$ 104.012. A further indicator of the inequality of income distributions in South Africa is the ratio of the top decile to the bottom decile. In the most recent income and expenditures survey year of 2005, the mean income of the top decile was 94 times that of the bottom decile.

Exceptionally high levels of income inequality are further illustrated by the Gini coefficient as illustrated in Table 6.2.[4] These estimates are

Figure 6.1: *Household Income Inequality: Lorenz Curve (1995–2005)*

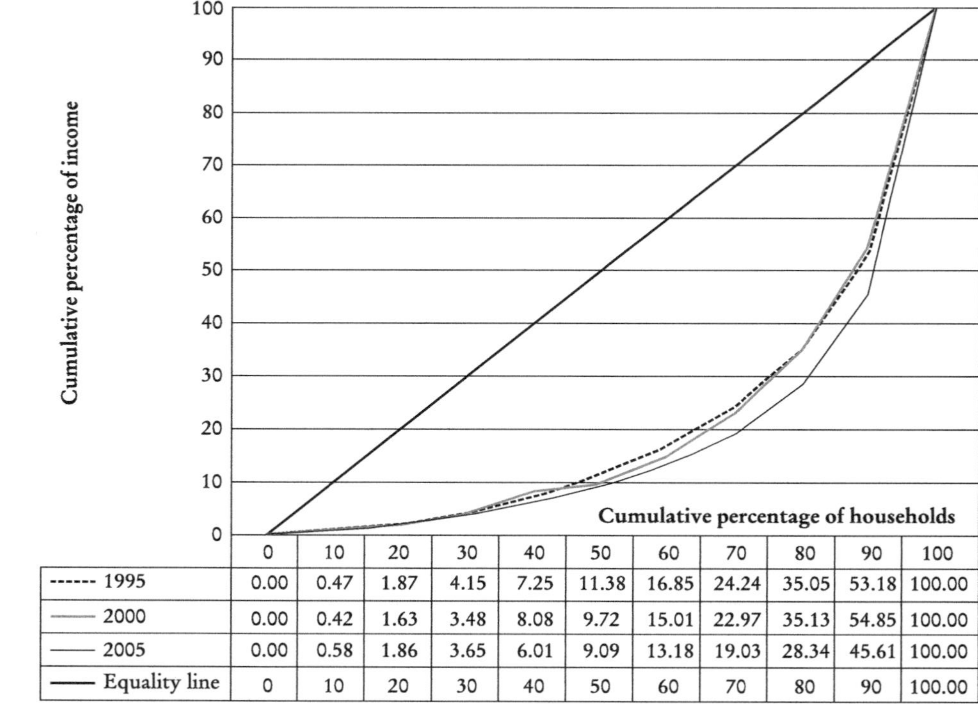

	0	10	20	30	40	50	60	70	80	90	100
1995	0.00	0.47	1.87	4.15	7.25	11.38	16.85	24.24	35.05	53.18	100.00
2000	0.00	0.42	1.63	3.48	8.08	9.72	15.01	22.97	35.13	54.85	100.00
2005	0.00	0.58	1.86	3.65	6.01	9.09	13.18	19.03	28.34	45.61	100.00
Equality line	0	10	20	30	40	50	60	70	80	90	100.00

Source: Calculations based on StatsSA (1995, 2000, 2005).

Table 6.1: *Mean and Median Income per Decile (2005)*

	Mean	Median
Decile	*US$ Per Annum (at PPP)*	*US$ Per Annum (at PPP)*
1	1,106	1,156
2	2,459	2,516
3	3,410	3,414
4	4,521	4,494
5	5,893	5,857
6	7,829	7,763
7	11,177	11,065
8	17,831	17,571
9	33,037	32,075
10	104,012	74,424
Total	**19,125**	**6,741**

Source: Table derived from StatsSA (2005).

Table 6.2: *Gini Coefficient Estimates of Income Inequality (1995–2008)*

1995	*2000*	*2005*	*2006*	*2007*	*2008*
0.64	0.68	0.69	0.685	0.66	0.67

Source: Bhorat et al. (2009), based on StatisSA (1995, 2000, 2005); SAARF (2006–08).

said to place South Africa in the position of greater inequality than Brazil in 2008 (Bhorat et al. 2009). The Gini coefficient assesses income inequality across all households as the ratio of the area between the Lorenz curve and the equality line, to the total area below the equality line.[2] While some change in the Gini coefficient is attributable to methodological and sampling revisions, overall a steady and increasing pattern of inequality is evident in these Gini coefficient estimates.

Income inequality has increased in the period since democracy, signalling the rise of a relatively large Black middle class, against a continued escalation in unemployment of the majority Black population, arising from job losses in historically important economic sectors such as mining and agriculture over at least two decades. Thus income inequality arises in part from the increase in intra-racial inequality. Greater inequality is also driven by a shift in the sectoral earnings shares from manufacturing and transport to government, the finance, insurance, real estate and business services (FIRE) and construction sectors, at lower average wage rates. The real growth in unit labour costs (ULC) evident in Table 6.3 is led by the mining and transport sectors.

Table 6.3: *ULC by Sector (1999–2010) (1999 = 100)*

	1999	*2000*	*2001*	*2002*	*2003*	*2004*	*2005*	*2006*	*2007*	*2008*	*2009*	*2010*	*Average Annual Rate (%)*
Finance, real estate and business services	100	98	95	96	97	93	92	94	99	100	103	106	0.5
Manufacturing	100	105	109	113	122	122	123	120	119	122	112	113	1.1
General government services	100	100	100	102	105	103	105	107	110	115	113	114	1.2
Agriculture, forestry and fishing	100	97	109	102	103	105	108	126	134	144	137	123	1.8
Electricity, gas and water	100	101	102	98	104	101	102	105	109	108	126	123	1.9
Economy-wide	**100**	**103**	**106**	**110**	**113**	**113**	**116**	**120**	**123**	**127**	**123**	**126**	**2.1**
Personal services	100	101	100	105	110	109	113	115	117	121	124	132	2.5
Construction	100	101	105	108	111	119	128	138	128	145	151	135	2.7
Wholesale and retail trade; hotels and restaurants	100	104	110	112	117	115	118	120	125	132	133	143	3.3
Transport, storage and communication	100	106	109	118	124	123	128	134	136	153	154	153	3.9
Mining and quarrying	100	111	122	134	126	123	135	144	149	164	148	158	4.1

Source: Calculations based on StatisSA (1999–2010a, 1999–2010b) estimates.

Bhorat, van der Westhuizen and Jacobs (2009: 57) argue that the increasing levels of wage inequality can be partly attributed to the 'ever increasing skill premium paid to highly skilled workers'. This is an important analytical insight for viewing the scientific workforce and the innovation system, as the existence of a premium may militate against funding allocations to increase the size of that workforce or to increase the value of innovation to society.

With total employment at around 13.1 million in June 2011, South Africa has a very small informal sector of around 2.2 million (excluding agriculture and domestic employment) or less than 17 per cent of the total employed, significantly lower than either Brazil or India (DBSA 2005; RSA 2010; StatsSA 2011c). Kingdon and Knight (2001: 4, 10) argue that this may be due to barriers to entry to the informal sector in South Africa, such as the costs of entry to market, licensing controls, restrictive municipal (city) by-laws and failure to provide requisite facilities and infrastructure for informal economic activity. The residual effects of apartheid segregation can be noted in the spatial distribution of population, where the unemployed still mainly live in townships far from industrial areas, from highly urbanised areas and from residential areas where they might earn an income from informal business and services. The cost of entry to these potential markets for informal services is therefore high in terms of transport costs, as well as capital costs for business infrastructure, e.g. the costs to an unemployed person of buying the equipment necessary to offer a one-person gardening service.

As regards consumption patterns, the most important asset class for the majority of South Africans is housing. In 2009, 76.2 per cent of households lived in a formal dwelling, 10.4 per cent of households lived in a traditional dwelling and 1.8 million households or 13.5 per cent living in informal settlements. In 2009, of a planned 3.9 million housing units, 3 million subsidised units were completed or were in progress (RSA 2010: 30) (see Figure 6.2).

There is significant demand for rental housing by individuals earning below US$ 1,660 per month, including people who cannot afford to own property, people who own property in rural areas but live and work in the city, and people who rent in informal settlements (FFC 2009: 59). Access to and quality of publicly funded housing is a good indicator with respect to reducing inequality in general household consumption patterns, as people who own a house are more likely

Figure 6.2: *Housing Units (1994–2009)*

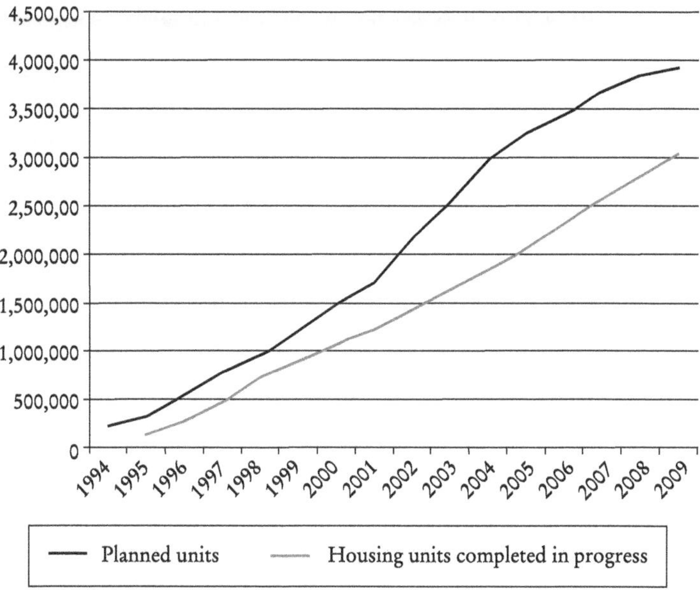

Source: RSA (2010: 30), based on National Department of Human Settlements data.

to have the requisite disposable income (even if it is small) to acquire other household goods and consumables, than those who do not own a house.

For a relatively low income per capita country, South Africa exhibits quite a good picture regarding the percentage of the population that owns housing assets. However, this belies the quality of much publicly funded housing. In 2009, the Minister of Housing and Human Settlements announced that several thousand houses built and subsidised through government housing contracts would need to be rebuilt because they are 'poorly constructed', highlighting corruption by construction companies and government officials (*Mail & Guardian Online* 2009). This alert points to the need for innovation activities to address the quality of housing assets, as regards at least three factors (*a*) basic quality assurance processes; (*b*) eliminating corruption in the process of asset creation; and (*c*) leveraging the value of government expenditure on housing assets by building houses that the owners will further invest in. Such an approach to innovation, aimed at increasing the efficiency and value of public spending, would enable low income households to spend a greater proportion of their limited disposable income on food, clothing, transport, electronic goods, and entertainment, rather than on remedying the defects in public housing.

With respect to services, a significant percentage of the middle and upper middle class chooses private schooling and private healthcare, amongst the range of personal services obtained from the private sector, where these services are obtained at a premium price as compared to public facilities paid for by the taxpayer. The public sector provides both economic and social infrastructure, as well as community and personal services based on a division of revenue to provincial and municipal government. These capital investments and transfer payments are an important redistributive factor, however, the redistributive impact is limited in terms of reducing structural inequality.

Interpersonal inequalities are strongly correlated with employment patterns, with inter-sectoral inequality and with inter-regional inequality, as examined later. Hence, South Africa experiences structural inequality as inequality is determined by the structure of the economy at the micro level, both as regards the shape and size of particular economic sectors, the business and wage models for each sector, and the geographic distribution of the productive economy.

Before the 2009 recession South Africa saw an upward trend in real per capita GDP growth between 1999 and 2008, providing the basis for a degree of redistribution through taxation and public expenditure (RSA 2010: 5). Social grants and non-cash social services funded by the government fiscus, such as public health and education, are major contributors to reducing interpersonal inequality. By March 2010, more than 14 million people received social assistance support grants to the value of more than 3 per cent of GDP (ibid.: 28). Social grants for the aged, children and the disabled appear to be highly effective in diminishing the impact of poverty, in an environment where more than 13 million people currently live on less than US$ 2.50 per day (ibid.: 26).[6]

In all, 76 per cent of government spending on social grants accrues to the 50 percent of the population that constitute the poorest two quintiles of households; moreover, grants raise the income share of the poorest 40 per cent of households from 4.7 per cent of pre-transfer income to 7.8 per cent of post-transfer income (FFC 2009: 63–64).

Important findings of a range of studies quoted by the FFC (2009), including studies on the impact of the child support grant and old-age pensions, show that social grants are used to purchase food, clothing and education, to relieve child poverty and enhance school enrolment. However, negative consequences of the grant system include a disincentive for unemployed persons to seek employment or create self-employment where they reside in households with at least one pension recipient (ibid.: 39–40). Thus social grants decrease interpersonal inequality for old-age pensioners and child grant recipients amongst others, but may drive interpersonal inequality for unemployed persons. Bhorat et al. (2009: 55–58) argue that, while grant income has been important to address the most negative effects of increasing income inequality, particularly for the African and rural populations, future policy measures should aim at strengthening education and labour market policies with a view to increasing employment as a long-term development strategy.

Inter-regional inequalities

As previously stated, the South African economy is dominated by the Gauteng province. This is evidenced by that province's consistent share of a third of GDP between 2002 and 2009. This share of output was significantly above a fifth of the national population which Gauteng composed during the same period. Comparison of the equality amongst provinces based on their relative output and population shares (see Table 6.4) is facilitated by computation of a Theil T statistic.

Trends of inter-provincial output inequalities between 1995 and 2009 are presented in Figure 6.3. Accordingly, output inequality among South Africa's provinces has declined from 0.11 to 0.06. Examination of the data in Table 6.4 indicates that part of this decline is caused by the relatively constant share of output in Gauteng (34 per cent) while its share of population has grown from 18 per cent in 1995 to 21 per cent in 2009. Similarly, while the Eastern Cape has had a constant share of output (8 per cent) during this period, its share of population has dropped from 16 per cent in 1995 to 13 per cent in 2009.

Figure 6.3 indicates that Gauteng and the Western Cape were consistently greater contributors in the value of their economic output relative to their population size. Similarly, five provinces — the North West, the Free State, Limpopo, KwaZulu-Natal, and the Eastern Cape — were consistently generating less output relative to their population shares. This can be explained partly by the relatively

Table 6.4: *South African GDP and Population: Provincial Distribution, South African GDP (US$ billion at PPP) (Top-Matrix) and Provincial Shares (Columns Annual percentage of Total)*

Province	*2002*	*2003*	*2004*	*2005*	*2006*	*2007*	*2008*	*2009*
Western Cape	14	14	15	15	15	15	14	14
Eastern Cape	8	8	8	8	8	8	8	8
Northern Cape	2	2	2	2	2	2	2	2
Free State	6	5	5	5	5	5	5	5
KwaZulu-Natal	16	16	16	16	16	16	16	16
North West	7	6	6	6	6	6	7	7
Gauteng	34	34	34	34	34	34	34	34
Mpumalanga	7	7	7	7	7	7	7	7
Limpopo	7	7	7	7	7	7	7	7
South Africa	**US$ 319**	**US$ 340**	**US$ 368**	**US$ 403**	**US$ 440**	**US$ 479**	**US$ 503**	**US$ 493**

South African population (millions) (bottom-matrix) & provincial shares (columns annual percentage of total)

Province	*2002*	*2003*	*2004*	*2005*	*2006*	*2007*	*2008*	*2009*
Western Cape	10	10	10	10	10	10	11	11
Eastern Cape	16	14	15	15	15	14	14	13
Northern Cape	2	2	2	2	2	2	2	2
Free State	6	6	6	6	6	6	6	6
KwaZulu-Natal	20	21	21	21	21	21	21	21
North West	8	8	8	8	7	7	7	7
Gauteng	18	20	19	19	20	20	21	21
Mpumalanga	7	7	7	7	7	7	7	7
Limpopo	13	12	12	12	11	11	11	11
South Africa	**45.5**	**46.4**	**46.6**	**46.9**	**47.4**	**47.8**	**48.7**	**49.3**

Source: Calculations based on StatsSA (2002–9a, 2002–9b).

higher concentration of urban populations for the former and rural populations for the latter provinces. For example, of the approximately 10.8 million population of KwaZulu-Natal (StatsSA 2011a), around two-thirds reside in rural districts with limited access to productive resources, infrastructure, services, or post-secondary education. In districts such as Zululand, with a largely agricultural base, unemployment has reached rates of 50 per cent of the working age population in the past decade (KZN DED 2006).

KwaZulu-Natal (KZN) can be used as a proxy to understand eight of South Africa's provinces other than Gauteng. Gauteng is a highly urbanised province incorporating three of the country's six metropolitan municipalities, whereas eight provinces have either a single or no metropolitan municipality. Gauteng is South Africa's financial centre and the home of the Johannesburg Stock Exchange. It hosts the administrative seat of the national government, the majority of national corporate headquarters including mining houses and the five largest banks, multinational corporate headquarters, as well as embassies and consulates. KwaZulu-Natal province, by contrast, has only three major productive centres: the coastal metro area of Ethekwini (Durban is the major city) which has a population of approximately 2 million, the inland town of Pietermaritzburg and the harbour town at Richards Bay (see Figure 6.4). The 400 km coastline is spotted with more sparsely populated urban towns and intermittent tourism and small-scale manufacturing, while the rural hinterland, with a population of more than 3.9 million people, has very limited infrastructure or opportunities for income generation (KZN DED 2006). The region contributes around 16.2 per cent to GDP with the main sectors being manufacturing, in particular automotive, chemicals and textiles; finance, real estate and business services; wholesale, retail, hotels, and restaurants; general government services; and transport and communication being the major contributors. Despite its coastal nature and vast rural geography, agriculture, forestry and fishing contribute only 4.4 per cent to gross geographic product (GGP) (StatsSA 2008a). Around 35 per cent of the population is employed, 14 per cent is unemployed and 50 per cent is not economically active. It has significant intra-regional disparities in income, assets, services, and infrastructure.

The Western and Eastern Cape have relatively smaller urban bases. The smallest provinces by population and GDP contribution, namely

Figure 6.3: *Theil Elements of Inter-provincial per capita GDP (1995–2009)*

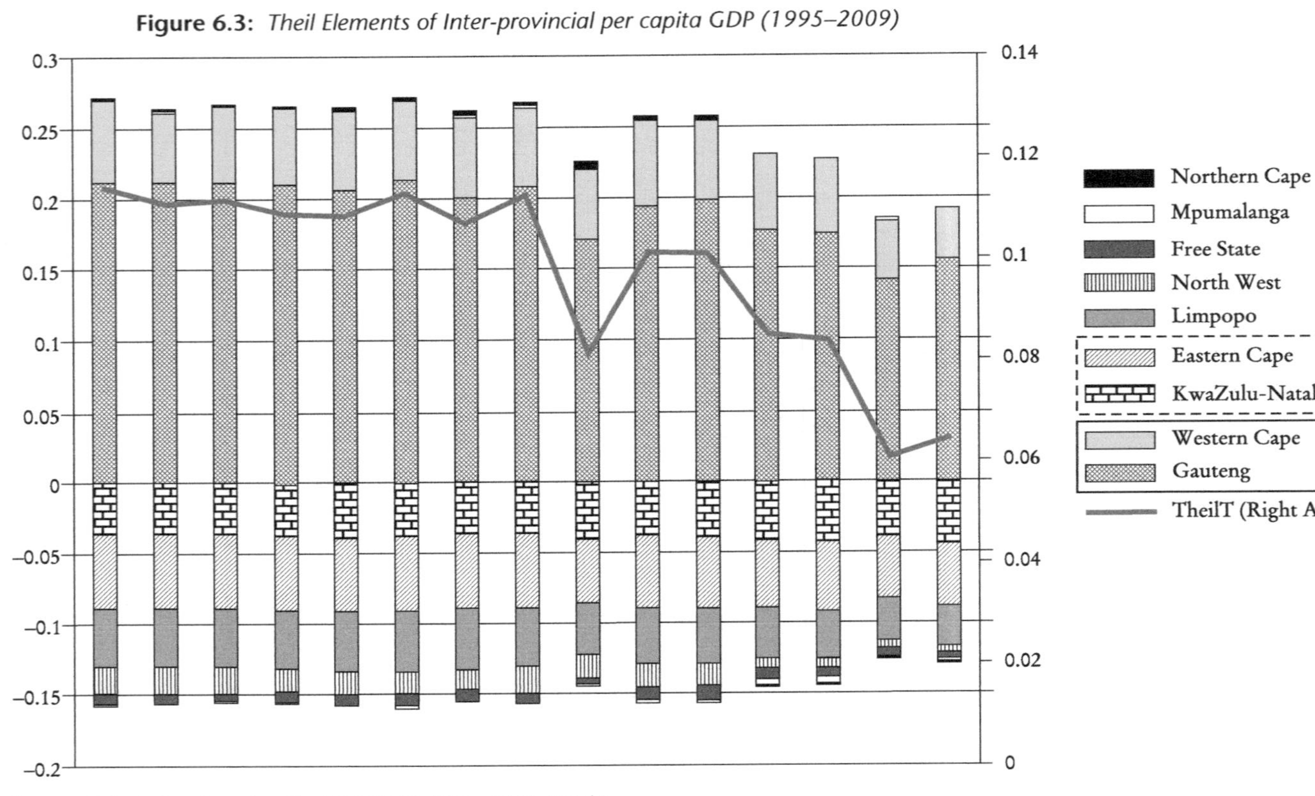

Source: Calculations based on StatisSA (1995–2009a; 1995–2009b).

Figure 6.4: *Map of KwaZulu-Natal Province*

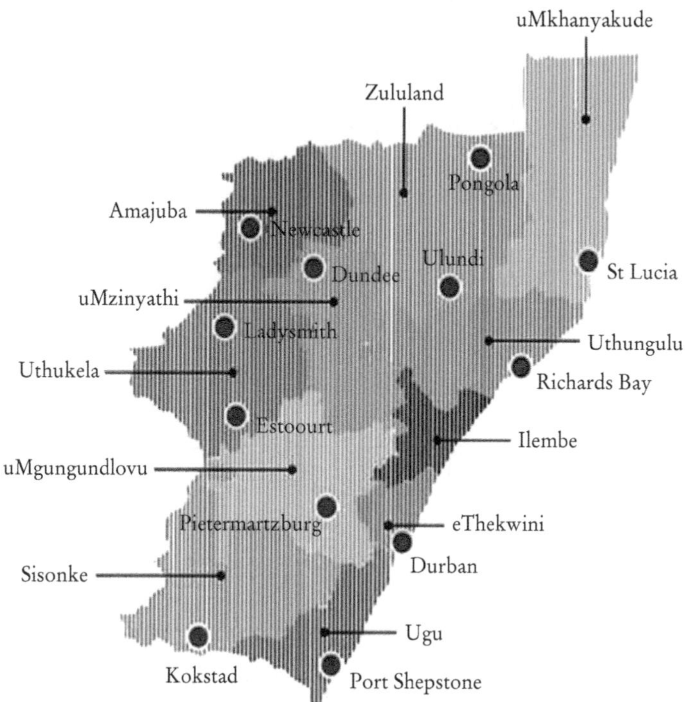

Source: Adapted from Ebandla Project, KwaZulu-Natal Provincial Government, available at http://www.ebandla.co.za/KZNGrowthCoalition_6.ca (accessed 9 July 2013).

the Free State and Northern Cape provinces, have a single major town, Bloemfontein and Kimberley respectively, with very limited industry or economic infrastructure outside these towns.

Provincial labour force participation rates for the period 2000–10 show positive rates for the Gauteng, Western Cape and Free State provinces, and negative participation rates for the remaining six provinces, with the Eastern Cape, North West and Limpopo provinces showing the lowest rates (see Table 6.5).

Another indicator of inter-regional inequalities is unemployment rates. Employment is a significant source of knowledge generation

Table 6.5: *National Unemployment Rate and Provincial Variations (2000–10)*

	KwaZulu-Natal	*Limpopo*	*Western Cape*	*South Africa (%)*	*North West*	*Gauteng*	*Free State*	*Northern Cape*	*Eastern Cape*	*Mpumalanga*
2000	–3	4	–3	23	8	2	–2	–8	0	–4
2001	0	7	–6	26	5	1	–2	–5	3	–5
2002	0	6	–5	27	5	0	–2	–7	4	–5
2003	–1	4	–3	25	6	0	–1	–4	6	–7
2004	–2	2	–2	23	4	0	2	–3	5	–4
2005	1	4	–3	23	4	–3	3	–4	5	–3
2006	–3	4	–5	22	10	–2	0	0	7	1
2007	1	4	–2	21	6	–3	0	0	4	–2
2008	–1	6	–3	23	4	–1	0	–1	4	0
2009	–6	1	–2	24	3	1	4	5	3	1
2010	–6	0	–2	25	3	1	4	0	2	3

Source: Table derived from StatsSA (2000–07, 2008b, 2009, 2010c).

and an indicator of the mobilisation of tacit knowledge. In aggregate, South Africa has a relatively high unemployment rate which has ranged in recent years from a high of 29 per cent in March of 2003 to a low of 21 per cent in September 2007 before registering a consistent rise, supported in part by the global recession of 2009, to above 25 per cent in 2010.

The dynamics of provincial unemployment have varied considerably during this period. The Western Cape generally reported a lower rate of unemployment than the national rate. After initially recording slightly higher than the national rate, Gauteng has also recorded consistently lower unemployment before again registering a rate above the national average. In contrast, Limpopo and the Eastern Cape have recorded consistently higher unemployment rates. Unemployment in the Free State went from a position initially lower than the national average to a rate consistently greater than or equal to the national average. KwaZulu-Natal and the Northern Cape have tended to record similar or slightly lower incidences of unemployment than the national average. Mpumalanga and the North West have had greater variation, but in general have recorded increasing unemployment with respect to the national average.

Class, race, gender, and inequality

Historically, inter-racial inequality has been an important characteristic of income inequality in South Africa and remains a factor for a large proportion of the population. However, decadal rates of change indicate that intra-racial inequality is also an increasingly important characteristic of income inequality in South Africa post-1994 (see Table 6.6). Among the four racial classifications for which data is provided in South Africa, intra-racial inequality increased for all populations — African, Indian, Coloured, and White. While difference in survey methodologies from past surveys to the current may explain some of the changes in values, the overall trend of increasing inequality within racial groups appears evident.[3]

This may be partly accounted for, by increases in class and gender inequality within these historically racial groups, as new opportunities in high-income jobs and business ventures began to determine the shape of inequality in South African society on a class and gender

Table 6.6: *Intra-racial Gini Coefficient Estimates of Household Income Inequality, 1995–2005*

	1995	*2000*	*2005*
Black African	0.52	0.49	0.63
Coloured	0.5	0.48	0.59
Indian/Asian	0.44	0.41	0.57
White	0.49	0.45	0.56

Source: Seekings and Nattrass (2005) based on StatisSA (1995, 2000 and 2005).

basis. Positions in corporate management, in the medical, legal and other professions were increasingly being filled by people from across the spectrum of South African society, though Black and White males appear to be the greatest beneficiaries of this opening up of economic opportunities. Seekings (2008: 23) argues that 'the evidence supports the unsurprising conclusion that the removal of racial constraints has led to continuing upward mobility among African people, in terms of both occupations and incomes, such that class differences within the African population are becoming more important as interracial differences decline'. While women participate widely in economic activity across all productive sectors and income levels, women form the bulk of the workforce in low-paid sectors such as in the clothing and textile sector, the public health sector and in domestic work.

Concluding remarks on trends in inequality

Public policy seeks to increase per capita income and to reduce unemployment. This requires a chain of actions. It requires facilitating greater impact of redistributive mechanisms on the capacity of society to move towards sustainable livelihoods through distributive means over the next two to three decades. In other words, social transfers, while necessary for now, must in the long term have the effect of growing future generations of people with productive capacities. In particular, productive capacities need to be geared towards making the benefits of science and technology more broadly available to society. A greater proportion of the benefits of investment in innovation must go to the 40 per cent of the population with the lowest income.

South African society requires political, business and community leadership to build sustained efforts to shift structural inequality as the only means of increasing income for the lowest quintile of the population and pushing the African mean income levels strongly towards the total mean income level. Given the current shape and size of the South African economy and its relative positioning in the global economy, strategies to address structural inequality will require major shifts in economic policy, charting a direction away from reliance on low-wage-labour resource mining towards medium-high technology production. Changing the history of centuries of dispossession and inequality will also require strategies to increase sustainable subsistence agriculture and to reposition South Africa's rural provinces with respect to participation in the local and global knowledge economy.

For each province, some potential for structural change exists. Though the change trajectory may occur over more than two decades, agendas can be set now. Such agendas are being formulated and acted on by, inter alia, Gauteng province through its global city-region 2055 approach and KwaZulu-Natal through its knowledge economy focus and building of an ICT and electronics cluster.[8] The comparative advantages of provinces such as Limpopo, Free State and the Eastern Cape in terms of their future positioning in the productive system must be assessed, theorised and strategised. The role of R&D and innovation in this strategic positioning must come under scrutiny.

Co-evolution of Innovation System and Inequality

This section analyses the co-evolution of inequality and the innovation system to highlight how the various elements of innovation in the production system and inequality mutually reinforce each other. It covers the private sector domination of R&D and unequal access to the global production network. Market-driven trade and investment under globalisation are briefly examined. It further reports on the public sector orientation towards supporting SET innovation in the production system for increased global competitiveness, as well as the limited but increasing drive for research to address social objectives.

A negatively mutually reinforcing relationship exists between the relative strength and particular focus of the innovation system and the state of inequality in South Africa. On the one hand, the low levels of R&D investment and the selective focus on innovation in manufactured goods over nearly three decades has contributed little to SME development, as the majority of SMEs operate in the broad services sector. This has meant that economic development amongst the historically disenfranchised communities has moved at a slow pace, despite the presence of democratic government. The policy emphasis in the past 15 years, and also the investment focus, has been on a Black economic empowerment (BEE) model based largely on asset structuring and deal financing, rather than on promoting innovation in Black-owned business, in small firms, in the informal sector or in social ventures. On the other hand, inhibitors in the education and health sectors have thus far resulted in limited progress towards fostering successive generations of researchers, knowledge workers and entrepreneurs. With respect to technology and knowledge inputs and innovation outputs, South Africa continues to advance slowly within the structural constraints of its economy, characterised by decline in the competitiveness of its manufacturing, mining and agricultural sectors.

National system of innovation and production dynamics

The structure of the South African economy is characterised by a large services sector, with services contributing 65 per cent of South Africa's sectoral value added between 2000 and 2010.[4] The finance, real estate and business services sector contributed over 32 per cent of the total service sector value added during this period. Between 2000 and 2010 the sectoral value in US$ PPP of services grew at a compound annual growth rate of 5.8 per cent. During this period, agriculture accounted for 3 per cent of value added, the mining and quarrying sector was a further 9 per cent and manufacturing contributed 17 per cent. Secondary industries which consist of manufacturing, utilities and the construction sector accounted for 23 per cent of national value added during this period. Secondary industries grew at an annualised rate of 4.3 per cent, which was less than that of services and the 6.5 per cent annualised growth in the primary sectors of agriculture and mining.

Formalised R&D and innovation operates in each of these sectors, with R&D performed by business, by publicly-funded scientific performing agencies and by universities. Business R&D performance constitutes the greater proportion of total R&D. According to Kahn and Blankley (2006: 280), there has been a high concentration of R&D expenditure in the four largest firms (40 per cent), in six universities (60 per cent) and in two science agencies (50 per cent). The public science system composed of 23 universities, 16 scientific performing agencies, eight national research facilities and eight scientific funding agencies exhibits the imprint of formation in a highly unequal society. Many of these institutions were formed in the cauldron of race and gender inequality that characterised the apartheid decades, though a few such as the Technology Innovation Agency were established since democracy or in the last decade. They continue to exhibit race and gender stratification in the demographics of the researcher populations, as well as in the student body and in the professoriate. This composition is changing very slowly as academic science attracts small numbers of knowledge workers as compared to careers in business and government.

The Council for Scientific and Industrial Research (CSIR) and the Agricultural Research Council (ARC) are valuable institutions in the national system of innovation (NSI), geared to contributing R&D for economic competitiveness and industrial and agricultural sustainability. The Human Sciences Research Council (HSRC) and the Africa Institute (AI) are key institutions collecting and analysing data and contributing to public policy formulation. The six research-intensive universities have built a strong knowledge base in a wide range of disciplines and in multi-disciplinary areas feeding competitiveness and societal development. These research-productive firms and public sector institutions provide the innovation infrastructure and exhibit the features of a newly evolving system, which includes the continuous reformulation of research agendas as the system adapts to its local and global knowledge context.

Next, let us see some important numbers regarding the size and shape of the R&D system: Between 1983–84 and 2003–04, the gross domestic expenditure on research and development (GERD)–GDP ratio fluctuated between 0.85 per cent and 0.6 per cent, with a median level of 0.76 per cent (Kahn and Blankley 2006). From 1993–94 to 2008–09, GERD increased from a relatively low 0.61 per cent of GDP (US$ 1.2 billion) to 0.92 per cent or US$ 4.6 billion (DST 2010: 7, 14).[10] The latter period saw an increase both in real expenditure and in GERD as a percentage of GDP. The South African innovation system includes business R&D performance of around US$ 2.7 billion at the latest available count, higher education expense of around US$ 928 million or 20 per cent of measurable R&D investment, as well as government contribution of just over 20 per cent. Total innovation expenditure including R&D was around US$ 13.53 billion in 2007 (DST 2011).

What are the trends in expenditure; what are the objectives that drive innovation-funding allocations? The purpose to which these funds were put can be observed from an analysis of R&D expenditure by major research fields and by socio-economic objectives (Kahn and Blankley 2006: 279). When viewed by research field, more than 87 per cent of expenditure has gone to the natural sciences, engineering and technology and just more than 12 per cent to the social sciences and humanities. The engineering sciences, medical and health sciences, and the ICT sector each received relatively high shares (between 13 and 20 per cent), while the environmental, materials and marine sciences received very small shares (less than 2 per cent) of R&D expenditure. When viewed by socio-economic objective, around 63 per cent have focused on economic development objectives including manufacturing, mineral resources and commercial services (each receiving a share between 8 and 14 per cent), whereas expenditure on R&D in key areas such as energy resources and supply, education and training, and environmental knowledge received relatively low shares of total expenditure (5 per cent or less in each case) (CESTII 2008). The e-fields (energy, education, environment) have become areas in which innovation is in great demand and where investment has been consistently low over too long a period, yet there has been no significant shift in funding priorities.

The private sector contribution derives from a range of fields including the banking and finance sector, the mobile telecommunications and information technology sectors, the pharmaceutical sector and innovations in business strategy and leadership. The largest proportion of this funded R&D activity is located in the Gauteng province. Analysis of the expenditure on innovation activities by business enterprises suggests that the major expenditure is on acquisition of machinery, equipment and software (65 per cent) and on other knowledge external to the business (7 per cent), while in-house R&D accounts for 20 per cent of expenditure (NACI 2008: 25). This has led to the assessment that:

> Knowledge intensive service industries (such as communication, financial, business, education and health services) and high-technology

> manufacturing industries (such as aerospace, pharmaceuticals, computers and office machinery, communications equipment and scientific instruments) are of particular importance in international trade and in knowledge-based economies. South Africa's international trade is still characterised by a tendency towards the export of primary products and resource-based manufacturing, with relatively low levels of high-technology exports . . . The business sector is the dominant force in funding and performing R&D. This is a positive factor from a business perspective, but it would appear that research efforts have not yet resulted in the increased development of medium- to high-technology goods and knowledge-intensive services (NACI 2008: 38).

A small country by population and geographical size, as compared with Brazil, India or China, South Africa's innovation system has undergone significant renewal in the past 15 years. The total research workforce (by full-time equivalent) of 30,802 people, includes 19,384 researchers, with women researchers comprising 39.7 per cent of all researchers (DST 2010: 7). The total number of researchers is 1.4 per thousand employed persons, comparable to Brazil and China, but low as compared to the Russian Federation at approximately 6.7 per thousand (NACI 2009a: 35).

What is the value of the innovation system for society? Despite the many innovative products and solutions adopted locally and exported abroad, the challenge to produce innovations that will contribute to changing the landscape of class, race and gender inequality and centuries of deprivation remains.

The history of innovation in South Africa can be traced to the early 1900s with the founding of institutions such as the Onderstepoort Veterinary Research Laboratories in 1908 and the CSIR in the immediate period post-World War II (Addison 2002; Mouton and Gevers 2009: 39–45). However, the early system was designed largely to service the economic needs of the minority White population and the participation of Black people in these institutions was typically at the level of low-income wage labour. Both the government and the private sector, for example, the mining sector, contributed to early knowledge infrastructure formation, funding the establishment of institutions which evolved to become today's universities. But here too, knowledge infrastructure formation was contaminated by apartheid logic, creating a highly differentiated higher and further education system with places reserved for people of different racial classifications. On this basis, research was largely excluded from the mandate and funding of historically Black universities.

During the period from 1960 to 1994, the government-funded research institutions focused largely on apartheid-sanctions busting by re-engineering global technology products for local consumption. By 1994 new science and technology production had gone into decline, as evidenced by falling investment in domestic experimental research and development (R&D) and a narrow focus on building tradable know-how in the defence and nuclear armaments sectors. Nevertheless, the eight science councils and the research active universities were well placed to participate in the creation of a national innovation system, though they required repurposing with respect to their missions and revitalisation of the scientific workforce.

Unsurprisingly, the majority of the research producing universities, as well as the scientific performing and the scientific funding agencies are based in South Africa's industrial heartland, the Gauteng province. While historically this is due to the science system developing around the attractive forces of economic demand and the seat of government, this clustering may today play a part in stagnation in the contribution of R&D to the local economies outside of Gauteng province. However, provinces such as KwaZulu-Natal and the Free State are seeking to reinvent their economies as 'knowledge-based' economies and are accordingly making the requisite infrastructure investments or considering new economic strategies. It has been noted that: 'Innovation is not a quick fix, it needs sustained efforts' (Xue 2009).

This dictum requires due attention in a small country, such as South Africa, whose infrastructure and resources are limited by its recent emergence (15 years) from a period of poor investment in productive innovation assets.

Post-1994, the innovation system has produced outputs across a wide range of economic sectors and technologies. This range includes productive activity in the transport manufacturing sector including automotive components for export, the opening of the South African Large Telescope (SALT) and other initiatives in radio-astronomy, nuclear medicine at iThemba LABS, eradicating alien plant species that threaten indigenous biological diversity in the Working for Water programme, the 'play-pump' introduced into schools to draw borehole water, and a wide range of social innovations (Addison 2005a).

As regards technological innovation and original manufacture or process development, the major contribution of innovation to economy and society has remained at the level of complex technologies for business and industry and commercial products for the middle classes, as evidenced by the greater proportion of GERD expenditure by business (53.5 per cent), compared to 20.3 per cent from the government and 0.4 per cent from the not-for-profit sector according to National Experimental Research and Development survey data for 2008–09 (DST 2011).[11]

While both private and public sector R&D investments have generally supported innovation for commercialisation in narrow product markets, some commercial outputs have benefitted society at large and some investments have had a social impact. Demand for innovation in services is visible across all income levels. For the public sector the most visible demand is with respect to health services (HIV/AIDS, tuberculosis, cancer, other), policing and crime reduction, public transport, energy, and electronic communications with government. As regards social innovation, which may be characterised as applying research and knowledge to address social needs, South Africa has witnessed some advances in the past 15 years. One such example is iThemba LABS which provides access to very expensive proton and neutron therapy for cancer patients referred by public hospitals.

For the private sector, demand for innovation in services is highly visible in banking and mobile communications. Innovation in banking channels has been an ongoing field of endeavour for around 25 years, commencing with the introduction of ATM banking in the 1980s and moving to telephone banking, Internet banking and mobile banking in the early 21st century. Innovations in ATM banking have seen the spread of non-cash machines to small rural retail outlets, where a withdrawal of funds involves an electronic transaction through the bank's computer system and the presentation of a receipt which can be exchanged for cash at the retailer. Innovative mobile phone products aimed at 'banking the unbanked' have been introduced into the market by Wizzit, a division of the South African Bank of Athens Limited (Fisher-French 2008).[12] Some electronic banking products are mature, while some are still in their infancy. Slowly, the banking industry is extending the benefits of innovation to a growing percentage of the population.

Another field which has seen value for all income groups is local innovations in mobile telephony, which has brought 21st century technology within the reach of millions of poor South Africans. Mobile voice and data services introduced communications access to poor communities in the context of an over-priced telecommunications market and a failure of the incumbent operator to successfully take fixed-line access to the majority of households (Esselaar et al. 2006: 39–40). The pre-paid system for SIM-cards and airtime has meant that communications can be maintained via voice or data (SMS 'texting') for as little as US$ 0.67 worth of airtime, with low-income users typically employing the 'please call me' SMS feature.[13] The state of access to and usage of information and communications technologies has advanced rapidly since 2000, with relatively high mobile penetration levels of 72 per cent of households in 2010 (StatsSA 2010a: 33). In the early part of the decade, mobile voice and Internet usage was stifled by very high prices and lack of effective competition in the market (Esselaar et al. 2006: 49–51), creating a 'digital divide' for the majority of the South African population. A 2010 Internet survey reports total broadband subscribers of 1.5 million out of a total of around 5.3 million unique Internet subscribers in December 2009 (World Wide Worx 2010: 136).

Low levels of mobile voice and Internet usage have been an obstacle to generating the social and economic information flows necessary to foster an innovative culture in society. However, this landscape appears to be shifting. With higher levels of mobile and Internet access being achieved after 2008, as the market begins to mature, it is reported that 39 per cent of urban and 27 per cent of rural users are accessing the Internet on their mobile phones.[5] The same study argues that the 'most dramatic shift' is that email has reached the rural user community (non-existent in 2009 and 12 per cent in 2010) and that mobile email is becoming mainstream (World Wide Worx 2011). Broadband infrastructure is an important enabler of access to knowledge in universities and research institutions, supported by the tertiary education network, TENET, and the national research and education network SANREN. However, household broadband has historically been limited by high prices, while schools and clinics are deprived of broadband access which would support innovations such as e-education and telemedicine.

South Africa is generally an importer of know-how and technology and has, until recently, had a negative technology balance of payments. It generally exports low and medium-low technology products, such as paper, food and textiles; and imports medium-high and high technology products such as aircraft, pharmaceuticals and electronic goods (NACI 2009a: 32–34). It is also engaged in designing mines and power generation systems across the continent, though this is not counted in the technology balance of payments. It may be argued that South Africa's current stage of development of its innovation system is as a stronger technology adopter than a technology producer. From the beginning of the 21st century, introducing innovations in public transport have featured high on the agenda — Gauteng province will introduce a high-speed rail service, the Gautrain; while bus rapid transit (BRT) systems are operating in at least two major cities, Johannesburg and Cape Town. In these cases, little of the productive innovation is of South African origin, with the infrastructure being imported from France and Brazil respectively. However, there is good absorptive capacity for advanced transport systems, with the ability to plan and design the integration of these systems, to project manage the integration process and to fund the acquisition of these complex technologies. The litmus test will be the value gained for commuters and the economy in terms of efficiency and safety.

As is evident in Figure 6.5, South Africa's historical competitiveness in the low-tech sectors is slowly being enhanced by competitiveness in the medium-high tech sector, driven largely by a decade-long upward trend in the export of automotive components and fully built-up motor vehicles. However, mining is still South Africa's largest export sector and its importance has risen since the 2009 recession. Participation in the global high technology production sector is minimal (2 per cent) and static. Given the structure of the economy and employment in low and medium-low technology intensive sectors, the South African labour force has witnessed limited adoption of medium-high and high technology tools and processes in the workplace.

The traded share of an economy is an indicator of an economy's openness and associated knowledge demand from domestic firms who may face a relatively larger challenge to innovate in a more open economic environment. In the period 1999 to 2010, South Africa saw a steady increase in its traded share of the economy, albeit marked by a notable contraction with the global recession in 2009 (see Figure 6.6).

During the stated period, the traded share of the economy grew at a compound annual rate of 1.2 per cent. While Rand depreciation appears to be correlated to the increase in the traded share of the economy, exchange rate fluctuations primarily appear to enhance or inhibit the overall upward trend. The increase is attributable to a number of factors, amongst which are (*a*) the dropping of sanctions and consequently greater participation in global trade, particularly

Figure 6.5: *Composition of Exports, percentage (2003–09)*

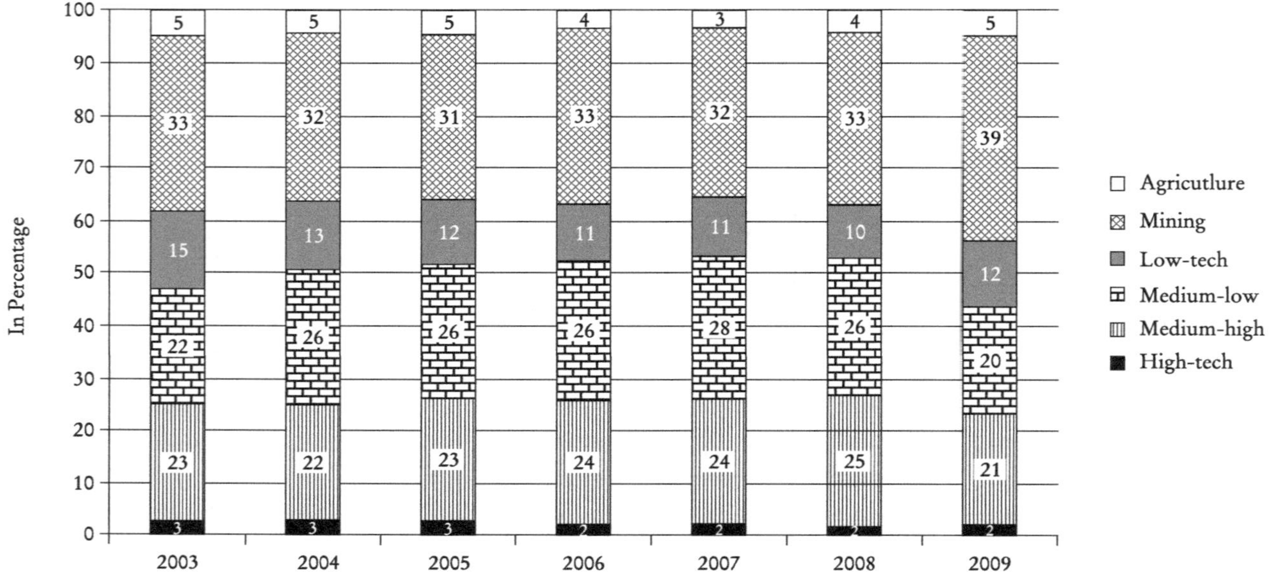

Source: Calculations based on annual data from the South African Revenue Service's Customs Trade Data (2003–09) following OECD guidelines (Hatzichronoglou 1997).

Figure 6.6: *Traded Share of South African Economy (1999–2010)*

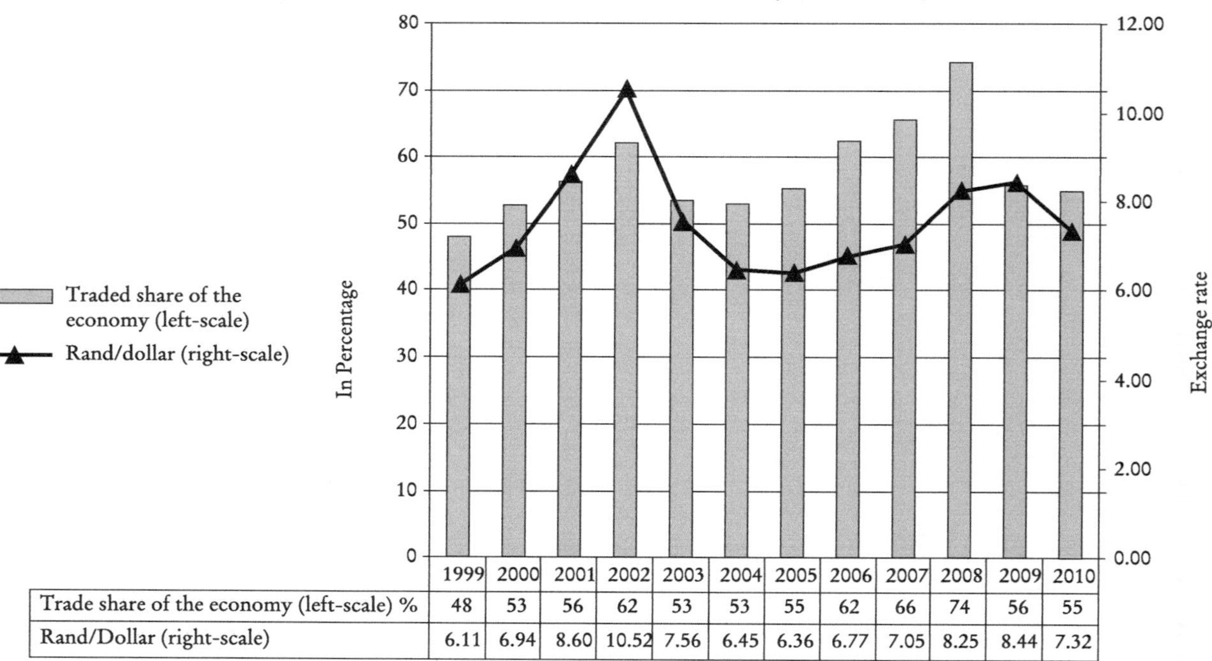

	1999	2000	2001	2002	2003	2004	2005	2006	2007	2008	2009	2010
Trade share of the economy (left-scale) %	48	53	56	62	53	53	55	62	66	74	56	55
Rand/Dollar (right-scale)	6.11	6.94	8.60	10.52	7.56	6.45	6.36	6.77	7.05	8.25	8.44	7.32

Source: Calculation of traded share of the economy based on StatsSA (1999–2010a) and South African Revenue Service's Customs Trade Data (1999–2010). Exchange rate based on South African Reserve Bank data for the annual middle rate in cents of the South African Rand to US Dollar (1999–2010).

with the United States and European Union post-1994; (*b*) new trade relations with Asian countries including Malaysia, Singapore and with countries on the African continent and (*c*) new trade relations with the BRIC countries. Though in most cases, the balance of trade is not in South Africa's favour, the improved trade relations have provided a stimulus for investment in innovation-based activity in, for example, agricultural biotechnology and information and communications technologies (ICT).

Access to health and education

The quality of health and well-being of the general population and the level of participation in higher education are contributing factors to the capacity of people to engage in R&D and productive innovation and to grow the country's knowledge base. In South Africa, inequalities in access to primary and tertiary healthcare and to education diminish the capacity of the country to build a robust national innovation system with appropriate levels of human capacity to conduct entrepreneurial R&D. These inequalities, particularly the low participation rate in higher education (15 per cent) (NACI 2009a:13) and post-graduate studies, create a major barrier to the ability of the current and future generations to participate in the evolution of an innovative productive system with the potential to increase household income and per capita GDP. The higher education participation rate for South Africa is at a similar level to that of India, though this would equate to only 0.04 per cent of the size of the Indian higher education population, while it is at a significantly lower level compared to Brazil (25 per cent) (ibid.).

Medical aid coverage varies considerably across racial groups. While on average 68 per cent of White households had medical aid coverage in the period between 2002 and 2010, only 8 per cent of African households had medical aid coverage (see Table 6.7). This reflects the still disproportionate participation of racial groups in industries with structured benefits as compared to the greater participation of African households in low income sectors such as agriculture, certain services, and in the small and medium enterprise (SME) and informal sectors.

Tables 6.8 and 6.9 reflect that a large proportion of the population live in relatively undeveloped conditions with respect to basic infrastructure and resources. The electricity sector performed reasonably

Table 6.7: *Medical Aid Coverage by Population Group (2002–10) (percentage)*

	2002	*2003*	*2004*	*2005*	*2006*	*2007*	*2008*	*2009*	*2010*
Total	16	15	15	14	14	14	16	17	18
African	8	8	7	7	7	7	8	9	10
Coloured	19	19	18	18	16	19	22	21	22
Indian/Asian	29	35	36	32	29	31	39	43	46
White	68	66	70	64	63	66	68	74	70

Source: Table derived from StatsSA (2002–10).

Table 6.8: *Household Amenities (2002–10) (percentage)*

	2002	*2003*	*2004*	*2005*	*2006*	*2007*	*2008*	*2009*	*2010*
Water in house or on site	70	70	72	72	73	74	72	72	72
Access to electricity	77	78	81	81	81	82	82	83	82
Toilet in dwelling	36	37	37	37	38	37	41	n/c	n/c

Source: StatsSA (2002–10).

Table 6.9: *Childhood Malnutrition (2002–08) (percentage)*

	2002	*2003*	*2004*	*2005*	*2006*	*2007*	*2008*
Percent of households in which children went hungry in last year	31	30	26	23	16	15	18

Source: Table derived from StatsSA (2002–08).

well, with 81 per cent of households nationally reporting electricity as a primary energy source for lighting in the period between 2002 and 2010.

While the percentage of households experiencing childhood malnutrition declined by slightly less than 50 per cent between 2002 and 2008, this belies the actual poverty levels experienced by children and the reality of poverty in child-headed households due to the effects of HIV-AIDS, given an estimated 2.01 million AIDS orphans in 2011 (StatsSA 2011a).

This continued divide between rich and poor is likely to undermine efforts to invest in the education of the younger generation and have negative consequences for the inclusion of young people from poor households in future generations of a skilled workforce. In addition, this failure to close the development gap may be detrimental to an economy that needs to grow and become increasingly competitive. Given its relative size, South Africa needs a significant proportion of its population to be highly skilled.

The statistics in Table 6.10 show a small decline in the percentage of the population with no formal education and a small increase in the percentage of the population who have completed a full 12 years of schooling. It is anticipated that this latter percentage will increase over time as the school age population benefits from compulsory schooling introduced post-1994. However, secondary certificate examination (SCE) pass rates reflect that just more than two-thirds of all learners writing the final examinations are successful (see Figure 6.7).

Table 6.10: *Headline Access to Education Indicators (2002–10)*

	2002	*2003*	*2004*	*2005*	*2006*	*2007*	*2008*	*2009*	*2010*
Percentage of persons aged 7–15 attending an educational institution	96.7	97.3	97.8	97.8	97.3	97.9	97.9	98.5	98.6
Percentage (aged 20 and older) with no formal education	10.3	9.8	9.6	9.6	9.5	9.3	8.8	7.4	7.0
Percentage (aged 20 and older) with matric/grade 12	21.1	21.5	23.4	22.5	23.9	23.6	23.9	25.6	25.8

Source: Table derived from StatsSA (2002–10).

Of the up to 350,000 learners writing SCE level biology, mathematics and physical sciences subjects, pass rates for physical sciences are higher than the SCE average, while pass rates for biology are marginally lower and for mathematics, significantly lower than the average (see Figure 6.8).

Of these, too small a percentage of school learners pass SET subjects with a sufficiently high grade to create a sizeable pipeline for higher education enrolments and successful graduations — around 40,000 for biology, 30,000 for physical sciences and just more than 25,000 for mathematics.

Figure 6.7: *Learners Writing SCE and SCE Pass Rates (2000–09)*

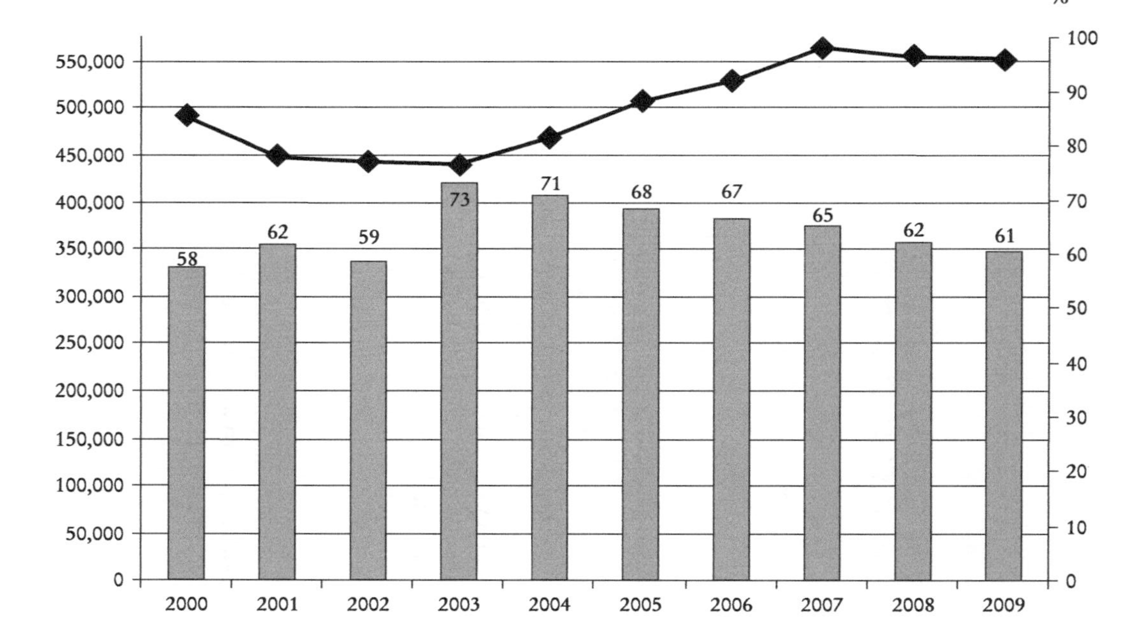

Source: Calculations based on Department of Education (2000–09).

Figure 6.8: *SCE and Select Subject Pass Rates (2000–09)*

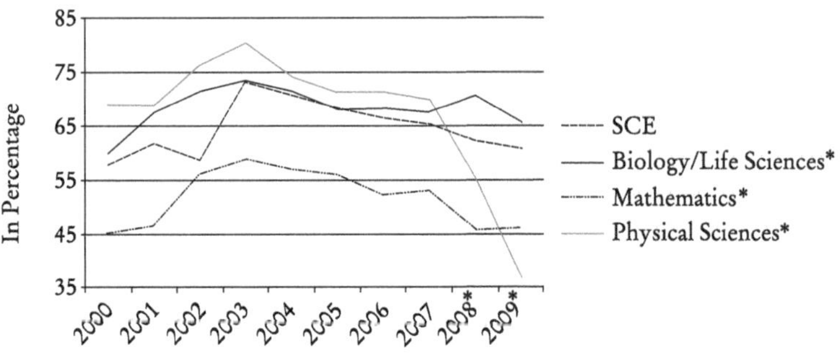

Source: Calculations based on Department of Education (2000–09).
Note: *In 2008, the subject exams were significantly revised. This should be considered with comparing subsequent results.

Current and future R&D capacity

Of particular interest, trends in inequality are to be observed in the production of SET human resources and in the workforce composition of the NSI. Few studies have been produced with respect to class, race and gender participation in higher education and in the public SET workforce, though some data is collected in the NRD and HEMIS surveys.[15] It has been argued that:'[t]he lack of critical mass of prominent women scientists as role models has hampered not only public understanding of science, engineering and technology, but also the participation of women at all levels within the science system' (Minister of Science and Technology 2004).

This comment is equally valid with respect to the participation of people from low-income communities, typically African, Indian and coloured (i.e., Black) communities, in SET education.

Data with respect to women's participation in the public SET sector workforce reveals that, while the proportion of female academic staff in universities increased for the period 1992–2001 and the proportion of female R&D staff in science councils increased in the period 1996–2001, both groups tended to be 'less qualified than their male counterparts, especially at the Doctoral level' (NACI 2004: 20–23). Furthermore, the upward trend in women's participation was marred by the low proportion of African, coloured and Indian women in universities (30 per cent) and science councils (33 per cent). In particular, women's participation in the natural sciences and engineering was very low, from around 9 per cent for instruction staff and 14 per cent for research staff in engineering and engineering technology to around 35 per cent and 29 per cent respectively in the mathematical sciences. Only computer science and data processing showed reasonable levels of participation at 46 per cent and 40 per cent respectively (NACI 2004: 26–27).

Higher education participation rates in South Africa are generally low at a gross enrolment ratio (GER) of 0.15 or 15 per cent of the population 'in the theoretical age group for the same level of education' (NACI 2009a: 4). This compares to 0.93 for Finland, 0.25 for Brazil and 0.12 for India (ibid.: 13). Data analysed by the National Advisory Council on Innovation (NACI) (ibid.: 9) illustrates that higher education SET enrolments and graduations hovered at between 26 per cent and 29 per cent of all enrolments and graduations between 2000 and 2008. However, post-graduate SET enrolments accounted for only 14.9 per cent of all post-graduate enrolments in 2008 and SET graduations for only 23.2 per cent of post-graduate graduations. For the same period, Black SET enrolments ranged between 62 per cent and 72 per cent, while graduations ranged between 53 per cent and 62 per cent (ibid.: 11).

The student pipeline for building human resources for the innovation system reveals problems with respect to stagnation in the percentage of the working age population graduating from higher education (see Figure 6.9).

Specifically, the gender distribution of post-graduate enrolments and graduations reflects the gender bias of inequality in higher education participation. While female students constituted the greater proportion of all university enrolments and graduations for the period 1992–2001, and while the percentage of female post-graduate enrolments increased in the same period, women's participation at the upper post-graduate (Masters and Doctoral) levels remained below the 50 per cent mark (NACI 2004: 8–19).

These observed trends appear to be changing with respect to the future SET workforce. Data for the period 2000–2007 (NACI 2009a, 2009b) indicates the following:

- 49 per cent of all higher education graduates are women
- The number of female graduates is increasing every year
- Women are approaching 50 per cent of enrolments and graduations at the upper post-graduate level

Figure 6.9: *Highest Education Level of Working Age Population (15–65 yrs) (percentage)*

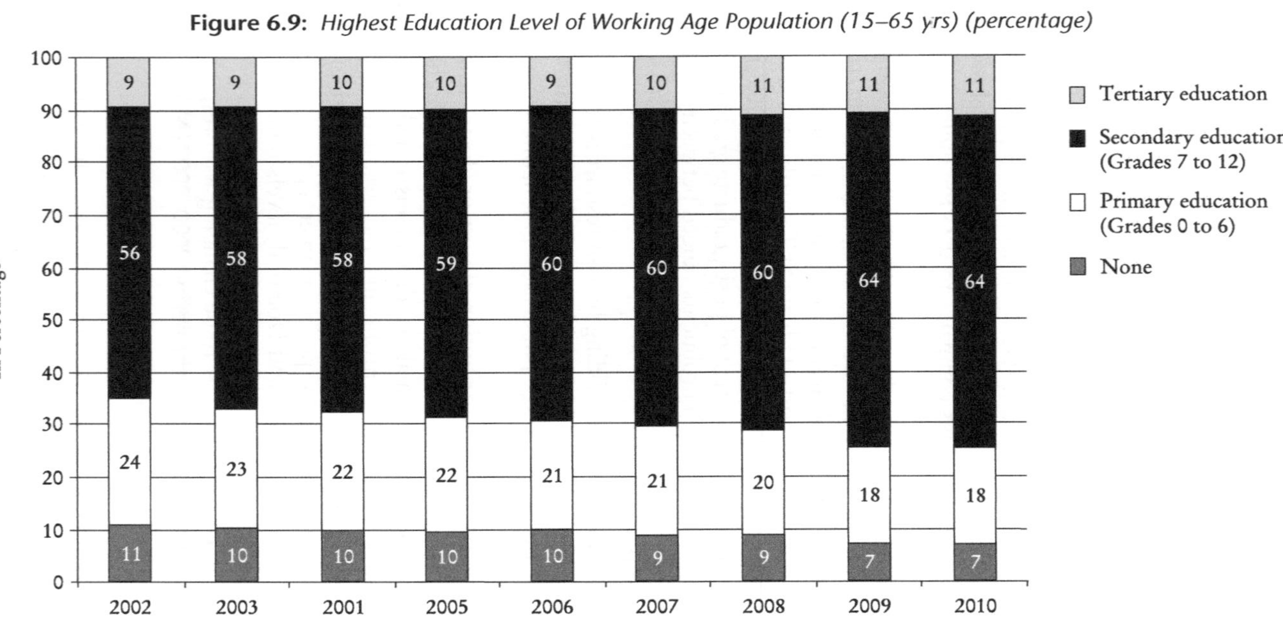

Source: Calculations based on StatsSA (2001–09).

A perspective on the distribution of participation across broad disciplinary areas at upper post-graduate level is given in the following statement:

> When viewed by broad field of study the proportion of female doctoral graduates increased most substantially in the Engineering Sciences and Applied Technologies (from 12 per cent to 19 per cent); in Humanities (from 30 per cent to 38 per cent); and in the Social Sciences (from 49 per cent to 53 per cent). In the Health Sciences, the female share of doctoral graduates declined from 60 per cent in 2001 to 57 per cent in 2005 (NACI 2009b: 16).

This shift may result from a cultural shift in society, where the engineering sciences are gaining popularity and no longer seen as men's work, while the humanities and social sciences are no longer seen as 'soft' options for further study. Nevertheless, women's sustained and increasing participation in the innovation system, as the basis for a high-performing system in a small country, particularly Black women's participation, constitutes a challenge for public policy and for societal change. South Africa's total researcher population is 39,955 by headcount, but only 19,384 by full-time equivalent (DST 2010). Despite policy intentions to increase GERD above 1 per cent of GDP, this will prove difficult without a significant increase in the numbers of men and women participating in the science system. In particular, this puts the focus on increasing the participation of African, Indian and coloured men and women, where barriers to participation have historically been experienced.

Access to financial infrastructure

Economic globalisation and foreign direct investment (FDI) are important factors in building a competitive innovation system. Inflow of foreign direct investment was US$ 7.2 billion in 2009, up from US$ 1.4 billion in 2000, but down from US$ 22.2 billion in 2008. South Africa experienced an outflow of FDI of US$ 11.1 billion in 2006 and US$ 928 million in 2004 (RSA 2010: 23). From at least the year 2000, inward direct investment stocks have generally been greater than outward direct investment stocks, a shift from 1995 where the reverse was true. However, the trend levels for direct investment stocks have been at the level of less than US$ 100 million (OECD 2009: 23).[16]

The private sector financial input to R&D is composed of investment by local and foreign firms. Public sector funding to the innovation system occurs through a wide range of institutions and includes tax incentives. The greater proportion of these funds circulates through the large-scale business sector, presenting limited opportunity for small, Black- or women-owned businesses to gain access. Table 6.11 illustrates the funding flows across the innovation system from funders to performers.

The private sector input includes significant investment in higher education research, accounting for nearly half a billion rands (US$ 100,502) or 4.1 per cent of all R&D spending, just higher than government spending at 3.4 per cent of GERD. It also includes investment flows from business to the science councils. All of these funding channels present opportunities for greater participation of Black and women researchers in R&D, though realising the opportunities is dependent on demographic change in the researcher population of universities, science councils and business R&D facilities. In at least a few instances, the next generations of graduates in scientific fields such as mining exploration and accounting illustrate a shift towards an increasing proportion of Black graduates.

As previously discussed, the bulk of funding to the public science system goes to six universities and two science councils, institutions which were historically the major research producers and which have continued to be research leaders post-1994. Such differentiation is apparent in all innovation systems. However, it can be argued that South Africa needs a critical readjustment in funding flows to a few universities that may not be among the current six research performers, but whose participation in R&D over time can bring economic benefits to their particular geographical regions. An example of such an institution would be the Central University of Technology (CUT) in the Free State province, which has built up a small but valuable R&D base in the period since 2003. The CUT's Centre for Rapid Prototyping and Manufacturing is already making a contribution to promoting innovation amongst SMEs in the major city of Bloemfontein, partly financed through the Tshumisano public funding initiative.

The major constraints for financial investment in innovation appear to lie not at the research stage, but in early stage funding for commercialisation. These funds were very limited before, but have now 'all but dried up' (Kaplan 2009).

Table 6.11: *Funders and Performers of R&D (2008–09) (US$ thousands at PPP)*

Performer ⇨ *Source* ⇩	*Business*	*Government Departments*	*Higher Education*	*Not-for-profit*	*Science Councils*	*Total*
Own funds	**1,799,009**	**164,400**	**438,948**	**2,135**	**84,338**	**2,488,830**
Government	**568,055**	**72,043**	**275,031**	**7,238**	**491,533**	**1,413,917**
Grants	438,006	71,679	N/A	4,807	291,419	805,911
Contracts	130,050	363	N/A	2,431	200,113	332,957
Agency funding	N/A	N/A	275,048	N/A	N/A	275,048
Business	**46,324**	**3,536**	**100,502**	**5,884**	**30,394**	**186,640**
Other South African sources	**6,519**	**403**	**22,232**	**6,262**	**1,222**	**36,637**
Higher education	469	19	3,696	762	150	5,096
Not for profit	4,240	62	8,097	4,309	545	17,252
Individual donations	1,810	322	10,438	1,191	527	14,289
Foreign	**308,913**	**11,805**	**90,733**	**31,731**	**86,743**	**529,926**
Parent Company	125,269	N/A	N/A	N/A	N/A	125,269
Foundations	1,552	N/A	N/A	N/A	N/A	1,552
All sources	182,092	11,805	90,733	31,731	86,743	403,105
Total	**2,728,820**	**252,187**	**927,463**	**53,251**	**694,229**	**4,655,950**

Source: DST (2010), with acknowledgement to Kahn (2009).

Data on investment provided by the annual KPMG and SAVCA (2008) 'Venture Capital and Private Equity Industry Performance Survey of South Africa' shows low levels of private equity investment (US$ 1–2 billion per annum) between 2000 and 2010 (see Figure 6.10). Investment increases sharply in 2007, effectively tripling in a year, but then declines sharply in 2008 and 2009 before recovering slightly in 2010. The composition of private equity investments is highly variable, with retail, manufacturing and mining leading investment and infrastructure taking a more prominent role after 2007.

Figure 6.10: *Private Equity Investment (in US$ millions at PPP) (2000–10)*

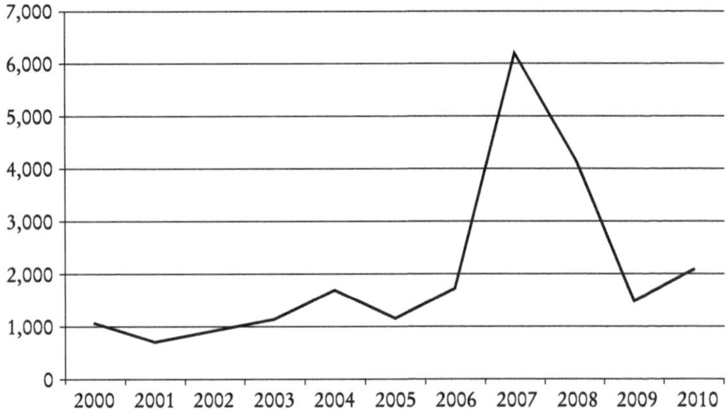

Source: Calculations based on KPMG and SAVCA (2001–10).

Venture capital (VC) intensity over the same period (2000–10), i.e., venture capital as a percentage of GDP, shows a gradual decline from 0.09 per cent in 2000 to under 0.03 per cent in 2010 (KPMG and SAVCA 2010). Comparative international data on venture capital intensity for 2010 puts South Africa in a stronger position than Austria, but in a weaker position than China, or India. Developing countries may exhibit a greater need for venture capital to finance their emerging innovation systems. Hence South Africa's VC intensity should converge towards that of Brazil and India.

As regards the composition of VC investments (Figure 6.11), it is predominantly for the start-up and early-stage commercialisation phases, with extremely limited seed capital funds, thus assuming advanced capacities for R&D and the availability of R&D funds.

Figure 6.11: *Venture Capital Investments (in US$ millions at PPP) (2000–10)*

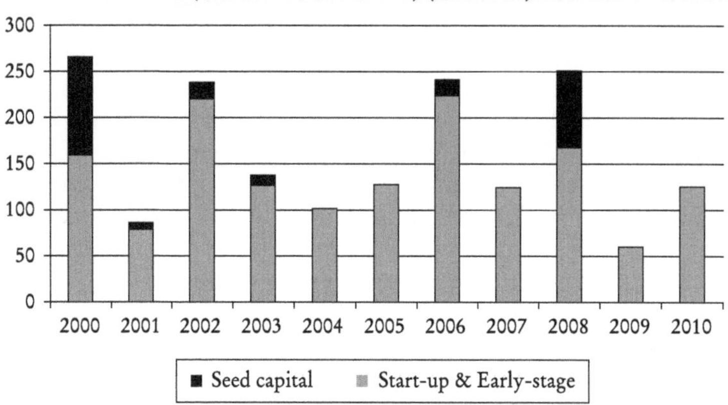

Source: Calculations based on KPMG and SAVCA (2001–10).

From a business perspective, it is apparent that large businesses dominate access to financial capital. The SME sector with enterprises of between five and 100 employees is vibrant in terms of innovative activity, 51 per cent of SMEs conducting innovation in-house. Despite this positive activity, SME innovation is poorly funded by the government at around 6.1 per cent (HSRC 2009).

From a race and gender perspective, the utilisation of financial infrastructure by Black and women graduates is not yet a major factor characterising the innovation system, though evidence suggests that this will be the case for the emerging generations of graduates, based on the changing demographics of the higher education student population.

Output and employment

South Africa's GDP is estimated at US$ 534.2 billion for 2010. Of its nine provinces, only three contribute more than 10 per cent to GDP (StatsSA 2011b). The period 2000–2008 showed strong growth in real GDP (at market prices) and a similar upward trend in real per capita GDP (at market prices) until 2009. The major growth for the period was in the tertiary or services sector, while growth was slow, yet consistent in the secondary industries and erratic in the primary industries. At certain times in the past decade, South Africa's growth was termed 'jobless growth', as just short of one million jobs were added to the economy, then lost in the economic downturn.

As presented in Figure 6.12, employment is dominated by trade and government services, followed by manufacturing, and finance, insurance, real estate and business services (FIRE). Domestic work in private households constitutes a larger proportion of employment than agriculture, construction or transport. Domestic labour is now regulated by labour law and can hence no longer be strictly defined within the informal sector, although the degree of legislative compliance may be open to contestation. Employment in the mining sector is a small percentage of total employment as thousands of jobs were lost through closures of marginal mines in the past two decades.

The Theil-T elements and statistics in Figure 6.13 report inter-sectoral earnings inequality in South Africa between 2001 and 2008.[17] The legend is organised with all sectors above the horizontal access in 2008, i.e. sectors with above average earnings, in the lower box. The lower box can be read in descending order from the right to left by row. As such the sector that contributed the most to inequality was general government services, followed by mining, and then the FIRE sector. Likewise, the upper box lists all the sectors that contributed to inequality from below average earnings in 2008. The upper box can also be read in descending order from right to left by row. Thus, the largest contributor to inequality having below average earning is the wholesale and retail trade sector followed by construction.

South Africa's output from the informal sector, excluding agriculture, was estimated in 1995 as representing only 5.4 per cent of total GDP (Jütting and de Laigiesia 2009). A comparison of informal and formal sector employment trends for the period 1995 to 2010 shows that income is earned largely in the formal sector of the economy, with around 2 million 'jobs' in the informal sector (Kingdon and Knight 2005: 8; StatsSA 1995–2007, 2008b, 2009). The composition of informal sector employment for the same period is dominated by trade, followed by community services, construction and manufacturing, and limited work in the finance and transport sectors.[18] Informal sector employment as a percentage of total employment is currently at 17 per cent. This is low even by comparison with a number of other African countries such as Egypt, Uganda or Tanzania (see Figure 6.14). In Egypt and the southern African countries of Uganda and Tanzania, informal sector activity developed alongside the formal economy, taking up the gaps that arose in the formal and public sector supply

Figure 6.12: *Sectoral Composition of Total Employment (2000–10)*

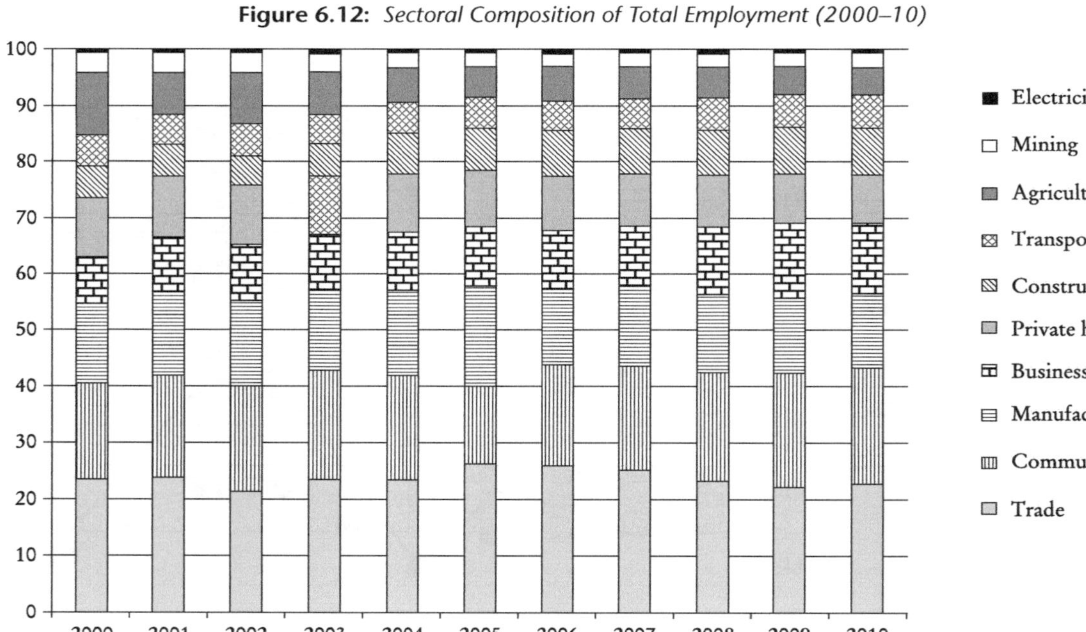

Source: Calculations based on StatsSA (2001–07; 2008b; 2009; 2010c).

Figure 6.13: *Theil Elements of Inter-sectoral Earnings in South Africa (2001–10)*

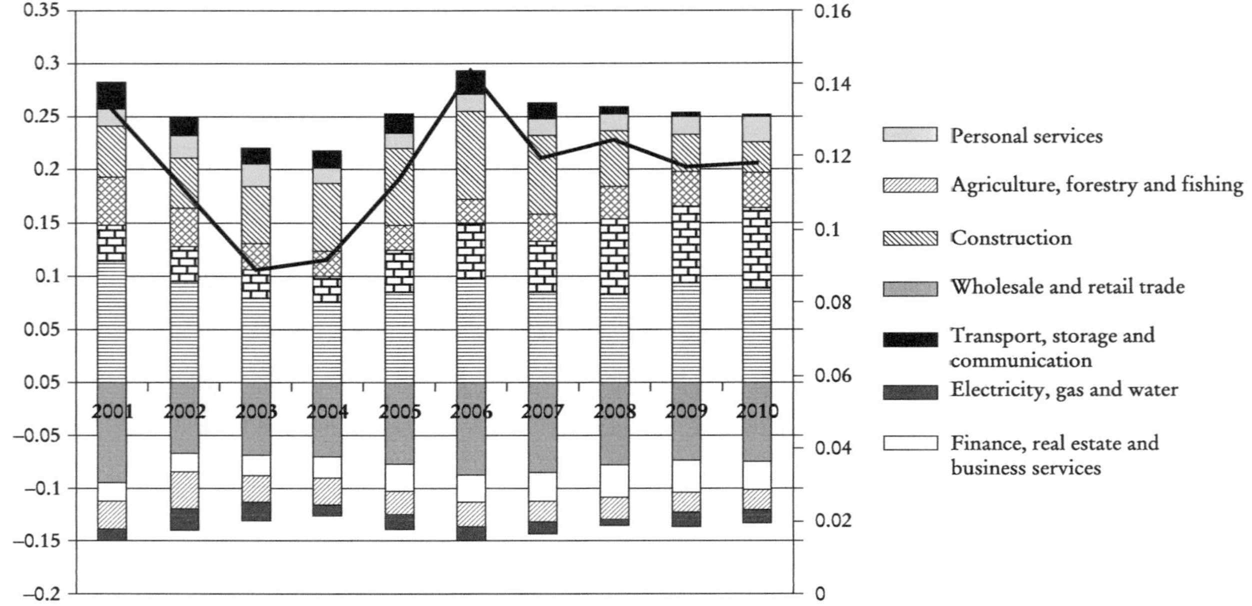

Source: Calculations based on StatsSA (2001–10a, 2001–10b).

Figure 6.14: *Informal Sector Employment as a percentage of Total Employment*

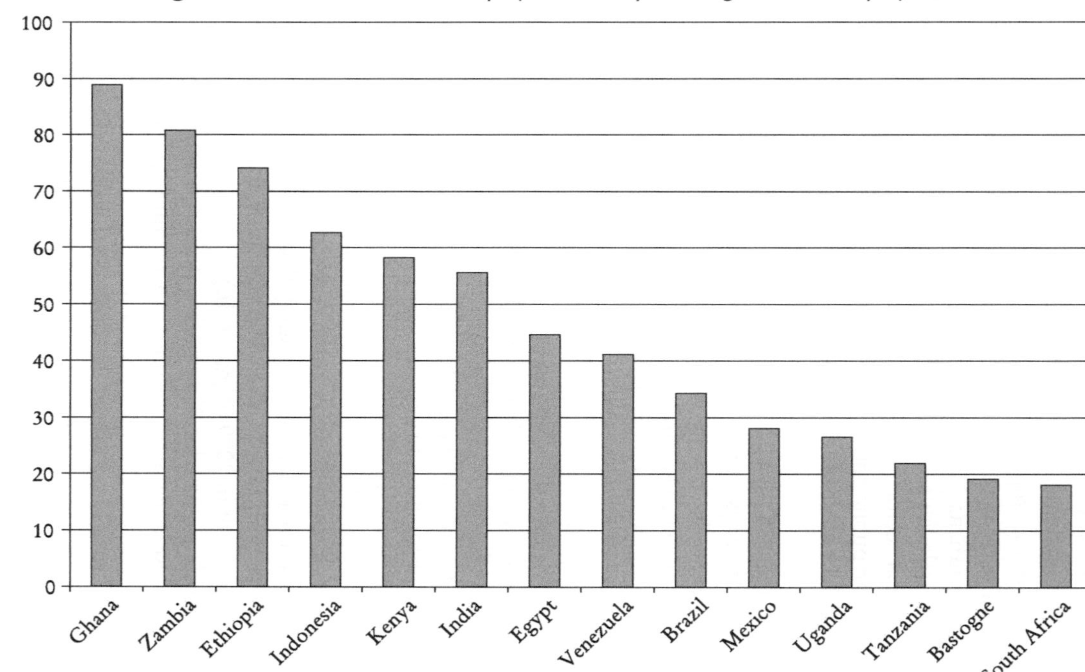

Source: Charmes (2004) and calculations based on StatsSA (2004).

side. In South Africa, the restrictive economic practices pursued by the apartheid government from 1948 through 1994 closed off many opportunities for informal sector trading and services by preventing activities such as street trading and informal trading in city centres or along national and arterial roads. On the other hand, high levels of informal sector employment, arising from lack of economic development in the resources, manufacturing and services sectors, such as witnessed in Ghana, Zambia or Ethiopia are not desirable.

Looking to lessons from the BRIC countries, which have relatively large informal sectors, it is apparent that, as a developing country, South African public policy should encourage informal sector growth as an important means for income generation and as a basis for future formalisation.

Employment in the agricultural sector has seen a decline over the past several decades from 1970, following an increase between 1951 and 1970.[19] This decline has occurred despite growth in the value of agricultural output. Data for the period 1980 to 2003 shows a structural shift in agricultural production, corresponding to an increase in the volume of horticultural products aimed at the export market (e.g. exporting fruit to Europe) and a reduction in the volume of field crops, side by side with adoption of less labour-intensive production methods (see Figure 6.15). This is attributed to the orientation of the agricultural industry towards global value chains, rather than towards innovations to provide cheaper bread and basic foods. The decline in agricultural production also means that there is a smaller production base for innovation to adhere to.

It is notable that there is a small, but steady increase in the education levels of the workforce, with respect to both secondary and tertiary education and a corresponding decline in the percentage of the workforce with low or no formal education from 24 per cent in 2001 to 19 per cent in 2009 (Figure 6.16).

However, current education policy does not sufficiently stress the value of science, engineering and technology education for increasing the size and value of economic production and for creating a nation of science and technology adopters in the workplace and in society. Consequently, educational investment in science and technology education is lagging in producing the next generation of knowledge workers with the capability and know-how to operate in new technology-intensive industries such as biotechnology and ICT. This partly explains the phenomenon of unemployed higher education graduates.

Figure 6.15: *Composition of Agricultural Output by Value (1980–2003)*

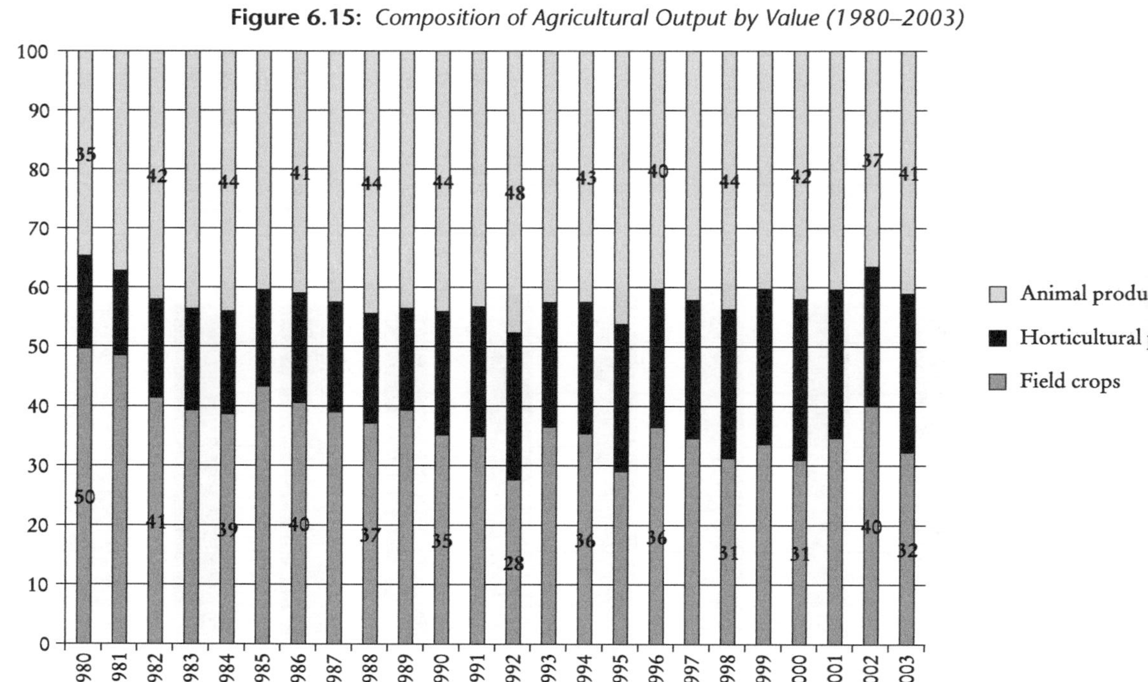

Source: Calculations based on data from StatsSA (1980–2003).

Figure 6.16: *Educational Attainment of Employed Population (2001–09) (percentage)*

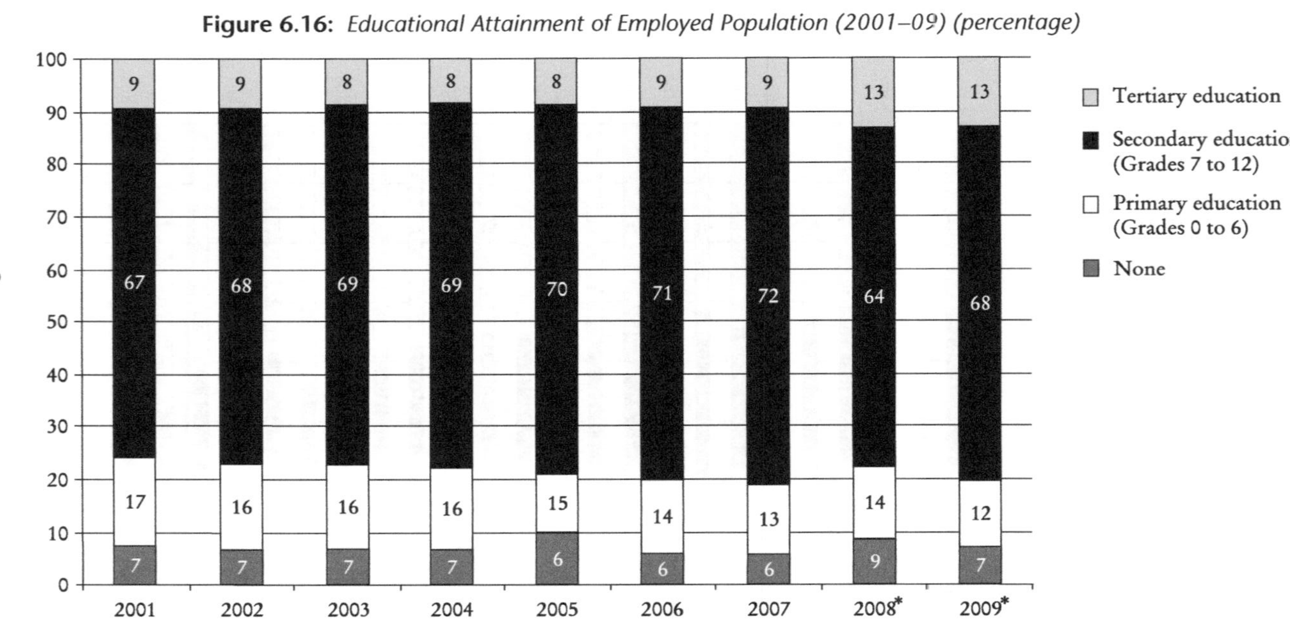

Source: Calculations based on StatsSA (2001–07; 2008b; 2009).
Note: *In 2008, the subject exams were revised and this should be considered when comparing results over time.

Race and gender characterise unemployment patterns, with women and Black Africans experiencing higher unemployment rates than the national average of around 26 per cent; and men, coloureds, Indians and Whites experiencing lower rates than the national average, see Figure 6.17.

Inter-regional disparities in innovation system

The contribution to production dynamics from the public science system, including science councils and scientific performing agencies, has increased in real terms over the period 1994 to 2009 and forms around 40 per cent of funding input to the innovation system, as measured by the proportion of GERD. Sectors relying on R&D and innovation for development include the mining sector with a dedicated geosciences research institute in Gauteng and research in the geosciences and minerals exploration based at universities in Cape Town and Johannesburg. The manufacturing sector is served by the Centre for Scientific and Industrial Research (CSIR), whose main base is in Pretoria, but which has historically had bases in Johannesburg and Cape Town and has recently opened a base in Durban. The other scientific performing agencies are mainly based in Pretoria, in Gauteng province.

The public sector contribution includes the provision of national experimental facilities such as the iThemba LABS and the South African Institute for Acquatic Biodiversity, aimed at sustaining and further enhancing South Africa's shared infrastructure for advanced research and technological development.[20] The eight facilities are based in Gauteng, Western Cape, Eastern Cape, and the North West Province, providing limited and expensive access to researchers, universities and public hospitals which require their services, even with public funding.

A few nationally funded initiatives are based in provinces which have little R&D infrastructure. This includes the South African Large Telescope (SALT) at Sutherland, whose services are used by international scientists and where the German and Japanese space science communities have installations. Sutherland is a small rural town in the Northern Cape which provides ideal surroundings for radio-astronomy data collection, inter alia, because of very low levels of light pollution. The Free State province, with a largely rural population of

Figure 6.17: *South African Unemployment Rates (2001–11) (percentage)*

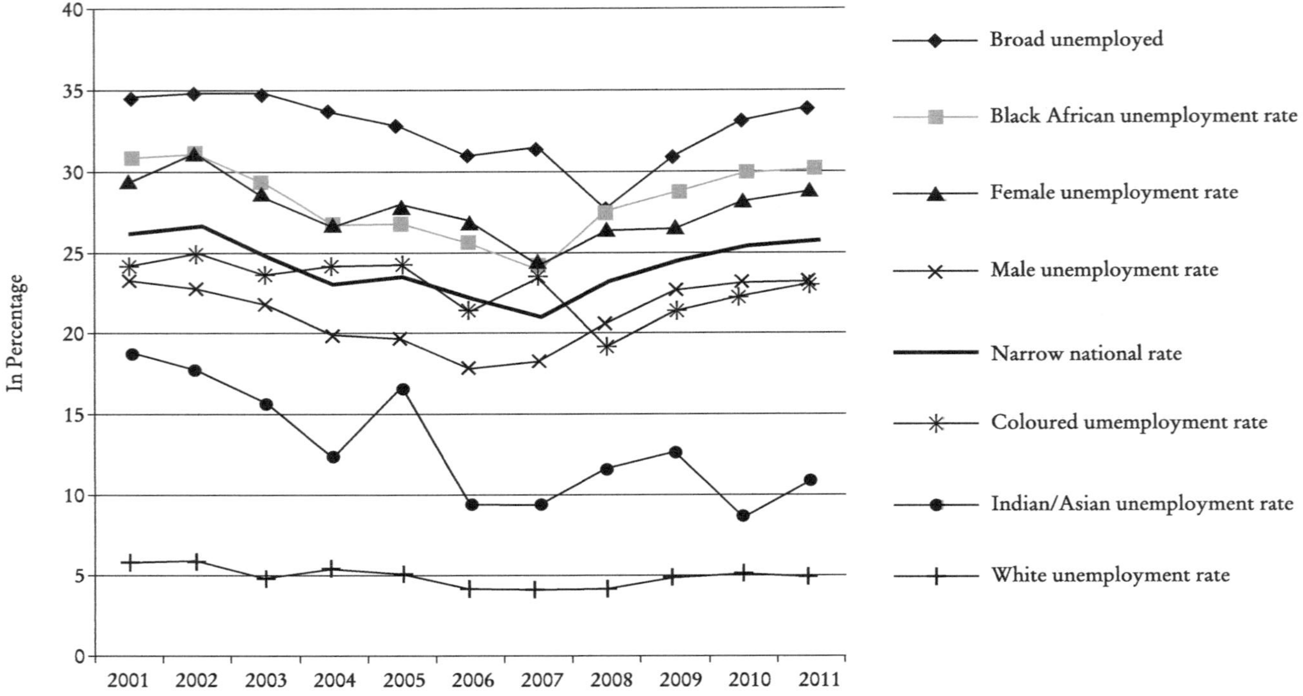

Source: Calculations based on StatsSA (2000–07, 2008b, 2009, 2010c, 2011c) Labour Force Survey estimates.

around 2.8 million people has a few important assets. These assets include the Centre for Rapid Prototyping and Manufacturing, based at the Central University of Technology, which has evolved as a government-funded platform for pre-competitive R&D in the period since 2003. Its increasing technology-intensive output is the basis for small-scale export-oriented initiatives and import substitution in a limited range of mechanical products (Ralebipi-Simela 2009). In the Free State private sector, the Farmovs-Parexel clinical research organisation participates in the global services market on drug trials and anti-viral therapy, but draws on a narrow science, engineering and technology (SET) human capital base from the two local universities (Abrahams 2004).

From the perspective of innovation infrastructure and assets, all eight provinces other than Gauteng are under-resourced relative to their needs and potential. Table 6.12 shows the provincial R&D split for 2008–09, with Gauteng and Western Cape having the highest funding inputs. Relative to population size, KwaZulu-Natal and Eastern Cape (and even the Western Cape) have low GERD inputs. This structural differentiation is defined by the comparatively rural nature of these provinces, each having one urban metropolitan municipality, while Gauteng by contrast has three large, highly urbanised metropolitan municipalities and a small rural population.

The economic dominance of Gauteng and the Western Cape is also reflected in Table 6.13 which sets out provincial shares of GERD. This indicator of inputs to the innovation system exhibits a consistency in inter-regional inequality from 2001 to 2008, with a slight rearrangement in shares between Gauteng and the Western Cape.

Provincial shares in GERD also indicate that the Eastern Cape experienced a moderate increase in its share, while Free State and the North West experienced a decline in their respective shares. Four provinces, namely Limpopo, the Northern Cape, Mpumalanga, and KwaZulu-Natal maintained a relatively constant share. However, of these, only KwaZulu-Natal has a share capable of impacting positively on economic development.

In 2001, Gauteng dominated inequality in R&D inputs, as measured by per capita GERD (Figure 6.18), but its previously mentioned increase in population share combined with a decrease in its share of provincial GERD from 55 per cent in 2001 to 52 per cent in 2005 led to its contribution to GERD inequities dropping sharply.

Table 6.12: *Provincial Split of R&D (2008–09)*

	Business Enterprise		Government		Higher Education		Not-for-Profit		Science Councils		Total	
Province	US$ '000	%	US$ '000	%	US$ '000	%	US$ '000	%	US$ '000	%	US$ '000	%
Eastern Cape	69,944	2.6	23,882	9.5	63,420	6.8	1,502	2.8	37,987	5.5	**196,735**	4.2
Free State	268,591	9.8	12,988	5.2	50,207	5.4	1,054	2.0	12,958	1.9	**345,798**	7.4
Gauteng	1,578,034	57.8	58,478	23.0	324,819	35.0	27,911	52.4	440,756	64.0	**2,429,999**	52.2
KwaZulu-Natal	277,818	10.2	25,514	10.0	125,686	14.0	8,960	16.8	51,123	7.4	**489,102**	10.5
Limpopo	16,745	0.6	12,226	4.8	19,171	2.1	1,137	2.1	14,041	2.0	**63,321**	1.4
Mpumalanga	44,599	1.6	8,653	3.4	16,063	1.7	2,286	4.3	12,291	1.8	**83,892**	1.8
North West	1,620	0.1	11,707	4.6	15,145	1.6	478	0.9	9,653	1.4	**38,603**	0.8
Northern Cape	49,263	1.8	15,654	6.2	33,220	3.6	518	1.0	9,192	1.3	**107,846**	2.3
Western Cape	422,206	15.5	83,084	33.0	279,733	30.0	9,404	17.7	106,227	15.0	**900,654**	19.3
Total	**2,728,820**	100.0	**252,187**	100.0	**927,463**	100.0	**53,251**	100.0	**694,229**	100.0	4,655,950	100.0

Source: DST (2010).

Table 6.13: *National GERD (US$ billion at PPP) and Provincial Shares (percentage) (2001–08)*

	Gauteng	*Western Cape*	*KwaZulu-Natal*	*Free State*	*Eastern Cape*	*Mpumalanga*	*North West*	*Limpopo*	*Northern Cape*	*South Africa*
2001	55	14	11	9	3	2	4	2	1	US$ 2.2b
2004	55	17	10	6	4	2	3	1	1	US$ 3.1b
2005	51	22	11	5	5	2	2	1	1	US$ 3.6b
2006	51	20	11	6	5	2	1	2	2	US$ 4.1b
2007	52	20	11	6	4	2	2	1	1	US$ 4.4b
2008	52	19	11	7	4	2	1	1	2	US$ 4.7b

Source: DST (2001/2–2008/9).

Figure 6.18: *Theil Elements of Inter-provincial per capita GERD (2001–08)*

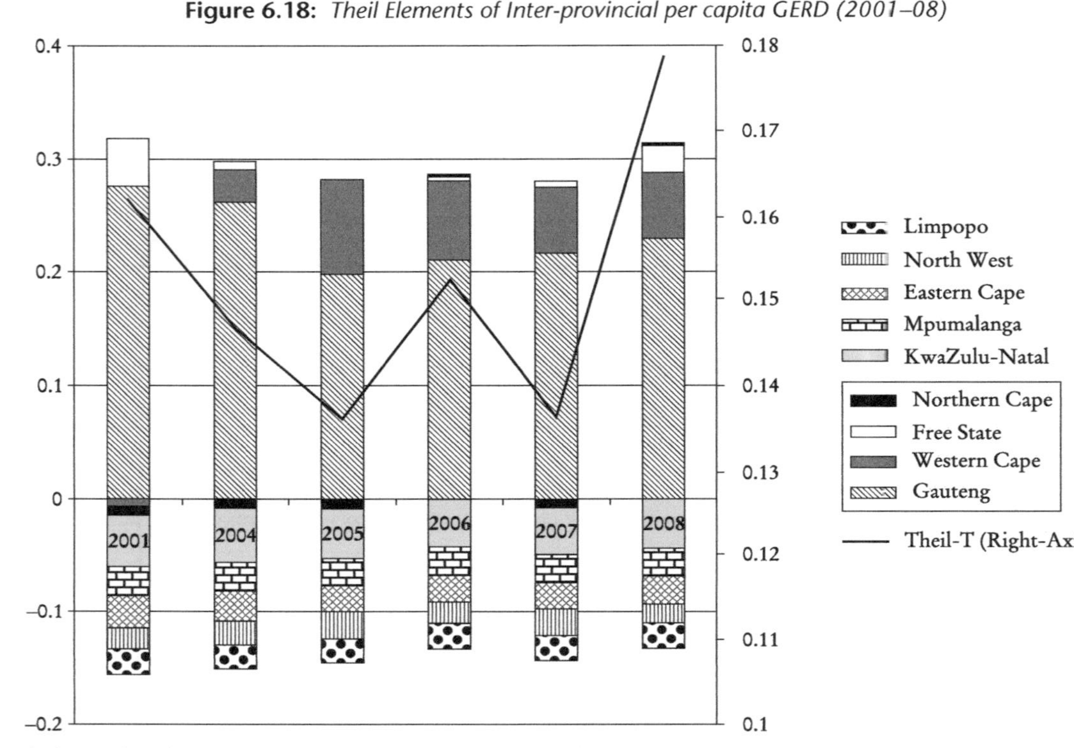

Source: Calculations based on StatsSA (2001a, 2001b, 2004–8a, 2004–08b)

Concluding Remarks

This brief analysis of South Africa's national innovation system shows that it is characterised by systemic inequality dating from its history of unequal development based on race, gender and geography. The inequalities of the past still greatly influence the present size, shape and performance of the system. Gauteng remains the only province with a sufficient combination of innovation infrastructure, SET and higher education institutions, human resources and access to finance for innovation to flourish across the sciences, creative industries, urbanisation processes, and economic sectors. Other provinces have some of these resources, but not the full suite of resources. For example, the Free State province has higher education institutions, but no science councils or local research funding institutions. Demand for innovation is low due to the limited development of manufacturing and services sectors and the decline of mining and agriculture. Innovators are far from markets in Gauteng and the Western Cape, and even further removed from global markets. With a relatively small population and an even smaller university graduate population, it is not an attractive destination for R&D investment. Nevertheless, South Africa's economy is growing. Cities or towns in provinces that have for many years been slow to develop, such as in the Eastern Cape, are showing increased urbanisation and increases in GGP.[21] This urban growth may create an additional stimulus for innovation in products, services and social processes.

Policy and institutional choices over the past 15 years have skewed the innovation system towards SET for the middle class and upper middle class parts of the economy and society. Current policies, such as the Ten-Year Innovation Plan (DST 2008), appear to aim at the static 3 per cent hi-tech sector, while South Africa's provinces need to focus on creating the innovation platforms for those parts of the economy that are performing well, where jobs are located and which need innovation inputs to support future growth and competitiveness. These include the low-tech and medium-tech sectors to support manufacturing, the construction sector and the services sector. Provincial and some metropolitan governments are seeking to address these needs. Amongst others, the KwaZulu-Natal provincial government has initiated programmes towards stimulating knowledge-based activity in the province, though with an emphasis on ICT as compared to SET innovation or innovation in the non-governmental development sector. It is exploring a renewable/alternate energy cluster and has established the ICT and electronics cluster at Pinetown, but these remain early stage ventures which still have to prove themselves.

Inter-regional inequality cannot be addressed by re-balancing existing levels of GERD input across provinces, as this would have the negative effect of reducing the value-creating capacity of the major research producers. Rather, the policy approach of promoting the provincial sub-systems, which is currently being undertaken by the Department of Science and Technology, requires the attention of all provincial governments and of the metropolitan and district municipalities. These institutions must consider funding inputs to technological and social innovation. Innovation system building in provincial sub-systems should seek strong linkages between investment in innovation infrastructure/resources and economic development strategies, as future economic development is unlikely to progress at the desired levels on the basis of the current historical path which is reliant on old technology.

The co-existence of inequality alongside the innovation system has a number of features, some of which have been outlined in the previous pages. The cross linkages between inequality and the evolution of the innovation system create a tension which must be broken, *but how*? In order to establish a future growth path based on the increasing incorporation of innovative ideas into economic and social activity, the education system will be required to rise to the challenge of creating an ever-larger human resource knowledge base with the requisite capacity to engage in productive innovation; while the innovation system will need to match that result with the capacity to absorb the new creative potential, in order to enable it to destroy those elements of the economy and society which remain retrogressive. These two levers, in combination, can promote the reshaping of society and economy towards the co-evolution of the innovation system with greater equality.

Given the analysis presented here, care should be observed in selecting innovation policy options with regard to what fields of innovation should enjoy public support, where new sites for innovation may be located, who will participate in innovation activities and for which segments of society innovation will be promoted. Strategic issues which require the attention of policy makers and decision-makers in all spheres of government, with a view to shifting the innovation system towards narrowing income, services and knowledge inequality in the economy and society, are:

(1) Promoting stronger articulation between innovation strategy on the one hand, and economic and social strategy directions on the other hand — with respect to the services sector, in the secondary and primary industries, and with respect to the SME and informal sectors. This includes focusing innovation in areas of large-scale consumption spending, e.g. major asset categories such as public housing; e-fields such as energy, education and environment; and process innovation in fields such as anti-corruption and public management of resources.
(2) Promoting access to R&D and innovation finance and reducing the costs of technology adoption, particularly for promoting technology usage and related innovation in the small business and the informal sectors.
(3) Enhancing access to educational resources through creating effective e-education and online content, thus improving the quality of the primary through tertiary education experience, particularly with respect to maths, science, technology, and language capabilities; and with due attention to closing the race, class and gender divides.
(4) Supporting current and future R&D capacity in the higher education sector and science councils as far as the fiscus will reasonably stretch, while encouraging business to increase R&D and innovation spend, as an investment in future economic growth and competitiveness, in ways that break the barrier of R&D spending of only 1 per cent of GDP experienced throughout the past two decades.
(5) Addressing frontier areas for research and innovation policy and practice: reducing inter-regional inequality in participation in the R&D and innovation system; increasing gender participation in the innovation system.

Given the history and structural nature of inequality in South Africa, the production and innovation systems are strongly influenced by inequality, in particular with respect to the availability of current and future R&D capacity. This is a challenge for advancing the competitiveness of the country and its ability to sustain economic growth through a combination of export orientation, import substitution and the development of frontier sectors such as the SMME and informal sectors. These modes of economic development require higher levels of and different thinking about innovative capacity than the status quo.

Notes

1. Based on StatsSA (2011) mid-year population estimates for the metropolitan areas and district municipalities.
2. Throughout the chapter all SA Rand (ZAR) currency figures are expressed as US dollars based on the adopted PPP exchange rates. These figures are derived from the population and GDP figures for 2010.
3. The Income and Expenditure Survey was last conducted in 2005, the next survey was started in 2010/2011.
4. There are a number of alternative Gini coefficient data sources which provide different data values, including the 2009 Development Indicators Report of the South African Presidency (0.66 in 2008) and the World Bank (0.578 in 2007–08).
5. The Gini coefficient can be a value between zero and one. If the Lorenz curve corresponded exactly to the equality line, the Gini coefficient would equal zero because there is no area between the Lorenz curve and the equality line. Conversely, if the single richest household possessed all of a society's income the Gini coefficient would equal one.
6. The poverty line is set at ZAR 283 per month.
7. For further discussion of the decreasing role race appears to have as a basis of inequality in South Africa, see Seekings and Nattrass (2005).
8. The Gauteng city-region approach seeks to recreate the Gauteng provincial economy as a globally competitive 21st century region based on economic activity in three large urban nodes and three urban-rural districts, aimed at advancing the level of economic development and reducing social exclusion and unemployment.
9. Calculations are based on StatsSA's Gross Domestic Product estimates.
10. The National Experimental R&D Survey bases its year of analysis on the government financial year April to March of the following year.
11. Note also that government R&D expenditure may translate into complex technologies for business and industry.
12. See http://www.wizzit.co.za. (accessed 2 December 2009).
13. Approximately ZAR 5 in 2011.

14. The data is sourced from a sample survey of 20 million South Africans above the age of 16, excluding 'deep rural' users.
15. The National Experimental Research and Development Survey (NRD) conducted by the Human Sciences Research Council for the Department of Science and Technology and the Higher Education Management Information System (HEMIS) of the Department of Education.
16. Inward stocks are the direct investments held by non-residents in the reporting economy; outward stocks are the investments of the reporting economy held abroad.
17. See Hale (2004) for further information about Theil's T Statistic.
18. Trends in informal sector employment are based on an analysis of StatsSA's Labour Force Surveys.
19. Trends in agricultural employment and output are based on an analysis of StatsSA's annual publication 'South African Statistics'.
20. Laboratory for Accelerator Based Services.
21. GGP is gross geographic product.

References

Abrahams, L., 2004. *The Free State in the 21st Century: Critical Linkages to the Emerging Knowledge Economy*, Report prepared for the Premier's Economic Advisory Council, Free State Province, 24 April 2004. Johannesburg: LINK Centre, University of Witwatersrand.

Addison, G., 2002. *The Hidden Edge: Quest for Progress, Innovation in South Africa 1900–2000*. Meyersdal: The Engineering Association.

———, 2005a. *The Competitive Edge: Creating Innovations, Lessons of South African Experience*. Meyersdal: The Engineering Association.

———, 2005b. *The Leading Edge: Dividends of Democracy, Innovation in South Africa 1994–2004*. Meyersdal: The Engineering Association.

Aliber, M., 2005. *Synthesis Report: Overcoming Underdevelopment in South Africa's Second Economy.* Development Bank of Southern Africa 2005 Development Report. Midrand: Development Bank of Southern Africa (DBSA).

Angang, H. and L. Chunbo, 2001. 'New Poverty during the New Century: Knowledge Poverty', *Social Sciences in China*. http://en/cnki.com.cn/Article_en/CJFDTOTAL-ZSHK200103007.htm (accessed 5 November 2011).

Bhorat, H., C. VanderWesthuizen and T. Jacobs, 2009. *Income and Non-income Inequality in Post-apartheid South Africa: What are the Drivers and Possible Policy Interventions?* Report prepared for the Second Economy Strategy Project, Understanding Inequality: Promoting Equity. Cape Town: Development Policy Research Unit.

Blankley, W. and M. Kahn, 2004. 'South African Research and Development: Preliminary Results and Indicators from the Latest Survey', *South African Journal of Science*, 100: 9–11.

Centre for Science, Technology and Innovation Indicators (CESTII), 2008. 'National Survey of Research and Experimental Development 2006/7'. Report prepared by Centre for Science, Technology and Innovation Indicators (CESTII), Human Sciences Research Council, March 2009. http://www.hsrc.ac.za/Document-3214.phtml (accessed 2 February 2010).

Charmes, J., 2004. 'Data Collection on the Informal Sector: A Review of Concepts and Methods Use Since the Adoption of an International Definition Towards a Better Comparability of Available Statistics'. Paper presented at the Delhi Group on Informal Sector Statistics, Seventh Meeting. New Delhi: United Nations Statistics Division.

Department of Education, 2000–09. Education Management Information System (EMIS). Pretoria: Department of Education.

Department of Science and Technology (DST), 2001/2–2008/9. *National Survey of Research and Experimental Development 2001/2–2008/9*, Report prepared by Centre for Science, Technology and Innovation Indicators (CESTII), Human Sciences Research Council. Pretoria: Department of Science and Technology.

———, 2002. *South Africa's National Research and Development Strategy*. Pretoria: Department of Science and Technology.

———, 2008. *Innovation Towards a Knowledge-based Economy, Ten–Year Plan for South Africa*. Pretoria: Department of Science and Technology.

———, 2010. *National Survey of Research and Experimental Development 2008/9: High Level Key Results*, Report prepared by Centre for Science, Technology and Innovation Indicators (CESTII), Human Sciences Research Council. Pretoria: Department of Science and Technology.

———, 2011. *South African Innovation Survey: Main Results 2008*, Report by Centre for Science, Technology and Innovation Indicators (CESTII), Human Sciences Research Council. Pretoria: Department of Science and Technology.

Development Bank of Southern Africa (DBSA), 2005. *Overcoming Under-development in South Africa's Second Economy*, Development Bank of Southern Africa 2005 Development Report. Midrand: Development Bank of Southern Africa.

Esselaar, S., A. Gillwald, and C. Stork, 2006. *Towards an African e-Index 2007: Telecommunications Sector Performance in 16 African Countries*, LINK Centre, University of the Witwatersrand. http://link.wits.ac.za/papers/Africa-SPR-2007.pdf (accessed 2 December 2009).

Financial and Fiscal Commission (FFC), 2009. *Submission for the Division of Revenue 2010/11*. Midrand: Financial and Fiscal Commission.

Fisher-French, Maya, 2008. 'Wizzit Strategy Works', *Mail & Guardian Online*, 24 September 2008. http://www.mg.co.za/article/2008-09-24-wizzit-strategy-works (accessed 2 December 2009).

Hale, T., 2004. 'The Theoretical Basics of Popular Inequality Measures'. UTIP Tutorial Guide. Austin: University of Texas Inequality Project.

Hatzichronoglou, T., 1997. 'Revision of the High-Technology Sector and Product Classification', STI Working Paper 1997/2. Paris: OECD.

Human Sciences Research Council (HSRC), 2009. 'Innovation Comes in Small Packages', *HSRC Review*, Volume 7 Number 4, November 2009, Human Sciences Research Council. http://www.hsrc.ac.za/HSRC_Review_Article-178.phtml (accessed 2 December 2009).

Jütting, J. and J. de Laigiesia (eds), 2009, *Is Informal Normal? Towards Better Jobs in Developing Countries*. Paris: Organisation for Economic Co-operation and Development (OECD).

Kahn, M., 2009. *Innovation, Finance and Funding in the National System of Innovation: The South African Experience*. Preliminary Report. Pretoria: Institute for Economic Research on Innovation, Tshwane University of Technology.

Kahn, M. and W. Blankley, 2006. 'The State of Research and Experimental Development: Moving to a Higher Gear', in S. Buhlungu, J. Daniel, R. Southall, and J. Lutchman (eds), *State of the Nation 2005–2006*. Pretoria: HSRC Press, 270–96.

Kaplan, D., 2009. 'South Africa: The Economic Crisis, Innovation and Development'. Opening Plenary Session, Globelics 7th International Conference: 'Inclusive Growth, Innovation and Technological Change: Education, Social Capital and Sustainable Development', 6–8 October, Dakar.

Kingdon, G. and J. Knight, 2001. *Why High Open Unemployment and Small Informal Sector in South Africa.* Mimeograph, October 2001. Centre for the Study of African Economies, Department of Economics, University of Oxford.

——, 2005. 'Unemployment in South Africa 1995–2003: Causes, Problems and Policies', Report prepared for the Global Poverty Research Group. Centre for the Study of African Economies and Department of Economics, University of Oxford.

Klynveld Peat Marwick Goerdeler (KPMG) and South African Venture Capital and Private Equity Association (SAVCA), 2008. Venture Capital and Private Equity Industry Performance Survey of South Africa. http://www.savca.org.za (accessed 7 August 2009).

——, 2001–10. Venture Capital and Private Equity Industry Performance Survey. http://www.savca.co.za (accessed 15 November 2011).

KwaZulu-Natal Department of Economic Development (KZN DED), 2006. 'KwaZulu-Natal Economic Overview', KwaZulu-Natal Department of Economic Development. http://durbanportal.net/kzn/Shared%20 Documents/KwaZulu-Natal%20Economic%20Overview.pdf (accessed 25 February 2009).

Mail & Guardian Online, 2009. 'Sexwale: R1,3bn to Rebuild Badly Constructed Houses', 16 November. http://www.mg.co.za/article/2009-11-16-sexwale-r13bn-to-rebuild-badly-constructed-houses (accessed 2 December 2009).

Minister of Science and Technology, 2004. Address by Minister of Science and Technology, Mr Mosibudi Mangena, at the 2nd Annual Women in Science Awards, Hilton Hotel, Sandton, 6 August. http://www.polity.org.za/article/mangena-women-in-science-awards-06082004-2004-08-06 (accessed 15 November 2011).

Moser, C., 1998. 'The Asset Vulnerability Framework: Reassessing Urban Poverty Reduction Strategies', *World Development*, 26(1), January: 1–19. http://www.sciencedirect.com/science/article/pii/S0305750X97100158 (accessed 5 November 2011).

Mouton, J. and W. Gevers, 2009. 'Introduction', in Roseanne Diab and Wieland Gevers (eds), *The State of Science in South Africa*, Pretoria: Academy of Science of South Africa (Assaf), 39–68.

National Advisory Council on Innovation (NACI), 2004. *Facing the Facts: Women's Participation in Science, Engineering and Technology*, Report of the South African Reference Group on Women in Science and Technology (SET4W). Pretoria: National Advisory Council on Innovation.

——, 2008.*Changing Perceptions of Women in Science, Engineering and Technology*. Report of the Science, Engineering and Technology for Women (SET4W) committee. Pretoria: National Advisory Council on Innovation.

——, 2009a. *South African Science and Technology Indicators 2009*. Report of the Innovation Indicators Reference Group. Pretoria: National Advisory Council on Innovation.

——, 2009b. *Facing the Facts: Women's Participation in Science, Engineering and Technology 2009*. Report of the Science, Engineering and Technology for Women (SET4W) committee. Pretoria: National Advisory Council on Innovation.

Organisation for Economic Co-operation and Development (OECD), 2009. *OECD Science, Technology and Industry Outlook: 2008*. Paris: Organisation for Economic Co-operation and Development.

Ralebipi-Simela, R., 2009. Presentation to the 2nd Regional Innovation Symposium, Free State Province by Deputy Vice-Chancellor: Academic, Central University of Technology, Free State, 31 July.

Republic of South Africa (RSA), 2010. *Development Indicators 2010.* Pretoria: The Presidency Republic of South Africa. http://www.thepresidency.gov.za/MediaLib/Downloads/Home/Publications/NationalPlanningCommission4/Development%20Indicators2010.pdf (accessed 4 August 2010).

South African Advertising Research Foundation (SAARF), 2006–8. 'All Media and Products Surveys 2006–2008'. Bryanston: South African Advertising Research Foundation. http://saarf.co.za (accessed 15 February 2008).

South African Revenue Service (SARS), 2003–09. *Department of Customs & Excise: Customs Trade Data.* Pretoria: South African Revenue Service. http://www.statsa.gov.za (accessed 15 February 2008).

——, 1999–2010. *Department of Customs & Excise: Customs Trade Data*, Pretoria: South African Revenue Service. http://www.statsa.gov.za (accessed 15 February 2008).

Satterthwaite, D., 2004. *The Under-estimation of Urban Poverty in Low- and Middle-income Nations.* Human Settlements Working Paper Series Poverty Reduction in Urban Areas, 14, International Institute for Environment and Development (IIED), London.

Seekings, J., 2008. *Poverty and Inequality after Apartheid.* CSSR Working Paper 200, Centre for Social Science Research, University of Cape Town. http://www.sarpn.org/documents/d003024/Poverty_inequality_Seekings_Spe2007.pdf (accessed 2 February 2010).

Seekings, J. and N. Nattrass, 2005. *Class, Race, and Inequality in South Africa.* New Haven: Yale University Press.

Statistics South Africa (StatsSA), 1980–2003. *South African Statistics.* Pretoria: Statistics South Africa.

——, 1995. *Income and Expenditure Survey* (Statistical Release P0100). Pretoria: Statistics South Africa.

——, 1995–2007. *Labour Force Survey.* (Statistical Release P0210). Pretoria: Statistics South Africa.

——, 1995–2009a. *Gross Domestic Product*, Third Quarter (Statistical Release P0441). Pretoria: Statistics South Africa.

——, 1995–2009b. *Mid-year Population Estimates* (Statistical Release P0302). Pretoria: Statistics South Africa.

——, 1999–2010a. *Gross Domestic Product*, Third Quarter (Statistical Release P0441). Pretoria: Statistics South Africa.

——, 1999–2010b. *Consumer Price Index* (Statistical Release P0141). Pretoria: Statistics South Africa.

——, 2000. *Income and Expenditure of Households Survey 2000 South Africa* (Statistical Release P0100). Pretoria: Statistics South Africa.

——, 2000–07. *Labour Force Survey* (Statistical Release P0210). Pretoria: Statistics South Africa.

Statistics South Africa (StatsSA), 2001a. *Gross Domestic Product*, Third Quarter (Statistical Release P0441). Pretoria: Statistics South Africa.

——, 2001b. *Mid-year Population Estimates* (Statistical Release P0302). Pretoria: Statistics South Africa.

——, 2001–07. *Labour Force Survey* (Statistical Release P0210). Pretoria: Statistics South Africa.

——, 2001–09. *General Household Survey* (Statistical Release P0318). Pretoria: Statistics South Africa.

——, 2001–10a. *Gross Domestic Product*, Third Quarter (Statistical Release P0441). Pretoria: Statistics South Africa.

——, 2001–10b. *Mid-year Population Estimates* (Statistical Release P0302). Pretoria: Statistics South Africa.

——, 2002–08. *General Household Survey* (Statistical Release P0318). Pretoria: Statistics South Africa.

——, 2002–09a. *Gross Domestic Product*, Third Quarter (Statistical Release P0441). Pretoria: Statistics South Africa.

——, 2002–09b. *Mid-year Population Estimates* (Statistical Release P0302). Pretoria: Statistics South Africa.

——, 2002–10. *General household survey* (Statistical Release P0318). Pretoria: Statistics South Africa.

——, 2004. *Labour Force Survey*, September (Statistical Release P0210). Pretoria: Statistics South Africa.

——, 2004–08a. *Gross Domestic Product*, Third Quarter (Statistical Release P0441). Pretoria: Statistics South Africa.

——, 2004–08b. *Mid-year Population Estimates* (Statistical Release P0302). Pretoria: Statistics South Africa.

——, 2005. *Income and Expenditure of Households Survey 2005/06* (Statistical Release P0100). Pretoria: Statistics South Africa.

——, 2008a. *Gross Domestic Product: Annual estimates per region 1995–2007*, Fourth quarter. Pretoria: Statistics South Africa.

——, 2008b. *Quarterly Labour Force Survey*, Third Quarter (Statistical Release P0211). Pretoria: Statistics South Africa.

——, 2009. *Quarterly Labour Force Survey*, Fourth Quarter (Statistical Release P0211). Pretoria: Statistics South Africa.

——, 2010a. *General Household Survey 2010 (revised version)* (Statistical Release P0318). Pretoria: Statistics South Africa.

——, 2010b. *Mid-year Population Estimates 2010* (Statistical Release P0302). Pretoria: Statistics South Africa.

——, 2010c. *Quarterly Labour Force Survey*, Quarter 2 2010 (Statistical Release PO211). Pretoria: Statistics South Africa.

——, 2011a. *Mid-year Population Estimates 2011* (Statistical Release P0302). Pretoria: Statistics South Africa.

Statistics South Africa (StatsSA) 2011b. *Gross Domestic Product, Second Quarter 2011* (Statistical Release P0441). Pretoria: Statistics South Africa.

——, 2011c. *Quarterly Labour Force Survey*, Quarter 2 2011 (Statistical Release P0211). Pretoria: Statistics South Africa.

UNDP, 2011. 'South Africa Country Profile: Human Development Indicators', http://hdrstats.undp.org/en/countries/profiles/ZAF.html (accessed 15 November 2011).

WorldWideWorx, 2009. *Mobility 2009*. Johannesburg: World Wide Worx.

——, 2010. *Internet Access in South Africa 2010*. Johannesburg: World Wide Worx.

——, 2011. *Research Notes*, 10 August 2011 (received by email).

Xue, L., 2009. '*China: The Economic Crisis, Innovation and Development*'. Paper presented at the Globelics 7th International Conference 'Inclusive Growth, Innovation and Technological Change: Education, Social Capital and Sustainable Development', 6–8 October, Dakar.

About the Series Editors

José E. Cassiolato teaches Innovation Studies and is the coordinator of RedeSist (Research Network on Local Productive and Innovation Systems) at the Institute of Economics, Federal University of Rio de Janeiro, Brazil. During 2011–12 he was the President of the Scientific Board of Globelics, Global Research Network on the Economics of Learning, Innovation and Capacity building Systems where he coordinated the Research Project — A Comparative Study of the National Systems of Innovation of BRICS countries. He has been Visiting Professor at the Université de Rennes (since 2001) and teaches at the Globelics Academy — School on National Systems of Innovation and Economic Development, Portugal and Finland (since 2004).

Maria Clara Couto Soares is Senior Researcher, Research Network on Local Productive and Innovative Systems-RedeSist, Institute of Economics, Federal University of Rio de Janeiro, Brazil. At the Ministry of Science and Technology as well as at CNPq-National Council for Scientific and Technological Development, she worked as Science and Technology Policy Researcher, participating in planning activities and policy proposals for science and technology development in Brazil. Her focus was the development of comparative analyses on international public policies to foster science and technology. She has also been Head of Policy, ActionAid International Americas, SA, and Head of the Brazilian Biodiversity Fund (FUNBIO) sustainable development programme. She is coordinator — with Jose Eduardo Cassiolato — of the BRICS Project on the scope of the Global Network for the Economics of Learning, Innovation and Competence-building Systems. She has a Master's degree in Economics and a Bachelor's degree in Sociology and Political Science. Her main research area is the evolution of innovation systems specifically focusing on social, environment and development issues.

About the Editors

Maria Clara Couto Soares is Senior Researcher, Research Network on Local Productive and Innovative Systems-RedeSist, Institute of Economics, Federal University of Rio de Janeiro, Brazil. At the Ministry of Science and Technology as well as at CNPq-National Council for Scientific and Technological Development, she worked as Science and Technology Policy Researcher, participating in planning activities and policy proposals for science and technology development in Brazil. Her focus was the development of comparative analyses on international public policies to foster science and technology. She has also been Head of Policy, ActionAid International Americas, SA, and Head of the Brazilian Biodiversity Fund (FUNBIO) sustainable development programme. She is coordinator — with Jose Eduardo Cassiolato — of the BRICS Project on the scope of the Global Network for the Economics of Learning, Innovation and Competence-building Systems. She has a Master's degree in Economics and a Bachelor's degree in Sociology and Political Science. Her main research area is the evolution of innovation systems specifically focusing on social, environment and development issues.

Mario Scerri is Professor of Economics, and Senior Research Fellow, Institute for Economic Research on Innovation (IERI), Tshwane University of Technology, South Africa. He is also Director, Institute of Comparative Studies in Local Development, Mozambique. His research focus is on the evolution of innovation systems, specifically within southern Africa, from a political economy perspective. He has worked and written on the measurement of innovation, on the teaching of undergraduate economics and the economics of innovation. He is the author of *The Evolution of the South African System of Innovation since 1916* (2009) and co-editor of *Measuring Innovation in OECD and non-OECD Countries* (2006).

Rasigan Maharajh is Chief Director, Faculty of Economics and Finance, IERI, Tshwane University of Technology, South Africa. He was previously Head of Policy, Council for Scientific and Industrial Research, following his deployment as National Coordinator of the Science and Technology Policy Transition Project for first democratic government of South Africa. He has a PhD from the Forskningspolitiska Institutet of Lund University, Sweden, and is an alumnus of the University of KwaZulu-Natal, SA, and Harvard Business School, USA. He has also been associated with the Kennedy School of Government, Harvard University, USA and the Institute for Policy Research in Engineering, Science and Technology, University of Manchester, UK. He is also an active member of the Global Network for the Economics of Learning, Innovation and Competence-building Systems. His areas of research include political economy, innovation systems and public policy.

Notes on Contributors

Vinoj Abraham is Assistant Professor,Centre for Development Studies, Kerala, India, since 2006. He did his PhD from Jawaharlal Nehru University, New Delhi, India, in 2006. His areas of research interest include Labour Economics, Economics of Technology and Innovation and Development Economics. He has published three books on related themes of employment, agriculture and industrial growth and has also published widely in peer reviewed international journals. He was awarded the young labour economist award for the year 2007 by the Indian Society of Labour Economics, New Delhi, India.

Lucienne Abrahams is Director, LINK Centre and Senior Lecturer, Faculty of Humanities, University of the Witwatersrand, University of Johannesburg, South Africa. She teaches public policy, strategy, innovation theory, knowledge management and e-government, all incorporating an ICT focus. She also conducts research on 'institutions and economic sectors in the network knowledge economy'. In addition to her academic work, Lucienne is a Commissioner on the Financial and Fiscal Commission, SA. She was a Council Member, Council on Higher Education; National Advisory Council on Innovation, a Board Member, National Research Foundation; State Information Technology Agency; and a Director, Development Bank of Southern Africa. In these capacities, her focus has been on thinking through a 'knowledge economy' perspective.

Ao Chen is a PhD Student, Graduate University, Chinese Academy of Science. His main research areas cover technology innovation management and technology economy evaluation.

Shucheng Han is Associate Professor of the School of Management, Wuhan University of Technology, Wuhan, China.

K. J. Joseph is currently the Ministry of Commerce Chair Professor, Centre for Development Studies, Kerala, India. He holds MPhil and PhD degrees from Jawaharlal Nehru University, New Delhi, India. Previously, he was Ford Foundation Fellow at Yale University, Visiting Professor at Jawaharlal Nehru University, New Delhi, Visiting Senior Fellow at Research and Information System for Developing Countries (RIS), New Delhi, and consultant to the United Nations Economic and Social Commission for Asia and the Pacific. He is the author of *Industry under Economic Liberalization: Case of Indian Electronics* (1997) and *Information Technology, Innovation System and Trade Regime in Developing Countries: India and the ASEAN* (2006). His co-edited volumes include the *Handbook of Innovation Systems and Developing Countries* (2002) and *International Competitiveness and Knowledge based Industries in India* (2007).

Maria Gabriela Podcameni is Professor, Federal University of Rio de Janeiro, Brazil. Her on-going PhD thesis, at the Institute of Economics at the same university, is on wind energy at the Economics Institute. She is also Associate Researcher, RedeSist (Research Network on Local Productive and Innovative Systems). Previously she was Associate Researcher at various organisations including the Brazilian Biodiversity Fund (FUNBIO) and the environmental economics group at UFRJ (GEMA). Her main research areas are national system of innovation, environmental innovations, wind energy, and sustainability.

Thomas E. Pogue is currently Assistant Director, Business Forecasting Center (BFC), University of the Pacific, USA, and Research Fellow, Institute for Economic Research on Innovation (IERI), Tshwane University of Technology, South Africa. While continuing work monitoring and evaluating innovation systems at various levels in South Africa, he has also developed analyses of the system dynamics of skills and economic growth in the Central California region. He has taught Economics at several higher education institutions, including Maastricht University, The Netherlands, the University of Cape Town, SA and the University of Nevada, Reno, USA. His research focuses on three inter-related themes — regional economic development, human resource mobility and systems of innovation.

Lakhwinder Singh is Professor of Economics, Punjabi University, Patiala, India. Prior to this, he has been faculty member of the University of Delhi and National Institute of Public Finance and Policy,

New Delhi as well as the Ford Foundation Post-Doctoral Fellow in Economics, Yale University, USA, and Visiting Research Fellow, Seoul National University, South Korea. His current research interest focuses on the national innovation system, international knowledge spillovers, pattern of development, globalisation and agrarian distress in developing economies. Apart from publishing numerous research papers in journals of national and international repute, he is also the founder editor of the journal *Millennial Asia: An International Journal of Asian Studies*, published by the Association of Asia Scholars, since 2010. He has co-edited the book *Economic and Environmental Sustainability of the Asian Region* (2010) and co-authored E*conomic Cooperation and Infrastructural Linkages Between Two Punjabs: Way Ahead* (2010).

Xielin Liu is Professor, Innovation Study, and Associate Dean, School of Management, Graduate University, Chinese Academy of Sciences. He did his PhD from Tsinhua University, China, in 1991. His research areas mainly cover innovation policy, catching-up, globalisation of technology and innovation. He has published prolifically in international journals and has also co-authored of *Innovation, Technology Policy and Regional Development* (2003).

Stanislav Zaichenko is Senior Researcher, Research Laboratory for Economics of Innovation, Higher School of Economics, National Research University, Moscow, Russia. He took part as expert in numerous international research programmes including GLOBELICS (BRICS and UniDev projects) as well as several national projects, initiated by the Russian government and enterprises. His academic interests, reflected in many publications, refer to NSI issues, university management reforms and other science and technology and innovation policy issues.

Index